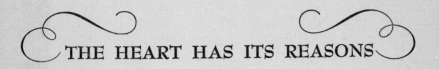

THE HEART HAS ITS REASONS

"Le cœur a ses raisons que la raison ne connaît point."

—BLAISE PASCAL, *Pensées,* iv. 277

THE HEART
HAS ITS REASONS

The Memoirs of
The Duchess of Windsor

David McKay Company, Inc.   New York

To DAVID

A Prefatory Note

MINE IS A SIMPLE STORY—OR SO I LIKE TO THINK. IT IS THE STORY of an ordinary life that became extraordinary.

The question has come down through the ages: Is our fate in our stars or does it lie within ourselves? The watchword of the hour is planning. Everyone and everything is supposed to work according to some master plan; few would have the temerity to admit that chance or mischance plays any part in the ordering of his or her life. Yet I often find myself wondering whether there has been some sort of plan that controlled my life.

The person who knows me best, my Aunt Bessie Merryman, enters a strong affirmative. Now forging resolutely into the nineties, with her wit and wits still about her and memories stretching across half the life span of the American republic, my Aunt Bessie insists that I have always had a plan germinating in the back of my mind for everything I have done. And to prove her point she can look backward down a long and complicated road, citing dates and episodes as far back, in fact, as my first young peoples' party, which must have been in Teddy Roosevelt's time. On that occasion, according to my ever-truthful aunt, I am supposed to have persuaded my mother, after a foot-stamping scene, to substitute for the blue sash she wanted me to wear with my white dress a bright red one. "I remember exactly what you said," my aunt now insists. "You told your mother you wanted a red sash so the boys would notice you." Whether I succeeded in producing the desired effect at the party, after having had my way with my mother, I do not now remember; I should rather imagine otherwise.

While conceding my aunt's point in the matter of the red sash,

I must disagree with her theory that I have operated under a succession of private Five-Year Plans. No one who succeeded in getting into as much trouble as I have managed to do, at one time or another, could ever be credited with having a clear-cut objective.

My endowments were definitely on the scanty side. Nobody ever called me beautiful or even pretty. I was thin in an era when a certain plumpness was a girl's ideal. My jaw was clearly too big and too pointed to be classic. My hair was straight where the laws of compensation might at least have provided curls. Moreover, I was prey to an unusual number of fears. Well into adolescence I was afraid of being alone in the dark. Thunder and lightning used to send me scuttling under the bed or into the protection of a closet.

No one has ever accused me of being intellectual. Though in my school days I was capable of good marks, I dreaded and evaded the subjects that did not come naturally to me. Having, for example, no ear for music, I hated piano lessons and by sheer resistance brought them to an early end—to my permanent loss. It was the same with mathematics, some capacity for which seems to have become a necessity even for women in today's world. That natural if unfortunate adolescent instinct of side-stepping the difficult and the stubborn until absolutely necessary I have carried with me into mature life. It made for a continuing, if precarious, pleasantness; and, if it induced problems, it also kept me from worrying about things until they finally hit me in the face.

These would hardly seem to be the ideal attributes for a biographer, even of one's self. In addition I labor under what my husband considers an appalling handicap: I am what he calls "undocumented," meaning that, living as I did, for the moment, I never saved letters, never kept a diary, never treasured personal documents or mementos. But perhaps this is an advantage for a woman; for the important things in a woman's life do not lend themselves readily to the ordered logic of the filing system so important to the male mind. So in my undocumented state my story cannot aspire to be a history; it can only be the simple record of my hopes, my thoughts, my dreams, my sorrows, my joys.

Acknowledgments

IN MY UNDOCUMENTED STATE I COULD NEVER HAVE WRITTEN THIS book without much and good help in refreshing my memories of the varied scenes and events of my life. One of the most rewarding experiences connected with the writing of my story has been the heart-warming co-operation I have received from everyone whose assistance I have sought. Here I can only list a few whose contributions have been major.

As in so many other things I am most deeply indebted to my Aunt Bessie, Mrs. D. Buchanan Merryman. She has been an inexhaustible source of information and recollection about innumerable happenings and incidents I should never have remembered without her help. This is also true of other members of my family, without whose aid I could scarcely have dealt with the Baltimore of my girlhood and the rather complicated family situations that played so large a part in my early life. I wish particularly to thank Mrs. George Barnett, Mrs. Zachary R. Lewis, and Mrs. George Murray. Also two residents of Baltimore have been most helpful in the same connection, Mr. William J. Casey and Mr. Karl F. Steinmann.

I wish to thank the following, all of whom either have played a part in the events of my life or have special knowledge of some aspect or other of it and who have not only given me information but have also generously reviewed for accuracy the manuscript in whole or in part: Sir George Allen, Lord Beaverbrook, Lord Brownlow, Mrs. Arthur Derby, Sir Walter Monckton, Admiral DeWitt Clinton Ramsey, U.S.N. (Ret.), Mr. Herman L. Rogers, Mr. Ernest Simpson, and Mr. Henry G. Walter, Jr.

For helping me check and verify factual details I am grateful to

Mrs. Doris G. Kinney; Mrs. Jean Leich; the British Information Services, New York; and especially to Mrs. Hildegard Meili Maynard, who has worked with me throughout.

For their help in the physical preparation of the manuscript I appreciate the unstinting services of Miss Helen M. Ferrigan, Mrs. Lelia B. Ryan, Mr. Delzell B. McMurray, and Mrs. Susan Kessler.

I owe a special debt to my husband for his constant encouragement and for his unflagging editorial help and advice. I also wish to acknowledge with gratitude the editorial counsel and aid of Mr. Charles J. V. Murphy.

Finally I want to record my deep sense of gratitude to my publisher, Mr. Kennett L. Rawson. His unfailing support and able assistance played no small part in the completion of these memoirs.

WALLIS WINDSOR

Contents

BOOK FOUR: *The Cresting Wave*

BOOK FIVE: *In the Eye of the Storm*

BOOK SIX: *In Search of a Life*

BOOK SEVEN: *The War Within a War*

BOOK EIGHT: *Of Women and Fate*

A sixteen-page section of illustrations follows page 116.

A sixteen-page picture story, "My Life Today," follows page 356.

BOOK ONE

A BALTIMORE CHILDHOOD

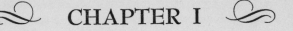 CHAPTER I

The Private War of the Montagues
and the Warfields

I WAS BORN AT A SUMMER RESORT CALLED BLUE RIDGE SUMMIT IN
the State of Pennsylvania, not far from the Maryland line and the
city of Hagerstown. My father's health was delicate; and he and my
mother had taken a small cottage at the Monterey Inn to escape the
summer heat of Baltimore.

The circumstances of my arrival appear to have been prophetic.
I started to struggle toward light and life somewhat in advance of
calculations and in an atmosphere of crisis. My mother's own doctor
being unavailable, a young Baltimore physician, Dr. Lewis Allen,
only just out of medical school, was called to the hotel cottage and
disposed of the emergency most efficiently.

In spite of the accident of my Pennsylvania birth, I consider myself
a Southerner. My father, Teackle Wallis Warfield, was a Warfield of
Maryland. My mother, christened Alice (although she often spelled
it Alys) Montague, was a Montague of Virginia; and the American
origins of both families go back to the earliest Colonial times. My
father and mother were both nearly the same age—twenty-six—at the
time of their marriage in June, 1895.

Now I am aware that the idea of a Southerner's being a special
type of American is rapidly losing validity. In fact, I would be hard
pressed to explain today precisely what makes a Southerner different.
But to be a Southerner was a matter of life-and-death importance
during my formative years. Baltimore looked upon itself as an un-
conquerable Southern peninsula in an encroaching Northern sea.

While the State of Maryland did not secede from the Union during
the Civil War, the sympathies of the principal families of Baltimore
and indeed of most of Maryland were with the Confederate cause.

My family was without exception on the Confederate side, and even four decades after Appomattox "the War Between the States" still supplied an honored topic of conversation at family gatherings. Indeed, my earliest perception of things past came from stories told me by my Warfield grandmother about the arrest of my Warfield grandfather by "Mr. Lincoln's men."

Grandfather Henry Mactier Warfield was quite a man. A member of the Maryland Legislature at the outbreak of the Civil War, he was among the first to call for the secession of Maryland from the Union. Along with a number of other prominent Baltimoreans, he was arrested the night before the Legislature was going to consider a secession resolution, by order of the Federal Department Commander in Baltimore, General John A. Dix. For a year and two months Grandfather was held a prisoner, initially in Fort McHenry, of "Star-Spangled Banner" fame. To the end he refused, unlike several others, to take the oath of allegiance to the Union in exchange for his freedom. He coldly informed Secretary of War Edwin Stanton, who tried to tempt him with certain conditions, "Sir, as I am confined without charges, I renew my claim to be discharged without conditions." Unable to break him, the Federal Government finally gave up, and he was released without taking the oath. He continued in his distinguished career, becoming one of the directors of the Baltimore and Ohio Railroad. He is reputed to have proposed the directors' resolution that led to the construction of the first grain elevator in the United States. I have no reason to doubt the story—the Warfields were always strong on resolutions.

Though my Warfield grandfather died eleven years before I was born, his formidable shadow still lay over his immediate descendants. There stands today, on Mount Vernon Place in Baltimore, a statue to one Severn Teackle Wallis, a distinguished lawyer, author, and Provost of the University of Maryland and long-time friend of my grandfather. My father was named after this man in honor of the deep friendship. Understandably, my father never derived much comfort from being called Teackle and as a young man chose to call himself T. Wallis Warfield.

I was christened Bessie Wallis—Wallis for my father, Bessie for my mother's older sister and also for her cousin, my godmother, Bessie Montague Brown. This was in keeping with the prevailing Southern custom of giving girls double names that were run together as one. Thus as a child I was called not Bessie but Bessiewallis. I always hated the name Bessie, for, as I told my aunt, "So many cows are called Bessie." Eventually I succeeded in persuading everyone but my grandmother to drop it.

Of my father I have no memory. He had had tuberculosis for some years and died in his mother's house in Baltimore, only five months after I was born. From the photographs of him that survive I would say that he had a poet's face—lean and angular, with piercing eyes set deeply in their sockets. A story is told in the family that at my father's request I was photographed for the first time only three days before his death. Contemplating the result, he observed softly, "I'm afraid, Alice, she has the Warfield look. Let us hope that in spirit she'll be like you—a Montague."

It may seem strange to say, but one of my early impressions is that I was somehow the product of two family strains so dramatically opposed in temperament and outlook as to confront each other with impenetrable mysteries. Beyond the fact that the Warfields and the Montagues shared the Mason-Dixon Line as a common frontier, they had almost nothing in common.

The Montagues were, and indeed still are, known to other Virginians as a magnetic, Bohemian clan. Their women were celebrated for their spirit and beauty, and their men almost invariably made reputations as wits and men-about-town. Unfortunately for them, in common with many another proud Southern family, the Montagues had little money, and it had been a painfully long time since any except the most venerable of them could remember having enough to support themselves in the style they considered traditionally their own.

By contrast, the Warfields of Maryland had prospered. For some generations they had been successful bankers, businessmen, and public servants. And as became so sturdy and industrious a line, they were noted for an almost puritanical rectitude, a strait-laced, unbending, never-forget-you're-a-Warfield attitude.

I gather that the union of these altogether dissimilar strains in my father and mother, as in the famous earlier encounter of the Montagues with the Capulets of *Romeo and Juliet,* was not only romantic but star-crossed. My mother was never considered a great Montague beauty like my godmother, the late Mrs. Alexander Brown of Baltimore, or my cousin, Mrs. George Barnett, the widow of a former commandant of the U.S. Marine Corps. But she was endowed with irresistible qualities of her own—a flashing wit, a bubbling gaiety, and a love of life that marked her a Montague through and through. Her shoes, size two and a half, were the smallest I have ever seen—a man could fit one into the palm of his hand. She had a tiny retroussé nose, bright blue eyes, and beautiful golden hair.

The Warfields were opposed to the marriage—and for sound reasons. My father had no real job because of his health; and his older brothers in family council were strongly of the opinion that he could not afford properly to support a wife. Understandably, the Montagues were even more strongly opposed. But my mother and father refused to be deterred. Without taking their families into their confidence, they slipped away and were married—according to one story in a church in Washington, according to another in a church in Baltimore.

So my legacy was this curious Warfield-Montague admixture, which had the effect of endowing my nature with two alternating sides, one grave, the other gay. If the Montagues were innately French in character and the Warfields British, then I was a new continent for which they contended. All my life, it seems, that battle has raged back and forth within my psyche. Even as a child, when I misbehaved, my mother taught me to believe it was the Montague deviltry asserting itself; when I was good, she gratefully attributed the improvement to the sober Warfield influence. However, it was my private judgment that when I was being good I generally had a bad time and when I was being bad the opposite was true.

In fact, this rather singular aspect of character was my only legacy. My father having left us almost nothing, my mother was thrown for support upon the generosity of relatives. On the urging of my Warfield grandmother, we stayed on with her at the Warfield house on Preston Street. That became my home for the next four or five years. But certain sad and probably inevitable circumstances that I shall presently relate made this arrangement impractical, and my mother moved with me to a hotel. At this juncture Aunt Bessie, who had recently been widowed and had no children, protested that it was silly for my mother to shut herself up in a hotel with a growing daughter when she had room for us in her house on Chase Street. So we went to live with her for a year or so, until my mother, who longed for a place of her own, finally decided to take a small apartment.

By then I was going on seven, and it seemed to me that we were always on the move. I desperately wanted to stay put, and the place I loved most, perhaps because it was the setting of my first conscious impressions, was the house on Preston Street, between Charles and St. Paul Streets, where I had lived with my grandmother. In the Baltimore fashion, the house was one of a row of almost identical structures—a red-brick affair, trimmed with white, of four stories, not counting the basement, where the kitchen was. It also had the typical Baltimore hallmark, white marble steps leading down to the sidewalk.

Here my grandmother lived with her last unmarried son, S. Davies Warfield, whom I called Uncle Sol, from his first name, Solomon. Uncle Sol was the eldest of my father's surviving brothers. (The first, Daniel, had like my father died young.) The third brother, Richard Emory, was married and had moved to Philadelphia, where he was prominent in the insurance business; and the fourth, Henry Mactier, named after my grandfather, had married a Baltimore girl, Rebecca Denison, and had a home at Timonium in Baltimore County. Uncle Sol, the bachelor, was head of the family. Cold of manner, with a distinguished if forbidding countenance, he was already, while still in his thirties, a banker of means and an entrepreneur of daring and imagination in numerous fields, such as transportation, public utilities, and manufacturing. About the time my mother took me to Preston Street, he was given the postmastership in Baltimore, a political appointment then held in high esteem. Of the Warfield brothers, Uncle Sol was to have the most influence upon me. For a long and impressionable period he was the nearest thing to a father in my uncertain world, but an odd kind of father—reserved, unbending, silent. Uncle Sol was destined to return again and again to my life— or, more accurately, it was my fate to be obliged to turn again and again to him, usually at some new point of crisis for me and one seldom to his liking. I was always a little afraid of Uncle Sol.

My feelings toward my grandmother were altogether different. Though from long immersion in the Warfield atmosphere she had absorbed many of the family's stricter virtues, she retained within herself some of the Emory softness and gentleness that warmed what otherwise would have been a cold house. She had a chiseled face, thin, aquiline features, and a fine aristocratic head over which the hair, by then gray, was tightly drawn back from a part in the middle. During my first years at Preston Street I was, of course, too young to notice very much about what went on there; but even after we moved away and until I went off to boarding school, there was hardly a day that I was not back at Preston Street to visit my grandmother, whom I loved. And since the house came to mean so much to me, chiefly because of her, I shall now describe what I remember of it and the good things that happened there.

The first floor had a long parlor furnished in the Victorian manner, with white lace curtains, gilt and mahogany furniture, and a marble statue of the Three Graces in a glass case on the mantel. Behind the parlor, down a short passageway containing a grandfather clock, was the dining room. At opposite ends of the dining room were mahogany sideboards on which gleamed pieces of Baltimore's famous Kirk silver. There was also a fireplace flanked by two long windows, which made the room the brightest in the house. I have reason to remember the good light, as the family doctor selected this room as the site for my first vaccination.

There was a library on the next floor running the full length of the front of the house, with bookshelves rising to the ceiling. In the back, over the dining room, my grandmother had her bedroom with a bath down the corridor past the library door.

On the third floor rear over my grandmother's room was Uncle Sol's bedroom and private bath. My mother had a room on the front and, connecting with it, a small room for me.

This arrangement was very pleasant for Uncle Sol, but highly inconvenient for my mother and me, as we had to use my grandmother's bathroom on the floor below. On the fourth floor the servants had their rooms, and there was also a small room reserved for the use of my cousin, Henry Warfield, when he came to town.

My grandmother was in her sixties when we came to Preston Street. The image of her that I carry in my mind is of a solitary figure in a vast, awesomely darkened room, rocking evenly to and fro in a large rosewood rocking chair with green velvet upholstery, and so erect that her back never seemed to touch the chair. She was still in mourning and wore black dresses with collars that rose tightly to her chin, surmounted by an edge of white collar, and a charming tiny white linen cap on which there were three small bows of black ribbon. The only jewelry she ever wore was a small pearl brooch and a black enamel bracelet. She ruled her world from a series of rocking chairs. In addition to the rosewood chair in the library, there was another in her bedroom and a small one in the dining room. The latter was her executive rocker; from it each morning she gave the servants their instructions.

There is a peacefulness, an air of reflection, about a rocking chair that attaches to no other moving object, and it may be that the sweet quiet so inseparably associated with my recollections of my grandmother and of Preston Street was due in no small measure to the countless hours I spent listening to her while she rocked and talked to me. However, there must have been occasions when I was a disturbing influence. In the library was a huge black leather sofa that had acquired an enticing slipperiness. I loved to squirm and bounce and slide on it. "Bessiewallis," my grandmother would say severely, "how will you ever grow up to be a lady unless you learn to keep your back straight?" Then, a moment later, "Bessiewallis, can't you be still for just a minute?" I seldom could. No doubt my grandmother put it down to that Montague streak.

These are clear echoes from a quiet Victorian room. Associated with them are the dim beginnings of understanding. For a woman who led so tidy and secluded a life my grandmother had developed an almost masculine appetite for politics, Maryland and national. Possibly because Uncle Sol was always active on the local political scene, she seemed to know everything that was going on, who the principal personalities were, the little scandals about them; and she was always as up-to-date as a precinct captain. Sitting in a corner of the parlor at teatime, I loved to listen to her exchange the day's grist of gossip with her friends.

To this odd worldliness of my grandmother was joined a profoundly religious spirit. She was an Episcopalian—"High Church," she would primly say so that there could be no mistaking her position on certain aspects of Protestant doctrine—and from her I assimilated the beginnings of an understanding of religion. Often I went with her to Christ Church on St. Paul Street for Sunday service.

As she grew older she sometimes had to miss a service, and she then expected me on my return to the house to give her verbatim the full text for the sermon. If she found I was misquoting, she would instantly and firmly put me right by reading from the giant family Bible that reposed on a table beside her rocker, the place where she had last been reading marked by a purple satin ribbon.

For all her common sense and kindness, my grandmother was herself ruled by occasional disconcerting prejudices. The implacability of her hatred for Yankees would have startled even Jefferson Davis. I doubt whether she ever knowingly invited a Northerner into her house. "Never marry a Yankee" went one of her fiercer injunctions. For her that idea was so patently treasonable as to justify banishment from the family hearth. She also laid down another rule: "Never allow a man to kiss your hand. If you do, he'll never ask you to marry him." Unfortunately, the exact meaning of this sage advice remained obscure to me, unless my grandmother meant to suggest that no virtuous woman should allow herself to be taken in by fancy foreign fripperies that could only lead to even more dangerous concessions. Still, whatever my grandmother said was law to me. She had equally strong views about coffee. "Don't drink the stuff," she decreed. "It will turn your skin yellow." For a long time I believed her, and I still have no fondness for the beverage.

My grandmother had a victoria, and on Saturday mornings it would be summoned to the front door precisely at eight o'clock to take her to the Richmond market, for the week's marketing. I had the privilege of going with her. For these expeditions she was decked out in her most somber widow's garb—a black bonnet trimmed with a little purple bow, a small crepe veil that hung from the bonnet down the back of her neck. The market money was carried in a black bag attached to her belt by an imposing silver buckle. Her horse, Gadfly, was beyond doubt the longest horse ever known. His front half would be halfway around the corner while the rear half would be contentedly on the straightaway. Going to Richmond market was for me as exciting as a trip to the moon. The market was open on all four sides to the heat of the summer and the winds of the winter. It was crisscrossed by aisles flanked with stalls heaped with every imaginable kind of produce and provender. On winter days the market glowed with the ruddy light of innumerable charcoal braziers. The bustle in the stalls, the clean, fresh country smell, the blazing braziers, and the spectacle of my formidable grandmother pointing a probing finger at precisely what she wanted have left in the recesses of my mind a memory of sounds and smells and color that still remains fresh. My grandmother would spend perhaps ten dollars for a week's food for the family; and, on finishing the marketing, she always led me by the hand directly to the taffy stand, where she would present me with a little bag of chewy yellow taffy.

There were two other personalities at Preston Street who also meant much to me. One was a wonderful Irish nurse who had taken care of my father and his brothers in their childhood. We called her Joe. She was tall, gaunt, almost toothless, and on occasion could bristle with Irish independence. When I was very young she wheeled me through the streets of Baltimore in a carriage. All the Warfields loved Joe. On her death, having no relatives of her own, she surprised them by leaving her lifetime savings, some seven thousand dollars, to the family.

Another important personage of my childhood was Uncle Sol's valet-footman, Eddie, one of the nicest people I have ever known. Eddie had worked for Teackle Wallis, the man for whom my father had been named, and on Mr. Wallis's death he had gravitated, according to Southern custom, to my grandfather and eventually to Uncle Sol. Eddie was a small, stooped, well-spoken Negro. In the morning on my way to breakfast I would meet him coming up the stairs to my uncle's room, an impassive figure in a black frock coat, gray trousers, and wing collar. When my uncle was away on a business trip, Eddie took care of me. There was only one flaw in Eddie's impeccable manner. He had a very bad case of asthma, and his breath came and went in whistles and wheezes that resounded through the house as he fought his way up the three flights of stairs.

Eddie did not live at Preston Street. Married, with grown children, he had a little house of his own some ten or twelve blocks away. Whenever I was judged deserving of a treat, my grandmother allowed Eddie to take me on the trolley car to his house to have tea with him and his family. The house was immaculately clean, with lace curtains, little vases of artificial flowers everywhere; and on the wall in the parlor was a sampler: "God Bless Our Happy Home." During one of these visits I remember Eddie's asking me, "Now, Miss Bessiewallis, where do you want to go?"

The question surprised me. "I don't want to go anywhere" was my answer. "I just want to stay here." That seemed to please Eddie very much, as usually, wherever I was, I wanted to be somewhere else. He never stopped working; living well into the eighties, he died in the service of the Warfields, to whom he had devoted most of his life.

In such comfortable if austere surroundings, I passed a happy childhood. However, I was to realize much later that Preston Street could hardly have been particularly happy for my mother. A young widow, with no resources of her own, she was under the steady surveillance of a stern mother-in-law and an even sterner brother-in-law who had opposed her marriage and upon whose bounty, grudgingly doled out, she was dependent. One source of friction was that my grandmother in her dozen years of widowhood had never so much as looked at another man; when, therefore, after a more than suitable period of mourning, my mother began to go out with suitors, my grandmother was sternly disapproving and no doubt blamed the Montague frivolousness. The situation steadily became more trying, and my mother decided that she could no longer remain at Preston Street. One sad spring day, when I was about four or five years old as nearly as I can remember, our things were gathered up, and Eddie took us to a hotel.

A subtly disturbing situation seems to have helped precipitate the separation. My Uncle Sol, perhaps against his will, perhaps without ever fully realizing it, appears to have fallen in love with my mother. She was young and attractive; living under the same roof, she and Uncle Sol were inevitably thrown much together. The Montagues are closemouthed about family affairs, and neither my mother nor my other relatives were ever explicit about what brought on the crisis. However, from scattered and enigmatic remarks I surmise that my grandmother sensed what was in the air and decided to stop it, in a firm Warfield way. It was not that she disapproved of my mother; on the contrary, she gave her affection according to her fashion. But by her stern standards, for her bachelor son to marry his brother's widow would have been the height of bad taste. Above all, I suspect that because of my grandmother's strongly possessive nature she could not bear to have her last son leave her alone in the house. Whatever the reason, her attitude toward my mother turned hostile. My mother found her most minor faults and shortcomings tartly criticized, and this she could not bear. Whether she was ever drawn to Uncle Sol I never knew. It would have been a union of the sun and the moon, of fire and ice.

CHAPTER II

"Outrageous Fortune"

OF OUR MONTHS AT THE BREXTON HOTEL I HAVE ONLY A BLURRED impression of a quiet family hotel, of a pleasant double room, of meals alone with my mother, and of rather forlorn afternoon excursions to the house on Preston Street, about which had so suddenly descended a mysterious and disturbing barrier. For the first time I came to know loneliness as loneliness can only be known in the excruciatingly sensitive perceptions of childhood. There is no way, in my opinion, of explaining how a child is able to sense the unhappiness and despair of grownups; but the phenomenon occurs—I experienced it. A shivery feeling comes, as when on a crisp fall day the sun is momentarily obscured; and the tenuous apprehensions that now assailed me took the form of a dread of being left alone, even for a few hours, as if my mother, too, might vanish.

This would have been an interval of quiet desperation for anyone less blithe of spirit than my mother. Independence exacted its price in the form of a continuing insecurity. Few jobs of any kind were then open to women, and these few were for the most part closed to women of gentle rearing. My mother had been raised in the manner of a young Southern lady; that is to say, she was completely but charmingly uneducated except in the decorous graces. Like most Southern women, she was a wonderful cook. She could also sew. Until I went off to boarding school, all my clothes were made by her, and afterward they were made by a seamstress from patterns selected and adapted by her. Now, in an effort to give me a few more nice things, she decided to put this one useful talent to work by making children's clothes for the Women's Exchange.

Fortunately, Uncle Sol was helping toward our support. Every month he deposited a sum of money in her account at his bank. The trouble was that the amount was almost never the same. One month it might be quite enough to take care of the important bills, the next month barely enough to cover the rent, and the following month it might have increased just enough to include a few amenities. Whether this was a banker's way of reminding a gay and (by Warfield standards) frivolous widow of the hazards of independence I shall never know. But however generous Uncle Sol's intent—and my mother and I had reason to be grateful to him—the ever-shifting contribution complicated things for us.

Nor did I ever know the exact circumstances that finally induced my mother to accept Aunt Bessie's invitation to make our home with her. At this late date there survives only the dim memory of thankfulness at escaping from the confinement of a hotel. Aunt Bessie's home was a typical gray-stone Baltimore house with a parlor, dining room, and kitchen downstairs, two bedrooms on the next floor, and a front bedroom and a servant's room on the third floor.

Although Aunt Bessie's husband, known to me as Uncle Buck, had died when I was only four, I can remember some things about him, as my mother often took me with her when she went to see them. Uncle Buck was a handsome man of unusual height, with a full beard. Had I been his daughter and my mother his sister, he could not have been kinder to us. And not the least of his desirable attributes was the possession of a handsome black buggy with bright yellow wheels, drawn by a high-stepping sorrel mare, in which he liked to take me spanking up Charles Street.

The Merrymans were and still are a distinguished Baltimore family. However, they used to say of themselves that they could resist everything but temptation—and my Uncle Buck was no exception. During one of these afternoon visits, when both my mother and aunt had gone out, he took me for a ride, as he had occasionally done before. This time, however, he stopped suddenly in front of a strange building. "Come with me, Bessiewallis," he said with a smile. "I feel a need to cut the dust in my throat. And there's a wonderful parrot inside that will talk to you."

We entered a large, badly lit room along the entire length of which ran what I took to be a sideboard with high stools in front and a man behind. Uncle Buck hoisted me to a stool, and calling for what I imagined to be a glass of sarsaparilla, he entered into a conversation with the man behind the counter, with whom he was obviously on the most cordial terms. The parrot was in a cage, which the other man put down on the counter in front of me, and I was astonished to have the parrot utter intelligible sentences. I repeated everything the parrot said, he echoed them to me; we understood each other perfectly. The only thing I did not understand was why, as I described to my mother on our return the wonderful things that parrot had said, she blanched and Aunt Bessie's expression went rigid. Uncle Buck never took me back.

From my Aunt Bessie's house I went to my first school. It was called Miss O'Donnell's after its founder, Miss Ada O'Donnell, now Mrs. Sanchez Boone, who still lives in Baltimore. The schoolhouse had been her own home, and she did most of the teaching herself, while managing some thirty or so restless boys and girls, all of whom came from the circle of families residing in the neighborhood centering on Calvert, St. Paul, and Charles Streets.

I went to Miss O'Donnell's for several years. While I don't recall too clearly just what we actually learned there, a single vivid memory suggests that I must have been very proud of what I did know. Miss O'Donnell liked to tell us stories from English history and ask questions about the stories the next day. One day she asked who had tried to blow up the Houses of Parliament. Remembering that it was Guy Fawkes, I proudly shot up my hand, only to have the boy sitting behind me shout out the answer. I was so mad I wheeled around and smacked him on the head with my pencil box.

While I was attending this school, my mother decided to move again. This time she took a small apartment in the Preston Apartment House on Preston Street, some three or four blocks away from my grandmother's house.

This move resulted in one of my mother's rasher economic experiments. Having got to know most of the tenants in the building, she discovered that there were a dozen or so who were in the habit of eating out. This gave my mother an idea. Tired of sewing as a source of pin money, she decided to try her other specialty—cooking. Therefore she invited these nonhousekeeping tenants to become paying dinner guests. Eight or ten accepted. With high hope, my mother engaged a Negro cook and began in a modest way. Unfortunately her culinary vanity soon ran away with her never-too-sound business sense. The simple dinners grew into banquets—terrapin, squab, prime sirloin steaks, and soft-shell crabs, fresh strawberries, elaborate pastries. The guests' enthusiasm spurred her on to the creation of still more elaborate and costly masterpieces. It was a matter of pride with my mother that the only complaint she ever received was from an elderly guest expressing concern for the state of her liver. The triumph was marred only by the realization, when the bills began coming in, that the guest aspect of the enterprise had completely eclipsed the paying side. My mother never dared to show her books to Uncle Sol, and it was Aunt Bessie who finally stepped in, settled with the tradesmen, and disbanded what had undoubtedly been the finest dining club in Baltimore history.

"The slings and arrows of outrageous fortune" never daunted my mother for long. Almost immediately she started to dabble in real estate—not too seriously and certainly without conspicuous success. It was in her nature to shed material concerns as birds shed rain. She lived for laughter; the gay quip was the only currency she really valued. Her mind was quick and her tongue even quicker. Half the time she herself seemed surprised by the delight and shock she produced. After a particularly devastating sally her face would assume an expression of mock contrition. "Lord," she would exclaim, "what have I said now?" Typical of her trigger wit was her reaction after she tripped and tumbled down the stairs in the five-and-ten-cent store. Up rushed a worried clerk who, as he helped her to her feet, inquired, "Madam, is there anything I can do for you?"

"Yes," replied my mother. "Just take me at once to the five-and-ten-cent coffin counter."

No one appreciated my mother's sense of fun more than did Aunt Bessie. But once, in a thoughtful mood, Aunt Bessie was heard to murmur, "We Montagues are very funny people to ourselves, but I sometimes wonder if other people really find us quite that funny."

Precarious as were our personal fortunes, my mother was determined that I should be brought up in the right way. Baltimore then had not more than two or three girls' schools for the small fry of its leading families. The most expensive and fashionable was Bryn Mawr, not to be confused with the college of that name. Arundell—the one to which I went, at ten—was not as expensive. It was on St. Paul Street facing Mount Vernon Place in what had been a private house— a small red-brick building the interior of which had been made over, not with entire success, into classrooms. The study halls and assembly room were downstairs, in what must have been the parlor and dining room. Classes were held on the upper floors in what originally had been the bedrooms.

Presiding over this establishment as headmistress was a remarkable woman—Miss Carroll, a strict, gray-haired despot who usually dressed in black. I was in her charge for six years and enjoyed nearly every day. The Arundell of my youth, like the Baltimore of my youth, was a remarkably sheltered little world. Their families all being more or less of a piece, the girls of Arundell were more or less similar. Whatever else Arundell may have done for us, it imparted in its calm routine a real feeling of being part of a group—an important thing for a child. And it was especially important for someone like me, an only child brought up by an indulgent mother and doting grandmother and aunt. At Miss O'Donnell's the shell of my self-containment had escaped unpenetrated. In fact, I lived, much more so I suspect than most children, in a make-believe world of my own devising. I used to pretend I was not just one but several imaginary characters. Aunt Bessie tells of finding me sitting on the floor, cutting paper dolls out of magazines, and telling wild stories about them. My favorite inventions were two imaginary people with whom I used to carry on long conversations on the telephone attached to the wall in the hall outside my grandmother's library, with the receiver hook held down. One was "Gubby"—he was a gadabout, and I used to call him up at the Maryland Club and say in peremptory tones, "Now, Gubby, you come right home." The other was "ABC"—he was the adventurous one and always in trouble.

Arundell dissolved the self-centered little world where I had everything my own way, and replaced it with the real people of my own age. I wanted to succeed in this new world as well as I had in the world of my family and the world of my own creation. In a surprisingly short time I longed to be just like all the other children but only more so. Because all the other girls wore what were called Peter Thompson suits—short pleated skirts, with a white middy overblouse, the feminine counterpart of the small boy's sailor suit—I insisted on having a Peter Thompson, too. My mother made mine; and the day I wore it to school, I hoped that everybody would notice me. The craving to feel at one with those whom I admired took other forms. On the same street with me lived another little Arundell girl named Mercer Taliaferro, pronounced, in Maryland and Virginia, Tolliver. Mercer and I walked back and forth to school every day. She had fine straw-colored hair set into long, sausage-like curls, which became an object of envy to me. "How I wish," I remarked to my mother, doubtless with a sigh, "that I had curls like Mercer's."

"Oh," said my mother, "that's no problem. All that it requires of you is the patience to sit still for a while." That evening, after supper, sitting on the side of my bed, she brushed my long brown hair until it shone. Then she painstakingly rolled the strands about strips of flannel. In the morning she disassembled this ingenious arrangement, tightly retwisting the little curls so contrived around her forefinger to reproduce the desired sausage effect. I was pleased to have Mercer, as she met me on the doorstep, stare at me with an astonishment she could not conceal. "Gracious, Bessiewallis," she exclaimed, "what has happened to your hair?"

"The same thing," I shot back, "that happens to yours." And then we raced off to school together, all the closer for being that much more alike.

In this and countless other ways my mother did everything within her power to clear the way for me. No doubt she spoiled me, and I realize now that I must have taken advantage of her. All the same, she had no inhibitions about resorting to old-fashioned measures whenever, in her judgment, something more salutary than a scolding was indicated. She possessed a rather heavy silver hairbrush, and more than once the back of it was applied accurately and vigorously to that part of my anatomy where a woman's hairbrush finds its only other important use. If I used a swear word, she would march me to the bathroom and scrub my tongue with a nailbrush.

So, if she gallantly interposed herself as a buffer between me and the adversities that had come to her, she also followed a rule of firmly thrusting me into those situations where a child was expected to make his or her own way. The manner in which she taught me to swim was characteristic. We were spending part of the summer at a hotel at Warm Springs, Virginia, of which one of the attractions was a large swimming pool. My mother decided the time had come for me to learn how to swim. But I was timid and refused to be coaxed beyond paddling range. "Very well," said my mother without changing expression. "There is another way to learn about these things." Taking me into her arms, she carried me to the edge of the pool and dropped me into water just over my head. Then and there I learned to swim, and the thought occurs that I've been striking out that way ever since.

I suspect that my mother had her own secret reason for sparing me from all possible strains and tensions while at the same time she sought to encourage in me both self-reliance and fortitude. Tuberculosis was then widely believed to be hereditary, and the fear that the disease that had killed my father might have been communicated to me induced her to subject me through my entire childhood to a regime that was a good deal more Spartan than that of my contemporaries. Fresh air, rest, and quiet were the sovereign remedies of the period, and these my mother reinforced with a therapy of her own invention. Because she was convinced that too much clothing made children susceptible to colds, I was always much more lightly dressed during the winter months than were my schoolmates. They went to school armored in thick, long, woolen stockings with heavy wool scarves around their necks while I shivered in short socks and a bare throat.

The process of building up what my mother called my "constitution" also included my drinking down, directly on my return from school, a tumblerful of juice squeezed from a large piece of raw beefsteak, the taste of which I loved. Whether because of these measures, or rather in consequence of my natural resistance, I seldom, if ever, lost a day at school because of a cold, although there were occasions when my blue legs as I made my way down Charles Street aroused the sympathy of passers-by.

It is my impression that the annals of schoolgirls are much alike, and I shall therefore keep mine short and simple. Because I was anxious to win the esteem of my teachers, I studied hard. If I was not the best scholar in my class, I was certainly among the most earnest. My desk was usually singled out as a model of neatness; I always did my homework. At five o'clock after our afternoon play period I would go straight to my room, shut the door behind me, and stay at my desk until I had finished whatever reading or composition I had been given to do.

But I do not wish to suggest that I was a bookworm or of a solitary temperament. There was a lively crowd of girls my own age in the neighborhood, and we used to gather at the houses of one or another of us almost every day to skip rope, play with our dolls, or play that unique game boys never learn and girls never forget—jacks. These games were often ended by a mass descent on Guth's pastry shop for *kossuth* cakes or meringues.

English and history were my best subjects in school. I usually got high marks in both. Nature had equipped me with a twenty-four-hour memory, and before an examination I would learn the essential points by heart. This small gift was useful in everything but mathematics. This subject defied me to the end. I can still see, in my mind's eye, those awful seven apples being divided or eaten in order to demonstrate the simple marvels of calculation. My inability to grasp even the simplest rules of mathematical logic was not only a trial to my teachers but a matter of continuing irritation in my relationship with Uncle Sol. We had reports every month, and after showing the card to my mother I was required to take it with me to Preston Street for inspection by Uncle Sol before Sunday dinner. He was naturally interested in appraising the results of what he was paying for. Being a banker, he was prone to attach more importance to a proficiency in mathematics than, say, in history or English. In a well-intentioned effort to show me how really simple mathematics could be, he turned the Sunday dinner into a kind of oral examination, firing questions at me and posing problems turning on questions of interest, simple and compound, freight loadings, bank deposits, and other useful details. But, inasmuch as I seldom got the right answers and was, moreover, under the disadvantage of being faintly terrified by Uncle Sol's stern insistence upon a snap answer, these Sunday family gatherings were on occasion a harrowing experience for me. Only once did I ever get the better of Uncle Sol. That occurred when I timidly seized the initiative after memorizing two sentences I had found in a geometry book, which struck me as dramatic though utterly unintelligible. We had sat down at the long table in the dining room, Uncle Sol at the head, my grandmother at the foot, my mother and I facing each other. As Uncle Sol rose to carve the roast, I announced loudly, "The square on the hypotenuse of a right-angled triangle is equal to the sum of the squares on the other two sides. The area of a circle is equal to pi-r squared." The carving knife clattered from Uncle Sol's hand to the plate. As he recovered it, he remarked with a rare smile that just escaped broadening into a grin, "Very interesting, Bessiewallis." There were no questions asked of me that day.

One of the best things Arundell did for me was to introduce me to athletics. Because of the scarcity of masculine influence in my family circle, I was no doubt inclined to be rather prissily feminine. The important sport the first year at Arundell was "Captain Ball," a little girls' version of basketball. The game provided the principal competition for the younger girls between Arundell and Bryn Mawr and other nearby girls' schools. The older girls played regular basketball. There was nothing I desired more fiercely in my childhood than to make these teams, and when my wish was granted, I experienced an elation of an intensity seldom equaled since.

I can't say that either "Captain Ball" or basketball made a tomboy out of me, but the fact of my being part of a team, no longer standing apart, gave me a real sense of belonging. In this mild metamorphosis a famous woman, Miss Charlotte Noland, played an important part— the same Miss Noland who later founded Foxcroft, the fashionable girls' school at Middleburg, Virginia. Miss Charlotte ran a separate athletic establishment of her own, known formally as the Gymnasium but to the rest of us more simply as "the Garage," in a rented building at the corner of Charles Street and Mount Vernon Avenue. Three afternoons a week we were taken there for games. Miss Noland was a strikingly handsome woman, with fine blue eyes and an outdoor, almost ruddy complexion. She had a wonderful way with girls—a mixture of gay, deft teasing and a drill sergeant's sternness. For many years she was my model of the ideal woman, cultivated of manner, a marvelous horsewoman, and a dashing figure in every setting.

Thus Arundell carried me through the mysteries and enchantments of childhood. My summer holidays were divided between my Warfield relatives in Baltimore County and my Montague relatives at Front Royal, Virginia. My three Warfield uncles all had farms in Baltimore and Harford Counties, all within fairly close range of one another— my Uncle Sol's at a place called Manor Glen, on My Lady's Manor, my Uncle Harry's and my Uncle Emory's in easy view of each other at Timonium, a suburb of Baltimore.

Of the three, the one I remember best, perhaps because I spent many summers there, was Uncle Emory's place, Pot Spring, to which he and his family repaired each year when warm weather came. The house itself was a lovely old structure surrounded by spacious verandas and graced in the front by a balcony supported by tall yellow columns.

My Uncle Emory was a true chip off the Warfield block, and my Aunt Betty, through long years of association, had become the equivalent of one. A Davies of New York, she was a great-grandniece of President Monroe and had several pieces of furniture, including a sewing basket, belonging to the former President. The life that revolved around them was stately, sedate, and regulated by daily reminders of Christian responsibilities. Tiny, finely boned, piercingly intelligent, my aunt was, if anything, even more strait-laced than my grandmother. She and Uncle Emory made a family ceremony of morning prayer; the servants were summoned from the kitchen to stand in the living room with the family while Aunt Betty read a chapter from the Bible and to kneel with us while Uncle Emory led the prayer. Grace was said before every meal. In the evenings, after I had gone to bed and my Aunt Betty had turned down the oil lamp—this was before electricity reached the countryside—on the table by my bed and tiptoed from the room, there would rise to me from the veranda, above the sound of the crickets, her voice and my uncle's in earnest discussion of affairs and morals.

[21]

Still, life with the Philadelphia Warfields also had its lighter side. My Aunt Bessie recently ran across a letter written during one of those summers that brings back to me some of the flavor of that existence.

Pot Spring
Timonium P. O.

DEAREST AUNT BESSIE

I have just gotten the book you sent me and as I have never read any Salt Lake City books before I am sure I will enjoy it. I can hardly realize that you are really going to traverse the world. I am so glad to know that Miss Adams is alright. I am wearing corsets now and am crazy about them. Do send me postcards. . . . I go riding every day and am becoming quite an expert. I play bridge all the time now and as I am dummy now I can write these few lines to my dear old aunt so far away. I don't think I have your address quite right, but hope I will get to you alright. I have to go back to the bridge table so will close with loads of love.

Yours affect.
WALLIS

P.S. Grandma sends love. Her mind is failing dreadfully.

P.P.S. Mother has just called up and told me about your accident and I am so sorry to hear about it. It must have been very embarrassing to have men look at you in your nightie.

In the midst of a nightmare, Aunt Bessie had hurled herself out of an upper berth on her way to the West Coast and the Orient and had cracked three ribs.

There were two sons in the family, my first cousins, Douglas, who was seventeen years older than I, and Henry, the younger one, who was only nine years older. Douglas lives in Philadelphia and has been a successful businessman in the Warfield manner. Henry, now dead, was one of my earliest masculine idols. I secretly adored him. Tall and with the Warfield litheness, he had brown eyes that danced with merriment. Though his features were irregular, his face gave an over-all impression of charm and personality. In the stable behind the house were a number of fine horses, and near the stable were jumps over which Henry practiced. He was a good horseman and taught me to ride. One day, as my Cousin Anita and I were jogging along the Bosley Road, just above Pot Spring, he came up behind us and gave both horses resounding slaps on the flanks. As a consequence, the animals bolted. Anita managed to stay on, but I was thrown—luckily into a ditch, which saved me from being trampled. This was scarcely calculated to fire me with love of horses, and in fact ever since I have been afraid of them. The little donkey and cart Henry's family provided for my exclusive use were much more to my taste. It was a tiny brown donkey cart, seating only two people opposite each other, and nothing was more satisfying to my first tentative feelings of grown-up independence than to set off down the long steep driveway to the turnpike for a call upon my Cousin Anita, Uncle Harry's and Aunt Rebecca's daughter, at Salona Farms, half a mile or so down the road.

Salona Farms was not just a gentleman's country estate. It was a working farm. A large herd of Hereford cattle grazed in the long meadows; a big dairy stood near the barn where the milk was collected in huge stone crocks. My Uncle Harry was always dressed as General—he was the Adjutant General of Maryland. He was also head of the insurance firm of Henry Warfield and Company, and was a much gentler, less reserved, Uncle Sol. My Cousin Anita, three and a half years older than I, was my closest friend. Like me, she was an only child. We talked endlessly together, although about what I cannot possibly remember. I greatly admired Anita and especially envied her assurance as to just where she was going and what she was going to do and what new dresses she was going to get. Now Mrs. Zachary R. Lewis, she still lives in Baltimore County.

Having Anita's family so close gave my summers at Timonium a big-family feeling. Altogether I loved Timonium and its peaceful meadows drowsy with the smells and sounds of summer. Anita and I, in my donkey cart, used to bump over the fields to watch the tenant farmers thrashing the grain. Pot Spring had its own icehouse where ice cut during the winter from a small pond at the foot of the hill was stored against the summer's heat under deep layers of straw. We considered it exciting to go there when the Negro farmhands were fetching ice for the big house and the dairy. A delicious coolness welled up from the dark depths as the straw was raked back; and often we were treated to an ice-cold slice of watermelon, of which scores were stored close to the ice. Now the Warfield connections with these wonderful places have, after several generations, been broken. Pot Spring was sold many years ago and has passed through several hands since. Salona Farms was recently sold by Anita and is now being made into a housing development. And Manor Glen also was finally sold by Uncle Sol's estate.

When I did not spend my summers with the Warfields, I usually went to Wakefield Manor, the Virginia country house of my mother's first cousin, Lelia Gordon.

She had been widowed at an early age, as had been the fate of so many Montague women. Her husband was Basil Gordon. His spine had been injured in a childhood fall, and he had been a cripple through much of his later life. He had had a brilliant mind and was, at one time, the youngest senator in the Maryland Legislature. He died before I knew him. Nonetheless, Cousin Lelia, who had been greatly influenced by his intellectual interests, carried them on after his death. Today she can still recite yards of poetry and almost all of *Alice in Wonderland*. She had four children: Basil, who was just my age; a younger daughter, Lelia, now Mrs. Newbold Noyes, whose husband was one of the heads of *The Washington Star*, and much younger twins, Katherine and Anne. Anne was until her recent death Mrs. Henry Suydam, the wife of a State Department official, but Katherine lost her life in an accident in Cousin Lelia's camp in the Adirondacks. A nurse put a candle under a mosquito net to look for a mosquito, the net went up in flames, and the child, only a year old, died the next day from the aftereffects of the fire.

Wakefield Manor was a typical rambling Southern plantation house, with white columns and two long wings flanking the main hall, and formal gardens distinguished by fine boxwood. It became not only a second home for me but also a gathering place for the Montague clan. Here gathered my mother's other cousins, the beautiful Corinne Mustin, wife of a young naval officer, Henry Mustin, and now the wife of Admiral George Murray, U.S.N. (Ret.), and Katherine Hill, wife of Philip Hill, in the electrical business. Here I had the same kind of family life that I had with the Warfields, except that the accent was strictly Montague. Among the Warfields there was a regulated life; the Montagues preferred to let life regulate them. At Wakefield I developed a glorious though competitive companionship with my cousins. One of our useful competitions was in collecting rose bugs off the bushes, for which we were paid five cents a quart. I was determined to be the high earner, but somehow Basil always managed to come up with a quart or so more than I did.

Soon after I started school at Arundell, another change occurred in my life. As I have said, my mother decided to try her hand at being a real-estate agent and being more optimistic of success than her transactions were later to justify, we moved out of the Preston Street apartment into a house at 212 Biddle Street, the first house of our own. It was of brownstone, one of several like houses joined to form an unbroken Baltimore block. Their brown marble front steps did not rise directly from the sidewalk to the doors; they went sideways up the front of the houses. There were exactly six steps, with an iron railing that also went across the steps at the top. Inside, on the first floor, were a library, a parlor, a dining room with a pantry and kitchen. My room was on the third floor. On the second floor in the front was my mother's room, and in the back were a small room and a bath; in between was a second large bedroom, which I thought was set aside for guests. But I was presently to learn, in a state of incredulity that constituted the first great shock of my childhood, that my mother had in mind another use for it.

One afternoon, on my return from school, she met me with the statement that she had something important to tell me. She gently informed me that after long reflection she had decided to marry again, putting the situation in eloquent terms in which I was given to understand that it was a case not of losing my mother but gaining a father. The man who wanted to marry her was one who had often visited us. His name was John Freeman Rasin. He was the son of the Democratic Party leader of Baltimore and a member of a wealthy and politically prominent family. If not exactly handsome, being on the heavy side, my mother's suitor was a very pleasant man. During his courtship he had been extremely kind to me, always producing little presents with a quick gesture from behind his back. He had an infectious laugh, and I had liked him until my mother told me of her intention to marry him.

I was dismayed. I was shocked. I burst into tears. The idea that my mother might one day marry again had never occurred to me. I could not bear to contemplate sharing her with somebody else. In a flash kindly Mr. Rasin was transformed in my mind into a sinister and hateful rival. The new house on Biddle Street, which had promised to be such a happy place because it was our own, now seemed to have turned into a deadly trap. In my shock and hurt I cried out to my mother that I would never let her marry Mr. Rasin, that I would run away. And nothing that she could say to me stopped my tears or assuaged my grief.

Perhaps I should have been spanked or at least have been sternly lectured for my selfishness. But the depths of my sorrow must have worried my mother. The argument between us went on for days. I had by this time abandoned the idea of running away and had fallen back upon my last pathetic weapon—a threat that I would not attend the wedding, which was imminent. Seeking another way to bring me

around, Mother summoned Aunt Bessie Merryman and Cousin Lelia
to add the weight of their arguments. It must have been a sad little
scene. Patiently they explained that my mother loved Mr. Rasin and
that since she no longer had my father she wanted and needed Mr.
Rasin to fill the void. Her love for him would not subtract from her
love for and her need of me. It was especially wrong of me, they said,
to think I could stay away from something that meant so much to my
mother's happiness. "She wants you to be at her wedding," Aunt
Bessie said, "more than she wants anyone else." I was miserable,
confused, and thoroughly ashamed of myself and was wondering how
I could retreat without loss of face from my unhappy position when
my aunt and Cousin Lelia, who knew me better than I realized, were
struck simultaneously by the same idea. They began to talk excitedly
about the plans for the wedding itself. It would be in our own house,
with all the Warfield and Montague relatives on hand, and everyone
all dressed up, and, best of all, a beautiful wedding cake. Hidden inside
this cake would be a ring, a silver thimble, and a bright new dime.
"Just think," Cousin Lelia exclaimed, "you'll be among the first to
cut the cake, and maybe you'll find one of these treasures."

That prospect broke down my last barriers of resistance and hurling
myself into Aunt Bessie's arms I tearfully agreed to do what was asked
of me. I still insisted that I did not see why Mr. Rasin had any right
to come and live with us afterward. The newspaper accounts of the
wedding list me as having "attended" my mother. This, however, was
a misleading picture of my actual role. More truthfully I was in attendance upon the wedding cake. While the ceremony was in progress
in the parlor I slipped out and made my way to the dining room,
where the cake stood unguarded on the table, ringed by white phlox
and smilax. It was never in my mind, I am sure, to damage the beauty
of the cake in the slightest. My only object was to determine the
precise location of the ring, the thimble, and the dime. And I had in
fact located the thimble and was probing for the dime when there
came a gasp from the dining-room door, through which my mother
and new stepfather were leading their guests.

The cake was not exactly a shambles, but neither could it be said
that its original beauty had survived unmarred, and there was I, caught
in the dreadful act. Then, as I whirled around, a roar of laughter
went up, and I felt myself being hoisted into the air, almost to the
ceiling. Finally I came face to face with a very red and happy Mr.
Rasin—and all he did, of course, was to give me a great big kiss.

CHAPTER III

The School of "Gentleness and Courtesy"

IN TIME I BECAME FOND OF MR. RASIN—I ALWAYS SO ADDRESSED him—but he remained something of a mystery to me. So far as I could tell he never went to the office, nor did he have any formal occupation. He would still be in bed as I left for school, and on my return I would usually find him in the library, reading newspapers and chain-smoking cigarettes. Having inherited a comfortable income from a trust fund, he seemed to have no ambition to do anything, but spent his time about the house, except for an occasional quiet afternoon at the corner saloon with his political cronies.

However, there was no mistaking the fact that with Mr. Rasin's advent our fortunes took a quick turn for the better. He was very good to me. I cannot remember his ever having scolded me or his even uttering a cross word in my hearing. As if I were not already spoiled enough, he tried to make me feel that I was his own daughter. One of his first gifts to me was an aquarium stocked with beautifully colored tropical fish. He also gave me my first pet, a French bulldog that I named "Bully." Meanwhile, my mother's life became secure, if not actually serene. She loved to give parties, and after Mr. Rasin moved in with us, the Biddle Street house was seldom empty. My stepfather had four married sisters, of whom two lived in Baltimore and the others in Philadelphia and Washington. They came often to our house with their husbands and friends, and these gatherings were usually celebrated with an elaborate terrapin dinner. Baltimore is famous for terrapin, and my mother was reputed to have a special recipe that was the admiration of her friends. Her preparation of such a dinner was a ritual marked at every step by reverence. The men

[27]

who sold terrapin from burlap bags they carried over their shoulders had a special cry to signal their appearance in the neighborhood—a high-pitched, singsong call. The terrapin were brought to the door, and my mother would pick out the ones she wanted. For four or five days the diamondbacks were allowed the run of the cellar, while they fattened on corn meal. On the day of the dinner my mother established herself in the kitchen; no one else was allowed to help. If we had a cook and the cook was good, she might be allowed to watch—but that was all. After the dinner there might be a poker game and perhaps music on the pianola. I remember creeping to the top of the stairs, in my nightgown, to sit there with my chin in my hands, listening to the voices in the dining room and trying to hear what was being said.

Along with the good things associated with Mr. Rasin was an innovation that failed of complete success. He and my mother decided that I should take piano lessons. Their choice of a teacher was a middle-aged lady named Miss Jackson, who had taught several gen-erations of Baltimore girls what they knew about music. She came to the house one afternoon a week to meet me on my return from school. The only fault with this worthy exercise in self-improvement was an immediate realization on my part that I was tone deaf. This made me so mad that on the afternoon Miss Jackson was due for the second or third lesson I tried to escape fresh embarrassment by hiding in a closet after the front doorbell rang. Miss Jackson was patient, my mother was determined, and before long my hiding place was disclosed, and I was led to the piano stool. In justice to Miss Jackson I must say that she did her best. It was the custom for her pupils to give in the spring a recital in the home of one or another of them at which each of us was supposed to play a piece. My selection was "To a Wild Rose," but before the fateful day came Miss Jackson thought better of presenting me as a soloist. When my turn came, I played a duet with a more accomplished student, receiving at the end what my mother described to my stepfather as "not exactly an ova-tion—a kind of gratitude that the thing didn't last any longer."

Perhaps in compensation for having subjected me to this ordeal, my stepfather announced that a special treat was in store for me. I was to be sent to a summer camp—if I wished to go. Forever, it seemed at that still impressionable age, I had been envying my Arundell friends when they were able to announce, as they did every spring, that their parents were sending them to this or that summer camp in Maine, New Hampshire, or Virginia. Summer camp had come to mean to me something remote and exciting and precious from which I was hopelessly excluded. My stepfather's announcement delighted me; yet pleasing as was the prospect itself, I think I was even more gratified to be able to tell my friends next day at school that I, too, was going off to camp. At any rate, doubly underlined in my memory book for the year 1911 are the words, "Yes, I am really going to camp."

The camp that my parents selected could not have been a happier choice for me. Called "Burrlands," it was near Middleburg, Virginia, and was run by Miss Charlotte Noland, who taught athletics to the Arundell girls, her mother, and her two sisters, Miss Rosalie and Miss Katherine. "Burrlands" was hardly a camp in the usual meaning of the word. It was the Noland family's country estate. The main house, where we had our meals, was a stately Southern mansion with six white pillars. Some distance away were two small buildings where we slept and had our lockers. The Noland sisters had a rare gift for keeping girls busy and happy. We swam; we rode; we played tennis; we went on picnics. On more formal occasions, wearing gay summer dresses and flowered straw hats, we were herded into an ancient but still elegant horse-drawn coach, known as the "Flying Yankee," to be taken to garden parties in the neighborhood.

"Burrlands" is also memorable for me for the reason that I associate it with the first sweet anguish of adolescence. A family called the Tabbs lived in a beautiful house not far from the camp; we had permission to go there for tea or Sunday supper, if invited. The Tabbs had a young son, Lloyd, and Lloyd was, or so I wished to believe, my first real beau. The romantic mists that had momentarily enveloped my Cousin Henry Warfield, who by this time was working at Uncle Sol's bank, had long since evaporated; Lloyd Tabbs, at seventeen, became my beau ideal. For two full and delicious months of daydreaming he occupied a permanent place in my affections. But his place was momentarily usurped by Philip Noland, Miss Charlotte's brother. Philip was very good looking, and though he was awfully old—thirty-five, I think—our relationship had all the more luster because of the tragic barrier of age. Once, Philip Noland took me driving alone in his two-wheeled cart, all unaware of the emotional storm he had aroused. To my mind it was exactly as if he had asked me to marry him, and when I came home from camp, I cried and cried over him. When my mother asked why I was crying, I told her I was desperately in love with a marvelous man.

"That's wonderful," my mother said. "But what are you crying about?" I told her I had of course expected him to write me every day, and the first day had come and gone without a letter. I do not remember just how my mother explained that it was only natural that a thirty-five-year-old man would be unreliable about writing to a fifteen-year-old girl, but she did. I got over Philip Noland in twenty-four hours. My mother always had the same effective treatment for puppy loves—it was to take them seriously. "If you step on a puppy's tail," she used to say, "it hurts just as much as if you step on a dog's."

In June, 1912, I was graduated from Arundell. All the girls I knew were headed for one or another of the two Baltimore County boarding schools, St. Timothy's or Oldfields. My choice was Oldfields, where my mother and Aunt Bessie had gone, and once more Uncle Sol generously came forward to pay the bills. The school is at Glencoe, Maryland, in the hills beyond Timonium, where I had spent many happy Warfield summers. My mother took me there on the train, and I was pleased to observe, as we drove up in a carriage, that it hardly looked like a school at all. The principal building had been a big country house, to which had been added a large wing that served as a dormitory. Grouped about it were a gymnasium, an infirmary, and on a low rise beyond stood a lovely gray stone parish church.

The coprincipal of Oldfields was a replica of my grandmother. We called her Miss Nan—her name was Anna G. McCulloh. Sharing the direction of the school was her brother, the Reverend Duncan McCulloch. They were a highly individualistic pair, even to the point of spelling the family name differently. The Reverend Duncan insisted that the best Scottish orthography called for a "c" before the "h," while Miss Nan rejected this as a corruption of the true Gaelic. I am glad to note, having seen so many of the important landmarks of my youth disappear, that the school is still flourishing, though now controlled by a board of trustees, but with a McCulloch of the "ch" persuasion still as the head.

When I went there, one of forty girls, Miss Nan was sixty-two years old. She was tall, spare, precise of movement and speech; her iron-gray hair was brushed into a severe pompadour; and like my grandmother she unfailingly wore black dresses with little white turn-down collars. Miss Nan was Oldfields, and the school was Miss Nan.

Boarding school is a memorable experience in any girl's life, and it was so for me, but I seriously doubt that the details of my sedate and really uneventful two years there could be made memorable for anybody else. Whatever happened to me at Oldfields, however fas-

[30]

cinating it may have seemed at the time, was exactly what happened to all the other girls around me. How much we actually learned was, of course, an open question. Perhaps the really important thing about a girl's boarding school, at least in my time, was its success in conducting its young charges across the threshold of adolescence. At Oldfields, the hazardous way was indicated by a stern commandment, *"Gentleness and Courtesy are expected of the Girls at all Times,"* posted on the door of every room in the dormitory.

"Gentleness and Courtesy"—these were the ideals toward which Miss Nan steadily inclined the green twigs given to her care. Even our two rival basketball teams were called, respectively, "Gentleness" and "Courtesy." I was a guard for "Gentleness," under the tutelage of Miss Rosalie Noland, the sister of the dynamic Miss Charlotte. When it came to basketball, Miss Rosalie's exposition of the rule of gentleness underwent a subtle change. A young lady, it appeared, should also harbor a desire to win; gentleness and courtesy were exhibited to best advantage in victory; and a certain aggressiveness, including free use of the elbows, was encouraged along the way, provided, of course, one stayed within the rules.

Along with its emphasis upon the rules of etiquette and comportment, Oldfields also attempted to inject a reverence for God. Every morning, after the rising bell and before breakfast, five minutes were given to school prayer, which followed the Episcopal Book of Common Prayer. Grace was said before meals, and in the evenings, after study hall, we sang hymns. Sunday morning each of us was required to memorize the Collect and the Gospel of the day before marching off to church. At five-thirty there was Evensong and then, after supper, an extra-long session of hymn-singing. Miss Nan looked upon Sunday as a day to be devoted to instilling into her young girls the meaning and obligations of the Christian faith.

Oldfields was a place of rules—there was a rule for everything, and a stated penalty for infractions. "Lights Out" and "No Talk" at nine o'clock for the younger girls and at ten o'clock for the "Old Girls." Two weekends at home during the entire school year and no more were allowed. No writing to boys or receiving letters from them. If, for example, one forgot one's rubbers on a rainy day there would be a summons to Miss Nan's office and a penalty—perhaps to memorize fifty lines of "The Lady of the Lake" by the next afternoon.

One of the inflexible rules laid down by Miss Nan was that no student could leave for the Christmas holiday until she had memorized a chapter of the Old Testament and had recited it word perfect standing before Miss Nan in her study. We were assigned the thirty-fifth chapter of Isaiah that contains the memorable lines: "Then the eyes of the blind shall be opened, and the ears of the deaf shall be unstopped."

Because, as at Arundell, I wanted to be well thought of, my years at Oldfields passed without involvement in serious crises, emotional or academic. I appear to have stood reasonably well up in my class, as shown by the following letter:

Miss Anna G. McCulloh
Rev. Duncan McCulloch
Principals

OLDFIELDS SCHOOL
GLENCOE, MD.

March 31, 1914

MY DEAR MRS. RASIN,

We will give Wallis the privilege of going into town on Wednesday afternoon on the 2-20 train to have her skirt fitted.

She has been such a faithful student and her averages have been so good we feel that she deserves some extra privilege.

Our chaperon will be at the Union Station waiting to bring Wallis back to school on the 5-10 train.

Hoping that you are feeling much stronger.

Yours sincerely,

A. G. McCULLOH

But I must confess that my progress was smoothed by a forehanded action that was less than meritorious. Early in my first year I discovered that algebra was an imminent course. I rushed off to my mother a frantic note telling her that I would die if I had to take that subject, that I couldn't master it. That desperate appeal brought a last-minute reprieve. Miss Nan summoned me to her quiet office to say that on my mother's request I was not to take algebra—English history was to be substituted in its stead. She did not tell me what reason my mother gave. However, Mother wrote me afterward, with wry humor, that she had given Miss Nan to understand that extreme nervousness induced by prolonged exposure to mathematics gave me the hives. To that white lie I owe much of the happiness I associate with Oldfields.

In the spring of my first year at Oldfields, the walls of my little castle of contentment were brought tumbling down by another family tragedy. My mother and Mr. Rasin had recently moved to Atlantic

[32]

City. My stepfather was suffering from Bright's disease, and the hope was that the sea air would help to restore him. One spring day— the date was April 4, 1913—Miss Nan called me out of the classroom and informed me as gently as she could that Mr. Rasin had died. My mother was bringing the body back to Baltimore for the funeral. Even through the surge of concern I felt for my mother, I realized how deep had become my affection for my stepfather.

Miss Nan took me to the railroad station on the morning of the funeral. From the train I went directly to the apartment of Mrs. Gatchell, one of my stepfather's sisters, with whom my mother was staying. The maid who let me into the apartment showed me into a front room. The curtains were drawn, and in the process of trying to adjust my eyes to the abrupt change from bright sunlight outside to the interior gloom, I thought the room was empty. Then in a corner I noticed a dark shadow—it was my mother, enveloped in a black crepe veil that fell to her knees. She looked so tiny and lost and pathetic that my heart broke. As I started toward her a sound of weeping made me turn toward the other side of the room. There, on a window seat, all in a row in front of the drawn shades, were three quite shapeless shadows—three of my stepfather's sisters, draped alike in heavy black veils and sobbing quietly in unison. They made me think of the Fates, and I was glad to find my mother's arms.

That sad day was a long time running its course. I spent the night with my mother at the apartment where I had found her. She was returning to Atlantic City to settle her affairs and close the cottage. It was the first time I had ever seen her dispirited. "I had not thought," she whispered to me, "that it was possible to be hurt so much so soon." Her second marriage had lasted not quite five years.

I returned to Oldfields. Through the first difficult weeks I came to feel that Miss Nan was watching me with unwonted solicitude, though from a distance. She had me in her rooms, which were in the old building, and several times she took me for walks along the paths behind the school. She talked to me quietly about my studies, Christian inspiration, the mixed joys and sadness of youth. The ache gradually went away. Soon my mother wrote to say that she was returning to Baltimore in search of another apartment.

One of the reasons I am grateful to Oldfields is that during my last year there a love of books overtook me with a rush. I read Thackeray, Dickens, Robert Louis Stevenson, Charlotte Brontë, and with an even more intense sense of discovery, came upon the French novelists, Zola, Anatole France, Victor Hugo, among others. Perhaps it was this

[33]

absorption in the exciting lives of others that saved me from more than passing involvement in mischief. The habit of intense reading, I regret to say, stopped with Oldfields and was a long time returning.

No doubt Oldfields was an old-fashioned school that was old-fashioned even for its time. But I cannot put down the feeling that a good word should be spoken in defense of its outlook and particularly the high importance it attached to "Gentleness and Courtesy." The granddaughters of my friends, who are products of today's so-called progressive institutions, strike me, from time to time, as rather brash and uninhibited. They suggest to me that the pendulum of reform has swung too far in the other direction. No doubt they, with all their comparative freedom, have a much livelier time of it at boarding school than did the girls of my generation. Still, I wonder whether with just a slight genuflection in the direction of the older and simpler female virtues, they might not have a better time afterward—that is, for the rest of their lives.

Among other things, I owe a number of enduring friendships to Oldfields. One of the deepest was with my roommate, Mary Kirk, who came to Oldfields from Baltimore. At school we swore eternal friendship, but in contrast to the usual boarding-school loyalties, ours did indeed continue. Our paths were afterward to cross at many and critical times. Mary Kirk was meant to be noticed. She had a gay, freckled face, a good sense of humor, blue eyes, and a comely figure. She was always good company, and I used to think that she talked a blue streak—until Miss Nan once remarked, with a mocking smile, that the only girl in the school who could outtalk Mary Kirk was Wallis Warfield. The rules forbade any talking after "lights out." Mary and I, however, through patient practice, developed a highly successful means of communicating across the room by whispering. It could be that Miss Nan had this talent in mind.

Next to Mary, my closest friend at Oldfields was Ellen Yuille. She was one of the handful of girls who were not Baltimoreans. Her family were North Carolinians, though originally from Virginia, and some years before Ellen entered Oldfields they had moved to New York. Mr. Yuille was in the tobacco business; he was associated with the Duke interests. There were four Yuille daughters; all of them, in the smug phrase of that period, made "good marriages." Ellen was first married to William Sturgis, and, later, to Wolcott Blair. One of her sisters married Harry Payne Bingham; another married Carroll Carstairs, of the Carstairs Gallery; the third married the Earl of Dunraven, then Viscount Adare.

Ellen was tall and handsome and as a schoolgirl exhibited a precocious taste for clothes. Beyond dispute she was the best-dressed girl at Oldfields; after the Christmas and spring holidays she could be counted upon to make a startling entrance flaunting the latest styles; and then, whatever it was—a new kind of skirt, belt, or even a new pair of shoes—we all wanted it, only to find out, of course, that it wouldn't necessarily do for us what it did for Ellen. But the impression of her arrival lingered, and the first letters home would recount with envy the details of Ellen's latest creations.

I spent several vacations visiting Ellen and her family—they were, in fact, responsible for my first trip to New York. I remember being driven with Ellen from the Yuille home in Bronxville to see Broadway light up—a phenomenon that was then regarded with amazement.

One summer I went to Boston's North Shore, and on another occasion I spent part of my holiday at the Maine resort of Prouts Neck. I also visited Martha Valentine in Richmond and Virginia Hughes in Norfolk.

Almost before I knew it, my Oldfields days were over. At that time there was no formal graduation, and the class of 1914 went out into the world without fanfare or celebration. By old school tradition, the one real ceremonial of the year was the May Day Festival. In my day it was still rather informal. The custom was for the girls to choose a queen, who, in turn, chose her attendants. Our queen was Renée duPont, now Mrs. John W. Donaldson. The day before the pageant we went into the woods to pick wild flowers, each of us forming her bouquet around a particular flower. I chose arbutus.

The day of the festival was hauntingly beautiful. The dogwood was in bloom, and the velvety green lawns were at their best. Our little pageant began with the singing of the "May Song," while in procession, led by the queen and her court, we marched down a hill into a pretty little wooded dell. In the dell was a Maypole, and after the procession had circled it, the queen escorted by her court took her seat on the throne—a chair covered with green baize and banked with flowers. For the rest of us the dramatic moment came when one by one we stepped forward to present our bouquets to the queen and to recite a special poem appropriate to our particular flower. I can still repeat the opening line of mine:

"Sweet Arbutus, youngest child of spring. . . ."

~ CHAPTER IV ~

"The World's Most Fascinating Aviator!"

MY MOTHER FINALLY FOUND A SMALL APARTMENT IN A BUILDING called Earl's Court, at the corner of St. Paul and Preston Streets, again not far from the Warfield house. We were as hard-pressed as we had ever been, for the income from Mr. Rasin's trust fund no longer came to my mother after his death, and she was once more on her own.

The thought of going to college never occurred to me—it just didn't exist for girls of my upbringing. In fact, not a single girl from my class at Oldfields went to college. Nor did I ever, at what might have been for me a fruitful moment of choice, give a thought to finding a job and earning my own living. Baltimore girls of my generation were not sent to school to learn vocational skills. Had we been forced to support ourselves, the only useful activities with which most of us could have claimed even the faintest familiarity were putting up preserves, baking cakes, and sewing a fine seam.

What, then, was life supposed to hold for us? The answer, in a word, was marriage. To be sure, Miss Nan McCulloh was far too wise and too gentle ever to imply that the principal purpose—and, indeed, for the great majority of her charges, the only purpose—of her sedate and well-regulated school was to prepare us for the marriage market.

Not only was marriage the only thing that we had to look forward to, but the condition of marriage had been made to seem to us the only state desirable for a woman—and the sooner the better. The fact that few, if any, of us were in love or were even the recipients of concentrated masculine attention had nothing to do with the case.

It was marriage itself, conceived in the most poetic and romantic terms, that we aspired to.

However, before a Baltimore girl could be considered eligible for marriage she had to make her debut. This presented a problem, in view of our straitened circumstances. Even though being a Baltimore debutante in those days did not have to be a costly and elaborate process, it would still entail new clothes, entertaining, and the innumerable incidental expenses connected with going out socially.

Fortunately, Uncle Sol came to the rescue. My mother's new difficulties had for the moment uncovered the vein of solicitude that lay under his granite exterior, and the kindlier side of his nature, which I had known as a child at Preston Street, was reassuringly in evidence. Uncle Sol was president of the Continental Trust Company. The bank was then housed in a handsome new fifteen-story building at the corner of Baltimore and Calvert Streets. Across Calvert Street was the banking establishment of his friendly rival, Alexander Brown & Co., run by Mr. Alexander Brown, who had married my godmother. The two institutions were known to Baltimoreans of that generation as "Solomon's Temple" and "Alexander's Tomb." One afternoon, Uncle Sol sent word that he wanted me to drop by for a visit.

My grandmother's victoria had by then been replaced by a new Pierce-Arrow, with headlights peering out from the fenders, and a chauffeur in a spotless linen duster. In this equipage I was driven to my uncle's office, feeling scared to death that I would take the wrong approach. But Uncle Sol was in a mellow mood. After telling me how pleased he was by my good showing at school, he remarked, "Naturally, your mother is making arrangements to bring you out this winter."

"Yes," I answered meekly. "At least, she hopes to be able to make the arrangements."

"Good," said Uncle Sol. "I want you to know the kind of life your father would have given you if he had lived. I shall help, of course." As I left his office, he kissed me on the forehead and pressed something into my hand, something crumpled into a small wad. I dared not open my hand until I was back in the car. There were two ten-dollar bills. This was the beginning of a strange, intermittent, and commendable practice. Whenever Uncle Sol thereafter gave me money, it was usually in that odd way—a small wad was pressed into my hand at the moment of parting.

To be presented at the Bachelors' Cotillion was a life-and-death matter for Baltimore girls in those days. This was a men's club, formed in the middle of the last century, that corresponded, in tradition and purpose, to the Philadelphia Assembly and Charleston's St. Cecilia Ball. The Cotillion exists for the pleasant purpose of giving cotillions, or as we used to call them, germans. In my time, when life was more leisurely, the club used to give several a year. By custom the first two were recognized as coming-out balls, and the first one was deemed the more desirable. The invitation list for the initial cotillion was strictly limited; and, as the Board of Governors' judgment concerning eligibility carried the finality of a Supreme Court ruling, the issuing of invitations was awaited in a state of suspense bordering on agony.

One morning in October, 1914, the mailman put into my hand a large envelope of fine texture that I instantly recognized. I was one of the fortunate forty-seven invited that year. From that moment until the cotillion on December 7, I was lost to all other earthly considerations.

The August before, the First World War had begun in Europe. The Germany of Kaiser Wilhelm II had invaded Belgium; Great Britain and France had sprung to Belgium's defense; and the newspapers were black with headlines of frightful battles. Baltimore's sentiments were all on the side of the British. Out of a praiseworthy desire to set an example of how young American women should conduct themselves at a time when other friendly nations were in extremity, thirty-four debutantes, of whom I was one, were inspired to sign a public pledge to observe, for the duration of the war, "an absence of rivalry in elegance in respective social functions."

However, my mother's limited budget made a certain austerity necessary. Our tiny apartment provided little space for entertaining. Nor was there any question of my ordering my ball gown, as did many of the other girls, at Baltimore's most fashionable shop, Fuechsl's. My gown was made for me by a Negro seamstress named Ellen. By tradition, debutantes wore white at the Bachelors' Cotillion. My choice was white satin combined with chiffon. The chiffon was to veil my shoulders and fall in a knee-length tunic banded with pearly embroidery—a style borrowed shamelessly from a ballroom gown in which Irene Castle was at that time dancing to spectacular success on Broadway. My mother and Ellen worked the idea into a pattern; but, before we were satisfied, my mother and I made many trips on the streetcar to Ellen's house.

By decree of the Governors, each debutante was permitted to

invite two or three partners chosen from among the subscribers to the cotillion. In common with most of the other girls, I chose two of my relatives. My Cousin Lelia Gordon had married a gallant Marine Corps officer, Major General George Barnett. I asked him to be one of my partners, no doubt also having in mind the dashing figure he would cut in uniform. My other choice was my Cousin Henry Warfield.

Memory would have the middle-aged believe that girlhood is a dreamy and unbroken waltz in a golden mist. But the teen-age stage of my generation must have been, in its way, just as chaotic and disorganized as is its modern counterpart, which today causes its elders so much anxiety.

We spent endless hours on the telephone, in prattle with our friends; a whirl of predebut luncheons at each other's houses; teatime dances and chitchat at the Belvedere Hotel, again with the same crowd—and always a mad rush from one enormously important trifle to another.

By the afternoon before the ball I was a nervous wreck. Ellen, the seamstress, came to the apartment to help me dress and to deal with any last-minute alterations in my gown. By the time she declared herself satisfied, she was as excited as I. "Miss Wallis," she declared, "I almost feel as if I were going to that cotillion myself." My mother, who had reveled in supervising the preparations, agreed that Ellen had come as close to perfection as one could hope.

I studied myself in the long mirror in my mother's bedroom, and my heart sank. My face stared back at me like a white mask. "But, Mother," I cried, "my face is so white—I look like a ghost. People will think I am ill. I look simply *awful!*"

"Now, Wallis," was the immediate answer, "it isn't *that* awful." My mother went to her bureau and picked up a small box. "This may be what's needed," she said, as she lightly brushed my cheeks with a puff. It was the first time I ever was allowed to use rouge. Even at that late date the use of rouge was considered a little fast. But the effect was magical. As I surveyed the faint glow of color a wave of self-confidence swept over me. Now at last I was grown up, or practically so.

Cousin Henry called for me on the dot, with Warfield punctuality. He bounced into the living room resplendent in white tie and tails. "How do I look, kiddo?" he demanded, whirling on his heels so that the tails flew out behind him in a wide arc.

"I'm not going to tell you," I said in a hurt voice, "until you tell

[39]

me how I look. A gentleman is expected to compliment a lady on her gown, especially when he's not seen it before."

Henry stopped his whirling, burst into a laugh, and slipping his right hand inside his coat, made a mock, jackknife bow that almost jerked his head to the floor. "Kiddo, I can assure you that you will be the most enchanting, most ravishing, most exquisite creature at the cotillion." But I doubted that Henry ever really noticed any difference in me. Rouge or not, I was still his kid cousin. However, in justice to him I must say that he now presented me with an enormous bouquet of American Beauty roses. They must have represented a full week of his salary at Uncle Sol's bank.

The cotillion was held at the Lyric Theatre. Uncle Sol had generously proffered the use of the Warfield Pierce-Arrow for the occasion. In it, with my mother, Cousin Lelia, General Barnett, and Henry, I made my progress in style to the scene. It is difficult for me to believe that anyone but me could possibly be interested in the details of a debutante ball that happened four decades ago. But on the theory that a young woman's first formal appearance in the world of society is probably just as important in her development as is the first skirmish to a young infantry officer or the first day in court to a young trial lawyer, I shall describe what happened that evening so long ago as to belong to a world now gone.

I entered the Lyric Theatre, one hand lightly resting on Henry's arm in an attitude that I was sure passed for the height of elegance, although my heart was pounding. The gilt and crimson interior had been transformed. Where the orchestra pit and seats normally were, a ballroom floor, polished until it shone, now filled the entire space. Forming a crescent around the room was a solid wall of boxes, one for each debutante and each banked with flowers of her choice. The stage had become a supper room with its vine-hung trellises symbolizing a magic forest bower. Along the steps leading to the stage were banked heaps of rich satin cushions of gold.

But would I measure up in the exacting test ahead—a test not only of poise and appearance, but above all of popularity? The specter of being a wallflower haunted me, and I whispered to Henry, "Don't leave me for one minute. If no one asks me to dance, you will just have to dance every dance with me."

Henry at twenty-seven was a veteran of the Bachelors' Cotillion and inclined to consider himself sophisticated. "I hope not," he said cheerfully. Then his gallantry rose to the occasion. "Kiddo, you will be the belle of the ball, and you won't even want me around after the first dance."

From General Barnett, on my right, rumbled a parade-ground growl. "Wallis! Henry! Dress ranks. We're approaching the reviewing stand." Directly in front of me materialized a group of Governors and their wives. After exchanging greetings and with the General in firm command of me, we made our way to our box. It was festooned with American Beauty roses matching the bouquet Henry had given me. A moment later the band struck up the first one-step, "Otaki." The cotillion was on.

General Barnett danced me out with the air of a soldier who is doing his duty. But one formality was necessary before I was officially "out." On the stroke of eleven the orchestra fell silent; from somewhere a whistle sounded—the signal for the debutante figure. The floor was cleared, then we forty-seven girls, each with our partners, and led by the Senior Governor, made a slow, measured march around the ballroom. What happened after that was all a dreamy haze of music and laughter. If Henry's prediction was not exactly borne out, at least I did not lack for partners, and gradually, as my nervousness wore off, I found myself hoping it would never end.

Suddenly it was all over, to the strains of *"Parfum d'Amour."* I remember thinking, as so many other debutantes must have thought before and since, that there must be something more to being recognized as an eligible young lady than this. Had I missed something in the excitement? Was there a mysterious ingredient that others had experienced but which had escaped me?

I did not have much time for thoughts like these, as the younger crowd adjourned to the Baltimore Country Club and danced until dawn. As we said good night at the door of the apartment, Henry smiled wryly and left me with the remark, "Hope Uncle Sol doesn't throw a fit in the morning when I turn up at the bank late for work."

In those days, before many girls had jobs to occupy their days, being a debutante was a full-time occupation for almost all of us, but an exceptionally harmless one, I hasten to add. From my experience I can say that it consisted, in its most reckless aspects, of being allowed to spend the night at another girl's house, and, after going to bed, of lying awake and exchanging ideas and hopes across the room and always about boys, the handsomest ones and the dumbest, which ones were perhaps dangerously fast and which were too stuffy to be worth a minute of a girl's time. This is not to say that it was all whispered speculations in the dark. There were plenty of real beaux on the scene, and while I won't suggest that I had my fair share—how could any young girl be expected to know what constitutes a fair share?—the truth is that I never lacked for company. Of those who, in the idiom of the day, would qualify as "attentive," two linger in memory. One, Carter Osborne, was on the short side, blond and voluble. Among his attractions was the privilege of using the family Packard, a concession equivalent, say, in present-day Texas standards of value, to being allowed to fly the family Lockheed. The other, Arthur Stump, was tall and dark and silent. Both I remember fondly, and Arthur perhaps with an extra touch of affection, inasmuch as he could always be counted on to clatter up in his Ford, while poor Carter's access to the more magnificent Packard was hedged by parental restrictions. Sometimes, on special occasions, Uncle Sol sent his Pierce-Arrow to take me to the dances at the Baltimore Country Club or to a dinner party at the home of my friends, and all this gave me a sense of really being grown up and truly "out."

The round of balls, dinner parties, and tea dances continued through the winter and into the spring. Looking back upon that season of 1914–15, and considering that most of us, before long, were to find ourselves classed as the first postwar or "lost" generation, I am struck by how simple, how decorous, how really calm our lives were. The word "date" had not then come into vogue; we spoke of "engagements" with boys. On gala occasions we formed theater parties and went to the Lyric to see the road version of a New York hit. I remember going to the Princeton Triangle Club's show entitled, *Fie! Fie! Fi-Fi!* and being amused by the clever lyrics of a young and attractive Princetonian named F. Scott Fitzgerald.

But the usual Baltimore evening was in a quieter tempo. A boy would telephone to ask whether one would be "home" after dinner. He could usually count upon a fairly breathless affirmative. The young man would appear about eight o'clock. There would be an interval of polite conversation with the parents, or, in my case, with my mother. Then the elders would withdraw, leaving the privacy of the living room to the young. But the privacy was only an illusion. Even though out of sight, the older generation hovered vigilantly in near proximity on ceaseless guard. I well remember spending a night with Mary Kirk when two boys came to call. Being more persistent than the average swains they remained beyond the traditional ten o'clock curfew. Suddenly there was a loud banging on the ceiling as Mr. Kirk very forcefully hurled one shoe and then the other on the floor. This sort of pointed hint, I might add, was not uncommon.

[42]

Our lives, in fact, revolved around a now all but departed institution—the chaperone. Even when two couples went out together, a chaperone was always included. I doubt that any Baltimore girl of my age—and I can certify the fact on my own account—ever went to a restaurant alone with a boy. It was the same when, with other girls, I went to proms at Princeton and to hops at the Naval Academy. The essential requirement was unassailable chaperonage.

Now that the institution has gone, I have a better appreciation of the role it played in our lives. The subtle effect of being under the surveillance of a chaperone, I see now, was to emphasize the importance of marriage and to stimulate the desire for it. Also, the gap between the generations was far deeper and wider than it is today. This was not only the case with family friends and relations but also with one's own parents. My mother was the exception. She never talked down to me; she never treated me like a child. We were more like sisters. Most of my friends had no comradeship with their parents. I think today's more natural relationships are far better, but something has been lost. Seldom do I witness nowadays the profound respect that my generation had for our elders. Whenever we were with them, we made our curtsies; we sat bolt upright at meals and paid strict attention to our manners. And we did all this not merely out of a desire to make a good impression but out of a genuine consideration for them.

It never occurred to us that we lacked freedom as today's younger generation now measures its freedom. And, anyway, the courteous conventions that regulated our lives provided their own compensations. According to a quaint Baltimore custom, the climax of a debutante's year was reached on Easter Sunday morning. All fashionable Baltimore turned out in force for a stroll along Charles Street after Easter services; and the measure of a young lady's popularity was the number of corsages that she was able to entice, lure, or otherwise chevy from her admirers, however distant or bashful, for display in the parade. These trophies—and the more the better—were pinned to the coat, like campaign ribbons; and a quick run of the eye down a rival's row of corsages would establish beyond doubt one's current relative position in the esteem of the other sex. However shy a Baltimore girl might be otherwise, she had no choice but to be conniving and deadly in arming herself in advance against her appearance on Charles Street, knowing well that her rivals were already up to their innocent necks in a feverish conspiracy to present themselves to their best advantage. The least favored of one's beaux had to be cultivated as a potential donor of a corsage. A bouquet of Parma violets was standard, but the addition of a costlier gardenia, where one could be coaxed, was proof of real devotion.

When on Easter morning I appeared on Charles Street with two of my beaux, Bryan Dancy and Harvey Rowland, and wearing three bouquets, each with a gardenia, I was confident of being able to hold my own without having to call out the additional two I had in reserve at home. And if really hard-pressed, I could have mustered two more that had been reluctantly promised, if the family prestige was endangered, by Cousin Henry and Cousin Basil, despite their own heavy commitments elsewhere. After half an hour of reconnoitering my rivals along Charles Street, my confidence was such that I felt able to send an emissary to Henry and Basil to release them from their pledges.

At the beginning of the season I had hoped that Uncle Sol would give me a coming-out party of my own. He had given one for my Cousin Anita four years before—a tremendous ball that had been the talk of all Baltimore. But Uncle Sol put his foot down—and firmly. As a prominent leader in various relief and charitable drives for the Allied cause, Uncle Sol did not consider it seemly for members of the Warfield clan to indulge in ostentatious show. And to make certain that his motives were not misunderstood, he caused to be inserted in the society column of the newspapers a notice to the effect that Mr. S. Davies Warfield would forgo the ball that he might otherwise be expected to give for his niece, Wallis Warfield, for the reason that "he does not consider the present a proper time for such festivities, when thousands of men are being slaughtered and their families left destitute in the appalling catastrophe now devastating Europe."

This was a blow to me. Wholly apart from my somewhat selfish desire to have a really grand party of my own, I had counted on the ball to repay my social indebtedness, which promised to reach embarrassing proportions. But in spite of my disappointment, I understood and respected Uncle Sol's motives.

But Cousin Lelia, who had planned to give a tea dance for me in Washington, was not deterred. The dance was held in April, 1915, in the ballroom of the flag-festooned Marine Barracks, with the Marine Band, some sixty strong, in gala red coats, providing the music. Dozens of my friends traveled to Washington from Baltimore. This was a period when hostesses insisted upon an extremely high ratio of males to females, so that no girl would be conspicuous as a wallflower. Cousin Lelia's precautions in this respect must have set an all-time high in the proportion of stags. "If there is an unmarried Marine officer stationed in Washington who isn't here," she informed me, "it must be somebody who has just reported in from the Fleet. I've rounded up all the rest." The girls from Baltimore had a glorious whirl, and I had fresh reason to be grateful to Cousin Lelia.

The end of my debutante year was marred by sadness. My grandmother suffered a fall and broke her hip. After the accident, she contracted pneumonia. One day as I sat beside her, she said, "Wallis, I shall never get out of bed again." She never did.

On one of my last visits she gave me a long story about the meaning of conscience. She compared it to a mirror. She said it was a mirror that only I could see, and that I must look into it carefully at least once a day. I have never forgotten that talk.

One morning, my mother awakened me with the news that my grandmother was dead. There came over me a feeling of sadness. Ours had been an extraordinarily deep and enduring relationship; and it was again, I think, intimately tied up with my whole feeling of respect for my elders. My grandmother had done much to try to give me some true wisdom about life. All her days she had practiced what she preached, and had herself been the best example of her teaching.

After my grandmother's death my family went into mourning. In those days there was much formality and convention connected with mourning, for an entire family. It was a very long and drawn-out affair. The entire family wore black and shunned all forms of public show.

Late in the winter, Corinne Mustin, my Cousin Lelia Barnett's youngest sister, invited me to visit her at Pensacola, Florida. Her husband, Captain Henry Mustin of the U.S. Navy, had recently been appointed commandant of the new Pensacola Air Station there. Aunt Bessie was summoned to Baltimore from Washington for a family council. Had Corinne asked me to join her in the heart of Africa, her invitation could not have been more carefully deliberated. The first judgment of my elders was that I simply couldn't go. It would be disrespectful to the memory of my grandmother in the eyes of the Warfields, particularly Uncle Sol's, for me to go out to parties. And obviously I could not go down there without taking part in the life of the Station. This was convention speaking, of course, but the convention of that day could also be rationalized, particularly by the Montagues.

On second thought, Aunt Bessie reasoned that it might not be such a bad idea for me to go to Pensacola after all. I certainly couldn't look forward to much fun in Baltimore, considering that all the Warfields were in mourning. Moreover, she suggested that perhaps it was time I discovered that the world consisted of something more than Baltimore. My mother was readily persuaded. The black was put away, the party dresses were taken out, and in the charge of a friend of the family I was packed off on the train to what was to be, although I did not know it then, the beginning of a new life.

The month was April, 1916. The day after I arrived, I wrote my mother a letter beginning: "I have just met the world's most fascinating aviator. . . ."

CHAPTER V

My Marriage to Lt. (j.g.) Earl Winfield Spencer, Jr., U.S.N.

"THE WORLD'S MOST FASCINATING AVIATOR"—OR SO HE APPEARED to me at the instant of our meeting—was Lieutenant (junior grade) Earl Winfield Spencer, Jr., of the United States Navy. We met casually, though perhaps Corinne Mustin had seen to it that our meeting was not entirely by accident.

Captain Mustin was in the habit of having some officers in for lunch several times a week to discuss the business of the Air Station. The day after I arrived Corinne casually remarked that three officers would be joining us for lunch; she gave me the names, and of course they meant nothing to me. Shortly before noon, as Corinne and I were sitting on the porch, I saw Henry Mustin rounding the corner, deep in conversation with a young officer and followed closely by two more. At that distance there was little to remark between them. They were walking in step and bore themselves with that indefinable erectness that is the hallmark of the Academy graduate. They were tanned and lean. But as they drew closer, my eyes came to rest on the officer directly behind Henry Mustin. He was laughing, yet there was a suggestion of inner force and vitality that struck me instantly. His closecropped mustache gave a certain boldness to his features that was arresting. A moment later they were on the porch and Henry Mustin was saying, "I want you to meet Lieutenant Spencer." He introduced the other two, but their names are gone from memory.

Until I went to Pensacola, I had never seen an airplane. The talk at lunch was mostly about flying, and although it was all foreign to me, I was fascinated. As the masculine opinions rumbled around the table, I became increasingly aware of Lieutenant Spencer. Whenever I turned away to listen to one of the others or to exchange comments with Corinne, the gold stripes on his shoulder boards, glimpsed out of the corner of my eye, acted like a magnet and drew me back to him. His gaiety and sense of fun were continually in play, though a certain undertone of sarcasm hinted at harsher forces working beneath the surface. The eyes were surprisingly intense and bright and quick to flash in response to a quip. Above all, I gained an impression of resolution and courage; I felt here was a man you could rely on in a tight place.

I was soon to discover that these first impressions were not altogether wrong. At the end of lunch while the other guests were leaving, and after he had thanked the Mustins, he returned to where I was standing to say that, if I didn't mind, he would like to call the next afternoon, after he had finished with his day's duties. The almost studied casualness of the request momentarily took me aback.

"That sounds very amusing," I answered hastily, "but I don't know what the Mustins have planned for me."

"Oh, don't worry about that" was the self-assured answer. "I really don't care what the Mustins have planned for you so long as the plans include me." Then he was gone.

I felt excited and moved as I had never been before. Here was a kind of man new to me, strong, assured, sophisticated—one who knew what he wanted and was confident of his ability to get it. I was dying to pump Corinne and Henry about him, but I was restrained by the fear that they might laugh at my curiosity about a total stranger.

Corinne gave me little time to dream about Win Spencer. Her cousinly warmth and her Montague gaiety saw to that. She was my mother's first cousin, and I had known her since childhood. Her natural blond hair was done in a high pompadour; she had enormous blue eyes and a soft, lazy, caressing voice that instantly evoked mental images of porticoed plantation houses, drowsy afternoons, enchanted evenings, and beautiful women in crinolines.

In spirit and manner her husband, who was nearly ten years her senior, represented an opposite pole. He was quiet, soft-spoken, and taciturn. He laughed a great deal at Corinne's jokes but made few himself—perhaps because, as was the case with all the men who had married Montagues, she was never silent long enough to give him much chance. He was something of an engineer and inventor as well as a daring flier. He had designed the then-famous Mustin gun sight and had also been, I believe, the first man to be catapulted off a battleship in an airplane. He gave the appearance much of the time of being absorbed in a private world of his own, wrestling with some deep problem. Often you could sense at dinner that his mind was not really following the conversation at all, and he was making perfunctory comments out of politeness. He was strict, though fair and just. He had an equable temperament, and his men both respected and liked him. He was devoted to Corinne and their three children and could not have been nicer to me, though I was always a little in awe of him. He died over thirty years ago from the aftereffects of his heroic action in jumping into a rough sea off a battleship to save a sailor who had fallen overboard. I am glad for his peace of mind that to the end he was unaware of the stormy aftermath of that innocent luncheon.

The day's activities on the Station were finished at four o'clock. At five, the following day, Win was back at the Mustin quarters, in a crisp new uniform, looking handsomer than ever. He was charming and attentive in an offhand way. His six years as a Navy officer had given him a maturity that made him seem far more worldly than the young men just out of college whom I was used to seeing at home. As dinnertime approached and he made no move to leave, Corinne bowed to the inevitable and asked him to stay. By the end of the evening I knew I was in love—in love at first sight, yes, but nonetheless completely, totally, and helplessly.

Undoubtedly his attraction for me was intensified by the glamour and novelty of flying. He and the other officers seemed to me, at that first meeting, to belong to another race of men—godlike creatures who had descended to earth from a strange and adventurous realm.

The art of flying was so new that the Navy had only one air station—the one at Pensacola—and there were then fewer than two dozen fliers in the service. Win himself, only six years out of the Naval Academy, was the Navy's twentieth pilot to win his wings, and embodied in himself a considerable fraction of all the U.S. Naval air skills then in existence. In spite of his low rank he was the senior instructor at Pensacola, and a key man in the naval air program, then just beginning to feel the quickening influence of the approach of war.

Every generation has its own set of heroes, and mine were the gay, gallant fliers of Pensacola. Many went on to distinguished naval careers. Among them were Admiral John Towers, who in 1919 commanded the first transatlantic air crossing in the NC-flying boats; Admiral DeWitt Clinton Ramsey; Admiral Marc "Pete" Mitscher; and Vice Admiral Patrick "Pat" Bellinger, all of whom held high commands in World War II. The executive officer was Lieutenant

Kenneth Whiting, later a captain, whose qualities of courage and leadership had already made him an outstanding figure even in that singular company. I knew them all as "Jack" and "Duke" and "Pete" and "Ken." There were others who were not so lucky—Lieutenant Godfrey de Courcelles Chevalier, Win's classmate at the Naval Academy, a daring flier who was killed at Norfolk in 1922; William Corry, Jr., another classmate, who was killed at Hartford in 1920; and a half dozen or more were soon to come to an untimely and sudden end.

I never pretended to know much about flying. Machinery of any kind, like mathematics at Arundell, was for me an impenetrable mystery. All that I ever understood was that I was in the presence of something novel and challenging and dangerous. In the early morning, with Corinne, I used to walk down toward the beach as far as the warning sign that barred civilians from the flying area, and watch the preparations for the day's flights. The green water of the bay was glass-still, at that time, and the airplanes were nothing more than flimsy, fabric-covered boxes, with bamboo outriggers. They were of the pusher type—Curtiss N'9's, I believe they were called. The engine was mounted on a metal rack just behind and over the pilot's head. In the event of a crash a pilot knew that the odds of his being crushed in the cockpit by the weight of the metal ripped loose from its fastenings were all against him.

The knowledge of the risks these young men so lightheartedly accepted used to tighten the cords of my throat as I watched their flimsy aircraft struggle and bounce across the bay in an effort to gain the air. There were awful accidents. Whenever one occurred, the atmosphere of the Station would shiver and reverberate to the blood-chilling sound of the crash gong announcing an emergency. Two fliers were killed before I left, and there were several other bad crack-ups. My dread of flying is associated, I am sure, with the terror that stabbed through me whenever the crash gong sounded. My heart would instantly ask, "Who is it now?" And always the fear was that Win might have been in the air.

Off duty, Win continued to see me at every opportunity, and I soon realized that he felt more than a passing attraction toward me. There were many attractive girls living in the town, in those days still a typical sleepy Southern port whose principal families had come down from Virginia and North Carolina in the early part of the last century. To my great relief I found that Win had made no commitments to any of the local belles and that the field was open.

In the late afternoons he tried to teach me to play golf on the little sun-baked course lying halfway between the Air Station and the town. I did not care too much for the game, but I pretended to, for it gave us one of our few chances to be alone. Other times we walked along the beach, looking for unusual sea shells. In the evening we often went with a group to the movies in town. There Win and I would try to find seats in the back of the hall so we could hold hands. Sometimes we would slip out briefly, and he would drive me in his Ford to the country club, where we could sit on the dark veranda, often deserted long enough for him to take me into his arms and kiss me.

On Saturday nights the officers nearly always made up a party to go to the San Carlos Hotel. Win liked to take me there, and I enjoyed dancing with him and his brother officers as late as Corinne, who was my chaperone, could persuade Henry to stay. The war would soon bring big changes in social conventions, but in 1916 it would have been the height of impropriety for a young girl to go out unchaperoned even with a group. And in fact the worst obstacle to our growing romance was the problem of how to be alone long enough to talk about ourselves and our thoughts and feelings toward each other.

The days went by in pleasant activity. The Bellingers were staying with the Mustins while they waited for their own quarters to be made ready. Pat's wife, Elsie, was a relation, I believe, of Henry's. Duke Ramsey and Chevvie Chevalier were particular favorites of Henry's, and they, too, were about the house a great deal. But I had eyes only for Win. The more I saw of him, the more certain I was that this was the real thing and that if he asked me I would marry him.

In addition to his own personal appeal there was something else at work. I was nineteen and eager to learn about life; I was becoming impatient with the restraints of the chaperone system. Spooning or petting, or whatever the present term for it is, was not then for any girl who wished to avoid the damning label of "fast," and few girls were brazen enough to risk their reputations and, as they were led to believe, their future expectations. Also, so impenetrable was the barrier of reticence around the "facts of life," as they were then known, that most of us knew nothing beyond the whispered conjectures of highly imaginative and unscientific schoolmates. Years later, after my marriage with Win had gone awry, Cousin Lelia once remarked jokingly: "You know perfectly well you just married him out of curiosity."

Sometimes doubts did assail me, and I tried to put on the brakes.

A few times, even though I knew full well that Win would be jealous, I forced myself to accept engagements with Duke or Chevvie or one of the other officers—afternoon excursions on the bay, dances at the San Carlos, or an evening of cards at one of the officer's houses.

But it was no use. One evening Corinne and I were playing rummy, and I failed to notice Corinne was rising from the table. I went right on and played my next card. Corinne laughed, and addressing me by her favorite nickname, said, "I hate to interrupt your daydreaming, Skinny, but the game is over."

She was right—the game was over. Later that evening Win led me out of the movies almost before the lights were down. On the country-club porch he asked me to marry him. I don't recall my exact answer—something banal to the effect that I loved him and wanted to marry him, but that I must be absolutely sure. And then there were my mother and Uncle Sol to consider; I would have to tell them and get their permission. But I am sure he knew what my heart's answer truly was.

"I never expected you to say yes right away," said Win evenly. "But don't keep me waiting too long," the latter remark accompanied by a broad grin.

My visit had only been planned to last a month or so. But now, of course, I wanted to stay indefinitely. Corinne obviously sensed that something more than an interest in collecting shells on the beach or improving my golf swing was making me so enthusiastically jump at her repeated suggestions that I stay another week. But I was lost to everything except Win, being with him and getting to know everything about him.

In the course of the next fortnight I came to know, if not everything about Win, at least a great deal. He had grown up in Chicago and had graduated from Annapolis in the class of 1910. While serving aboard the battleship U.S.S. *Nebraska* of the Atlantic Fleet, he had become engrossed with the new art of flying and, against the advice of his superior officers, had become a flier. Shortly after the Pensacola Station was organized, he had wangled an assignment there. There was no question of his competence. It was said of him by his brother fliers that he possessed "a fine pair of hands," meaning that he had an intuitive, a natural feeling for airplanes and flight. He was already marked, at twenty-seven, as a highly competent officer of unusual promise.

There was also something else about him. Deeply imbedded in his nature, under the surface layer of jauntiness and gaiety, was a strange brooding quality that verged on bitterness and even cynicism; a word or gesture could change his manner in a flash. The laughter that crinkled the lines around his dark eyes would be gone as if a blind had been drawn across his mind; he would become silent and morose. He could be, I learned, unaccountably jealous for a man otherwise so sure of himself. If I danced too long with one of his brother officers, he would sulk at the table or confront me on my return with noncommittal detachment. These strange and sometimes bewildering alternations of mood fascinated me even more than his undoubted good looks. His was the most subtle, complicated, and dramatic personality I had known until then. Lost in the perfume of the oleanders and azaleas, I was too inexperienced to realize that the shut-in, bitter side of Win Spencer's nature was the stronger side, that even then he was struggling to hold it in check. In the years to come it would gain the ascendancy and destroy him and also the life we tried to make together. But all that lay in the unforeseen future.

At last in all conscience I could not prolong my stay; the one month had already stretched to two. Reluctantly I wrote my mother that I would be home in a week's time and tackled the dreary business of packing.

When Corinne and I pulled up at the station in the Commandant's car, Win was pacing the platform. He helped me aboard the train with my luggage, and then, to my consternation, as I held out my hand to say good-by, he pulled me half down the steps and kissed me full on the mouth, indifferent to Corinne's presence.

"I shall be in Baltimore for my summer leave," he said, "and I expect my final answer then."

"I promise," I replied, and fled flustered up into the train.

There were two thick envelopes, addressed to me in a firm male hand, waiting on the table at my mother's apartment. They were both postmarked Pensacola, Florida. Win must have written them the day before I left.

"I take it," my mother said, "that these are from 'the world's most fascinating aviator.' "

She already knew a great deal about Win Spencer from my occasional letters. I told her at once that he wanted to marry me and that I was in love with him. To my astonishment, my mother was not surprised at all.

But as that day wore on she maneuvered adroitly about a mother's duty. In the process of asking about Win Spencer she made her points: I had known him eight weeks, and during that interval I had learned something about the terrible hazards of flying. Would I marry him only to find myself, as had she, a widow before the echo of the wedding bells had scarcely died away? I should have learned something about the heartbreak of such a lot. I was nineteen years old, and it would be foolish of me, with so much of my life before me, to allow my common sense to be swept away by what might prove to be a passing emotion. The life of a Navy wife, she noted, would be hard enough at best—no permanent home, constant change of station, little money, and long and lonely waits for a husband to return from the sea.

All that, I responded, was what appealed to me. However chancy, that kind of life, I insisted, was more to my taste than the dull, placid rounds of a Baltimore matron of that day.

My mother replied, "The Navy, too, requires conformity to its own code. I fear you may well be too spirited, too independent to take easily to so regulated a life."

But I was in love, and her worries seemed unreal and irrelevant.

Seeing that nothing could shake my determination, she sighed, and using a familiar expression from my childhood, concluded, "Well, I suppose it is another case of 'must-have, got-to-get.' "

Although my love for Win Spencer was real enough, there also lay in the back of my mind a realization that my marriage would relieve my mother of the burden of my support. I did not tell her so. Such a thought would have shocked and dismayed her. But it was there.

True to his promise, Win came for a visit. He had great charm—there was no doubt of that—and my mother and Aunt Bessie and the rest of my family were not unmoved by it. Even Uncle Sol gave, in his way, his blessing. He stated as his opinion that my young man struck him as having his feet on the ground.

Win was able to arrange another short leave late in August, and I went to visit him and his family in Chicago. They lived in Highland Park, a pleasant suburb a few miles north of the city. Win's father was a member of the Chicago Stock Exchange. The family lived in a large frame house, with a wide veranda and an ample lawn. They were all extremely nice to me, though perhaps a little baffled.

I, too, was slightly stunned when we all sat down to our first meal together. I had never anticipated such an overwhelming array of prospective brothers- and sisters-in-law as ranged themselves about the Spencer table. Win was the eldest of four brothers and two sisters. The next brother to Win was blond and gay, and the youngest was

[54]

dark and quiet. There was one sister who was pretty and the other was not—that was the kind of family it was.

Mrs. Spencer was British, from Jersey, largest of the Channel Islands. At first her attitude toward our marriage was very much that of my mother's. She, too, made a serious point of the precariousness of the situation we proposed to enter. We could not, she warned, count upon much help from Win's father—so big a family already taxed all his resources. But these kindly warnings apart, the visit was pleasant and reassuring. So long as Win was certain in his own mind, the family wished us all possible happiness.

Little though I suspected it then, the Spencers were to prove to be an even more ill-starred family than the Montagues. In less than a year one brother, Dumaresque, was shot down and killed while fighting with the Lafayette Escadrille in France; another brother, Egbert, was to die in a riding accident; a sister, Ethel, was to commit suicide; and Win's mother was to be killed in an automobile accident. As for Win himself, he endured a succession of personal tragedies in his later life. He married four times, and died in 1950 at the age of sixty-one.

Our engagement was announced in September, 1916. Privately, of course, Win and I had been engaged all summer; but the actual public announcement was an exciting event, for I was one of the first debutantes of my coming-out year to become engaged. I went all over Baltimore, waving my left hand at every opportunity—on the third finger there was, of course, a diamond. It had cost Win many months of pay as well as a month or two of our future income, but he said it was worth it to him.

The wedding date was November 8. That left less than two months' time for all the things a bride-to-be must do—shopping, fittings, invitations, and parties. The time was gone while I was still trying to accustom myself to the pleasure of being formally engaged. Emily McLane Merryman gave a luncheon for me at "Gerar," her home near Cockeysville; Mrs. Aubrey Edmunds King, a lifelong friend of my mother, gave a luncheon at the Baltimore Country Club; and my Cousin Lelia Barnett gave still another party for me in Washington. This one was, of all things, a breakfast dance, and if I cannot say we danced until dawn, we certainly danced until dusk—with once again the Marine Band playing for us. My wedding presents were beautiful. Uncle Sol gave an exquisite silver bowl, and the Spencers gave flat silver and a tea service—all of them in the "Repoussé" pattern of the famous Samuel Kirk silverware of Baltimore. While Win held his bachelor's dinner party at the Belvedere, the bridal party went to see the Dolly Sisters in *His Bridal Night*.

The wedding took place at six-thirty in the evening in Christ Church, the church in which I had been confirmed. I was married by our minister, the Reverend Edwin Barnes Niver. The altar was banked with Annunciation lilies, and the church was a profusion of white chrysanthemums. My bridesmaids wore orchid-colored bouffant gowns of faille with wide girdles of French-blue velvet. They carried yellow snapdragons, and in each of their hats, which were blue velvet with orchid-colored faille silk crowns, there was a single silver rose. Besides Mary Kirk, my attendants were Lelia Gordon, Mercer Taliaferro, Mary Graham, Emily McLane Merryman, and Ethel Spencer. The ushers, all naval officers and fliers, resplendent in full-dress uniforms, were Chevvie Chevalier, Harold Perry Bartlett, George Martin Cook, John Homer Holt, Duke Ramsey, and Ken Whiting. Win's best man was his brother, Dumaresque, while my matron of honor was Ellen Yuille, then Mrs. William Sturgis, who had been my good friend at Oldfields. She wore Lucille blue with touches of silver and a large hat of blue satin that had a single orchid-colored plume, and carried orchids. I wore a gown of white panne velvet made with a court train and a pointed bodice of elaborately embroidered pearls. My skirt fell over a petticoat of heirloom lace. I carried a bouquet of white orchids and lilies of the valley, and I had a spray of orange blossoms arranged in coronet fashion around a veil of tulle, which was also edged with old lace.

There was a breathless moment before the wedding march; and then, after it began, I wondered if I could possibly remember the responses correctly and whether my voice would be quavering and too choked up to be heard. My Uncle Sol, who was to give me away, marched stiffly beside me. Suddenly I felt oddly remote from everything that was going on around me; that sense of detachment was still with me as I drew near Win. When I saw his face, I was reassured. He was calm and confident enough for both of us.

And so I was married, among my family and friends. The reception was held at the Stafford Hotel. The Spencer family had come on from Chicago, and I was happy to see that they were mixing well, if a little clannishly, with the assorted Montagues and Warfields, who probably were not mixing so well. The reception was very gay— it could hardly have been otherwise with my mother present. Finally, the time came to throw my bouquet. To my delight it was caught by Mary Kirk. A year and a half later, she was to marry Captain Jacques

Raffray, a French officer who came over to this country on liaison duty after war was declared. As Win and I came down the old spiral stairway on our way to the car, the guests showered us with rose petals.

We drove away to Washington with Cousin Lelia Barnett. She deposited us at the Shoreham Hotel in characteristic Montague style.

"It seems all wrong," she said, "to leave you here with this strange man."

❧ BOOK TWO ❧

NAVY WIFE

CHAPTER VI

A Time to Reflect

BECAUSE OF HIS TRIPS NORTH DURING OUR COURTSHIP, WIN COULD get only two weeks' leave for our honeymoon. We therefore decided to divide the time between the Greenbrier Hotel in White Sulphur Springs, West Virginia, and New York, seeing the sights and taking in a few shows. So the day after the wedding we went on to White Sulphur by train, arriving at the hotel late in the afternoon. Here at the outset of my married life, an odd incident occurred upon which I had good reason to reflect later.

Win and I had gone to our room to change for dinner. While he was dealing with the luggage, I went to the window, raised it, and looked hopefully over the grounds. "Do you know, Win," I finally said, "my mother brought me here one summer as a child? The funny thing is that I now find I scarcely remember anything about the place."

An instant later I was turned around by an explosive nautical oath. Win was stooped over the dressing table, peering at something under the glass top. "Imagine this happening to a man on his honeymoon," he chuckled, pointing at the table. I went over to see what he meant. It was a printed hotel notice stating that West Virginia was a dry state and therefore no alcoholic beverages could be sold on the premises.

"That's hospitality for you," said Win. "We certainly can't stay here."

Although he was joking, his irritation was authentic. Win flung open one of the suitcases. From under the shirts he produced a bottle of gin. "Just enough left," he said with relief, "to get up flying speed until I can locate a local source of supply."

It may sound odd, but at twenty I had yet to have my first drink of anything alcoholic. My mother always had a small tray of assorted liquors on the sideboard for those who cared for a drink. But the only liquor that was ever served in the Warfield house was a touch of champagne at the Christmas dinners—just enough for a toast. My grandmother had strong convictions on the evils of alcohol, and these I took as gospel.

To be sure, I was to become aware, before our brief honeymoon was finished, that the bottle was seldom far from my husband's thoughts or his hand. Once when I mildly commented upon this preoccupation Win laughed. "Now don't be a prude, Wallis," he said. "Just because you look askance at a cup of coffee is no reason to believe that other people shouldn't enjoy it." And because no unpleasant effects were in evidence, I rationalized his thirst away on the theory—ill-founded, as matters turned out—that a flier was entitled to relaxation, especially on his honeymoon.

In point of fact, we were both relaxed and happy at White Sulphur. Win had a highly developed sense of fun, if not exactly a wit himself; and, while we did not know a soul at the hotel and November was not a particularly active season there, we enjoyed both the beauty and the comfort of the place. White Sulphur was, then as now, a famous golfing center; and Win, who had never had much time for the game, went at it with characteristic determination. He hit a tremendously long ball but with little control of direction. Consequently we spent much of our time looking for lost balls in the woods. One day, after a particularly woodsy round, he asked me why I didn't play along with him. I had puttered around the course at Pensacola, but without seriously trying to master the game. But this time I was fired with genuine enthusiasm and the belief that I could be a finished player in no time at all. So I told him I would, and the next day I began to practice in earnest. I realize now that no one in her right mind would think that she could be a good golfer without years of practice, but I was determined to be the shining exception. When I found out this was not to be, I promptly stopped—at least for the time being. I regret to say that my attitude toward golf is typical of the impatient, importunate way I go about all too many things. I start with a rush, and if I don't get immediate results I stop right away.

After a week we went on to New York, where we spent a few busy days, the high light of which was the Army-Navy game at the Polo Grounds. Then we returned to Pensacola. It was exciting to be accepted as a definite part of a fascinating world to which, only a few months earlier, I had come as almost a total stranger—I can still see Corinne Mustin running along beside the train before it stopped, waving and shouting, "Hi, Skinny!" During the next few days all the officers' wives gave parties for the newly arrived bride.

The Air Station was really an old Navy Yard that had been practically inactive for some years before it was turned into a seaplane base. As in most old Navy Yards the officers' houses were situated along a street leading from the main gate down to the water front, with the Commandant's quarters on a knoll near the bay, where the view and the breeze were at their best. The house was very handsome with large verandas and formal gardens. There were several two-story houses for the senior officers; the rest of the quarters consisted of a line of identical, one-story, white frame bungalows, each with an identical veranda. They stretched back from the Commandant's house toward the gate in a neat hierarchical progression by rank to that of the most junior lieutenant at the inland end. On the beach were hangars, workshops, ramps, and various other installations. The setting itself, despite the architectural monotony, had a certain picturesqueness. The oleanders and the roses were in bloom. The view over the bay was lovely, and I was young and wide-eyed in a world that was not only new but brave.

Since Win was the sixth-ranking officer ours was the fifth in the row up the street from Corinne and Henry's house. It was, like the others, basically a simple bungalow. From the veranda the front door opened into the living room, directly off which were three bedrooms with two baths sandwiched among them. To the right of the living room and toward the back were steps leading down to the dining room and the kitchen—apparently a later addition. The only change I made was to have the furniture painted white and to hang bright chintz curtains at the windows. The whole house was tiny and could easily have been put in the parlor of a large house.

As a Navy wife, I settled into a surprisingly easy if somewhat confined routine. In those days servants cost next to nothing, and we were able to start with a cook and a maid for somewhere around $32 a month in all. This was a great boon to me as Win took all his meals at home, including lunch, and I had never previously even boiled an egg.

The horizons of our interest scarcely extended beyond the mile-square perimeter of the Station and the town of Pensacola. So, in the immemorial fashion of Service wives, we invented an existence within the orbit and indeed the very sounds of our husbands' duties. The evening diversions were limited to visits to the quarters of other officers for dinner or having them and their wives at our house, with bridge afterward or a poker game for modest stakes. My mother loved poker and fancied herself expert at it, but I had been too young to learn the game in Baltimore. Now I took up poker in earnest; and, if I do say so, I became a rather good player. The skill acquired at Pensacola was to stand me in good stead later on a critical occasion, as I shall relate.

There was a strict regulation at Pensacola forbidding pilots from taking a drink during the twenty-four hours before they were scheduled to fly. Since the majority of officers were in the air every day, this order meant in effect that they were supposed to be off liquor from Sunday through Friday, at least. But they played a little game with this order. Before supper, in the quarters of the gayer officers, there would be enacted on occasion a mock ceremony called "preparing the consommé," a rite that was curiously the male prerogative. This was attended by mysterious disappearances of the men into the pantry, from which issued presently muffled laughter, shaking and smacking sounds, and eventually a tray of ice-cold "soup" in regulation cups, on saucers as well. The consommé—it was really Martinis—was gravely drunk down, to the accompaniment of appreciative comments on the excellence of the flavor and calls for "a second helping."

What we Navy wives really lived for was Saturday night. Then all restrictions were off, and we went to town literally and figuratively. Dressed in our best we descended on the San Carlos Hotel for a night of wining, dining, and dancing into the small hours.

Win had an inexhaustible zest for horseplay and practical jokes. Typical of his pranks was one that he played on Henry Mustin. While conducting Captain's inspection one Saturday morning, Henry opened the mess-hall icebox, to find staring at him a Gordon's gin bottle well filled. Henry was shocked and demanded an explanation from the officer in charge, who of course was utterly flabbergasted. After allowing his brother officer to stammer and stutter for a suitable interval, Win came forward and nonchalantly announced that perhaps he could explain it: He had filled the bottle with plain water to cool for drinking before going down to the hangars the previous day and had forgotten to take it with him. There was nothing Henry could do under the circumstances, but he was furious nonetheless.

Win also fancied himself a mimic. With a borrowed cane wildly twirling and a straw boater at a rakish slant on the side of his head, he would throw the other guests at the hotel into convulsions of laughter by suddenly dancing out in front of the orchestra and rendering an impromptu impersonation of some Broadway vaudevillian of the hour, his favorite being George M. Cohan. I was never too comfortable during these solo performances. They were a side of Win's character that had not been conspicuous during my earlier stay. However, in any case, I looked upon these parties as a kind of thanksgiving that another week was safely past.

Frightening as the crash gong had seemed to me before, it became terrifying when, as a wife, I had to live with it. Whatever else we might be doing on our own account, our subconscious was always waiting for it to sound. Then, once it had sounded, the first frightening thought was: "Has it sounded for me?" All of us women knew that awful period of waiting to learn whose husband had crashed. The first impulse of course was to rush to the telephone, but that was not permitted. It was the rule of the Station that whenever the crash gong sounded the telephone system was to be kept free for emergency traffic. Sometimes it was an hour or so before the women, back in quarters, could learn from the grapevine what had happened down on the bay, or who had crashed. And the first tentative tidings would often be followed by another dreadful interval of waiting before one learned how badly the man was hurt. Soon after our arrival Win turned over while landing in a choppy sea on the Bay. Fortunately he wasn't hurt and was rescued almost immediately by the Station launch.

I remember a friend from Arundell days who came down for a visit and heard the gong for the first time. After it was all over, she sat shivering. "Wallis," she said, "I just couldn't go through that for any man." There were times, I confess, when I couldn't bear even to look into the sky and when the evening talk of planes, planes, planes put me on edge.

We were waiting, too, for something more. We were waiting for war. Week by week and even day by day it was coming closer. By the beginning of 1917, there was no more talk among Navy people about whether the United States would enter the war; now it was just a question of when. As the news from the European battlefields became more and more alarming, the activity at the Station mounted toward crescendo. It seemed impossible from one week to another to drive the tempo any higher. Yet every train into Pensacola brought more cadets. Win was busier than ever and complained bitterly over

[65]

the shortage of airplanes, though it seemed to me that the air over the bay and the ramps at the water's edge were swarming with them. Finally, on April 6, Congress declared war on the Central Powers: the United States had joined the Allies in body as well as in spirit. The news, after so long a wait, was almost a relief to Pensacola.

Very soon after, Win was promoted to lieutenant, and in a short time he received orders to proceed to Squantum, Massachusetts, near Boston, to take command of a new naval air station he was to organize.

It was an important assignment and an undoubted recognition of Win's administrative ability. But the transfer disappointed him, nonetheless. What he had expected and wanted was an overseas assignment with the prospect of combat flying. "Squantum!" he snorted. "What a place to fight a war!" As we set out from Pensacola, late in May, he had only one thought: to wind up the new job as quickly as he could, and wangle orders for Europe.

We took a small apartment in a hotel in the Back Bay section of Boston. Win's day was long. He was up every morning at six o'clock, and by seven, after bolting the breakfast I prepared for him, he was on his way to Squantum. He was seldom back before eight or nine or even later—too tired, as a rule, to want to do anything but have a quiet dinner in the hotel dining room and go to bed. This was Win's best period. He stopped drinking. The more work that was piled upon him the sturdier was his response.

Win literally created the Squantum Naval Air Base by sweat and will power. The only trained personnel the Navy was able to assign to him was a handful of petty officers and mechanics. The staff consisted of young gentlemen, Reserve Officers, from Boston, who knew little or nothing about airplanes. Win's executive officer, for example, was Lieutenant M. J. Pierce, whose name was pronounced in Bostonese as "Purse." His aide was another proper Bostonian, Ensign G. R. Fearing, Jr., a well-known court-tennis player. Among the ensigns was a Cabot—Norman Cabot, who had captained a Harvard football team. Studying the roster of his Squantum command, with its high proportion of blue bloods, Win remarked wryly, "War is certainly shoving aviation up the social ladder."

At the same time, as a career officer, he greatly admired these young men for the lightheartedness with which they accepted the hazards of the air and the rigors of training—hazards and rigors that were all the greater because of the forcing methods necessary to produce pilots in quantity. Among the Navy professionals the new crop of aviators were known as "Eight-Week Wonders." The name derived from a telescoped course of instruction in seamanship, navigation, gunnery, signaling, meteorology, aerodynamics, and the principles of aviation that was crammed into the students in eight weeks, preparatory to flight training. But unlike some regular officers, Win never used the term in a derogatory or contemptuous context. He was proud of his "Eight-Week Wonders."

Living in Boston in those days was regarded as a difficult accomplishment for an outsider. Indeed, no American city, I believe, had a more forbidding reputation in this respect. I can only say, on the basis of my brief stay there, during the summer and early fall of 1917, that I was fascinated by Boston, though for reasons peculiar perhaps to me. Not having a car and being excluded, in any case, from the activities connected with the Station, I entertained myself during the day by taking excursions on the streetcars to historical landmarks. After I had exhausted the accessible supply of monuments, a sudden impulse opened up a new and absorbing source of entertainment. Being so much alone I formed the habit of reading the Boston newspapers from front to back, including even the want ads. Among the principal topics of journalistic attention at that period was a rather lurid murder case. Finding myself one forenoon in the vicinity of the Middlesex Superior Court in East Cambridge, where the case was being tried, I decided to go inside and watch the drama. It was the first time I was ever in a courtroom. My curiosity was instantly engaged, and I remained until the end of the day's proceedings and returned the next morning. In fact, I was a spectator until it went to the jury. A whole new view upon life, which happily cost nothing but carfare, having been presented to me, I extended my inquiries to include the Suffolk County Courthouse as well.

I may not have known much about the stately houses of Beacon Hill, but before Win's tour of duty was over, I was momentarily an expert upon some of Boston's sleazier characters. In the evening I would describe to Win the fine points of the day's proceedings, tally the score on the cut and thrust of the cross-examination, and render my judgment on the innocence or guilt of the defendant.

In late October, or thereabouts, my new hobby was summarily interrupted. Win was ordered to California with instructions to organize a naval air station on North Island, near San Diego, much bigger than the one at Squantum. That assignment almost broke his heart. Throughout the stay in Boston he had pulled every possible wire inside the Navy Department to arrange for a berth overseas. But the answer always was the same: he was too valuable where he was. North Island was a big job. Win was to have responsibility for the construction of a huge base and the training of hundreds of pilots and mechanics. But to find himself being sent, not to Europe, but in the opposite direction, was another bitter disappointment.

My recollection is that, having crossed the country by train, we arrived in San Diego in November. Compared to the busy metropolis it has become today, San Diego then was a small, leisurely, semi-tropical community. The palm trees and hibiscus, the tile-roofed, Spanish-type bungalows with flower-covered patios combined to make it a reasonable facsimile of the California publicity folders. I did not see how Win and I could fail to be happy there.

As matters turned out, it was quite a long time before we had a chance to find out. If I had seen little of Win during the Squantum period, I now saw almost nothing of him. For the first three months until the Station buildings were erected on North Island the offices were downtown in San Diego. Even so, he was off at the crack of dawn. He came home for lunch and then was off again not to return before dark.

Our first home was a furnished two-room apartment in the Paloma Apartments. I was taken with its spacious patio and general look of a private home; the whole atmosphere was pleasant and inviting. The rent was a bit higher than we felt we should pay, but I decided to forgo a cook to make up the difference. The management provided Japanese houseboys to whom could be delegated the general cleaning and the dishwashing. This decision to do my own cooking proved to be an impetuous one. I took it for granted that I had inherited some of my mother's talent as a cook. The flaw in this reasoning was that before my marriage I had never taken much interest in being her apprentice. My only equipment was a vague recollection of the way my mother used to do certain things and a copy of Fannie Farmer's *Boston Cooking-School Cook Book,* which had been a wedding present.

I gave my first dinner party as soon as I felt I knew Fannie Farmer well enough to get an entire meal ready to come off the stove at the same moment. My choice of victims was a young Army couple who lived nearby. The menu, I confess, was one that will surprise no young bride—Campbell's cream of tomato soup, roast beef and gravy, roast potatoes, artichokes with hollandaise sauce, and ice cream with chocolate sauce. The hollandaise sauce aside, this was certainly a cautious introduction to the hazards of cuisine. Yet, for all my careful preparations, beginning with a most conscientious reading of Fannie Farmer's directions, the experiment would almost certainly have ended in disaster had it not been for a prescription recommended by Win—one not to be found among the kitchen aids enumerated by Fannie Farmer, at least for the cook.

The morning of the dinner I went to the butcher's to pick out the beef. While dressing the meat the butcher ran a skewer clean through his hand. Some time later I found myself propped up in a chair with a cluster of strangers around me. I was covered with sawdust—somebody explained that I had fainted. Happily the butcher was not badly hurt, but it was an inauspicious start, and the developments of the afternoon augured no better for the dinner. By the time Win came home I was as nervous as a witch. I was sure that nothing would be ready on time, and if it was, it would not be on time with anything else. Win burst out laughing.

"Only one sure way of getting through this crisis," he decided after an examination of the stove and the oven, such as he might have given his flight instruments. Disappearing briefly, he returned to the kitchen bearing two cocktail glasses.

"One for the cook," he announced, pressing the glass into my hand. "A sovereign recipe."

I had never had a cocktail. And I was dubious of the wisdom of trying my first. But, as I appraised the simmering pots, I concluded that desperate measures were called for.

I do not know to this day what Win gave me—later acquaintanceship suggests that it was a double Martini. I do know that I finished the glass, and before long my apprehensions concerning the dinner miraculously dissolved. In due course the guests appeared; Win had cocktails for them; the need for hurry, or indeed for spending too much time over the kitchen range pleasantly evaporated. The hollandaise took on a creamy consistency under my masterful stirring, and I was not the least concerned to see flecks of it flying off my spoon and dotting the walls. When the time came to serve dinner, I returned briskly to the kitchen, and whisked through the final stirrings and bastings with scarcely a look at Fannie Farmer. Perhaps to everyone else's surprise, but not my own, the beef was done to a beautiful shade, there were no lumps in the gravy, and even the hollandaise was without a trace of curdling.

From then on I was converted to the cocktail as an occasional kitchen aid, but I never again allowed it to obscure my dependence upon Fannie Farmer. She became my Bible. I followed her to the letter. If she told me to tie the asparagus with two pieces of string I tied it with two, not one or three. Whatever reputation I may since have acquired as a hostess began with her.

For all my desire to fit myself into Win's world, I found myself at loose ends. The simple, closed pattern of Pensacola had flown apart under the pressure of his work. He was gone all day, and even nights and weekends his mind was never far from flying. I kept busy with household chores, marketing, and cooking three meals a day. Actually I only had a few hours in the afternoon to fill. These were pleasantly occupied with bridge, sight-seeing, or just visiting the friends I came to know. By five o'clock in the afternoon I would be home starting the dinner preparations. Once or twice I was tempted to resume my visits to the courts; but, San Diego being then a small community, I decided that it would not be seemly for the wife of the Commanding Officer of the new North Island Naval Air Station to become identified as a "buff" of local court proceedings.

My life would have been quite happy if only I had been able to convince myself, after a year of marriage, that Win and I possessed in ourselves the capacity for mutual understanding and compatibility. The painful truth is that, even though I could not bring myself to admit the fact, our marriage was already in serious trouble.

When Win's offices were moved to North Island in January, 1918, we took a double room in the Hotel del Coronado on Coronado Beach, so that Win would be nearer his work. There, for a little while, matters between us improved. The worst part of Win's job was behind him; the Station was now a going enterprise, and the training program was in full swing. As the wife of the Commanding Officer I was drawn into the official functions that went with the position. There was a steady incursion of high Navy "brass" in whose honor small cocktail and dinner parties had to be arranged. Win and I were brought together again, and something of the joy we knew during the first months at Pensacola was momentarily recaptured.

Best of all, I found in Coronado a little house whose owner was willing to rent. It was a typical California bungalow all on one floor except for an enormous living room that extended up an extra story. The front door was on the side and opened directly into the living room. Back of the living room across a small hall were the dining room and kitchen. Down this hall were our bedroom and bath and across the corridor two guest rooms and another bath. However, what I liked best about the house was a charming patio where we could have most of our meals and entertain our friends. There was little I could do or really needed to do in the way of decorating. The place was completely furnished when we rented it and most attractively so.

Just as I was settling down to the war pace of Coronado the Armistice came, on November 11, 1918. The celebration was a wild one. All day and far into the night most of the population of Coronado and San Diego—men and women, officers, enlisted men, and civilians —danced in the streets. Win could justly look with pride on what he and his instructors had accomplished. The men under his command had flown 35,000 hours, equal to 2,360,000 miles, without a single fatality, without a single student's being taken to the hospital, and without a single plane totally destroyed. It was a fine record.

But I could see Win's faith in himself disintegrating because of the Navy Department's failure to send him overseas, even though he had been promoted to lieutenant commander early in 1918. A suspicion grew in him that he was being sidetracked in favor of less experienced men. As he withdrew deeper and deeper inside himself, it became harder and harder for me to reach him.

Although we still had good times together on occasion, Win's drinking was also growing worse, and this intensified the jealous and sadistic streak in him. As is so often the case, he turned on the person he loved and made me the victim of his own inner aggressions. At parties he would go out of his way to direct at me a running barrage of subtle innuendoes and veiled insults. Outsiders were not supposed to understand these clever thrusts, but I certainly did, and they made my evenings terribly uncomfortable. I am naturally gay and flirtatious, and I was brought up to believe that one should be as entertaining as one can at a party. I have always loved to dance, and I was seldom left sitting at the table when "Avalon," or "A Pretty Girl Is Like a Melody," or other haunting tunes of that era when jazz was new and exciting were being played. My gaiety, and even more the response of others to it, made Win jealous; and, as the evenings wore on and he drank more and more, he either became loud and assertive or slumped into a moody silence while he thought up new and more wounding taunts. Often he would disappear, and friends would have to take me home. Sometimes these absences would last well into the next day, and no apologies or explanations were ever forthcoming.

While Win was interested in meeting people and impressed them on first acquaintance as being a genial extrovert, at home he was just the opposite. When we were alone, a whole day might pass without his ever speaking a word to me. Or if he did choose to speak, it was usually to tax me with being a flirt and ignoring him. His propensity for playing practical jokes now took a sadistic turn. One of his favorite diversions was to lock me up in a room while he went out—often for hours on end. Our life together became a succession of quarrels —bitter flurries over nothing really important, but all the more difficult to compose in the immemorial fashion of lovers because the root cause was Win's festering discontent with himself. The erosion of a marriage is a harrowing experience, and I shall not chronicle all the details; they cannot be unusual.

I desperately cast about for some solution to our difficulties. With the war over and the Navy demobilizing, there seemed to be a shrinking scope for Win's talents. Moreover, it was by now clear to me that he had made several powerful enemies in the Navy's higher echelons of command. I therefore suggested in a most tentative manner that he think about making a career in business, possibly in the newly born field of commercial aviation. I was also thinking perhaps selfishly of myself as well. Much as I respected the Navy, I had seen enough of it to realize that it was not really for me. I was simply not made for the mode of life that went with a Service career—gypsy pilgrimages to new stations for brief sojourns in rented bungalows or tasteless Government housing, endlessly repeated associations with the same people conditioned to the same interests, and always the struggle for promotion. We should both do better, I was sure, in a less ingrown, not quite so self-contained way of life where our respective temperaments would be less at war with the prevailing state of things.

But Win would have none of that. He was Navy through and through, and to him such thoughts were heresy. So I put them out of my own mind and reconciled myself to facing, with all possible grace and in good heart, whatever assignment the Bureau of Navigation might have in store for him.

No new assignment was forthcoming for a year and a half. Beginning in February, 1920, Win was put in charge of a detachment of naval aviators who were taking instruction in flying land planes. This assignment took him to March Field, at Riverside, California, and then to Ream Field at Imperial Beach. I stayed on in Coronado.

Meanwhile, things did not improve between Win and me. Our marriage now began to break up in earnest. In the hope of rousing him out of himself I attempted to draw more people into the contracting orbit of our marriage. I had made a number of friends, among them Rhoda and Marianna Fullam, the gay and attractive daughters of the late Rear Admiral William Fullam, and Rita Chase, the young wife of a rich Easterner from New Jersey who had settled in Coronado.

They knew everybody; and through them and other friends Win and I received many invitations—polo at Del Monte; beach parties at La Jolla; weekends at Santa Barbara. Maurice Heckscher appeared with a string of polo ponies. The Spreckels of San Francisco resumed entertaining in their handsome houses. And the Hotel del Coronado became even more popular as a gathering place. It was there, for example, that I met John Barrymore and Charlie Chaplin, but not, as one popular story has it, the Prince of Wales, when he called in at San Diego aboard the *Renown* in April, 1920, on his trip to the Antipodes. But these attempts at gregariousness only intensified our private difficulties.

During this unhappy period my mother came to stay with us. Although I had been careful not to mention a word of our difficulties, she may have read between the lines of my letters. She stayed about a month. Win and I put the best possible face upon our situation. He was charming to her and, in her presence, to me. If my mother finally surmised how matters really stood between him and me, she did not let on, nor did I tell her.

The morning she started back to Baltimore she said, "Wallis, the thing that worries me most about you is that you give your friendship too easily; you always feel you know people right away—or think you do—and I'm afraid it's going to get you in a lot of trouble someday." I looked at her in some surprise, but my mother smiled quickly. "I know, dear," she said. "I do, too."

A temporary truce in our personal struggle was brought about by Win's being ordered back to Pensacola, in November, 1920, for a short tour of duty as senior instructor. It was agreed between us that I should remain in Coronado until he received permanent duty. A whole winter went by in this uncertainty. Finally, in May, Win received orders to report to the Navy Department in Washington, as assistant to Rear Admiral William Moffett, who was preparing to set up the new Bureau of Aeronautics. Now Win wrote me exultantly, saying, "I'll have my chance to do something useful." I was happy for him and for myself.

CHAPTER VII

The First Separation

ACROSS THE YEARS I AM STILL UNABLE TO EXPLAIN WHY I WELCOMED so eagerly Win's new tour of duty. Did I really believe that a change of scene would shore up the crumbling foundations of our marriage, make whole again the damaged fabric of love and mutual trust? The truth is, I suppose, that wounded and disillusioned by countless indignities, I was almost in a state of shock and beyond reason. All that was left to me was to hope against hope for a miracle. I had been brought up in the ancient belief that marriage represented ultimate fulfillment for a woman; and the realization that my marriage with Win was a failure, or at the edge of failure, was more than I could admit to him or to myself. I had to go on trying.

Life has since taught me that a change in material circumstances has little effect upon love that is securely established, but love that has been weakened and undermined is at the mercy of every incident and irrelevancy. Far from having the good effect I had hoped for, our move to Washington only made the wreckage complete.

Win's assignment with the Navy's Bureau of Aeronautics could have been a wonderful opportunity for an airman of his experience and ability. It brought him back into the fold of the Navy's ruling hierarchy. He was in an excellent position to attract the favorable attention of his superiors, press for the adoption of his own ideas, and overcome whatever unfavorable impressions his eccentricities might have caused. For myself, I hoped for something not quite so complicated. It was that once Win was able to concentrate the power of his will upon matters that were really meaningful to him, the inner tensions that drove him so mercilessly would be set at rest. I was soon to be disappointed.

Actually, Win was never cut out to fight either a war or a peace from behind a desk. He had always loathed the routine and paper-shuffling connected with administrative duties; he drafted reports and memorandums in a mood of baffled fury. Again, Win was dedicated heart and soul to flying, and this was the era of the famous controversy between the battleship admirals and the Army Air Service, led by Brigadier General Billy Mitchell. Though he was devoted to the Navy, Win deplored the attitude of the "black-shoe" Navy toward the airplane, even more than he deplored the brash claims of the Army Air Service. As time went on, he grew more and more unhappy and demoralized.

To make matters worse, one of his superiors in whom Win had always placed especial faith and confidence turned against him. I myself had never shared my husband's esteem for this officer; and, although I tried to avoid an I-told-you-so attitude, Win included me somehow in his self-anger at having misjudged his man. And as so often happens, since nothing was right at the office, nothing was right at home. Whatever I did was wrong in Win's eyes, and in this unhappy situation, he did what was so easy for him—he took to the bottle.

We were living in a service apartment in a hotel called the Brighton. Win was not a quiet drinker, and the walls of the hotel were not particularly solid. I had the humiliation of having our private difficulties become known to our friends.

I pleaded with my husband to save such remnants of dignity and self-respect as were still left to us. Brought up as I had been in families ruled by a code of considerate conduct, I could not bear any public indelicacy. And I was aghast at the deterioration of his character that daily confronted me, transforming a brilliant officer into a mixed-up neurotic.

Then, one Sunday afternoon, Win locked me in the bathroom of our apartment. For hours, I heard no sound from beyond the door. Whether Win had gone out or whether he was still in the apartment, playing a practical joke, I could not tell. I tried to unscrew the lock with a nail file, but I had to give up when I found I could not stir the screws. As the afternoon wore on and evening came, I was seized with panic at the thought that Win might mean to keep me a prisoner all night. I wanted desperately to call for help, but held myself in check. Our situation was already distressing enough without my drawing attention to so sordid an episode.

After an interminable time, I heard the sound of a key turning in the lock. But the door did not open, and I was afraid to try the handle myself. When I finally got up enough courage to do so, the apartment was in darkness. I could hear Win's breathing from the bed. The rest of the night I spent on the sofa in the living room, endlessly reviewing the events that had led to my personal catastrophe. Of only one thing I was certain: I had somehow become the symbol of Win's frustrations, and to leave matters as they were going could only result in the final destruction of his career and of my life along with his. There was no solution but to leave him.

Next morning, after Win had left for the Navy Department, I went to see my mother, who was now living at 2301 Connecticut Avenue. I dreaded telling her what I had in mind. Once I left him there was only one honest course for me—a divorce. My mother, Aunt Bessie, and Cousin Lelia Barnett all had a horror of divorce, and I had grown into womanhood sharing their views. Throughout my family, in all of its ramifications, there were deep-seated religious scruples against divorce, no matter what the grievance. It was a matter of stout pride to my mother and aunt that there had never been a divorce in the Montague family, whatever its other misfortunes. Nor, so far as I knew, had there ever been a divorce among the Warfields. My mother and her sister believed that marriage was indissoluble. And they themselves had always been prepared to act in strict keeping with the terms of this code. How could I ever face these uncompromising women? How could I hope to win them to my side?

As simply as I could, and leaving out the most painful details, I told my mother what had been happening to my marriage with Win. She was upset. But when I told her what I intended to do, she was appalled.

"Oh, Wallis," she cried, "you can't be serious! Getting divorced would be the most terrible mistake you could make—one that you would never live down."

"I can think of a worse mistake," I said grimly. "That would be for Win and me to go on as we are."

It was rarely my mother's way to force me to accept her decisions. Rather, she counted on reason to bring me around. "Don't be so foolish as to imagine that divorce will end your difficulties," she told me. "Of course, it's easy enough to burn one's bridges—I've seen many of my friends set fire to theirs—and I can understand how love can turn to hate or loathing. But I've observed, too, that many of them found the road ahead to be even more difficult. They would gladly have turned back, but the bridges were gone."

My mother talked on quietly, trying to persuade me to abandon the idea of divorce, at least until I had tried again to keep our marriage together. In any event, she warned me, the Warfields would be anything but approving if I divorced Win, and I would have to look to them for financial support unless I was prepared to earn my own living. "Nor will your Aunt Bessie be pleased to hear what you have in mind. You know her views very well. She isn't going to welcome the idea of your being the first Montague to be divorced."

"Perhaps the Montague women have been lucky till now," I said with a cynicism I did not intend. "You just became widows. Besides, people's ideas about divorce are changing. It's the only solution for a marriage that has become unbearable."

My mother touched my hand. "Wallis, I know how very hard all this must be for you. Let's stop thinking about it for a little while. Let's go out to lunch."

All through lunch, mother talked gaily about a number of things quite unconnected with my problems. Then, just as we were separating, she observed quietly, "I've been married to two men. Neither was continuously easy to live with. Being a successful wife is an exercise in understanding."

"A point comes," I said bitterly, "where one is at the end of one's endurance. I'm at that point now."

My mother urged me to talk to Aunt Bessie, so that afternoon I called on her. She had some shopping to do, and we walked down Connecticut Avenue together. If she suspected what was on my mind, she gave no indication of it, talking briskly in her usual intemperate way about the latest act of "that outrageous government of ours." When an opportune moment presented itself, I told her that I had made up my mind to leave Win and intended to get a divorce.

Aunt Bessie came to a dead stop in the middle of the street. "Divorce!" she exclaimed. "It's unthinkable. Surely you and Win can't be contemplating so dreadful a thing."

I told her that, dreadful though it might be, I saw no alternative. Aunt Bessie shook her head angrily. "You must try again. Or go away for a while, by yourself, and let the dust settle. Or, as a last resort, agree on a temporary separation. But whatever you do, don't get a divorce."

Aunt Bessie said much more. I had been too young to know what I was doing when I got married, and I was still too young to appreciate what a divorce meant. If I persisted in my folly, my future would be worse than uncertain. As a divorced woman, I would be entering a wilderness—the shelter, support, and companionship of marriage

[77]

would all be behind me; and, as a woman who had failed already as a wife, I could scarcely hope to achieve these things again. Had I even considered where I would go and what I would do? Was I not in reality giving up something for nothing? Suddenly, Aunt Bessie stopped. At last she said, in a tone of absolute finality, "The Montague women do not get divorced."

It was too much. "Aunt Bessie," I cried, no longer in control of myself, "how can you possibly appeal to that old-fashioned convention when it's a question of saving or sacrificing what is left of the lives of two unhappy people? How can you urge me to live my life in a relationship that is destroying us? How can you urge me to do this to Win? We're both young. We still have a chance to make something of our lives." This I remember. And I imagine there was a good deal more about the mockery of a separation for appearances' sake.

By way of an answer, Aunt Bessie reminded me that I would have to see my Uncle Sol. "If your mother and I can't knock the idea out of your head, possibly your Warfield relatives can. You'll have to tell them, you know. Your Uncle Sol is as opposed to divorce as the rest of us. You had better tell him before he hears about it from someone else." And on that note she turned away.

Bewildered, momentarily shaken in my resolve, I went back to the apartment. That evening Win did not come home for dinner. Long after I had gone to bed, I heard him come in, but he did not speak to me. And when I woke in the morning, he was gone. I faced the day torn by doubt and uncertainty. Though I had spoken out bravely the day before, it was hard to put aside the knowledge of the pain that my choice was sure to bring my family, so proud of its ties, so sure of the fortitude of its women. And yet, the more I thought about the advice of my mother and Aunt Bessie, the clearer it seemed to me that their outlook rested on a conception of women's status that was rapidly ceasing to be true to the facts of modern life. I could imagine circumstances that would make divorce indefensible. But the idea that two people, without children and responsible only to each other, should attempt to preserve a marriage that was destroying both of them seemed to me just as indefensible.

If ideas like these are common enough today, they were revolutionary in the early 1920's. Nevertheless, I had to take my courage in my hands and go to Baltimore to see Uncle Sol.

I called on him in the afternoon at his bank, a setting in which he was always at his most formidable. Before many minutes had passed, I knew that if I had sown the wind with my Montague relations, I was reaping the whirlwind with the Warfield side. Not that Uncle Sol was particularly stirred by the recital of my trials. He reserved his emotion for the disclosure of my intention to profane the family traditions. "I won't let you bring this disgrace upon us!" he announced. The Warfields, he exclaimed, in all their known connections since 1662, had never had a divorce. "What will the people of Baltimore think?" I had always been aware of my Uncle Sol's preoccupation with what people thought. His steely attitude strengthened my resolve. Though I was trembling, I sat bolt upright in my chair, as my grandmother in her own house had taught me to do, prepared to rise and take my leave without a word when he had finished his lecture.

But perhaps this deportment struck some nostalgic chord, for his mood changed abruptly. He seemed to regret his vehemence. "Never having been married myself," he said gently, "I may be a little dogmatic about these things. I've seen the marriages of my friends go to pieces—yes, I think I can understand how circumstances may make the idea of going on with some marriages seem quite intolerable." I was more moved by this unexpected flash of sympathy than I had been frightened by his harshness. When he suggested that I return to Washington and make another effort to stay with Win, I meekly agreed.

I kept my promise and returned to our apartment. Win may have guessed what was up, and for a fortnight or so our relationship was almost tranquil. Then the trouble began all over again, and everything I did rubbed him the wrong way. One evening he did not return until after dinner. I had a long time to think, and the more I thought about the advice of the members of my family, the more it appeared to me that they could not possibly understand what I was going through both physically and mentally. In my mother's case, the plain fact was that two deaths, sad experiences though they were, had relieved her of the necessity for testing her own stern principles. As for Aunt Bessie, her conception of marriage was so absolute as to have no relevance whatsoever to my own unhappy situation. I recalled how in happier times, my mother used to tease Aunt Bessie about remaining a widow despite the fact that there were several men who were anxious to marry her. She had worn mourning for so long that my mother had been moved to say a number of times, "Honestly, Wallis, do you think your Aunt Bessie is ever going to take off that veil?" And to whom had I been sent as to a court of final appeal? To a confirmed bachelor, a bachelor on principle. My conscience was clear.

When Win came home, I told him of my decision. Whatever his

faults, he was still essentially a gentleman. "Wallis," he said slowly, "I've had it coming to me. If you ever change your mind, I'll still be around."

That very night I went to my mother to ask whether I might move in with her until I could find a place of my own.

"You are absolutely sure," my mother asked, "that this is what you really want?"

"If I've never been sure of anything before, I'm sure about this," I told her.

"In that case," she said resignedly, "you may stay with me."

Aunt Bessie was summoned to yet another family council, this time after the fact. I thanked my aunt and my mother for their well-meant advice and told them how much I regretted the pain I was causing them. But I made it clear that I would set about getting a divorce with no feelings of guilt, and that get it I would—with or without the help of my family. Then I went to my room.

Before going to bed, I wrote a long and, I suspect, overwrought letter to Uncle Sol. His answer was formal, almost stiff. Any divorce action that I might contemplate I must undertake entirely with my own resources; no help of any kind would be forthcoming from him.

CHAPTER VIII

The Slow Unraveling

NOT LONG AFTERWARD, IN FEBRUARY, 1922, WIN WAS ORDERED TO the Far East as commander of a gunboat on what the Navy then called the Asiatic Station. This was in accordance with the Navy practice of regarding its fliers as sailors for whom the air was only a second medium. The regulations of the service prescribed long tours of sea duty at intervals for every line officer, whatever his field of special competence, and to Win's distaste his turn had come. I continued to hear from him. Every now and then, there would be a letter from Hong Kong, where his ship was based—laconic letters telling of sweltering patrols up and down the Pearl River, which flows through Canton, of bumping into fellow officers we both knew, of the enervating heat and unending squalor of China. He was unhappy—and not only because he was alone. Win was out of his medium. The command of a small ship, which Navy men of his day considered the pleasantest berth in the service, had no attractions for him. He looked upon sea duty as a sentence of exile, to be served out to the last prescribed day and hour, before the Navy would allow him to return to the air.

I was unhappy, too, but it was because I was alone. Loneliness descended upon my spirit, an emptiness I had not counted upon. A marriage, even one that goes awry, generates claims and needs that persist like an afterglow long after the emotional fire is burned out. The mind and the heart continue to remember the happy and cozy times together, and the unpleasantnesses recede. Now, having separated—as far as I could tell forever—I began to learn that a marriage is not so easily uprooted, that divorce itself is no escape. There is no evading what has been lived through together. The habit of mutuality intrudes itself upon the simplest arrangements and judgments of the day. One begins the most ordinary project, only to realize that it must be done alone, or with a stranger—and that is an altogether different thing. The real essence of any marriage that has struggled, however unsuccessfully, toward happiness lies in the growth of a wordless understanding that what is acceptable to one partner will be acceptable to the other. Between the storms, Win and I had briefly known a sharing of this kind. And the habit of shared experience makes the process of detachment inexpressibly difficult. There can be no summary and dramatic end to a marriage—only a slow and painful unraveling of a tangled skein of threads too stubborn to be broken.

A woman in this situation becomes a kind of female Crusoe, a castaway upon an emotional sea. And it is remarkable how many "men Friday" will emerge from the underbrush to help a lonely woman. The 1920's were, I recall, a particularly hazardous era for American women, especially on sofas and in rumble seats. But there is a safe strategy for women, applicable to their situation in every stage of history, and that is for a woman to have a code by which she is determined to live. I had such a code, which was never to allow myself to drift into light affairs of the moment. But one must pay the price—many evenings alone. I was determined to wait until I was sure I had found a deep love that would engage both my mind and my emotions.

There was good company in the Washington of the early 1920's, perhaps the most charming, exciting, and cosmopolitan company to be found in the United States. Those were the days of the administrations of Harding and Coolidge when the personnel of government was restricted in numbers to an extent that is almost unimaginable today. The entire Federal bureaucracy in Washington could have been housed quite satisfactorily in two of today's Pentagons. Washington in those days was much more like a provincial capital than a national seat of government—certainly it bore little resemblance to the commotion-ridden, world-power center of the present. Congress, as it assembled and adjourned, seemed to be imitating the comings and goings of a flock of migratory birds. Meanwhile, quite indifferent to the legislative flurries at the far end of Pennsylvania Avenue, the permanent community of old families, who called themselves the "Cave Dwellers," carried on their graceful Southern existence, accepting or rejecting mere officialdom as the spirit moved them. Revolving around this core, and less like satellites than like stars in their own right, was the group known as the "diplomatic set." Compared to the present *corps diplomatique* in the capital, it was a small and relatively uncomplicated society.

When I first came to know these people, in the role of an "extra" woman, diplomacy was still a profession carried on by men of cultured background. And because its devotees had known one another in various parts of the world, they formed a subtly interlaced group of their own, one that to a young woman newly arrived from the parochialism of a naval station seemed incomparably urbane and luxurious. That group, before the advent of the economic adviser, the agricultural expert, the cultural attaché, was still so small that a second or even a third secretary of a legation was a personality in his own right, a young man of charm, an accomplished dancer, worldly wise without being world-weary, sophisticated without being cynical. And the surplus of attractive, unattached men of this stamp made the diplomatic set a special paradise for women on their own.

What delighted me about this world was its easy mixture of the formal and the charmingly informal. Elaborate evening receptions— white-tie affairs, with the women in their most splendid clothes—and protracted dinners sometimes followed by dancing in the embassy ballrooms alternated with teas and cocktail parties in which the conventions of the European drawing room were just beginning to crumble before the assaults of the Charleston, the Lost Generation, and the American Flapper.

Some of my women friends had also gravitated to Washington. Marianna Sands, whom I had known in San Diego and Coronado, was back in Washington; and Marianna, like me, was separated from her husband. Among others I made friends with Ethel Noyes, whose father was president of the Associated Press. She, too, was separated from her husband, and she was later to marry Willmott Lewis, the distinguished correspondent of the London *Times,* and like him regale Europe and America with her uninhibited wit. (She will long be remembered for her remark apropos of the knighting of her husband: "Well, it took King George to make a lady of me!") We were all about the same age, had the same interests, knew the same people, and our lives became gaily intertwined. Together we went to the same round of embassy parties, Sunday-night suppers at the houses of friends, impromptu excursions to pleasant little country restaurants, picnics in the Virginia countryside. But some of our gayest times occurred at the very special luncheons given by the "Soixante Gourmets." This famous club, composed of sixty of the younger set, met once a week at midday at the Hotel Hamilton, and each member was expected to bring a lady. One lunched in leisurely fashion, seated at a long table that extended down one side of the dining room. The conversation always struck me as brilliant, and not the less so because it was conducted in at least four languages, only one of which I fully understood. Everyone has observed how the half-heard remarks of strangers and the half-understood comments of foreigners are always so much more interesting than the conversation of the people in one's own party. Something of this spirit must have colored my vision of those luncheons, for I see them to this day in a kind of rich golden haze.

The change from my Pensacola and Coronado days was very stimulating, and yet this new life was so easy and charming that before I realized what was happening I was already part of it. The most celebrated wit of the "Soixante Gourmets" was Willmott Lewis. He shared a house with Harold Sims of the British Embassy. Bill Lewis was famous for his subtle characterizations of politicians and celebrities on the national scene. When he started to tell a story, whether on politics or last night's party, everyone stopped talking and listened. I remember his saying that everyone should be married to a Montague once in his life, and he liked to greet what he considered my sometimes whimsical inconsistencies with, "Oh, the Montaguity of it." Rose Nano, wife of the Counselor of the Rumanian Legation, was the great beauty of the Diplomatic Corps. Prince Caetani, the Italian Ambassador, was the handsomest, most-sought-after bachelor of the group. Jules Henry, a secretary of the French Embassy, gave many amusing parties. Juan Francisco Cardenas, the Counselor of the Spanish Embassy, later an ambassador, was a serious diplomat but with great charm and a sense of fun. Henry Hopkinson, then Third Secretary of the British Embassy, now Lord Colyton and recently Minister of State for Colonial Affairs, gave the impression that he took nothing seriously, but his career has disproved this.

These are only a few of the group who happen to stand out in my memory; there were many more. If one judges from the unhappy condition in which the world would all too soon find itself, the diplomacy practiced by these witty young men of the embassies and legations may not have been so effective as events nowadays demand, but it certainly imparted a gloriously civilized aspect to the comity of nations. So far as I was concerned, the male population of the eastern seaboard at that time consisted almost exclusively of military attachés, diplomats, and other cosmopolites. These young men were in the vanguard of what was called—first in hope and later in cynicism—the Brave New World. It was a world, I remember, in which all problems were to be solved out of hand by a generation that was sure it knew all the answers.

Naturally the day was never long enough for a generation so worthily occupied. It was mystifying to me how quickly it could disappear, and the best part of the evening as well. I was often out quite late. Whatever the hour, my mother was always waiting for me, sitting up in bed, reading or sewing, when I came in. She never failed to ask me where I had been, what I had done, and with whom. I always told her. But having herself been brought up under a convention that held that no self-respecting woman should be out after midnight with a man not her husband, my answers must have been strangely disquieting to her. One evening she asked, more curious than angry, "I wish you'd explain to me, Wallis, exactly what you do when you stay up until two o'clock, night after night."

There was a scene, not serious, but yet painful for us both. With the arrogance of youth, I insisted that I was a grown woman, quite able to take care of myself, and at an age when it was humiliating to be compelled to punch a time clock. "Mother, if you're going to worry about me whenever I stay out, and if I, on my part, have to worry about your sitting up to wait for me—"

As if to end the argument, my mother put out the light over her bed. Her last words, spoken in the darkness, were friendly in tone, but quite unmistakable in their intention. "I know very well that you will do exactly as you choose. But as long as we are under the same roof, I shall continue to tell you what I think is right."

An unquenchable desire for freedom had sprung up within me. I really had no idea of exactly what I intended to make of my life, but I was determined to make it a success within my capacities. It was not quite enough for me to be, or at least try to be, the life of the party, or to spend my existence merely taking part in good conversation. I wanted something more out of life. I could not feel that one unsuccessful marriage was the end of the road. I still believed in marriage and that within its framework lay my true destiny and my happiness. At this stage of my life the thought of any other career had no appeal. In my mind I had the picture of the sort of man I wanted. Ideally he would be a young man who was making his mark in business, diplomacy, or one of the professions. He would like and understand people and above all appreciate me. I wanted someone who would make me a part of his life and whom I could help in his career. I wanted a man who would draw me into the full circle of his existence in all its aspects.

I met several men who came close to measuring up to my ideal—interesting, successful men who also seemed more than passingly attracted to me. But a funny thing happened: much as my mind told me that I should encourage them, my heart held back. Its dictates proved far more compelling than those of my reason, and I found myself unable to consider marriage without being completely committed, emotionally as well as mentally.

This is not to say that my heart was never stirred. It became involved in Washington. There was a young diplomat attached to the embassy of a Latin American country. Only a little older than I, he was already marked as a man of great promise. He was intelligent, ambitious, subtle, gracious—in many respects the most fascinating man I have ever met, with principles of steel and a spirit that bubbled like champagne. For a time he was only a gay escort, somebody to take me to this party or that. Then he came to mean much more. Perhaps without realizing it, he acted as both teacher and model in the art of living. He took me out of the world of small talk and into the wider world of affairs and diplomacy.

This may well have been what was worrying my mother. I was not yet divorced—indeed, I had made only tentative gestures in that direction. I was conscious of drifting dangerously, and yet I was reluctant to free myself from so beguiling a current. I knew that I could not continue to have it both ways. I must either go through with my divorce or return to Win.

As my mother was planning to move, I left her apartment in the summer of 1922 to share a little house in Georgetown with a friend, Mrs. Luke McNamee, the wife of a naval officer who was abroad on a mission. Thus passed another pleasant but rather aimless year. At this point, Corinne Mustin re-entered my life. Henry had died during the summer of 1923, and after several months of mourning, she wrote to me, asking me to go abroad with her. I leaped at the idea. Corinne wanted to go to Paris, and this was particularly appealing. At the back of my mind was a vague notion, picked up from my newspaper reading, that a Paris divorce would be simple. There was one small difficulty: I had very little money.

Win gave me $225 a month out of his Navy pay. The sum was adequate for my needs in Washington but permitted no such excursion as the one Corinne was planning. There was no choice but to throw myself on the bounty of Uncle Sol. This I did most apprehensively, in the light of our last formal exchange of sentiments; but on the other hand, I reasoned that he was my father's brother, that he had always been generous to me, and that I was fond of him. I learned that he was staying in New York, at the Plaza Hotel, where he kept an apartment. Having first written to say that I regretted not having seen him for so long and was in need of his wise counsel, I took the train for New York, bracing myself for what I was reasonably sure would be a difficult interview.

Uncle Sol was occupied with an important business call when I was ushered into his apartment, which I had never seen until then. His preoccupation gave me the opportunity for a brief glimpse of the New York side of his life, which, though vaguely rumored, had remained successfully partitioned off from his family side. As I looked around, I could scarcely believe what I saw. The puritanical banker had covered the walls of his sitting room with photographs of actresses and opera singers—all of them affectionately or respectfully autographed to Uncle Sol by the donors. Almost all were strikingly beautiful women. Something stirred in memory—a vignette from childhood of a much younger Uncle Sol in the gloomy parlor of Preston Street, listening with raptness to operatic arias issuing from the horn of the Victrola. Could it have been that Uncle Sol's seemingly incongruous fascination with opera even then extended beyond an appreciation of the music alone? There was, then, beneath the sternness a hidden aesthetic, possibly even a Bohemian, side.

While I was admiring the photograph of a particularly attractive woman, Uncle Sol materialized at my side.

"She's very beautiful," I said.

"Ah," said Uncle Sol.

"French?"

"No, Italian."

From Uncle Sol there issued a faint sound that I would have been forced to identify as a sigh had it proceeded from anyone else. "A tragic story," Uncle Sol said. "She was a coloratura—lovely voice, a graceful figure, one of the most promising singers I've heard in a long time. Now she's dying in Italy."

"Uncle Sol, I'd always heard that you were interested in the theater and the opera. But I'd never realized that your interest was so extensive."

"Wallis," said Uncle Sol reflectively, "I long ago concluded that banking, while a convenient way to make a living, can be extremely dull." His glance swept appreciatively over his gallery of beauties, and for my part, I was still staring, wide-eyed and fascinated, when he took me by the hand and led me to a chair.

He reverted briskly to the banker-uncle role, and I set about explaining my call. I told him about Corinne's plan, mentioned that I had never been abroad before, and placed particular emphasis on what I knew would appeal to him the most—the scant attention that a foreign divorce would attract in Baltimore. I got no farther than the word divorce. Uncle Sol still did not approve of my getting a divorce anywhere, and he could not bear the thought of what might happen, on such a long trip, to two unaccompanied women.

"We're not going unaccompanied, Uncle Sol," I pleaded. "We're accompanying each other. Corinne is older than I. She'll be my chaperone."

Uncle Sol was not impressed. He gave me to understand that he had as little faith in the widows of the present generation as he had in the divorcées. And indeed, Corinne was a very attractive young widow. She wore a tiny tight-fitting black crepe hat faced with a narrow white band, to which was attached a flowing black crepe veil that hung to just below her shoulders. With her blond hair and big blue eyes she was simply ravishing. With Montague flippancy we called this her hunting cap. If Uncle Sol could have seen her, his apprehensions would have multiplied. At last, he asked me where we proposed to go. I told him Paris.

At this there was a real explosion. "Good God!" my uncle said. "Why Paris? Paris, of all cities!" Uncle Sol was on his feet. He launched into a denunciation of Parisian morals that led me to reflect fleetingly that he seemed very well informed on this subject. At the height of his outburst, he came to a halt directly under a particularly provocative photograph—I can still see the alluring pose and tender inscription. Suddenly, the whole thing struck me as very funny. When he paused for breath, I mildly suggested that perhaps any city might be immoral if one chose to make it so. I had never said anything like that to Uncle Sol before, and I do not think too many people had. But I could not help it—there was something really ludicrous about receiving a lecture on morality from a man standing squarely in front of such a picture. For a moment I did not know what was going to happen. Then, slowly, Uncle reached into his pocket and took out some money. I did not look at what he had given me until I was in a taxicab. There were five brand-new hundred-dollar bills.

Corinne Mustin and I sailed in January, 1924, on a small American ship. While Corinne had some insurance money and a Navy widow's pension, she was far from affluent. We knew no one on board, and it was a terribly rough trip. Corinne was seasick most of the way across, and I was timid about wandering around the ship by myself. But we two Montagues had so much fun laughing and joking with each other that we scarcely noticed the other passengers.

It was dark when the boat train arrived in Paris; and, having neglected to arrange for our hotel rooms in advance, we taxied all over the city in search of a place we could afford. Near midnight—and still supperless—we finally pulled up at a gloomy and dilapidated little hostelry on the Avenue MacMahon. It no longer exists, and I am not surprised.

After two or three days of coping with the extras that multiply so mysteriously in the arithmetic of French hotels, we decided that even this establishment was beyond our means, and we had to renew the hunt. This time, after an all-day search, we found a tiny hotel in the rue Pierre Charron. It was far from elaborate, but it seemed like a haven of comfort to two lone women in a strange city.

Fortunately, we were not two lone women for long. Corinne, who knew people almost everywhere, suddenly remembered a friend in Paris, a bachelor officer who had been a close friend of her husband. His name was William "Imp" Eberle, and he was the Assistant Naval Attaché at the American Embassy. Commander Eberle invited us to dinner at once, and with him was Elbridge Gerry Green, then First Secretary of the Embassy, also a bachelor. The dinner proved the happiest kind of beginning. We became a foursome.

Our escorts were extremely knowledgeable about cathedrals and châteaux as well as cafés and restaurants, and soon our evenings were taken up with exploring the city while our weekends were solidly booked for trips through the French countryside. Corinne was a wonderful companion. Gallant and indefatigable, she was the kind of person one could count on to hop into the car and not care in the least where she was going or how long it would take to get there. One day, however, after she had several times looked out and seen the sign *Ralentir*—French for "Slow Down"—she did protest. "Skinny," she said, "are you sure these men know where they are going? This is the third time today we've been through Ralentir."

One day, not to be behindhand with our hosts in hospitality, we asked them up for a drink. The next morning the hotel manager called us on the carpet. We were not to have men in our room. We were outraged. Immediately we called Imp and Gerry and explained what had happened. Then we hurriedly packed our things. If the manager was going to take such an attitude, we, in turn, would give him something to think about. We removed to the lobby and sat there for more than an hour, awaiting our knights errant, surrounded with bags, parcels, half-opened boxes, and even an ironing board.

Our friends moved us to the Hotel Matignon, where we remained until Corinne returned to America—with several new hunting caps, this time with Paris labels. I myself decided to stay. By this time I had many friends, not to mention several beaux, in Paris, so the decision was easy enough to make. Also, Ethel Noyes had come over to Europe, and she and her friend Isabel Bradley asked me to share the apartment they had rented. This I was delighted to do, the novelty of my tiny room in the hotel having long since worn off.

Ethel was in the process of getting a divorce, preparatory to her marriage to Willmott Lewis, and the prospect of getting mine at the same time and having the benefit of their guidance was too convenient to pass by. After joining them, however, I got a rude awakening. Of all the lawyers to whom I talked, none was the least bit interested in undertaking my case for less than several thousand dollars. To me, the figure was astronomical. Discouraged and disillusioned, I abandoned entirely my efforts to secure a divorce.

To tell the truth, my legal shopping had been somewhat half-hearted. All this time, Win had continued to write to me from the other side of the world. He kept urging me to forget the past, to join him in China, and give him one more chance to rebuild our marriage. My resolution began to weaken. The bitter memories of strife and unhappiness had begun to fade with the lapse of time, and besides, I was no longer quite so enthusiastic about the abstract benefits of freedom. I had recently been spending much of my time in the company of women who were separated from their husbands or actually divorced, and my eyes had been opened to the fact that these women were far from happy. A divorce was an admission of failure, no matter how one looked at it, and I was unutterably cast down at having failed not only myself, but Win, in the most important venture of our lives.

Now, Win wrote pleading with me to return to him and suggesting that I could board a naval transport at Norfolk and travel to China at Government expense. While I was considering all this, Ethel Noyes told me that she was going home on the *France*. She invited me to accompany her, and I said yes—with such unexpected eagerness that I had to recognize it as evidence of feelings that I had been stubbornly refusing to acknowledge, even to myself: the long-suppressed yearning for a half-forgotten tenderness and the warm presence of someone I loved. So be it, I thought. Win and I have failed in the West. Perhaps in the East we can find our way to a new life together.

CHAPTER IX

Reunion and Parting

JUNE, 1924, FOUND ME BACK IN WASHINGTON WITH MY MOTHER, who was now living at the Woburn Apartments, which she called the "Woebegone." There was a letter from Win, saying that he had notified the Navy Department that I was joining him in Hong Kong and that I was to arrange through the Department for passage aboard a Navy transport. My mother was slightly startled though delighted that we were going to try a reconciliation. But she was concerned over my going so far away on such an uncertain mission. "You were very sure before you left him," she said, "that you could never live with him again. Do you think you can make a go of it now?"

I confessed frankly that I wasn't sure; there was no way of telling. The only thing about which I was sure was that something inside me kept urging me to give our marriage a second try. "And the truth is, I suppose, I still love him," I told my mother.

Through the Navy I booked passage on the U.S.S. *Chaumont,* a transport bound for the Philippines. On July 17, 1924, I boarded her at Norfolk, Virginia, as part of a cargo of Navy wives. I say cargo advisedly: quarters, which is to say cabins or cabin space, were rigorously allotted to wives on the basis of their husbands' rank. There was the usual representation of senior officers on board, with their families, and therefore the wife of a lieutenant commander was naturally in the middle of the scale of accommodations, on the second deck. I shared a cabin with two other women, one the wife of a Navy captain, the other a young woman on her way to marry a Marine officer in China. The hierarchical gradation extended even to the tables in the dining room.

It was my bad luck to arrive at Panama in a state of prostration, half-dead from a combination of cold and fever. By a fortunate coincidence, a friend of Coronado days, Kay Manly, the wife of a Navy captain stationed in the Canal Zone, learned of my plight and arranged to have me taken off the ship and brought to her house. She also found a remarkable doctor for me. When the ship sailed two days later I was well enough to continue the voyage.

More passengers disembarked at Honolulu; and I began to move upward, literally and figuratively, as regards the quality of my accommodations. As the *Chaumont* approached Guam, I calculated that at the previous rate of improvement I should be able to count upon completing the final stage of the voyage comfortably on the top deck.

The *Chaumont* was the original slow boat to China, and the voyage seemed interminable. By the time we reached Guam six of us unattached wives felt a great urge to get off the ship, so we rented a thatched native hut ashore while the ship was discharging cargo. Although the Captain was inclined to view our departure as most unorthodox, and possibly as a breach of Regulations, Guam being a closed port, he must nevertheless have been privately relieved to be rid of us if only for a couple of days. He finally relented enough to take me to lunch with the Governor. The native hut turned out to be a great success, and we had lots of fun. For the first time I ate breadfruit, mangoes, and custard apples.

Eventually, six weeks out of Norfolk, the *Chaumont* reached the Philippines. There I said good-by to her forever, with more regret than my first impressions of her had led me to expect. I then boarded the *Empress of Canada*. She was a beautiful white ship built for the tropics, and my two nights aboard her were pleasant indeed.

Hong Kong has one of the loveliest harbors in the world, and the beautiful vision it offered to me from seaward was confirmed by the almost unreal, don't-touch-it quality of the island itself. Win was on the dock to meet me. He looked better than I had ever seen him since our first meeting at Pensacola—tanned, clear-eyed, and charming. When I commented upon how well he looked, he said, quietly, that he had not had a drink since he had received my letter saying that I would join him again. However, I did have one moment of sinking doubt that first day of reunion. Win had a little apartment in Kowloon, on the Chinese mainland. After he had deposited me there, to return to his ship, I was horrified to find in the bathroom, beside the washstand, two half-empty gin bottles. I did not know what to do. Summoning the number-one boy I asked him to explain the presence of the gin in the bathroom. The question induced a spasm of Oriental

[93]

head-bobbing, back and forth, up and down. Finally, he made a brushing motion across his mouth. It was sterilized water, I gathered, for brushing the teeth.

We had two utterly satisfying weeks together, really a second honeymoon; and my heart was reassured. Win commanded the *Pampanga,* one of three gunboats that constituted the China patrol. When not actually at sea, he was able to come home each night, and we often dined together in the apartment building, which had its own dining room, run by a charming English lady. Then one evening something happened. We were to have dinner with friends of his. Win did not return to the apartment at the time he said he would. I waited. Still no word from him. Well after the time of our scheduled appearance I sent the house servant padding off to our host to say that Win had been unexpectedly delayed by his work and they were not to wait for us. It was long past midnight when Win clattered into the apartment. He looked as I had seen him all too often before.

In the morning there was no explanation. That had never been Win's way. But having lost his self-control he seemed incapable of regaining it. He was to leave in several days with the *Pampanga* on river patrol. I saw little of him until the time for him to pack his clothes. It is not my habit to cry, but I was close to tears then.

"What is it, Win?" I asked. "Have I done something to start this all over again?"

"I can't explain it," was the answer. "It's just me. Something lets go—like the control cables of a plane."

But I wondered. Was it not the two of us together that set off the chain reaction?

It had been understood between us that I would join him in Canton a few days later, after he had finished his patrol of the Delta. As U.S. Navy regulations forbade women traveling on our warships, Win had arranged with his opposite number on a British gunboat—the Royal Navy had no such stuffy attitude toward women—for me to travel to Canton aboard his vessel. This I did, and on my arrival I moved into a hotel in the Foreign Concession, where Win joined me. Almost immediately I came down with a severe kidney infection; this was accompanied by a high temperature, and for several days I was almost delirious. Win dropped everything and devoted himself night and day to nursing me. Then the nightmare of fever and pain left me almost as quickly as it had come. I was surprised and touched by Win's unexpected solicitude. It brought back momentarily into view a side of his character that I had not seen for a long time.

[94]

As soon as I was able to be up and around, Win left to resume his patrol; and I returned to Hong Kong by passenger ship, heartened by his devotion. My apprehensions receded; with my usual gaiety I entered into the wonderfully easy life of the Occidental in China—a life where even the small pay of a naval officer commanded almost princely luxury. Win returned presently. For a few weeks all was well. Then, without warning and, I must say, without cause, the old jealousies and resentments began to reassert themselves. He accused me of having "carried on" with the officers aboard the *Chaumont* and with men in Hong Kong during his absence. Before long, I was shocked, not because I had anything to conceal, but because of the indignity of being put in such a position, to find that he was opening my letters. To his already formidable repertory of taunts and humiliations he now added some Oriental variations. I gathered that during our time apart he had spent a considerable amount of his leisure ashore in the local singsong houses. In any event, he now insisted on my accompanying him to his favorite haunts, where he would ostentatiously make a fuss over the girls. All this was bad enough; but when he began drinking before breakfast, while off duty, I realized that whatever there had been between us of love and respect was gone beyond hope of recall.

During the day in our apartment in Kowloon I had much to think about. During our long separation we had grown apart—we were now strangers to each other. I finally told Win that our attempt at a reunion was a failure. Reluctantly, he agreed. There was no scene; the final unraveling was singularly without emotion; not even the capacity for anger remained.

I had heard of the U.S. Court for China in Shanghai, and decided to try to get my divorce there. Without being asked, Win promised to resume my monthly allotments. He provided me with money and saw me off on the steamer to Shanghai. As he said good-by at the gangway, his parting words were: "Pensacola, Boston, Coronado, Washington, and now Hong Kong—we've come a long way, only to lose what we began with." I was to see him only once again.

In Shanghai, once more on my own, I established myself in the famous Palace Hotel on the Bund. This was a favorite stopping place for Navy wives whose husbands were away on sea duty, and I was sure of running into an acquaintance. Occupying the room next to me was one of these wives, whom I soon got to know. A rather plain woman, the daughter of a minister in a small Midwestern town, she had acquired a heroic capacity for gin. There was always a bottle in her room. I never saw her drunk, but I never saw her really sober, either. "Gin," she noted one day, "is supposed to be the beachcomber's drink. It is cheap, companionable, and effective. But, since it looks like water, and is frequently mistaken for water, it makes a very satisfactory drink for respectable women." Although I tried to get her to join me on short walks and shopping excursions, she almost never left the hotel. It was her preference to remain hermitlike in her tiny room, with the bottle of gin on the table, typing long letters to her husband, who was on sea duty. I wondered how she could find so much to write about. "No problem at all," she assured me. "I live two lives —the one in this room, my secret life, and another imaginary. I tell my husband about all the fun I'm having, the parties I go to, the interesting people I meet. It makes my husband happy and surprisingly enough, I half believe it myself."

I have a particular reason to be grateful to my friend next door. Before leaving Washington, I had been given a letter of introduction to an Englishman working in Shanghai. One afternoon I happened to run across it in my writing case. I asked my friend in the adjoining room whether she thought it might be amusing to send it to him. "What can you lose?" was her airy advice. "If he's a bore, you can shed him easily enough. Anyway, it will be fun to see what he's like. I'm going down to mail some letters of my own. Let me have it and I'll put it in the box."

A day or so later a nice basket of mangoes arrived, to be followed shortly by a telephone call. It was from the man to whom the letter had been so offhandedly sent. He had an attractive voice. Would I care to have a cocktail with him in the bar later in the afternoon? I said I would be delighted. Then arose the question of how we would recognize each other. On impulse, I said I would wear a single red camellia on my shoulder. About six o'clock, so adorned, I entered the bar, somewhat apprehensive over what I might be letting myself in for. Then a man came toward me—young, handsome, beautifully dressed. His name does not matter; I came to know him as "Robbie."

We had a drink together, very pleasant. Then he suggested dinner, and it proved to be even more pleasant. This was the simple beginning of a delightful friendship. Robbie knew everyone in Shanghai. He and his business partner had a large house where they entertained the more amusing members of the foreign colony, then predominantly British.

From knowing nobody I was drawn swiftly into a totally different kind of world—garden parties, race meetings of the Shanghai Race

Club, and dinner parties in the lovely old Majestic Hotel on Bubbling Well Road, where in a bower of flowers one danced in a sunken courtyard by the light of colored lanterns. It was here, in the company of Robbie, that I first heard Vincent Youmans's "Tea for Two," and the combination of that melody, the moonlight, the perfume of jasmine, not to mention the Shangri-la illusion of the courtyard, made me feel that I had really entered the Celestial Kingdom.

No doubt about it, life in Shanghai in 1924 was good, very good, and, in fact, almost too good for a woman under a dangerous illusion of quasi independence. It was also purposeless. Robbie put me in touch with a lawyer from whom I learned that, given Win's circumstances and mine, the process of getting a divorce would be complicated and costly. I therefore abandoned the idea. So a clean break with the past was once more out of reach. Perhaps wrongly, I also saw no reason for being in a hurry.

Among the Navy wives at the Palace was another with whom I was to have a short and curious acquaintanceship. She was inclined to be rather stiff and formal, and in that respect at least was as unlike me as anyone could be. Whether it was a case of opposites attracting, or whether it was the spell of China acting on two women far from home, we became close friends. One day she invited me to join her in a shopping trip to Peking. This involved a journey of nearly a thousand miles and was not an easy trip either by land or sea. It is characteristic of my state of mind at that time that I promptly said yes, thank you, as if she had asked me to dinner.

However, I did have my reasons. My Aunt Bessie and Cousin Lelia had both traveled widely in China, and I had been fascinated by their descriptions of Peking. Moreover, the officer commanding the U.S. Legation Guard at Peking, Colonel Louis Little, of the Marine Corps, was a close friend of the Barnetts, and I had known him in Washington. I had also learned from friends in the American colony in Shanghai, that the first secretary of the Legation was the same Gerry Green who had squired Corinne Mustin and me in Paris.

Going to Peking, then still the capital, involved taking a coastal steamer to Tientsin and transferring there to a train. The vessel was a creaky, leaky, rusting tub. There was a frightful storm—memorable to me for the reason that the only passenger who preserved his aplomb in the din and clatter was an elderly, bearded Chinese. While the rest of us sat trembling in the dining room, sure that the next heave of the ancient hull would be its last, he sat unmoved; and we were not surprised to learn that, in recognition of some signal public service, he was a Knight Commander of the Order of the British Empire.

Our unlikely vessel finally docked at Tientsin, but our problems had just begun. The American Consul informed us that a local war was in progress, trains were being raided daily, and we should be proceeding to Peking very much at our own risk. Encouraged by the fact that the Consul was advising rather than prohibiting, I urged my friend to join me in insisting on our desire to go on. The Consul turned stern. He replied stiffly that if we should become involved in an "international incident" it would be his duty to report to the Navy that we had disregarded the advice of the U.S. Government's representative and had wilfully placed ourselves outside of the protection of the Government. My friend capitulated. She said, "My husband would never forgive me if I went against the Consul and then something awful happened." But, since my relationship to the United States Navy had become perfunctory, I took the opposite view. Having come so far, I did not propose to be stopped by a mere civil war, and accordingly informed the Consul that I was sure my husband would have no objections to my going on, and there could be no question of the Government's being held responsible for me. In fairness to the Consul I must record that while he was not impressed by my logic he did bow to a woman's whim. In fact, he was an extremely nice man. The morning I left Tientsin he sent a sailor from his office to the station to hold a seat for me on the train, and he himself was on the platform to make sure that I got off safely. His parting words to me were: "Well, if it should be your bad luck to run into trouble, I fancy the bandits will be the ones to regret it. You'll not be a comfortable hostage, that's sure."

The train was late in getting under way. As usual, the aisles were crowded with Chinese passengers, chiefly occupied in eating oranges and spitting out the pips. Seated across from me, the only other Occidental in the carriage, was a rather plump, middle-aged man whose obliviousness to the rain of squirted orange seeds marked him as one to whom travel could present no further surprises. Introducing himself as Eddie Mills, an American living in Peking and working for the Salt Gabell, he politely helped me with my luggage.

As the train clanked and huffed out of the station, I told my new friend of my brush with the Consul. "Do you think I did wrong?" I asked anxiously. "Should I have stayed in Tientsin?"

"Oh, well," was the languid response, "it's the inalienable right of American travelers to make life impossible for their consuls. You have only been unusually impossible." He refused, however, to be drawn into any prediction as to the outcome of the immediate journey. "The trick about living comfortably in China," he remarked, "is to recognize the inconvenient as the normal. But I am inclined to believe that we'll get there all right, after the usual nonsense."

"No bandits, then?"

"Of course. But, as bandits go, the Chinese are the most courteous in the world."

In the company of my worldly, phlegmatic acquaintance my journey to Peking proceeded—but not uneventfully; several times on the way the train jerked to a violent stop; evil-faced men in shabby uniforms and armed with rifles pushed into the crowded vestibules. Imitating the example of Mr. Mills, I assumed an air of utter indifference. Nothing ever happened; after a quick look around the soldiers disappeared.

When the train finally arrived at Peking, eight hours late, I was startled to see Colonel Little striding down the platform to meet me. In spite of his threats, the Consul at Tientsin had wired the Legation that I was en route. I detected at once an unmistakable leatherneck grimness underlying the surface heartiness of his greeting that made me realize my victory over the Consul had not been received with official approval.

"Oh, Louis," I said, "have I really done a terrible thing in coming here? I did want to see you and meet your wife."

The Marine in Louis Little began to thaw. "Well, maybe you shouldn't have done it. But you're here, and what might have happened is no longer important."

CHAPTER X

My Lotus Year

I ESTABLISHED MYSELF AT THE GRAND HÔTEL DE PÉKIN, LOCATED near the Legation Quarters. My intention then was to stay in Peking perhaps a fortnight, seeing the sights and shopping around for silks and porcelain. But now occurred one of those chance encounters that so often sharply influence the entire course of one's life—one that, in my case, at another and far more critical turning point, would provide me with sanctuary when almost every hand seemed raised against me.

The encounter took place at a dance at the Grand Hôtel de Pékin at which I was a guest of the Littles and Gerry Green, who had gallantly offered to be my escort for the evening. Across the ballroom I spotted a friend of Coronado days—Katherine Moore Bigelow, who was then a young widow. We recognized each other instantaneously. In that telegraphic manner peculiar to women we succeeded in communicating to each other, in the instant of mutual rediscovery, the essential facts about each other: that Win and I were separated and that she had remarried. A moment later her husband, Herman Rogers, came up, an unusually attractive man, with a lean, handsome face, brown wavy hair, and the bearing and look of an athlete.

Because Katherine and Herman Rogers were later to play an important part in my life—to be the source of the most loyal of friendships and kindness immeasurable—I must interrupt this narrative to tell about them. Theirs was a truly romantic marriage. Katherine's first husband had died at the beginning of the First World War. She joined the Red Cross and was sent to France. She was strikingly handsome with a slim figure, shining golden hair, and slate-blue eyes; in her Red Cross uniform she must have summed up simultaneously the essence of Florence Nightingale and Greta Garbo. One afternoon a troop train moving up to the front stopped at a station where Katherine and several other co-workers were dispensing coffee and doughnuts. Herman Rogers, a major in the artillery, was on the train. He was afterward to say that his fleeting glimpse of her as she stretched on tiptoes to hand him the Red Cross bounty was so unnervingly enchanting that he exclaimed to a brother officer, "That's the most attractive girl I've ever seen. In fact, I'm going to marry her if ever I catch up with her again."

The train moved on. More than a year later, after the war was over, Herman was introduced to a young woman at a cocktail party in New York. Even without the Red Cross uniform, the face, the smile, the carriage were as he remembered and cherished them. Tentatively he inquired whether she had been by chance in the Red Cross during the war. She had. In France? Yes. In 1918? Yes. And was it possible that she might have been at such-and-such a town on a certain afternoon distributing coffee and doughnuts to American troops? Why, yes. "Ah," said Herman, "then you are the girl I promised myself I would marry."

Herman's family had a large estate on the Hudson River, close to the Hyde Park property of Franklin D. Roosevelt. Herman was a Yale man, class of 1914. He rowed, I believe, in the crew. In the natural progression of young men of his background and connections he would have gone into Wall Street and become, like his brother, a successful banker. But the war had given Herman other ideas. He turned his back on finance, and it was very much in his mind to become a writer. More interesting still, he and Katherine had made up their minds, at the time of their marriage, that before they settled down they would search the world for a setting that in their agreed judgment was the most beautiful on earth; and there they would make their home. When I encountered them in the ballroom of the Grand Hôtel de Pékin, they were on their second trip around the world, trying to decide whether Peking or the south of France or possibly Florence was their ideal.

Katherine insisted that I leave the hotel and come to stay with them. They had me for luncheon next day. Their house was in the Tartar City, near the Hatamen, one of the many gates of the city, on what was called a *hutung*—the Chinese word for a small street that is really not a street but a crooked lane of houses set behind blank gray walls and completely hidden from the possible scrutiny of passers-by. Behind such a blank wall, entered through a tiny door, was the Rogerses' house, an ancient but lovely one-storied structure roofed with old gray tiles arranged in an intricate herringbone fashion, and approached through a spacious garden court paved with gray stones. The house was constructed of sun-baked gray brick. Its most distinctive feature was the large central courtyard around which were arranged in rambling fashion a series of small rooms separated one from another by doors cut in the shape of large keyholes or portholes. Both Katherine and Herman had excellent taste and the means to exercise it. The stone floors were covered by thick multicolored Peking rugs, and the walls were hung with beautifully embroidered tapestries and with ancient Chinese pictures. It was purely a matter of arbitrary selection which rooms were used for bedrooms and which were used for living and dining. When therefore they pressed me again to join them, I yielded, without serious struggle, and after insisting that I be allowed to pay my own way. Katherine assured me that this would impose little strain even upon my small purse. Like a fairy godmother, she waved her wand and there instantly materialized, for my personal use, an amah, a handsome black ricksha with rubber tires, and a ricksha boy—all, I believe, for about $15 a month.

However, that evening I had my doubts that all was necessarily as simple as it appeared on the surface. The Rogerses had some friends in for dinner and poker afterward. When Herman told me what the chips cost, I was horrified and reluctant to play.

"You've played before, haven't you?" Herman asked. "You know what a straight is? And a full house?"

"Oh, yes," I said. "I learned to play with the Navy."

"That should make you almost a professional gambler," said Herman. "You join us. If you lose I'll assume your losses."

My rather considerable education in the principles of Hoyle that had begun at Pensacola now stood me in good stead. I was not tempted to fill inside straights. I was not afraid to stand by good cards. By the end of the game, I had an impressive pile of chips in front of me, but I had no idea how much I was ahead. When Herman totted up the sum, it amounted to exactly $225.

"Good Lord!" I exclaimed in genuine shock. "That's what I have to live on for an entire month."

A quizzical look came into Herman's eyes. "Wallis," he said severely. "You need no protector in this game. Hereafter you'll be on your own."

Thanks in part to this windfall—modestly increased, I must in candor confess, in later sessions—there now began for me, without conscious plan or foreknowledge, what was beyond doubt the most delightful, the most carefree, the most lyric interval of my youth— the nearest thing, I imagine, to a lotus-eater's dream that a young woman brought up the "right" way could ever expect to know.

Life in Peking in the mid-1920's, before the great Chiang Kai-shek upheaval, before China became a modern nation, before the name of Mao Tse-tung was even a whisper in that age-old land, was for foreigners like me a special experience. Peking was a walled city; at night the gates in the great walls were made fast, heightening the illusion of utter separation from the outer world. Within this city the foreign community formed an island of Western culture, a world apart and self-sufficient as an island is separate from the surrounding sea. The foreign colony was itself unlike any other on earth. There was a considerable commercial infusion of bankers, traders, manu-facturers, and the like. But it was essentially a diplomatic enclave that centered upon the Legation Quarters—a spreading conglomeration of ancient temples cheek-by-jowl with handsome new houses and chanceries ringed by formal willow-bordered gardens. The life that revolved around the *corps diplomatique,* reflecting the then pre-eminence of British power and influence in China, was not merely Victorian but mid-Victorian. Except for the motorcars (still quite rare), the trams, the telephones, and the fashions, one might have been back in the third quarter of the nineteenth century, when a sunny optimism suffused the world and human perfection patently bore a British label.

Peking was, in any case, an ideal place for a woman with time on her hands and a secret sorrow in her heart. I never made an analysis of the exact proportions of the sexes; but my impression is that the bachelors outnumbered the unattached women by a ratio of at least ten to one. To be sure, the incidence of honorable men with dis-honorable intentions was undoubtedly higher than a Sunday-school teacher of that period might knowingly have tolerated for long; but such perils, if prudently recognized in advance, are readily manage-able. The point is that for women Peking could be and was perhaps not so much a metropolis as a point in time where every woman could be Cinderella and midnight never struck.

Yet, at the same time, there was a simplicity, a still-deep peace-fulness about life in Peking that imparted an air of timelessness to one's thoughts and actions. No one ever seemed to be in a desperate hurry about anything. If diplomacy was ever arduous or exacting, if the selling of salt or matches or gasoline ever gave rise to vexing difficulties, the evidence of stress and strain seldom showed on the surface. Time was not something to be carefully apportioned and doled out by electronic counters as is the case in what now passes for civilization. In Peking it was a prodigal substance to be lavished on the whims of the moment; and the whims, now that I reassess them in the perspective of a more complicated life, were by and large as mild and stylized as episodes on a Chinese screen.

The Rogerses had several saddle horses. Every morning Herman, Katherine, and I went riding on the glacis, an esplanade surrounding the Legation Quarters. Afterward, a leisurely breakfast in the courtyard, if the weather was mild. Thereafter, at least in the summer, the day would take its casual unfolding. Perhaps a swim before lunch at the big new pool of the American Legation. Or tennis at the British Legation. Three times a week there would be polo at the Polo Club. Evenings one went to dinner parties at the legations, or at the homes of friends, or to a fine Chinese restaurant. The necessary to and from was accomplished by ricksha, a form of transportation so pleasant as to be its own reward.

Weekends were an experience so novel as to border on fantasy. They were spent, at least until winter came, in our temple, in the Western Hills, the name given to a series of foothills that lay outside the city gates. The countryside in this direction abounded in temples of every imaginable description and configuration, dozens and dozens of them, mostly empty and deserted. Those nearest the city gates could be rented from the local priests who were their nominal proprietors, and fixed up as weekend lodges. The temples farther out, in the Western Hills, were abandoned and could be appropriated by anyone.

The Rogerses had such a temple, a fabulous place, with a tiled roof of many colors and vermilion eaves from which hung tiny bells that tinkled in the wind. Presiding over the central chamber was an enormous Buddha, originally gilded but now peeling and leprously discolored. Along the back wall was a kang, a huge Oriental bed platform covered with a brilliantly brocaded rug that Katherine Rogers had found in a shop. Two small rooms adjoined the central chambers; and these, one for the men and the other for the women, were furnished with cots and camp chairs. The plumbing facilities were strictly of the Ming Dynasty. Candles provided light, and the cooking was done on charcoal braziers.

I had many joyous weekends with the Rogerses at their temple.

It was our custom to set out Friday after lunch in a motorcar. Some fifteen miles out, in the lower foothills, the road disintegrated into impassable ruts. Here servants dispatched in advance would be waiting for us with donkeys, and aboard these docile creatures we would complete the climb. Another convoy of servants dispatched the night before would have preceded us to the temple with food, bedding, and saddle horses. In the twilight we picnicked around an open fire, in front of the temple. It might seem incongruous to have a modern picnic in surroundings whose beauty spoke of bygone splendor and ageless serenity. But, when the sun went down and we were left in candlelight, the incongruity faded, and the spirit of the place settled down upon us.

Our leisure pursuits were simple. During the daytime we explored the countryside on horseback. Every eminence, every outcropping, was graced by some kind of temple—Buddhist temples, temples of Confucius, Taoist temples, Lamaist temples, most of them crumbling into dry ruin, their once lovely courts choked by weeds, their monstrous, obese gods toppled off their pedestals, and everywhere a silence broken only by the lonesome, forlorn tinkling of the few surviving temple bells. Herman was deeply read in ancient Chinese history; he and Katherine loved to roam among these forgotten ruins, and I was delighted to tag along with them. I cannot claim to have profited as much as perhaps I should from these excursions; but I did attain something that was even more important to me at that stage of my life: the nightmare of my last association with Win faded from my mind.

For that I shall always be grateful to Herman and Katherine Rogers, although, as will become evident, I am irretrievably in their debt for additional reasons. The Rogerses belonged to that rare species, people who live up to their highest ideals, and possibly that is the reason for their having been so uninterruptedly happy with each other. Through a Peking summer and winter and spring I was privileged to share their happiness; it did much to steady me. Although the Rogerses entertained a great deal, they took their pleasures with restraint. Herman had a thoughtful side. He was working on a book—about a character in mythology, I believe. Every morning he disappeared into his study to read and write. He and Katherine also took a daily lesson in Chinese. A Chinese scholar in a long black gown, known to us only as Mr. Wu—all Chinese gentlemen, it seemed to me, were called Mr. Wu—would appear in the forenoon for the instruction. I joined the lessons for a while, only to decide, characteristically, that since there was no hope of my mastering Chinese in ten easy lessons, I could get along quite well enough with pidgin English, in which I had already begun to develop considerable fluency.

Herman had the latest books sent to him by his bookshop in New York. In the afternoons he used to read to Katherine and me. New and startling ideas were astir. I remember a long and warm discussion among us over a moral dilemma posed by a forgotten novel— whether a wife who had been momentarily and bewilderingly unfaithful should tell her husband of her slip from grace. Katherine and Herman prided themselves on being modern and sophisticated; they held that relations between the sexes should be based on forthrightness and candor; that the old conventions had become hopelessly outmoded; and that any intelligent relationship must take into account the human drives and foibles. But I argued contrariwise. I held that every interesting life, however circumspect, contained its little secret compartments; and that if the true relationship was the continuing relationship then these small secret compartments, holding that which was finished and dead, should be left undisturbed.

I cannot say that I was meanwhile creating new secret compartments of my own. But I was nevertheless adding to my store of memories. We were young; we were gay; and, cushioned as we were by the vast amorphous mass of China, the happenings of the outer world came to us only as faint and implausible echoes. There was a dashing British military officer and a gallant Italian naval officer who whirled briefly in and out of my life. The Italian, who later became an admiral, is now dead; among his effects was found a poem written during his youth in which he left to me "the sea, the sky, and the sun"—surely the noblest of bequests.

For many reasons I came to love Peking as I have loved only one other city—Paris. In fact, the two cities have much in common. Both are old; each sums up a culture and cosmopolitanism of near perfection; they are cities of light and color. The winter days were especially beautiful; sometimes the skies over Peking were incredibly blue; other days the winds off the Gobi desert would permeate the atmosphere with a thin yellowish film of dust through which the sunlight would fall as through a golden filter. I even became accustomed to the smells of Peking, which were scarcely imperial. But most of all I rejoiced in its sounds—the intricate cries and signals of the street hawkers; the tinkle of bells; the clack of wooden rattles; the blowing of reed flutes and trumpets; the banging of the iron-pot

[106]

vendors; the strange, reedlike notes of the pigeons as they circled over our garden in the morning, turning the air to music with the bamboo whistles ingeniously fastened to their tail feathers; and the rhythmic slap-slap of the ricksha boy's slippers against the pavement as he trotted me home in the evening through the dim streets. Sometimes in the late afternoon Herman would take me walking along the broad parapet of the great wall around the city. As we looked out over the ocean of gray and yellow tile roofs, the myriad voices of the metropolis welled around us to form a tapestry of living sounds. And from this height, looking out across the golden plain, one would sometimes see camel caravans, heavily burdened, making their way toward the city at the end of their journeys from Inner Mongolia or Manchuria.

Actually, I never did get much closer to the real Peking than these views from the top of the city walls and my occasional encounters with dealers in jades and porcelains and the can-do tailors who made my clothes from patterns obtained from British and American magazines or from designs of my own invention. I seldom saw either a Chinese woman or man at the countless parties I went to. Indeed, the only time I ever came into close proximity to a Chinese family was on a particularly sad occasion. One day when Gerry Green was visiting us his chauffeur went off on some errand; Katherine's ricksha boy, eager to show his mastery over the machine, cranked the car while it was still in gear; it lunged forward, pinning one of my ricksha coolies to the wall, crushing his body terribly. A Chinese doctor was summoned. The next day Katherine and I visited the boy. He lived with his family in a little house at the gate. A sickening smell assailed us as we entered the darkened room. Gangrene had already set in. The boy's family was grouped around the cot in attitudes of silent resignation, and the Chinese doctor was applying herbs to the dreadful wounds. Katherine tried to persuade the family to let her bring a surgeon from the Rockefeller Foundation, but the family refused. The boy died before the week was out.

In later years I was to reflect upon how much I missed in China. Actually chance had directed me there at a critical turning point in history. The great revolution begun by Dr. Sun Yat-sen (he died while I was in Peking) and carried forward by Chiang Kai-shek was even then gathering momentum in the southern provinces. But few of the people I knew in Peking attached much importance to what was happening. The newspaper reports of increasing turmoil were shrugged off as only evidence of the hopeless chaos of China. However, one unexpected development in the early spring of 1925 gave the new movement a more serious aspect. An unfortunate incident occurred; the new revolutionary government proclaimed a boycott against the British, and students in the universities promptly engaged in noisy public demonstrations against British establishments, in Peking and elsewhere. Other foreigners, to distinguish themselves from the targets of the crowds' abuse, marked their rickshas with their national colors. But Katherine and Herman, who were stanch Anglophiles, refused to turn their backs on their British friends in their adversity. No American flag appeared on their ricksha, and though I was not so courageous and felt quite uncomfortable when out alone, I followed their example. One day I was out shopping, and while I was inside a shop, a group of students wrote in chalk on my ricksha, notwithstanding my coolie's protest that I was a "Melican lady." When I emerged from the shop, they looked angrily at me, but did nothing more serious. I went directly to our Legation to have the inscription on my ricksha translated. It turned out to be surprisingly mild.

The British themselves naturally experienced a good deal of embarrassment and inconvenience during the crisis, but even that strained situation had its lighter side. An attaché at the British Legation learned just before dinner that his number-one boy was forsaking his post. "I say," he protested, "you can't do that. I have people coming in, you know."

One quiet summer evening, in the Rogerses' temple in the Western Hills, while watching the sun go down, an inner voice, which I suppose was the voice of conscience, began to speak to me. It spoke rather severely. It said that I was deluding myself; that I was beginning to confuse a lotus-eater's illusion for reality; that I had better give thought to returning to my own people and winding up the unfinished business of my marriage to Win.

I did not want to listen, but I did. And in the end the proddings of conscience took command of my reason. Deep inside me was a disturbing realization that a life without purpose or responsibility was doing me no good. I was improving my sense of enjoyment but not my mind. I finally told the Rogerses that, hard as it was to leave them, the time had come for me to start back home. So, in the early summer, somewhat in the mood of a female Ulysses, I left for Japan to take a ship to the West Coast.

CHAPTER XI

A Meeting and a Portent

AT THIS PERIOD OF MY LIFE, I SEEMED FATED TO MAKE SEA JOURneys that ranged from trying to catastrophic. En route across the Pacific, I became ill with an obscure internal ailment. Once more, chance brought me a remarkable physician, this time the ship's doctor, who struggled valiantly with a very puzzling case, and then had me removed to a hospital when the ship docked in Seattle. There it was decided that an operation was necessary. It was not a long operation, but an ordeal nonetheless and one more thing I had to go through alone in a strange city.

Still weak from my illness, I traveled across the continent by train. Win was now back in the United States. He was on leave, staying with his parents in Highland Park. Having learned of my illness, he insisted upon boarding my train in Chicago and accompanied me all the way to Washington. I never saw him again.

Once in Washington I went directly to my mother's apartment and stayed several months. In the meantime, after my strength returned, I delved seriously into the business of securing my divorce. Having investigated the matter on the far shores of the Atlantic and Pacific Oceans, I now found that a divorce could be obtained practically at my front door and at a price I could afford. A family friend who was a lawyer advised me that in Virginia I could apply for a divorce after one year's residence and could obtain a decree on the grounds of desertion at the expiration of three years' separation from my husband. He estimated the total legal cost at around $300. My adviser recommended Fauquier County, and, in particular, the little town of Warrenton, which possessed a small but comfortable hotel where I could live on my Navy wife's allotment. Moreover, Warrenton was not far from Washington by rail, so that I would not be completely isolated from my friends during the long wait.

My mother did not like the idea of my staying alone in a commercial hotel. I suppose she had heard too many traveling-salesmen stories. But I firmly rejected her offer to accompany me to Warrenton.

So one hot October morning I took the early train. The Warrenton of that day was not the prosperous and glittering community it is now. Although it had always been a traditional center for hunting—the Fauquier Hunt was the oldest in the country—its glory was in a state of decline during my stay. Its renaissance came into full flowering some time later after the New York hunting set took over in force. Certainly the little town itself had a shabby post-bellum look in the shimmering heat of the afternoon.

The dusty, rattling train journey had left my flowered chiffon dress as dispirited as I was myself. Standing on the station platform in the blinding sun, I did not have the resolution to lift my bags. In this extremity, an affable Negro porter came up, introduced himself as "Jake from the hotel," and asked me to follow him. I would have followed him anywhere. As we marched down Warrenton's main street, Jake plodding doggedly in the lead and I tottering behind him on my precariously high heels, we made a curious procession. The flowered chiffon may have been responsible, but from the stares of undisguised appraisal directed at us from store windows, I decided that my mother knew what she was talking about. A young woman arriving unaccompanied and unmet was still a phenomenon in the American country town.

The Warren Green Hotel boasted only one room with its own bath, and I did not receive it. The room went by seniority, and was then being occupied by an ancient Southern lady, widowed, I should judge, since the McKinley administration. Eventually, she went off to spend her declining years with her grandchildren, and I succeeded to her room, having outstayed all other claimants. Meanwhile, however, I lived in a single room, second floor back, fifteen feet by twelve, with faded flowered wallpaper, a high brass bed, battered night table, imitation mahogany bureau, enameled washstand, large black easy chair in cracked leatherette—a classic example of what my mother used to call inferior decorating.

The Warren Green was primarily a commercial hotel, and its clientele was drawn chiefly from the corps of traveling salesmen—drummers. in the idiom of the period. Their sudden arrivals and departures, announced by the appearance and disappearance of a clump of sample cases in the lobby, seemed as mysterious as the visitations of locusts. One day the hotel would be silent and empty as a country church on a Wednesday afternoon; twenty-four hours later, the Warren Green would come alive, every room would be taken, and the lobby would be buzzing with the chatter of the trade. From my observation of the fraternity, I concluded that the folklore characterization of traveling salesmen was greatly overdrawn. Those who passed through the Warren Green Hotel were a serious lot— though it is always possible that they were in a rush to wind up their business there and make tracks for livelier surroundings. As time went on, I came to recognize the steady callers, and nodding acquaintanceships developed. Sometimes one would stop at my table, after luncheon or dinner, to say hello, and perhaps chat a moment about the weather or the state of business on the road. I suppose they looked upon me as a permanent fixture of the place.

Another fixture of the Warren Green was a gentleman in his middle sixties about whom there was an air of mild mystery. His name was Jack Mason. Like me, he had a table in the dining room reserved for his exclusive use. The hotel staff knew little about him except that he was an American who had lived abroad most of his life. They were inclined to regard him as an eccentric because of his habit of taking a long brisk walk before breakfast. He spoke with a British accent; and his clothes, especially the tweeds, were patently of Savile Row origin. But the clothes also had the look of being well worn; and the encroachments of seediness that careful grooming could no longer disguise, combined with the British mannerisms and a worldliness that was distinctly out of place in a drummer's hotel, were signs of a man who had come down in the world.

Since there were occasions when Mr. Mason and I were the only people in the dining room, we struck up a kind of shipboard acquaintance. He proved to be the best of company—a ready and fluent talker, witty, and well informed. At the same time he was reticent about himself. However, from clues he dropped here and there in his conversation, it appeared that he had lived in Great Britain much of his life, that he had been something of an adventurer who had married a rich woman, that she had left him, and that now—perhaps pensioned off—he was quite content to be, as he put it, "a retired black sheep grazing on a harvest of wild oats."

Occasionally, in the afternoons, I took walks with him along the country roads behind Warrenton. Traffic was not the horror that it is today; and the surrounding countryside, especially in the spring, with the dogwood in bloom, was peaceful and lovely. On these leisurely excursions Mr. Mason, in a reminiscent mood, would turn back to random episodes in his life—riding to hounds in Leicestershire, the Ascot race meeting, the life revolving around the country houses of England, the time he lost his shirt at Monte Carlo. He was, I suppose, something of a snob and, as such, a cynic. Once he said, "The trouble with a social life is the sheer weariness of continual deceit. You have two faces, the one you were born with and the mask you wear over it all the time. Sooner or later a time comes when an intelligent person feels a desperate need to breathe. That happened to me. I took the mask off. The results, needless to say, were catastrophic."

On the whole, my first year at Warrenton was the most tranquil I have ever known. I simply rusticated; and, when I wasn't rusticating, I vegetated with equal satisfaction. I read more than at any time since leaving school—lots of poetry, which I have always loved, the novels of Sinclair Lewis, Somerset Maugham, and John Galsworthy. The Warren Green had an upstairs veranda. On warm days I used to sit there for hours in an easy chair, soaking in the sun and reading a book through a whole afternoon. Hoping to enrich my mind, I even tackled Will Durant's *The Story of Philosophy* and other similar works.

However, I do not want to give the impression that Warrenton was for me a distaff Walden where my days were dedicated solely to books, solitary meals, and afternoon walks with the philosophical Mr. Mason. After a time I ran into an old acquaintance, Hugh Spilman, who worked in the local bank and whom I had known in Baltimore. He took me in tow and launched me in the social whirl of the local horsy set. He was also possessed of an old three-pedal, rattling flivver. The two of us must have made quite an impression as we rolled up to the porticoed mansions for formal dinners.

Nor did I ever really cut my ties to the city, which I preferred to the country. I used to take the train to Washington every now and then to spend the night with my mother, or perhaps to dine with friends. More rarely I went on to New York to shop for clothes at the small, side-street specialty shops. Mary Kirk and her husband, Jacques Raffray, now had a charming apartment in Washington Square, on lower Fifth Avenue, a section which seemed to me then the most attractive part of the city. I used to stay with them. Not far from Washington Square were two delightful hotels with famous restaurants, the Brevoort and the Lafayette, both now of hallowed memory. Our custom was to dine at one or the other and perhaps go afterward to a show, or more usually to spend the evening at bridge.

Among the Raffrays' friends were Mr. and Mrs. Ernest Simpson. Ernest was in his family's shipping business. His father, an Englishman, had come to the United States as a young man well before the turn of the century. He had opened a ship-brokerage office, which had prospered, and had married an American woman. Ernest was born in New York and had been graduated from Harvard. To prevent a complete obliteration of the British blood ties, Simpson Senior had given his son the opportunities to learn to know England and Europe almost as well as he knew the United States. His summer holidays were divided between England, where he had an older married sister, and the continent, where his father, himself a tireless traveler, took him on a series of Grand Tours. The father had proposed that Ernest, on reaching twenty-one should choose for himself whether to be a British subject or an American citizen. During the last year of the war, while still an undergraduate at Harvard, Ernest had crossed the Atlantic and joined the Coldstream Guards as a second lieutenant. He had come to love his father's country, and he elected to become a British subject.

If I remember correctly, it was while visiting the Raffrays one time that I first met the Simpsons. They invited us to dinner in their home. Ernest was married to an American woman. Mary gave me to understand that their marriage was in difficulties, and Ernest was turning to her circle of friends. Reserved in manner, yet with a gift of quiet wit, always well dressed, a good dancer, fond of the theater, and obviously well read, he impressed me as an unusually well-balanced man. I had acquired a taste for cosmopolitan minds, and Ernest obviously had one. I was attracted to him and he to me; several times, on my visits to New York, Mary Raffray had him in for dinner and as a fourth for bridge. However, with each of us caught up in a personal dilemma of some complexity, the friendship for a long time was nothing more than one of those casual New York encounters between the extra man and the out-of-town friend who find passing pleasure in each other's tastes. Moreover, with my divorce becoming more imminent, and uncertain how I would support myself, I was determined not to allow myself to become emotionally involved until my life was straightened out. In fact, it was very much in my mind.

as I neared thirty, to look for a job and perhaps try my wings as a career woman.

The position of women in the social order was certainly being revolutionized by the middle 1920's; an increasing number of well-born young women were opening little shops, or taking selling and semiexecutive jobs in department stores, or starting off bravely on careers of their own in the theater, law, journalism, and even medicine. The new interest in careers, not necessarily as an alternative to marriage, was an exciting expression of the growing independence of women. To my mind this was one of the most important social contributions of my own generation.

The trouble was that I had no readily marketable talent, and my confidence in being able to find a good job was undermined by powerful reservations about the depth and scope of my education—notwithstanding Miss Nan's gallant efforts. Department-store selling, the obvious job for a woman having no special training, had little appeal for me. My natural impatience, I was sure, would get me into trouble sooner or later at such a job. My true forte, if indeed I had one, was I decided, on the creative side—perhaps in designing, or even in writing about fashion.

At about this time, a fashion magazine announced a competition for prospective fashion writers, the winner of which would be appointed to the magazine's editorial staff. The subject chosen was spring hats, and I composed my essay on this challenging topic at Mary Raffray's apartment, staying up until dawn to complete the final draft, and polishing it to a state that I judged, with customary optimism, to be perhaps just short of perfection. I knew no one on the staff of the magazine, so I merely committed my masterpiece, with a prayer, to the mails. Some weeks later, long after I had returned to Warrenton, I received a form letter from the editors saying that, while they appreciated my interest and effort, my contribution was not quite up to their standards. Nothing more. In consequence of that heartless rejection the world of *haute couture* would in due course gain a good customer while losing a reporter and critic. On balance, the fashion industry was probably the gainer, but my ego was flattened.

The idea of entering the fashion field may have been suggested to me by the example of several of my friends who were working as saleswomen in dress shops in New York. It was also perhaps stimulated by a charming young Southern girl, Jane Derby, who, with her husband, Arthur, came to the Warren Green in the spring of 1926, as I was beginning my second half year there. Part of the vanguard of the horsy set that was now taking over the estates of the Virginia gentry, the Derbys bought an interesting old place in Warrenton and took up temporary quarters at the hotel while they supervised the work of reconstruction and renovation. Jane was an unusually attractive woman and always beautifully turned out. She later put her knowledge of clothes to good use by opening a dress shop in New York and today is a highly successful designer. Casting a knowing eye over my things, acquired for the most part at New York sales and made over under my direction by my mother's colored seamstress in Washington, she was nice enough to say that I had a good eye for fashion.

This was particularly generous of Jane, in the light of a dreadful thing I unwittingly did to her. Whenever she came down to Warrenton alone, she usually moved into the room next to mine. This permitted us to share my bathroom, in which I had my telephone. Since both Jane and I had many friends in Warrenton, that particular connection was undoubtedly the busiest in the Warren Green. Jane and I were usually scrambling wildly for it.

One evening we went out together to a dinner party that afterward showed all the signs of developing into an extremely late affair. Feeling the need for a good night's sleep, I slipped back to the hotel, leaving Jane behind. Not long after I fell asleep, the telephone in the bathroom began to ring. I thought that it must be our friends at the party trying to lure me into returning. Not having too much resolution about such things, I decided to be prudent, so I buried my head into the pillows and let the thing ring. It stopped after a while, only to begin again more insistently than ever. I was still determined not to be drawn into a losing argument and would not have answered it had the night porter not banged on my door to cry: "Mrs. Spencer, ma'am, you better answer yo' telephone. It's a 'portant call for Miss Derby. Her new old house's afire and it's doggone near bu'nt to the groun'. If she don' get there right quick there ain' goin' to be nothin'."

I leaped out of bed and grabbed the phone. The porter was right. The call was from a neighbor who was trying to reach Jane with the bad news. I called Jane at the party, and she arrived on the scene in time to see the remains of her house crumble into smoking ruins. Although there was nothing that Jane could possibly have done to save the house—the fire department had been summoned by the neighbors—I nevertheless felt sick at not having answered the phone.

To this day, if there is a telephone ringing anywhere, I rush to answer it first and ask questions afterward.

Meanwhile, an opportunity came my way that, if seized at the flood, might have transformed me eventually into a female tycoon. I had a friend, Elizabeth Schiller, whose husband, Morgan, was an established Pittsburgh industrialist. This gentleman had an interest in a company manufacturing tubular steel scaffolding for construction purposes. Now commonplace, the invention was new on the market at the time my friend's husband became involved in it, late in the Coolidge administration. Its advantages over wooden scaffolding, as well as I can recall at this late date, were that it (a) could be put up and taken down quickly, (b) could be used over and over again, and (c) was free from fire hazard.

My brief connection with this promising invention came about in a simple way. The Schillers happened to come to New York. Not wishing to impose further on the Raffrays, I had taken, for a few days, a tiny garretlike room, without bath, on the top floor of the New Weston Hotel, while I looked about for a job. Elizabeth knew of my quest, and one evening, after dinner, surprised me and startled her husband by suggesting that he hire me as a saleswoman.

"Selling what?" Morgan demanded.

"Your tubular steel," Elizabeth said, firmly. "Nobody else seems to be able to sell it. Maybe Wallis can."

Morgan turned to me. "Know anything about construction?"

"No" was the honest answer.

"Ever study engineering?"

"Never."

"Can you use a slide rule?"

I had seen Win Spencer solve problems with one, but that was as far as my knowledge of the gadget went. "No," I said.

"Do you know any construction engineers?" Morgan continued.

"Not that I can recall offhand," I said. "But are they different from other men?"

"Only that they're twice as hard-boiled as anybody you've ever met."

Then he stopped, to look at me sharply. "Maybe Elizabeth's got an idea, after all. Maybe what this product needs is not just another salesman, in shiny blue serge, with an order book and a slide rule, but a girl who looks as if she's stepped out of a bandbox, and with her head full of hard-rock figures. Let me think about it."

The outcome of that casual conversation was an invitation from

My mother, Alice Montague
Warfield

My father, Teackle Wallis
Warfield

My grandmother, Mrs. Henry Mactier Warfield

An early photograph with my beloved Aunt Bessie, Mrs. D. Buchanan Merryman

With my Uncle Sol (S. Davies Warfield) and, between us, my Cousin Anita (later Mrs. Zachary R. Lewis)

With my first pet, "Bully," given to me by my stepfather, John
Freeman Rasin

At school at Arundell

This hat was the height of fashion in my debutante days.

With my husband, Lt. Earl Winfield Spencer, Jr., U.S.N., at the Mexican Border

During my Navy days with my friends at Coronado, left to right: Mrs. Neustadt, myself, Mrs. Sands (Admiral Fullam's daughter), and Mrs. Chase

This is the living room of the Peking house of my good friends, Herman and Katherine Rogers, with whom I stayed.

With Herman Rogers on the way to the temple in the Western Hills that the Rogers used for the weekends

In the courtyard of the temple

The local merchants used to bring their wares for us to make our selections. Here I am looking over fabrics with Katherine and my friend, Alberto Da Zara, the Naval Attaché of the Italian legation.

On a vacation with Aunt Bessie in Marienbad in 1929

With Aunt Bessie and Ernest Simpson at Baden-Baden

Photo from European

One view of the living room at 5, Bryanston Court

These photographs of David and me were taken by members of our party, during our memorable cruise on the *Rosaura*.

Two views of Fort Belvedere, the "Grace and Favour" house turned over to David for his country residence. David completely remodeled the castle and laid out the informal gardens surrounding it.

This is the *Nahlin,* in which we cruised the Adriatic and Aegean when David was King.

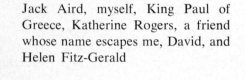

On board the *Nahlin,* left to right: Jack Aird, myself, King Paul of Greece, Katherine Rogers, a friend whose name escapes me, David, and Helen Fitz-Gerald

On our return from the *Nahlin* cruise we stopped briefly for a visit with Prince Paul of Yugoslavia.

Kemal Atatürk loaned David his private train for the trip from Istanbul to Vienna. King Boris, assisted by David, drove the locomotive for part of the way through Bulgaria.

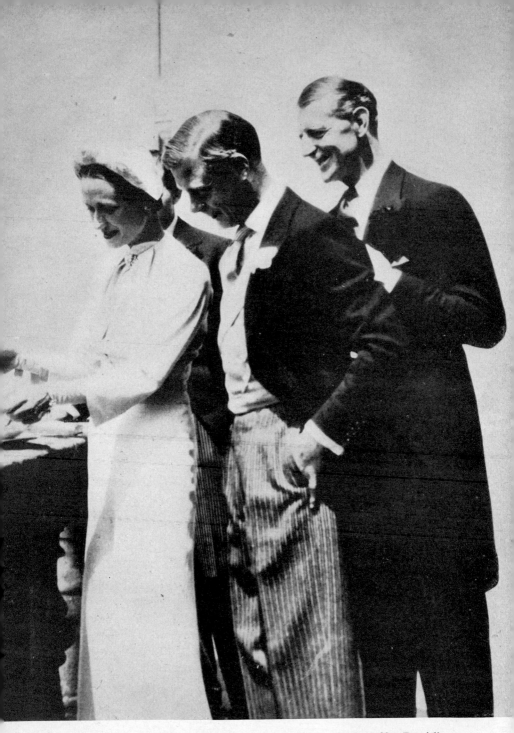

Our wedding day. Back of David is Major Edward Metcalfe, David's best man and a former A.D.C.

On our honeymoon in Venice

It was a tremendous task coping with vanloads of David's possessions, when we moved into Château La Cröe.

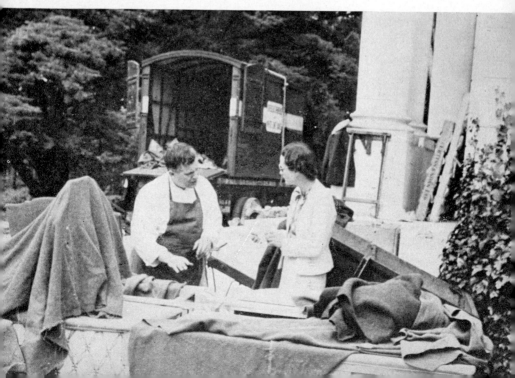

During the early part of World War II I worked with the *Section Sanitaire,* French Red Cross, and David was attached to the British Military Mission at Vincennes.

Later when David became Governor of the Bahamas, I became head of the local Red Cross and devoted a great deal of time to the job.

One of my favorite pictures of David and me taken by a member of our shooting party at the Tallahassee, Florida, plantation of our good friend, Mrs. George F. Baker, in the winter of 1955-56.

Elizabeth and Morgan to come and stay at their house in Pittsburgh while I decided for myself whether or not I had any aptitude for selling tubular steel. I took them up on the offer, more from bravado than from any conviction that I could possibly be of use to Morgan. But I must confess that I was filled with enthusiasm at the prospect of becoming part of the exciting world of big business. What attracted me about it was the idea of doing something different, something out of the ordinary for a woman, a job in which I could pit my wits not against other women but against men in a man's world.

Thus it happened that I spent three weeks in Pittsburgh learning all about tubular steel—how it was made, how it was put up and taken down on the job, its economics, and its rationale. Nobody could have been kinder to me than Morgan. Listening to him, I gathered that all I had to do to make a satisfying sale was to walk into the office of the Vice President of the Cosmic Construction Company, present my card, sit down, and floor him with an M.I.T. graduate's command of pertinent statistics while he was still slightly overcome with the unexpected emanations of my Chanel No. 5.

But in the end Morgan failed to convince me that I could be a sales executive. Tempted though I was, I finally drew back in the face of my old adversary, mathematics. Negotiating a sale required lightning calculations of price and cost—so much a foot, so many feet, freight rates, and the like—the same vexing variables that had always defeated me at school. With Morgan playing the part of skeptical prospect and I that of confident salesman, I struggled through the selling routine again and again, carrying the drama to the critical point where I whipped out the order book—only to lose the sale because my arithmetic never came out the same way twice. Discouraged, but by no means dismayed, I returned to New York. For a few days I toyed with the idea of taking a secretarial course, then abandoned it partly because I felt that I was probably too old to begin, and partly because of a distaste for the typewriter. Then, by chance, something happened that may have had an unappreciated role in diverting my attention from the chances of a career.

One day, while I was debating whether or not to throw in the sponge and return to Warrenton, I had lunch with a Baltimore friend, then living in Westchester, who, after one disastrous marriage, had married a stockbroker. Apropos of nothing at all, she told me of a wonderful experience she had had, at a critical point in her life, with a woman astrologer whom she described as the favorite pupil of the famous Evangeline Adams. "She's really clairvoyant," my friend exclaimed. "She did my horoscope, and you just wouldn't believe the number of things she had right—my breakup with Don, my meeting Jim, his coming into an inheritance, all kinds of fascinating predictions. It can be very comforting, Wallis."

"But I don't believe in that rot. I'm too much of a realist," I said, using a term in wide currency among the incurable romanticists of the period.

"Oh, you don't have to believe in it," said my friend brightly. "The real satisfaction comes in just sitting there while somebody talks seriously about you and your future for half an hour. It's extremely flattering—and much cheaper than going to a psychiatrist."

We separated at the door of the restaurant. I had a tentative engagement with another friend who had volunteered to introduce me to a dress designer on Seventh Avenue, a prospect for which I had little zest on that particular afternoon. A number of old Navy friends from Coronado days had come to New York on a training cruise; their warship was anchored in the Hudson River. There had been a very, very late party the night before, and at that point in the early afternoon, I did not feel capable of mustering up the brisk self-confidence expected in a job-seeker. On a sudden impulse, I returned to my room, found the address of the astrologer in the telephone book, and made an appointment with her, in spite of what I considered her exorbitant fee of ten dollars.

As my friend had discovered, there is something enormously flattering in having one's character and prospects made the subject of half an hour's undivided attention. Among other things, the lady astrologer wanted to know not only my birthday, but the exact hour of my birth. Years before, out of curiosity, I had once asked my mother the same questions, and she had answered impatiently that she had been far too busy at the time to consult the calendar, let alone the clock. The astrologer said that the information was not indispensable. Many of the details of the horoscope she cast, of course, have long since disappeared from my memory. But certain points I clearly remember. One was that I would have two more marriages in my life. Another was that I would have a normal life span but would die unexpectedly and in an unusual place. And still another was that in middle life, between the ages of forty and fifty, I would exercise "considerable power of some kind."

The marriage and death predictions seemed to me fairly stereotyped, and I did not linger over them. But the last prophecy fascinated me.

"What kind of power?" I asked, hopefully.

"The aura is not clear," the astrologer said. "But the power will be considerable. You will become a famous woman."

"Will the power be connected in any way with a job?"

"Oh, no. Absolutely not. There is nothing in your aura to suggest an association with a business career. The indications are all strongly in the opposite direction. You will lead a woman's life, marrying, divorcing, marrying again, with several serious emotional crises. The power that is to come to you will be related to a man."

Thanking her, I paid the fee to the receptionist at the desk and walked out in the daylight. I was not aware of feeling more encouraged, or, for that matter, any more disheartened. So I do not suggest that the episode had any effect on my decision to forget about trying to find a job and to return to Warrenton, my books, my afternoon walks, and my simple reflections. But perhaps our conscious decisions are not always based on conscious reasons.

Something much more easily identifiable did undoubtedly contribute to the sudden deflation of my ambition. I was seeing a good deal of Ernest Simpson. He and his wife had decided on a divorce, and by this time the action was all but completed. Ernest asked me to marry him after we were both free. I had come to admire him for his high qualities of mind, stability of character, and cultivation. But I was not altogether sure that my Southern temperament was exactly suited to such a man. Still, for the first time in a long while, I felt myself falling unmistakably in love; and, when I left Pennsylvania Station to return to Warrenton, I carried an armful of books that Ernest had chosen for me.

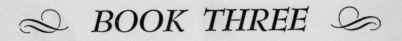

BOOK THREE

I MARRY AN ENGLISHMAN

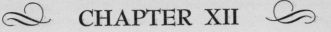

CHAPTER XII

London Wedding

WHILE MY AFFAIRS HAD BEEN TAKING THESE VARIED TURNS, MY mother remarried. Her new husband was a charming Washingtonian, Mr. Charles Gordon Allen. My mother was then fifty-six years old, but she was, characteristically, as gay and excited as a young bride. It was a small family wedding—only Aunt Bessie, Cousin Lelia, Corinne, now the wife of Lieutenant Commander George Murray, several Allens, and I were present. Some weeks later Cousin Lelia had the bride and groom down to Wakefield Manor on the Fourth. My mother signed the guest book in her usual impish way: "Here on the Fourth with my third."

The following spring during my second year at Warrenton, Aunt Bessie, deciding I had been rusticating quite long enough, wrote me a letter that was like a reprieve. She was thinking of taking a summer trip to Europe. Would I like to go with her as a companion? "I can promise nothing very exciting," Aunt Bessie warned. "But the change may do you good, and, anyway, having you with me would do me good."

I could not telephone her quickly enough to ask when we should leave, and where we should go.

"H-rrmph" was Aunt Bessie's answer. "Your mother tells me that you think you may be falling in love again. You don't sound like it to me."

"Perhaps I am, perhaps I'm not—I can't be sure yet," I said. "But being abroad for a while may help me to make up my mind."

In the midsummer of 1927, Aunt Bessie and I sailed from New York, taking the southern route across the Atlantic and into the Mediterranean, with stops at Naples, Palermo, and finally, up the Dalmatian coast to Trieste, where we left the ship. From Trieste we traveled, sometimes by train, sometimes by hired car, back across southern Europe, stopping at various places on the way—Monte Carlo, Nice, Avignon, Arles—and arriving eventually in Paris. Aunt Bessie was, as always, the perfect traveling companion, shrewdly observant, amusing, and incorrigibly independent.

Aboard ship was a very sedate young Philadelphia lawyer who decided, once the Main Line had safely receded behind the western horizon, that life was meant to be lived and that even for Philadelphians the allotted span was hardly enough. He traveled with Aunt Bessie and me from Trieste to the south of France. He introduced the Black Bottom to Villefranche, demonstrated the Charleston in Juan-les-Pins, and by Cannes had become almost human. Then, in the vicinity of Avignon, he wistfully departed, to hurry back to the law, with the air of an escaped convict being returned to the chain gang.

Rather late one evening at the Hotel Lotti in Paris, having stolen into Aunt Bessie's room to say good night, I was sitting on her bed happily recounting the chronology of the evening, when from a ventilator in the wall there issued an angry Middle-Western voice. "From what we've heard so far, the subject can wait until breakfast. Will you please keep quiet and let the rest of us go back to sleep?"

"I'm very sorry," I shouted at the ventilator. "But you're going to miss the best part of it."

"We've heard it all before," the voice growled back. "We've got four daughters."

A few days later Aunt Bessie had to return to Washington. As I had just been invited to join a party of friends going to Lake Maggiore, I decided to remain. The trip in the company of Mr. and Mrs. Augustine Healy and Mr. and Mrs. Henry Tompkins was enlivened by the presence of a very amusing young Irishman named Rowland Byers. On my return to Paris I moved back to the Hotel Matignon, where I had stayed with Corinne on my previous trip. Coming out of a restaurant one evening, I picked up a copy of the early edition of the *Paris Herald*. On the front page was a dispatch from Baltimore announcing the death of my Uncle Sol. Terribly upset, I rushed back to the hotel and there awaiting me was a cable from my mother confirming the newspaper story and giving the date of the funeral. Even though I booked the first passage available—on a ship running to Boston and not leaving for several days—I could not possibly arrive in time for the funeral.

Many memories flooded my heart. During the years since I had told

Uncle Sol of my intention to divorce Win Spencer, there had been little communication between us. By his coldness he had made it plain that whatever survived of his original affection for the only child of his dead brother had by my action been sadly shaken. In his eyes I had become the black sheep of the family, and the recollection of that harsh judgment made me shiver. But what had I really done to earn his settled disapproval? I remembered the gallery of photographs in his apartment in New York. My uncle had clearly been drawn to women whose interests and tastes were in dramatic contrast to the standards that he laid down for the women of his own family. Why did he object to my so much more modest show of spirit and independence?

I had mentioned this to Aunt Bessie. She had quietly replied, "Sol always had an eye for a pretty woman. But I doubt that he ever credited us with much sense or principle—that is, a man's idea of sense and principle, which is a highly flexible and self-accommodating apparatus." It was an acute saying, perhaps, but not a comforting one.

Saddened in spirit I sailed for home. My mother met my train at the Washington Station. Uncle Sol was sleeping his last sleep in the Warfield vault in Greenmount Cemetery. The will had been read to the family. The bulk of his fortune, grossly overestimated at five million dollars, together with Manor Glen, was left to found and support, as a memorial to my grandmother, a home for impoverished ladies of gentle birth. Manor Glen was to remain as it had been in my grandmother's day, with the same furniture, the same silver in its accustomed place, and the same servants to the end of their days. Thus Uncle Sol with this romantic salute to a fading tradition proposed to perpetuate his code beyond the grave.

All would have been well if he had been content to stop there. But the trouble was that in his desire to make Manor Glen a fitting abode for the large number of indigent ladies whom he was determined to care for he had overreached himself.

His plans called for the erection of a fine new building, and above all the creation of an atmosphere so genteel that his charges would never have reason to be reminded that they were the objects of his charity. This project miscarried because it was his misfortune to die at an awkward juncture in his financial affairs, and his estate was worth only a fraction of its hoped-for value. Since there was not enough income to build the building and support the ladies, the Court finally permitted the executors to abandon the Manor Glen aspect of the plan and use the revenues of the estate for the direct support of the beneficiaries. This work is still being carried on under a corporate form of the Anna Emory Warfield memorial fund.

I was left with only a small trust fund that was to cease in the event of my remarriage. On the advice of other members of the family, I appealed this to the Court, and an equitable settlement was made with the executors.

However, I am getting ahead of my story. From Washington, on my return from Europe, I continued to Warrenton. A month later, on December 6, 1927, my divorce petition was submitted to the Circuit Court of Fauquier County. Four days later the petition was heard and granted. Since there was no other place for me to go, I stayed on at the Warren Green.

Ernest Simpson had by agreement with his father and his other business partners arranged to transfer to the London office with the object in view eventually of taking charge of the firm's British offices. This was what Ernest had always wanted. He had always yearned to take up permanent residence in England and follow the ways of his father's people. We were now both free. Ernest again asked me to marry him. This time I said yes.

But over the winter I had a momentary attack of doubt. My original misgivings assailed me. It was not so much a question of Ernest's not being the right man for me as of my not being the right woman for him. Temperamentally, we were at opposite poles—and from watching the married lives of my friends I had lost confidence in the old axiom that opposites complement each other.

My old friends, Katherine and Herman Rogers, having meanwhile left Peking, were living on the Côte d'Azur, in a villa called Lou Viei, on a hill behind Cannes. They invited me to spend the spring with them. I returned to France early in May to spend a little time in their company while pondering my personal situation.

The spring enchantment of the Riviera and my deepening loneliness combined subtly to turn me around once more. I wrote to Ernest, now established in London, telling him that I was now sure in my heart —I was ready to marry him. Toward the end of May, 1928, I went to London, taking a tiny flat at Stanmore Court. Ernest had everything arranged for the marriage. He had bought a new yellow Lagonda touring car and hired a chauffeur, a Welshman named Hughes, for our honeymoon trip to Paris. "Later on," he said, "there'll be time to look for a place to live. All that matters now is getting married and agreeing on where we'll go on our honeymoon." I was very happy.

Ernest Simpson and I were married in London on July 21, 1928, at eleven o'clock in the morning. It was a perfect July day, sunny and warm. I wore a yellow dress and a blue coat that I had had made in Paris. Ernest sent the car for me, and Hughes drove me to the Chelsea Registry of Marriages where Ernest; his father; and Ernest's nephew, Peter Kerr-Smiley, who was almost as old as Ernest himself, were waiting for me. The Registry is one of those gloomy Victorian piles in which so much of London's business is transacted. Ernest hurried me through grimy corridors bustling with activity. The setting was more appropriate for a trial than for the culmination of a romance; and an uninvited sudden surge of memory took me back to Christ Church at Baltimore, and the odor of lilies and the bridesmaids in lilac and the organ playing softly.

We were married in a cluttered office with bare walls by an official standing beside a battered desk. His bored tone and manner conveyed the impression that he had been through his role much too often to have the slightest interest in those whose lives he so briskly and bureaucratically united, for better or worse. A rattle of words, a simple "yes" in response, a kiss—"a cold little job," Ernest was later to say. We fled back into the July sunlight. Ernest's father had arranged for a wedding breakfast in his sitting room at the Grosvenor Hotel, a rambling, soot-stained structure near Victoria Station. There was excellent champagne. Then Ernest and I, with Hughes very smart in his new livery, left in the car for the Channel ferry and a honeymoon in France and Spain.

We began with a week in Paris, that most enchanting of cities for a honeymoon, stopping at the Hotel St. Regis, on the rue Jean Goujon. Ernest knew Paris well, especially the amazing little out-of-the-way restaurants with the checked tablecloths and good food and wine. We dined at a different one every evening. I had realized, of course, that Ernest was a man of wider reading than most of my friends; but in the course of our honeymoon I discovered, to my pleasure, that he was a highly cultivated and many-sided man. He spoke French fluently, with a good accent. He knew a lot about French history and possessed more than a tourist's acquaintanceship with art and architecture. He took me to the Louvre again, to Chartres, and to Beauvais, among other places, to show me what is in my opinion the most beautiful apse in Christendom. Later we motored briefly into Spain. I was avid for information; Ernest was a Baedeker, a *Guide Michelin,* and an encyclopedia all wrapped up in a retiring and modest manner. This was a blissful existence; and, for the moment, I felt a security that I had never really experienced since early childhood.

CHAPTER XIII

The Good Life in London

ON RETURNING TO LONDON WE MOVED INTO A SMALL HOTEL WHILE I searched for a house. Ernest's sister, Maud Kerr-Smiley, came to my assistance, and with her help I finally found one in the West End, at 12, Upper Berkeley Street, near Portman Square and not far from Marble Arch. We rented it for a year, furnished, from Lady Chesham, intending in due course to find a place of our own. Upper Berkeley is a short street; and the house, of yellowed stone and of indefinite vintage, was one of a row of small houses, of the kind that abound in the West End of London. Stone steps led from the sidewalk to a green door fitted with a brass knocker. The dining room, with walls of pale striped wood, was on the first floor. From the entryway a flight of stairs shot straight up to a large **L**-shaped drawing room, painted Georgian green and providing a warm, effective background for the Chippendale furniture. My bedroom was on the third floor, a sunny room looking out upon the street. Practically everything in it, except my clothes and my family photographs, belonged to Lady Chesham. There was an enormous bed, with a fine brocaded headboard; the entire effect spoke of a completely feminine woman. Indeed, having lived so long by myself, I recognized this as the house of a woman who had also lived alone. Adjoining the bedroom was a bathroom, with a commodious tub, and a smaller room Ernest used as a dressing room.

By American standards the house had most of the usual drawbacks of old British houses, with the kitchen in the basement, which was as dark as the hold of a ship. Still, for a rented house it was altogether charming, and I was enchanted with it. In spite of the fact that not a stick of furniture in it was mine or Ernest's, I came to think of it as my own. After my years as a wandering Navy wife, living in standard Navy dwellings with government-supplied furniture, and my one-room existence at Warrenton, my home on Upper Berkeley Street seemed almost a palace. I had a butler, a cook, a housemaid, and a chauffeur. Compared to what I had known since I had left my grandmother's home, this was luxury. But who would come to my house?

I knew scarcely a soul in London, and I approached the business of making a new life for myself with trepidation. Ernest's sister was an understanding woman. I was a stranger, and she took me in. She was eager to fit her long-absent brother and her new American sister-in-law into her secure, well-ordered, entirely British world. A tiny, pretty woman, she was separated from her husband and lived in a big house near Belgrave Square. Her daughter, Betty, was a debutante, and I was invited to the parties given for her. In addition, Maud gave small luncheons and bridge parties in order to introduce me to her own circle of friends. Nevertheless I had the feeling, at times, of being a somewhat awkward American relation who had turned up unexpectedly, and to whom the English connections were expected to be considerate. Moreover, it was difficult for me to adjust myself to British ways.

The observation has been made that the English-speaking world consists of a single race divided by a common language. I was to discover for myself, during my first months in London, the truth of that generalization. Even the minor differences of language made me feel as much out of place among the British as an Eskimo on exhibition before the Royal Geographical Society. A man who came to wash the windows started to leave with the muttered explanation that he had forgotten his "pile."

"Your pile?" I asked. "What on earth has a pile to do with washing my windows?"

It turned out that what he had to fetch was his pail. When in a shop I asked for a *pitcher* the shopgirl stared at me blankly. Only after I had explained that I wanted a glass container for water did she perceive, as by an act of revelation, that it was a *jug* I had in mind. Maud introduced me one afternoon to the British housewife's glossary; *endive* for *chicory; patterns* for *samples; grill* for *broil.* I also discovered, in the course of my apprenticeship in the London idiom of the hour, that *darling* as used by the British was not necessarily a term of endearment but only another way of saying hello. In the London of that day, everybody was darling—*Darling, so glad to see you! Darling, could you possibly come to dinner tomorrow evening?*

Being endowed with strong powers of assimilation, I succeeded in time in mastering enough of these Anglicisms to be able to communicate with my British friends.

I was further confronted by a disconcertingly different etiquette of eating. At the British table the left hand is brought into play far more briskly and usefully than is the American practice. British eating is carried on with a continuous motion, and the method, I concluded, was much more efficient than the one to which I was accustomed. Another peculiarity of the British table, which at first dismayed me, was the custom of starting to eat as soon as one is served, instead of waiting, as Americans do, for all the guests to be served. The virtue of what to American eyes looks like an act of rudeness is that one may taste one's food while it is still hot.

No doubt, in the first flush of my discovery of Britain, I arrived at conclusions that Ernest must have privately judged somewhat unsound. The awe in which the average Briton, at least of that period, held a title, struck me as odd, and, indeed, almost irrational in a country otherwise so democratic. The phenomenon was most conspicuous among the shopkeepers. If one was a Lady Vere de Vere there was never any difficulty about opening charge accounts, and salespeople fell over themselves for the privilege of serving a title. A friend of Maud Kerr-Smiley advised, when she heard I was engaging a new maid, "You'll find that it will make quite a difference in her attitude if you carelessly drop a few titles into your conversation."

Seeking a key to the British riddle, I formed the habit of reading most of the London newspapers. I studied them from front to back; and there was one organ of the British press that instantly absorbed my curiosity—the Court Circular, which recorded the movements, engagements, and appearances of the Royal Family. The stately language, suggestive of another epoch, delighted me: "His Majesty graciously replied. . . ." "His Majesty is pleased. . . ." He was never ungracious, I was sure; but was he never displeased, I wondered. It surprised me, an American, that an entire nation should follow with such rapt attention the purely formal goings and comings of a single family. Even Ernest, for all his long residence in the United States, was under the spell. He would mention in hushed tones something the Queen had done at a charity bazaar, or something the King had remarked to a disabled war veteran while inspecting a hospital. It seemed to me that every British household, from highest to lowest, unconsciously patterned itself upon the royal example. Queen Mary had only to change her coat to start a new style. And King George was the national model of propriety and decorum.

Never having previously lived under a monarchy, I found it difficult to fathom the state of mind that accepted it as an axiom that the King could do no wrong. And compounding my bewilderment was the voracious English appetite for gossip about the Royal Family. Long before I had met the Prince of Wales, or had had even the most passing encounter with members of his family, I had formed a strong impression, from the gossip shuttling across the bridge tables, that he was a gay blade; that his brother, Prince George, was often in hot water for one thing or another; and that the King was rather strict with his sons.

Indeed, and it is strange to have it come back to mind after so many years, one of Maud Kerr-Smiley's favorite stories about the British Royal Family was that, at a ball she gave in her house in Belgrave Square, toward the end of the First World War, the young Prince of Wales, then a soldier Prince on leave, had met a beautiful young woman who became his first true love.

Few of the internal secrets of the British Royal Family and the troubles that are usual in any large family and that understandably remained uncatalogued in the Court Circular appeared to escape the riveted curiosity of the King's subjects; and it was difficult for me to reconcile the appetite for unflattering gossip with the genuine awe.

Perhaps the great root of my difficulty in adjusting myself to English ways was my habit of speaking my mind, which my mother would have described as congenital. I was accustomed to say whatever popped into my head. My American outspokenness seemed to amuse, and occasionally to startle, Ernest's sister and friends. No doubt they classed me as a representative product of the American era of the twenties. But the world of which I was a product was not that of F. Scott Fitzgerald or Ernest Hemingway. I had been shaped in the circle of naval officers and their wives, where a woman learned to maneuver furiously for her husband's promotion and where an American woman of my generation judged it important to be a little different, or, in any case, interesting, and was prepared to pit her ideas spiritedly against those of the male. The emancipation of the American woman had not necessarily contributed to the improvement of American affairs; it had intensified rather than assuaged the animus of the war between the sexes; but perhaps on that account a woman's life was all the more exciting. By contrast, English women, though formidably powerful in their sphere, were still accepting the status—

to borrow a contemporary term—of a second sex. If they had strong opinions they kept them safely buttoned up; confidences were seldom given or encouraged. The British seemed to cherish a sentiment of settled disapproval toward things American—when they were not too insignificant for notice of any kind. The only contemporary Americans, outside Hollywood, of whom British women appeared to have heard were all named Vanderbilt, Astor, or Morgan. By and large they seemed mildly regretful that the continent had ever passed from the control of the Indians. American slang was practically never heard in Mayfair drawing rooms; and it was not, in any case, welcomed as a desirable import. When with characteristic impulsiveness I agreed to something with a cheery "O.K.," my sister-in-law stared at me with an expression of shock and disappointment that could not have been more in evidence had I dropped an *h*.

There used to come over me an icy feeling that Maud's friends were wondering, "What strange ideas will be coming out of that woman's mouth next?" The realization that I was different from them, that I was looked upon almost as an ethnological curiosity, had a dampening effect upon my natural exuberance. I withdrew into myself.

Under these circumstances, perhaps it is not surprising that I was some time finding a place for myself in London. For one thing, Maud Kerr-Smiley was somewhat older than I, as were most of her friends. Then, again, I was afraid that I offered a kind of instinctive resistance to the body of English views and customs that Maud so stanchly represented and that threatened, I felt, to cancel out my own personality and substitute an artificial one, made to an English pattern. Maud was a strong-minded woman, and for the sake of her brother, whom she cherished, she tried to ensure that his wife conformed in every particular to the standards of the people of her set. But, grateful as I was to Maud Kerr-Smiley for these well-intentioned efforts, they had an unfortunate effect. I recognized the genuinely helpful spirit underlying them, but nevertheless they intensified my sense of being a stranger in a strange land. The result was that I clung the more fiercely to my own American ways and opinions— possibly to the point of exaggeration.

For a long time, I was very lonely. I knew no other Americans in London—no one, that is, whom I could call an intimate friend, chat with over the telephone, lunch with, or drop in on for tea. And the British practice of never introducing a stranger at parties was hardly calculated to put a new arrival at ease. When I had finished with the household chores in the morning, the day sometimes stretched vacantly before me. The winter of 1928-29 is even yet remembered by those who experienced it as one of the bitterest in London's history. The Atlantic cold settled over the city like a glacial blanket. So did the winter fog. Oddly enough, I did not mind the cold so much, although my British friends shivered and grumbled in their ancient houses and referred wistfully to the advantages of central heating. On the contrary, having been through a Peking winter, when my only source of heat was a tiny brazier, I rather welcomed the change. It made me grateful for the snugness of my own house and the coal fires burning ruddily in the grates. And, indeed, the cold contributed to what was perhaps the most amusing episode of that winter. The plumbing at 12, Upper Berkeley Street, being of either late Victorian or early Edwardian vintage, left much to be desired. The drain for the guest bedroom, for example, was an open standpipe that ran down the outside of the house. We had a friend staying with us, Merritt Swift, who was attached to the U.S. Legation at The Hague. Leaving the house one morning, Merritt had the misfortune to slip on a patch of ice on the sidewalk. Limping back to the house to recover his breath and to determine the extent of the injury, he inquired of the butler, Robert, about the source of the water. "I'm afraid, sir," said Robert, "that the drainpipe was frozen, and your own bath water overflowed and froze as it ran down. To put it bluntly, sir, you've skidded on your own bath."

What depressed and at the same time fascinated me about my first London winter was the incredible grayness and gloominess that clamped down over the vast metropolis, until the atmosphere, the silent buildings, and even the people in the street merged into a sooty gray dinginess.

The fog, which was especially dense and persistent that particular winter, was for me a new and even exciting experience. I had never seen anything like it. It was almost a living thing, something touched with mystery and malevolence. On bad days, it crept into the house under the doors and through the cracks in the window sills in visible tendrils, gradually filling the room with a yellowish, acrid haze. If the front door was suddenly opened, the smog in the street poured into the hallway like water spilling through a riven bulkhead. I loved to walk in the streets on such days, watching the dark-yellowish shadows coiling and uncoiling about the houses, listening to the honking of the traffic feeling its way through the murk.

The gloom of London that winter was deepened by a sad circumstance. King George V was seriously ill; he had been stricken by a streptococcus infection and was fighting for life at Buckingham Palace. The Prince of Wales had raced back to London aboard a warship from East Africa. His dramatic reappearance added to the general apprehension. All England seemed to be hanging on the doctors' bulletins; my friends talked of nothing else. On a rainy afternoon, as I was driving past St. James's Palace on the way to the City to pick up Ernest at his office, I saw the scarlet-coated sentries at the entrance suddenly stiffen to attention and present arms. A black motor emerged into St. James's Street. As it passed my car, I caught a fleeting glimpse through the side window of a delicate boyish face staring straight ahead, the whole expression suggesting the gravity of a deep inward concern.

I knew it must be somebody important. The chauffeur turned around, to say in awed tones, "Madam, that was the Prince of Wales."

My loneliness that first winter, coupled with my natural curiosity, served a useful purpose. Instead of being caught up in the usual round of bridge parties and luncheon parties, I used my empty afternoons to learn about London. By myself I visited, one after the other, Westminster Abbey, the Tower, the Houses of Parliament, St. Paul's, the Inns of Court, and all the other famous landmarks, having first, at Ernest's suggestion, read something about them.

I began by not liking London at all. It seemed to me, a stranger, the most unfriendly community I had ever known—all cold gray stone and dingy brick, ancient dampness and drabness, and a purposeful hurry and push in the streets. Indeed, an honest description of my original response to London would be that it evoked in me a bone-deep dislike. There was about the city a pervading indifference, a remoteness and withdrawal, that seemed alien to the human spirit. And my sense of alienation was all the more acute for hearing around me my own language, without being able to relate it to my own experience. One can be more alone in London than in any other city in the world; and coming to know it is a far more complicated process than, for example, coming to know Paris. That city is a feast to the eyes, something to be immediately savored and shared. The difference between the two cities, as has been remarked before, is that Paris is like a woman while London is like a man.

In time, as my knowledge of English ways deepened, I was to change my first emotional impression of London. Like a weathered rock, the character of London partakes of the climate that envelops it. Beneath the unpromising exterior lies the warmth of a banked fire. The British reception of other human beings I discovered to be the reverse of the American. The American practice is a lavish, spontaneous outgiving of hospitality, followed all too often by an equally dramatic consignment to total oblivion. The British invitation is not so quickly forthcoming but, once extended, is perpetual. Still, I was some time learning this fact, and consequently spent many a miserable hour wondering what would become of me, and whether, like a bottle of champagne kept too long in an icebox, I would find that the bubbles had been chilled out of my spirit.

It was understood between Ernest and me, from the beginning of our marriage, that he would keep the family books and I would run the house and buy my clothes within a weekly budget to be arrived at through trial and error. Living on a budget was, of course, no new experience for me. I suppose, too, that I really had no cause to worry. Ernest's father was generous; had our expenses been momentarily overwhelming, he would no doubt have come to our assistance. But it was a matter of pride with Ernest and with me that we should stand on our own feet. Moreover, the sum that Ernest turned over to me for the week's marketing seemed a great deal in comparison with what I had previously been accustomed to. And life in Britain was extraordinarily cheap by American standards. One could live well indeed in the England of that period on an income that in the United States would have meant a grinding struggle. Our house, with its four servants, cost little more than would a small apartment in New York, with a single day servant. The wage of a good cook, I believe, was only six pounds a month, and of a maid four pounds.

In London I continued to do my own ordering for the kitchen, as my grandmother and mother had done before me. I never considered marketing a chore. On the contrary, it was always fun to me. Quite aside from the advantage it gave me in keeping my budget under control, it grew to be part of my education in British customs. There was nothing then in London corresponding to the American grocery store. One went to the fishmonger for fish and chicken and game, to the butcher for meat, to the greengrocer for vegetables and fruit; and each was a little world in itself. I started my rounds at ten in the morning and would spend an hour or so within the confines of four blocks in Paddington. The fishmonger's and the butcher's were all staffed by men; only at the greengrocer's did one find women assistants. In the cheeriness of their natures they all might have bounced straight from the pages of Dickens; and among them, even more than among my new friends, I came to feel that I was at last getting acquainted with England.

I had my own fixed ideas about food. For example, in planning a dinner, I wanted each item whether it was trout, partridge, or grouse to be of the same size. I had noticed that this small detail, besides making for symmetry, has the merit of reducing a hostess's area of possible embarrassment. With everything the same size, there is no chance of the platter's arriving at the far end of the table bearing only a token; and, conversely, there is no necessity for the hostess to make conversation while the guest of honor probes an irregular assortment for a modest helping. I cannot say that my fishmonger was immediately sympathetic to this desire of mine; nor was he visibly elated by my habit of pressing the breast bone of a fowl to see whether it was tender, nor was the greengrocer other than disapproving at my punching and squeezing the fruits and vegetables to determine their quality. I knew all the cuts of beef; and, when the butcher failed to cut me the T-bone steak I wanted, I produced for him my *Fannie Farmer* cookbook, with a diagram showing how to cut a steak the way I liked.

No doubt they considered me an eccentric. Once my fishmonger inquired, after ransacking his rows of partridge for a half-dozen birds of identical size, whether all American women insisted on having their meat and fish in matching sizes.

"I doubt it," I said. "The idea is probably peculiar to me."

"A good thing, I'd say," muttered the fishmonger. "Otherwise they'd have to stamp these things out like Morris cars."

Ernest and I set aside one evening a week to go over the household accounts together; his rule was to pay his household bills weekly. The fishmonger, the greengrocer, the butcher, and other tradesmen would each send a little book or ledger—hideous things, in cramped handwriting—listing my purchases. Ernest was extremely meticulous. He would run down the list, scrutinizing each purchase. I was seldom over the budget, and to be able to splurge at Fortnum & Mason on a jar of caviar, brandied peaches, or avocados was a special treat. Whenever any unusual expense was in prospect, perhaps a dinner party or going to the theater, which we did fairly often, the additional outlay was carefully budgeted in advance. We lived frugally but well.

My second husband was as different from my first as day from night. There was no trace of the skylark in Ernest Simpson. He was regular in his habits, with a temperament as steady and dependable as the trade winds. Because he worked hard and seriously he disliked staying out late at night. For him a pleasant evening's relaxation consisted of going to a friend's house or having friends at ours for

[136]

dinner and bridge. He was up at half past seven in the morning, and off to the city at nine. And he was seldom back before seven in the evening.

Ernest, too, was readjusting himself to British life after his long absence in the United States. It may be that Manhattan and Harvard had also left their stamp on him. He never appeared to me an altogether typical Englishman, despite his ingrained faith in the correctness of British ways of doing things and his pride in having served in the Coldstream Guards. He had none of the Englishman's passion for sports. He did not ride or often play golf, and he did not shoot. The shipping business was his principal interest. In the beginning, at least, our dinner guests were for the most part people connected with his work—shipping men and their wives, from Norway, Sweden, or the United States. However, I would not like to suggest that he was solely a man of business. He is a man who might well have found his true métier as a scholar. He never lost the habit of reading the classics; and one evening after dinner, I was astonished—and, needless to say, impressed—to come upon him and a friend in the drawing room, sitting over their coffee and reading to each other in Latin. His grasp of history, the dates securely embedded in his head, made me conscious of the deficiencies of my own education, the more so because he had a far greater knowledge than I about the history of my own country. He also had an informed love of the theater, the opera, and the ballet. We saw most of the good plays in London, sometimes dropping in at the Savoy afterward for a bit of supper.

Thus Ernest and I began in London what I am tempted to call, despite my initial pangs of loneliness, the good life—a normal married life, comfortable in its unjarring repetition, untroubled by the pinch of money, and revolving around the interests of a businessman husband who was secure in his position in a successful and highly respected shipping firm. My days were ordered—housekeeping in the morning, and occasional luncheons and bridges with other women, all within the orbit into which I had been introduced by Maud Kerr-Smiley.

However, my family situation was not without its complications. Ernest's parents were separated. His mother lived in New York; his father, then well into the seventies, made London his headquarters. He was the most restless man of his age I have ever known, always off on the spur of the moment to a different place—the French countryside, Rome, New York, Switzerland. Ernest had been born to his parents some years after the birth of his sister. They had called him their "afterthought." Ernest was devoted to both of them, and their separation was painful to him. Whenever his father was in London, Ernest and I always dined with him Sunday evenings at Grosvenor House, not far from where we lived. Mr. Simpson was a tiny, almost dwarflike figure, with an unusually intelligent face, a goatee, and piercing eyes that seemed to go right through one. Semiretired, he nevertheless continued to take a keen interest in the business he had founded. Uncompromising to the point of sternness where questions of principle were concerned, the father had, like Ernest, a lighter side. He used to make up amusing little verses about small incidents connected with us and send them to me. The difficulty in the relationship was that Ernest's mother expected us to be with her whenever she came to London. She put in her annual appearance toward the end of winter. Ernest's father, whose policy it was to leave England during her visits, would quietly vanish in the direction of the Continent. Ernest's mother came to see us, and I was under the impression that she took a decidedly dim view of things British. The situation called for the continuous exercise of tact, and Ernest and I had to be on our guard not to exhibit favoritism toward one parent at the expense of the other.

However, the family situation was a minor discord, and my life as it slowly developed suited me very well after my years of wandering. The restlessness left me; there came in its place a reassuring consciousness of sinking my roots into solid earth.

Then, the following spring, just as Ernest and I were planning to leave for a short holiday on the Continent, there came a cable from Aunt Bessie in Washington saying that my mother had been taken seriously ill. Ernest would not hear of my going back alone. We left aboard the *Mauretania* in May.

CHAPTER XIV

My Mother Dies

MY MOTHER WAS STILL LIVING WITH HER HUSBAND IN WASHINGTON in a house on Woodley Road, facing the Wardman Park Hotel. Aunt Bessie, whose fate it has been over many years to watch over and nurse her more vulnerable connections, was with her. I was alarmed by my mother's appearance. She was thin to the point of emaciation; and the clear complexion that she had carried serenely into middle age was now overlaid with an ashy grayness. For the first time that I could remember she looked old and worn. As I entered her bedroom on the second floor and went to her, she cried, "Oh, Wallis, why did they bring you so far? Have you come to see me die?"

She had awakened one morning to find the sight strangely gone from one eye. Thinking that her eyesight might be failing, she went with her husband to an oculist. The oculist sent her to a physician who diagnosed a more serious trouble—a thrombosis. The examination revealed that hardening of the arteries had been an aggravating cause; since my mother had little confidence in doctors and had avoided them for years, it had developed unnoticed. The doctor told her that she was a lucky woman; if the blood clot from which she was suffering had lodged in her brain, she would have been paralyzed. "Guess it was up there first," my mother answered, "but couldn't find the poor thing."

Yet her spirit remained bright, and even with only half her sight she missed nothing. After I had kissed her, she asked me to move away from her bed so that she might see me better. "Isn't that a brown dress you have on?" she asked. It was a brown checked dress that I had bought in London.

"Yes, Mother," I said.

"Thought so," she said in the dry, ironical tone she had often used when I was being difficult as a child. "Whatever made you choose such an unbecoming color!"

It was heartbreaking to see reduced to helplessness a woman who had always been so self-reliant and so seemingly invincible. She was under strict orders not to leave her bed. And the prospect of being bedridden was all the more difficult for her to endure because she had been seriously ill only once before in her life, when she had had typhoid fever as a child. Suspecting that this would be her last illness, she never fully recovered the buoyancy of her nature; an unwonted depression claimed her spirit. There were occasions, I imagine, when she suspected that I might realize how close to the breaking point she really was. More than once I entered her room to find her face buried in the pillow. Yet, summoning up those reserves of will and fortitude that I as a young girl had seen in her, she always managed to turn to me without showing a trace of self-pity or despair.

My mother met Ernest for the first time under these melancholy circumstances. She seemed to like him instantly. From her response to him, I knew that it meant much to her peace of mind to know that I was safely and happily married. She said to him, "You must remember that Wallis is an only child. Like explosives, she needs to be handled with care." Ernest replied that he was well aware of the explosive content but had no misgivings. "I'm glad," said my mother. "Still there have been times when I was afraid of having put too much of myself into her—too much of the heart, that is, and not enough of the head."

After a week or so Ernest had to return to London because of his business. I stayed on for another fortnight, never leaving my mother during the day and only occasionally visiting my old friends in the evening. She and I had many long talks together. She asked about the house in London, how I spent my days, the people I had come to know. It was as if she were trying to reach out across the sea and to understand through my descriptions the kind of life into which my marriage had taken me.

One day she asked, "Are you ever lonely?"

"Sometimes," I answered. "But never for long."

"Well, never be afraid of loneliness. I've been lonely, too. Many times. Loneliness has its purpose. It teaches us to think."

My mother's condition did not improve, but neither did it grow worse. The doctor advised me that she might continue in the same condition, with no additional impairment of her faculties, for two or three years. I was in a dreadful quandary, torn between my desire to be with her and what I felt to be my responsibilities toward Ernest. Where did my duty lie? Did it require me to stay with my mother, who would never get well, or to return to London to be with my husband, with whom my life was just beginning?

I thrashed out the problem with Aunt Bessie and the doctor. Both urged me to return to London. There was no immediate danger of another crisis. If my mother should take a turn for the worse, there would be time for me to return by fast steamer.

The sadness that I carried back to London was a long time in lifting. My mother had supplied me with continual support throughout my life. I could not imagine life without her. For all the years of separation, we had always been close; to her I was both daughter and sister; I had looked to her, in my spells of defeat and frustration, for courage and direction. She understood me; the mixture of Montague and Warfield in my character, so confounding to others, was no mystery to her. Now she was going, and with her would disappear the fragile thread of purpose and meaning that had led me through the labyrinth.

Perhaps sorrow had turned my thoughts away from myself. In any event, I returned to London in an entirely different mood from the one in which I had left. The notion of London's being a vast, implacable, and unfriendly place, bent upon suppressing a stranger, had become preposterous. London was now my home, and during the humid May nights in Washington, when I was unable to sleep, I had found myself longing for my quiet house and the simple rounds of my English day.

Ernest met me at Southampton. It was June again, and the meadows were one bright surge of growth and flowering. On the drive back, Ernest outlined his plans for our summer. He was eager to show me the real England, beyond London, the more so, perhaps, because after his years in the United States he wanted the fun of rediscovering his own country with me. I had explored the nooks and crannies of London; now he wished to take me into the English countryside, into the sea hamlets of Devon and Cornwall, the Lake Country, the Cotswolds, the moors.

With characteristic methodicalness, Ernest had laid out an elaborate program of sight-seeing that would take us every weekend to a different part of England. Needless to say, the focal point of all of these excursions was either a famous cathedral or a castle. Although I had not been able to muster on our honeymoon quite the same enthusiasm for flying buttresses, Gothic arches, and naves that animated Ernest, the prospect nevertheless delighted me. New places, new things, new experiences had always drawn me. And in addition I was inwardly relieved to know that I would not have to endure the interminable weekends of a London summer, with the metropolis all but deserted and our friends away from Friday afternoon through Monday.

Thus we passed the summer of 1929. One weekend, for example, we motored down to Oxford, to visit the ancient and beautiful colleges. Another time we went to Stonehenge to see the Stone Age monuments. We spent a weekend in the Lake District and in August had ten days in Scotland, stopping one night at the famous Gleneagles Hotel in Perthshire, and then continuing up to the Highlands, an eerie, pixy world that enchanted me.

Ernest made quite a ceremony of these weekend excursions. Since our destination was usually a full day's drive away, we would start from London early Saturday morning. Ernest was something of a gourmet. From his earlier holidays in England he knew the little places along the way that were notable for their cuisine. We would stop at one for lunch, and, since Ernest liked to linger over his food and ale and to savor the atmosphere of a place, the afternoon portion of the drive was usually completed at breakneck speed in order to arrive in time for dinner at the inn where he had engaged rooms for us, which was near the site of his historical objective.

Ernest was never happier than when roaming around ancient buildings, searching out for himself the architectural details he had read about in preparation for the visit. He would have me up early Sunday morning, and directly after breakfast we would leave for a day of sight-seeing. Whenever Ernest came upon something that he considered particularly significant or unusual, he would take me to it and discourse learnedly upon the significant features. Possibly Ernest decided that these weekend excursions, with their predominantly historical tone, were a relatively painless way of teaching me English history. If so, he must have known a teacher's moments of despair with a pupil's wandering attention. Though I was always stirred by my first sight of something new, it was the outward look of things, and the internal effect it stimulated, rather than the subtleties of details, that usually stayed with me. And, by and large, I was satisfied to leave ruined castles, crumbling abbeys, and gloomy cathedrals to scholars whose blood was better fortified than mine to withstand the dampness and chill associated with such relics. Far more fascinating to me were the rural inns where we stayed, and the life connected with them. In these remote places there lingered, even at that late date, a Victorian calm and regularity that seemed ages removed from the bustle and rush of London. Dinner usually began at six-thirty, and precisely at seven-thirty the dining-room doors were closed. If one was a second late, one went hungry, and on many occasions, because of Ernest's disinclination to hurry a good lunch, there was barely time on arriving at the inn for me to rush upstairs to wash my face and fix my hair, and race downstairs again before the doors were slammed behind us.

There was an extraordinary ritual connected with some of these inns of which I had observed no exact counterpart elsewhere in my travels. After dinner the guests all repaired to the lounge for coffee, served by waitresses in stiff black alpaca dresses. Husband and wife, paired off like the species in Noah's Ark, would head purposefully toward what were obviously their favorite chairs, title to which was theirs by right of long and undisputed occupancy. The faces, and indeed the entire heads and torsos of the men would disappear instantly, behind the long white pages of the *Times,* which they devoured in deadly silence, inch by inch. The women sat beside them in the enveloping silence, knitting or reading a magazine. Nobody ever spoke; once in such surroundings my handbag, through pure inadvertence, slipped from my lap to the rug, making a sound that could have been no more grating than that of a swallow landing on a roof. Immediately the room became charged with menace; above a dozen chairs the *Times* was lowered in a concerted movement, and a dozen pairs of eyes were trained upon me in cold disapproval. I fumblingly retrieved my bag, opened it, and hastily took out my handkerchief.

Seldom in these surroundings did we encounter another couple as young as ourselves. The occupants of these ancient inns were mostly retired Indian Army colonels, naval officers, civil servants, or plantation managers who, after a lifetime in the colonies or faraway places, had returned to pass their retirement in their English countryside. A great English poet is authority for the noble conception that "no man is an island, entire of it self." But after studying this particular breed of Englishman, in his chosen habitat, feeling no need to communicate with or even to acknowledge the existence of others and coldly resentful of all intruders, I decided that the generalization was far too sweeping. Ernest and I hardly dared to talk aloud until we were safely back in our own room.

Yet, deepfreeze and all, these weekends in the country hotels were fun. The food, though simple, was always good—excellent sole, the

[143]

best roast beef in the world, delicious cold Yorkshire ham, and Cheddar and Cheshire cheese of delicate flavor. I, for one, was never able to understand, after coming to know the English countryside, how English cooking had acquired its bad reputation. To be sure, the spelling on the menus was not always according to Escoffier. It was at one of these inns, for example, that Ernest and I encountered, with delight, a course described as *Sole O'Grattin* and another called *Cold Chicken in Aspect.*

Thus the summer passed quickly, and the variety of experiences into which Ernest conducted me as wife and companion gave new depth and scope to my life. He and I had found happiness together. It was hardly the happy-go-lucky, helter-skelter, semidelirium of a naval aviator's existence into which Win Spencer had rushed me. Flux and change had been my previous lot as a Navy wife; overshadowing every family decision and plan was the realization that out of the blue was certain to come an order requiring us to pick up our things and move. My English life was secure, fastened down to earth, with quiet rhythms of change. In its prevailing sedateness it was the kind of life my Warfield ancestors would have understood and approved; and, if my Montague side occasionally yearned for a gayer circle of friends, I was nevertheless quite happy with what I had.

Through the summer- and into the fall, Ernest and I continued the search for another house. When our lease at Upper Berkeley Street ran out, we moved temporarily into a furnished flat in Hertford Street, off Park Lane, with the idea of using it only as a *pied-à-terre* while continuing the search for a place pleasing to both of us.

Then in October, 1929, came the summons I had been dreading. My mother was failing. Because Ernest could not leave his business, I crossed the Atlantic alone. Mary Raffray met me in New York, having been asked by Aunt Bessie to prepare me for a shock. "I am sorry," Mary said, "to have to tell you that the news is bad. Your mother is in a coma." Mary took me to Pennsylvania Station, and I left for Washington. My mother died three days later, on November 2, 1929.

She had never regained consciousness; and, though there were fugitive moments when she seemed to be struggling back to lucidity and my name sounded among the vague whisperings, I doubt that she ever knew I was close by.

Fortunately for the human race, pain, however piercing, is not a lasting emotion. The recollection of happiness lingers, but the consciousness never retains for long the first thrust of tragic loss. The details of daily life crowd in upon the mind. So it was with me. On my return to London I threw myself into the business of finding a house, and Ernest helped me to look for things with which to furnish it.

Ernest and I decided that, to the extent that our budget allowed, we would collect antiques. The more famous and therefore more expensive shops like Partridge's on New Bond Street or Mallet's on the same street were beyond our reach. I had, however, by this time discovered the small, out-of-the-way, but interesting shops in Kensington and Chelsea. During the winter of 1929–30 I haunted these places, looking for good furniture. On Saturday afternoons Ernest joined me in the search.

Through my persistence and Ernest's judgment we eventually came across a number of nice things at prices we could afford; a handsome eighteenth-century Dutch secretary; a lovely Italian table, painted yellow and black; a William and Mary walnut chest; and several Queen Anne pieces, all in good condition. In addition, we had the fun and excitement of finding them, and this is beyond argument the true reward of the amateur collector. Then, by chance, we stumbled upon the kind of place we wanted. Having reluctantly given up the search for a house, we started to look for flats, and toward the end of the winter found one only a few blocks from our first house in Upper Berkeley Street. It was on the first floor (or second floor, by American numbering) of a fairly new apartment building, 5, Bryanston Court, on George Street, not far from Marble Arch. It had a drawing room, dining room, three bedrooms, and a modern kitchen, as well as four servants' rooms elsewhere in the building.

I had a wonderful time furnishing the new flat. For the first time in my life I had the means and the opportunity to create the kind of setting I had always wanted, a place where good things out of the past would intermingle gracefully with good things of the present, with the accent on color and a pleasing symmetry. To help with the decorating, I enlisted the services of a talented young man named Schreiver, who worked for the well-known shop of Eldon off Grosvenor Square. The drawing room, which was square, had pale green walls, curtains of cream damask, and a beige carpet. The Dutch secretary that I had found, as well as the William and Mary chest and the long Italian table, which had been bought with no particular room in mind, fitted perfectly—or so I decided in the first fine flush of creativeness. When to these good pieces were added two comfortable sofas and chairs, of no particular value, and the bookshelves along one wall had been filled with Ernest's books, the effect was of a bright and comfortable room.

The dining room, however, did not come off so easily. For one thing, it was quite small and could seat only ten people without excessive crowding. For another, it had only one window, at the end of the room. So I had to solve the double problem of assuring adequate ventilation while disguising the blank, boxlike aspect of the room itself. The question of ventilation was the trickier because I preferred to dine by candlelight, which always throws flattering shadows. With candles in sconces on the wall and candlesticks on the table, the temperature in so small a room was certain to become uncomfortable before the end of a dinner, and my solution was a purely practical one. Being myself virtually immune to a draft on the back of the neck, which is the bane of most people, I simply decided to reverse the normal order of the head and foot of the table, sit with my own back, rather than Ernest's, to the open window. The arrangement worked out very well; I never caught cold, nor can I recall that any of my guests was ever a casualty. Moreover, I was in a strategic position to direct the service and to make faces at the parlormaid if anything went wrong.

With the idea of brightening the dining room and giving an impression of spaciousness, I decided to cover the walls with a paper copied from a pattern the French call *toile de Jouy*—scenes of grazing sheep, shepherds, and spreading meadows, and rust-colored figures. The fashion then was to apply a clear glaze to wallpaper, to impart a shiny look, and I made the mistake of trying it. Once it was done, and I was committed beyond recall, I realized my mistake. The glaze gave the room a hard glitter, defeating the soft pastoral effect, and, moreover, the rather busy meadow scenes had the unexpected result of pushing the room in rather than out. My first instinct had been to paint the walls in a light pastel color, and I would have done much better if I had followed its promptings. Unfortunately, having exhausted my budget, I had to live with my mistake. Syrie Maugham, the wife of the novelist, helped me with the rest of the dining room. Having inaugurated the vogue of white rooms, she had established herself as a leader of the *avant garde* of the modern school of decorating. She was a delightful person to work with, although almost too formidable, brooking no interference. From her shop I acquired two good Adam pieces—a sideboard and a console, painted blue-green and white. In another place I found a lovely table of uncertain origin, possibly

Italian, to go with these two pieces. Syrie Maugham's workmen made for me a dozen matching chairs with tall backs, upholstered in white leather, and studded with nails. When the various pieces were finally brought together, the table laid for the first time, and the candles lighted, the effect (except for the unhappy glaze) was soft and charming.

My bedroom was the last room in the flat, a rather large room on the corner, overlooking Upper George Street. The walls were aquamarine; the bed and curtains were aquamarine and pink. My secretary, which might have been French provincial, was of an off-white shade, and the chaise longue was upholstered in pale pink. The room was compact, comfortable, and bright. Next door was another bedroom, which Ernest converted into a dressing room for himself; and adjoining the dining room was another small bedroom that served as a guest room.

For me, the move to 5, Bryanston Court, was a landmark. My desire to give expression to my feminine interests—to create a home embodying the amenities and tastes of twentieth-century life, yet resting on the charm and goodness of the past—came to the surface. I cannot say that I was ever wholly satisfied with my Bryanston Court flat. I was always changing and replacing things or shifting them into new positions. Ernest, whose good taste entered into the composition, was delighted with what gradually evolved. Watching me moving things about and flecking off imaginary dust with a finger tip, he laughingly named me "Madam Mahogany." My days were full; there was excitement and satisfaction in the knowledge that I was making a place for my husband and myself in London.

It was certainly not a conspicuous place. It was not socially important in the Mayfair meaning of the term. But in time it came to have a rather special quality of its own. The process of forming friendships in a strange community had run through its first and most trying phase. I began with only one person, besides my husband, to sponsor me—Maud Kerr-Smiley. She introduced me to her friends. Among these I was drawn to several who seemed to like me. They led me into their own circle, where Ernest and I found several new acquaintances to whom we were attracted, and who in their turn brought us into touch with their friends. Ernest's maritime associations added a cosmopolitan flavor. And thus by the time the flat in Bryanston Court was finished and we were ready to entertain, there was no lack of attractive friends to welcome.

Eventually perhaps my group came to have a stronger American coloration than I realized at the time. In a variety of ways Ernest and I had been thrown in with the American colony in London, which then, perhaps more than today, was a self-sufficient community, made up chiefly of young diplomats, the resident managers of American banks having branches in London, and the representatives of other American business interests. Intermingled with them was, of course, that early type of American expatriate who, in contrast with his more intellectual counterpart on the Left Bank in Paris, found escape from the presumed brashness of American life in England, the fox hunting, the shooting, and the stately social ritual of the British Court and the great country houses.

Among the pleasant acquaintanceships that developed was one with Benjamin Thaw, who was then First Secretary of the United States Embassy, and his charming wife, the former Consuelo Morgan, whose sisters were Thelma, Viscountess Furness, and Gloria Vanderbilt. I had known Benny's brother, Bill, at Coronado. He had served with the Lafayette Escadrille and had been a beau of Katherine Bigelow before she had met Herman Rogers. We had also come to know Major Martin "Mike" Scanlon, the Assistant U.S. Air Attaché, who later became a general. He was then a dashing bachelor; he had a tiny and charming house at Chesham Place, where he gave gay cocktail and dinner parties that had a bright infusion of British and foreign aviators. A little over two years after I came to London Corinne's husband, Lieutenant Commander Murray, was assigned as Assistant Naval Attaché at the Embassy. Having a member of the family nearby, and one of whom I was so fond, made me feel even more at home in London. Also the transatlantic ships, beginning in the spring and continuing through the summer, could be counted upon to discharge a succession of old friends.

Naturally we had many British friends as well. Among those with whom there developed a most agreeable relationship were George and Kitty Hunter, friends of Maud Kerr-Smiley. The Hunters had an extremely attractive flat in Sloane Street in Belgravia. They were both very British, very charming, and wonderful hosts. Florid, portly, and hearty, George was the epitome of the English country squire; a man of means, he never had to work, as far as I was able to judge, and was therefore never bothered by the nuisance of having to go to the office every day. Both he and Kitty, having traveled widely, knew as much about food as any amateurs I have ever had the good fortune to meet. George himself did the marketing; whenever an unusual dinner party was in prospect, he would joyously devote the morning to the task. In consequence of this unstinted expenditure of effort, a dinner at the Hunters was always a rewarding experience. Kitty had accumulated, with the care of a banker salting away a portfolio of gilt-edged securities, a marvelous collection of recipes. A few of these she confided to me, virtually with a reverent laying on of hands. Added to my own inventory of Southern and Chinese recipes, they helped to found the modest reputation for skill as a hostess that my friends were kind enough to accord me.

Meanwhile, by a stroke of luck, I found a very good cook, Mrs. Ralph, who had been kitchen maid to Lady Curzon's French chef, who in turn was considered one of the best in London. Mrs. Ralph was herself no chef, as the kitchen hierarchy is graded on the Continent; but being observant, she had quietly absorbed her master's tricks, and in the matter of preparing sauces and pastries, she could have had few equals. Another quality that endeared her to me was her willingness to concede, without a soul-searing battle, that the British method of preparing vegetables could be improved. The essence of this method is to drown them in a big pot of water. I preferred to have my vegetables steamed in the French way. With Mrs. Ralph in charge, I seldom had to worry about the kitchen. My staff at Bryanston Court also included, as at the house on Upper Berkeley Street, an excellent Scottish parlormaid, Mary Cain; a housemaid; and a part-time personal maid, Mary Burke, a girl of fine character and high intelligence who presently came to work for me full time and who was to be both devoted servant and friend in my period of trouble.

There was nothing elaborate or glittering about the life that materialized around Ernest and me at Bryanston Court. Compared to the magnificent parties to which we were from time to time invited by our British friends—huge affairs for forty and fifty people, with liveried servants and tables blazing with silver—our way of life was fairly simple. Yet for us and our friends it represented an informality and ease that were still somewhat novel in social London, though the staid traditions were already bending grudgingly before the gathering forces of change and soon would yield altogether.

No matter what might have been on my schedule during the afternoon—a bridge party or a scouting expedition to Fulham Road for antiques—I was always home by six o'clock. This habit gave rise to what before long became a most agreeable diversion. The people we knew fell into the habit of dropping by at that hour for a cocktail and an hour or so of light conversation. No one in London ever "dropped in" without invitation, as Americans are accustomed to do. There would be a telephone call, asking if it would be all right to come by for a drink, perhaps with a friend. I had a low cocktail table in front of me and would mix the drinks, a trifling but widely appreciated knack. The cocktail party was, of course, the invention of others. That institution, in London as elsewhere, is usually little better than a milling, babbling mass all talking at once. My slight contribution was to transform mine into a small group gathered in a circle and drawn into a general conversation in which all took part. Whether for this or other reasons, my flat became, toward the end of the day, a pleasant influence in the life of our growing company of friends— young diplomats of many countries, bankers, military attachés, barristers, a sprinkling of M.P.'s, rising young men of the city, several journalists, and the gay young people of Mayfair.

Yet, at the moment that our city life was beginning to order itself so agreeably, we also began to be drawn into that most traditional aspect of British life—the life of the country gentry revolving around the great houses. While Ernest and I had been making our motor trips about rural England, on our way to and from the ancient castles and abbeys that fascinated him, I had noticed with awe and curiosity the vast estates that lay behind the ancient villages—seemingly endless expanses of verdant meadowland and wooded copses, and their entrances guarded by high walls and iron gates. Beyond, barely visible from the lanes and through the shielding trees, one would obtain a flashing glimpse of enormous piles of stone, turreted, towered, or spired, presiding majestically over carpetlike lawns. As I had speculated about what might go on behind London's forbidding gray stone, while poking about the city during my first winter, so I had found myself wondering about the way of life associated with these stately establishments. They were larger than many an American township, each a little rural kingdom, complete with its own tenantry, gardeners, gamekeepers, and other retainers, the whole passing down from generation to generation in a manner that had scarcely changed since feudal times.

My passport to this world came about through a typical British introduction. One evening at a dinner party at Mike Scanlon's house on Chesham Place, after we ladies had withdrawn, I was engaged in conversation by an attractive woman, with brown hair and dancing blue eyes, whom I judged to be an American of about my own age. In the course of our conversation I mentioned Ernest's efforts to educate me in the geography and history of England. Her response to this was a startling non sequitur.

"Do you play bridge?" she asked airily.

"Yes, a little" was my puzzled response.

"Does your husband?"

"A little."

"Do you play golf?"

"Yes, a little."

"And your husband?"

"Once in a while."

"Good—then you must come to Knole this weekend."

It was only then that I realized I was talking to Lady Sackville, chatelaine of one of the most historic houses in all England. I could hardly wait to tell Ernest about this invitation, knowing how pleased he would be at the opportunity to realize so fully and under such hospitable circumstances an antiquarian's dream.

So on Saturday afternoon we took the Dover Road into Kent, through a countryside dozing in the still-lingering warmth of an early autumn day. During the week Ernest, with his usual care, had read up on the history of Knole and its most famous occupant, Archbishop Cranmer, the great Tudor cleric who had played so prominent a part in leading England away from Rome. I, on the other hand, had made it my business to find out something about the Sackville-Wests. Lord Sackville, the fourth baron, had inherited the property and title from his older brother who had died without issue. Lord Sackville was a major general who had had a distinguished military career. He had recently been Lieutenant Governor of Guernsey. He had married Anne Meredith Bigelow, who had been on the stage in the United States for some years before her marriage. Just before dark we swung into the ancient town of Sevenoaks, behind which lies Knole. Almost before we realized where we were, we had turned off High Street, taking a winding road that suddenly terminated at huge iron gates suspended from two great stone pillars. The driveway led through a vast park; as we passed a stand of ancient beeches, I was startled to observe the white flash of deer's tails as they scampered away on our approach.

Now, it would be useless and, indeed, presumptuous for me to attempt to describe again a house that has been the subject of so many learned and exhaustive volumes of history and reminiscence. I will only say that it is a castle of surpassing beauty and a treasure house of great art. I loved my hours there—I was to return many times—and never tired of gazing at the magnificent paintings on the walls, or at the exquisite silver gleaming in the soft light of many candles. Several times we found ourselves occupying Archbishop Cranmer's own room, a gloomy chamber that seemed eerily in keeping with the dark deeds associated with the times of Bloody Mary. I used to lie awake at night, fancying that the small creaks and groans of the ancient woodwork represented a ghostly stirring and impatience at this unwelcome intrusion.

While Knole itself was the most formal of houses, the life that went on inside, thanks to the lively spirit Anne had brought with her, was the essence of informality. Mornings were given over to golf on the estate's own private course; afternoons were devoted to leisurely walks among the great gardens and through the stately park, followed by a rubber or two of bridge. On Saturday evenings, after dinner, there was always dancing in the famous Colonnade Room, to music supplied by a gramophone and by the light cast by myriad candles burning brightly in the magnificent Charles II silver sconces and the Queen Anne chandeliers. Our host had taken up dancing after his marriage to Anne; he had come to love it with the fervor of a belated discoverer. With his white hair, slim figure, and courtly manner, he was the acme of grace as he danced with each woman in turn. Saturdays, with dinner, there was always champagne; Sundays, it was burgundy—this rule was never broken all the time I was there.

In time I came to know many other famous houses, but none ever quite held for me the magic of Knole.

Thus my life was changing in many ways. So far England had encouraged the ascendancy of the Warfield side in me. But now I felt an unmistakable resurgence of the Montague inheritance.

CHAPTER XV

I Meet the Prince

MANY STORIES HAVE BEEN TOLD OF MY MEETING WITH THE PRINCE of Wales. The facts are as I shall now relate them. In the course of so doing, I have no choice but to correct, in the interest of accuracy, the recollections of my husband, as recorded by him several years ago in his memoirs, *A King's Story*. David is justly famous for a flawless memory for names, places, and historical dates—a truly royal gift. But this accomplishment apparently does not extend to occurrences of a mildly romantic connotation, a deficiency that is not unusual in husbands. He thinks that we first met in the fall of 1931. He was right about the season but a whole year off in the date. Actually we met late in the fall of 1930. I am sure I am right because of a dramatic experience that took place that summer.

It had been arranged for Aunt Bessie to visit Ernest and me, and the three of us took a motor trip on the Continent. From England we went to The Hague. There we stopped at the Hotel des Indes. The first night we were there, after we had gone to bed, I was suddenly awakened sometime after midnight by the sound of running feet in the corridor, a banging on doors, and a cry of *"Brand"*— fire. Shaking Ernest into wakefulness, I jumped out of bed, threw a coat over my nightgown, and rushed to Aunt Bessie's room. By now there was a strong smell of smoke, and people were pouring down the main stairway. Aunt Bessie had already heard the alarm and was up. Taking her firmly by the arm, I hurried her into the corridor. As we passed my room, I saw Ernest methodically folding his shirts and placing them neatly in a suitcase.

I yelled at him to forget our clothes and get out while there was still time.

[153]

"You take Aunt Bessie to the lobby," he said calmly. "I'll be right along."

The lobby was full of guests in all conceivable states of undress, and the firemen had already taken charge. The fire appeared to be in the upper stories of the hotel. Minutes passed; there was no sign of Ernest. I started back up the stairs to find out what had happened. A fireman stopped me. Then, just as I was growing desperate, an immaculate figure appeared at the head of the stairway—Ernest, complete with bowler hat, Guards' tie, handkerchief neatly folded in his breast pocket, his suitcase in his right hand, and in his left the inevitable umbrella.

"Good Lord!" gasped Aunt Bessie. "The best-dressed man at the fire!"

Actually the fire turned out not to be much, and we were able to return to our rooms.

After leaving The Hague, we motored through western and southern Germany and finally ended up in Paris.

All this while I had kept Uncle Sol's legacy untouched. Now I decided to indulge myself in a little splurge, and buy a dress from each of the three or four leading couturiers. Ernest and Aunt Bessie were disapproving of such extravagance; they strongly advised me not to dip into the principal—a piece of advice that was all the more appropriate considering the source of the legacy—but rather to put it into blue-chip investments. But the prospect of at last having a few chic clothes from the great couturiers was more than I could resist.

It was because of this incident that I am sure of the year of our meeting.

As I have mentioned before, Benny and Connie Thaw had become my close friends, and I was aware that Connie's sister, Thelma, Viscountess Furness, was greatly admired by the Prince of Wales and was widely reputed to be the object of his interest. One day in November, 1930, Connie called up in some agitation to ask my help. Her sister was having the Prince of Wales and several other guests down for a weekend's hunting at Burrough Court, her husband's country house at Melton Mowbray, in the hunting country of Leicestershire. Connie and Benny were to have been the chaperones. Unfortunately for that arrangement, Benny's mother had been taken ill in Paris; and, because Benny was tied up with some business at the Embassy, Connie would have to leave for the continent alone. Would Ernest and I take her place? Benny, she promised, would take us down to Melton on the train and be on hand to supply whatever counsel might be needed.

My first reaction was a mixture of pleasure and horror. With the exception of Benny Thaw, all the other guests were certain to be strangers. Like everybody else, I was dying to meet the Prince of Wales; but my knowledge of royalty, except for what I had read, had until now been limited to glimpses at a distance of King George V in his State Coach on his way to open Parliament or on other great occasions.

I scarcely knew Thelma Furness, except for having exchanged polite greetings with her at one or two parties. She was strikingly attractive with big brown eyes, brown hair parted in the middle and drawn softly back into a chignon. Her skin was camellia-like, and she had a thin, lovely figure.

The responsibility of taking Connie's place as chaperone scared me. I gasped that I couldn't imagine anything that would be more fun, but—but I wouldn't know anybody there; I didn't hunt; I wouldn't know what to say to the Prince of Wales, or how to curtsy. Thank you very much, Connie, but—

"Don't be silly," said Connie. "You can't let me down now. There'll be no difficulty with the Prince—he doesn't stand on ceremony, he's never stuffy, and, besides, he likes Americans. May I tell Thelma that you'll do it?"

"Oh, Connie," I said, "I just can't."

"Benny will see you through," said Connie. "Now be a dear and call up Ernest and tell him that I want you to do it as a favor to me."

I called Ernest at the office to repeat the invitation. He was delighted. "Of course, we'll go," he said, firmly. "It's really a great honor."

"But, Ernest, I'm really scared," I protested. "I haven't the faintest idea of what's expected of me."

Ernest laughed at my apprehensions. "All that's expected of you, darling, is that you be yourself."

I called Connie back to say that Ernest and I would do what she had asked but that I, personally, would dread every moment of it. "You'll have a marvelous weekend," Connie promised. Then she added, "I forgot to tell you that the Prince of Wales's younger brother, Prince George, will drive down to the country with the Prince of Wales, but he won't be staying in the house."

"Connie," I begged, "how can you expect me to manage two curtsies?"

"One at a time," she said gaily, "will be quite enough."

A little later Thelma Furness telephoned to thank me for taking her sister's place. She was very sweet, but my misgivings remained. The one bright spot in my prospects was the new winter wardrobe that I had acquired in Paris. Among my acquisitions was an attractive blue-gray tweed dress with a cape of the same material edged with nutria, which I had bought during my shopping spree. This, I felt confident, would meet the most exacting requirements of both a horsy and princely setting, and would give me the added assurance that came from the knowledge that in the dress was a little white satin label bearing the word Molyneux. And I also had several new evening dresses.

So one Friday afternoon Ernest and I met Benny Thaw at St. Pancras Station, where we boarded the train for Melton. I have never felt worse in my life. Possibly from the onslaught of excitement I had come down with a dreadful cold. My head was stuffed up; my body ached; my voice rasped in my ears. In my despair I saw nothing but disaster ahead: a sniffling chaperone boring the Princes and the other guests.

As the train sped into the English countryside, I addressed myself to the first difficulty that would have to be met. "Benny," I said, "I feel awful. I wish I were dead. But if it's the last thing I do, I intend to make a proper curtsy. Start showing me how."

Benny was startled. "Where did you ever get the idea that I know anything about curtsying? Needless to say, I've never had occasion to curtsy."

"Connie said you'd teach me. It was the condition of my going. If you're not going to help me, I'm getting off this train at the next station."

Benny was amused by my concern but slightly unnerved by my seriousness. However, having attended many Court functions and being an observant man, he had a general knowledge of the fundamental mechanics of the act. Rising reluctantly to his feet he attempted to demonstrate what was required. Even conceding Benny a certain manly grace, and allowing for his being handicapped by the lurch and sway of the train, the example was anything but adequate. "The trick," Benny tentatively suggested, "is, or appears to be, to put your left leg well back and behind the right one."

"Now, if you'll do it once more, this time more slowly, I may catch on."

Under any other circumstances the scene in the carriage would

[156]

have been extremely funny, but I was in no mood to see its humorous side. After Benny had gone through the ritual once more, with something less than the grace of a Pavlova, I tried it myself.

"I'll never be able to do it," I moaned.

"Now, calm down, Wallis," said Ernest. "That was really a very nice curtsy—much more to my taste, I can honestly say, than Benny's."

We arrived at Melton Mowbray about five o'clock in the afternoon. A pea-soup fog had clamped down over the countryside, and as the car that met us at the station crawled into its cold, wet embrace I found myself wishing that it would swallow me without a trace. At Thelma Furness's house we were met by her stepdaughter, Averill, who told us that the rest of the party had been delayed on the road by the fog but were expected shortly. The house was a hunting lodge of fairly recent date. It was spacious, and comfort was the keynote. It was furnished in typical country-house style— mahogany furniture and gay chintzes. We were taken into a drawing room where there was a round table in front of the fireplace laid for tea. My cold was worse, if anything. I knew from the burning sensation of my skin that I had a slight temperature. More than anything else I wanted to slip upstairs to my room and go to bed. We made small conversation and had tea. A maid entered the drawing room and quietly drew the curtains. Night had come. Still no sign or further word of the others. We sat and we sat and we sat. I saw Ernest glance nervously at his watch. Then about seven o'clock there was a sound of voices in the hall, and Thelma appeared with the two Princes. She introduced me to both of them. I summoned my fading courage and made my first curtsy to the Prince of Wales. To Ernest's surprise and my own it came off very well as did my second one to Prince George. Thelma led us to the tea table, and we had tea all over again. Only then did I dare to scrutinize the two Princes.

The Prince of Wales, as I remember, had on very loud checked tweeds. His younger brother was similarly dressed, but his clothes were more conservative in pattern. I remember thinking, as I studied the Prince of Wales, how much like his pictures he really was—the slightly wind-rumpled golden hair, the turned-up nose, and a strange, wistful, almost sad look about the eyes when his expression was in repose. But I was surprised on seeing him for the first time to discover how small he was. From the photographs I had seen of him in uniform I had somehow formed the impression that he was fairly tall, but he could not be, I realized then, more than two inches taller than I, and I am five feet five. Prince George was considerably taller, with neatly brushed brown hair, aquiline features, and dark blue eyes. He gave an impression of gaiety and *joie de vivre*.

What attracted me at once about the two brothers and especially the Prince of Wales was their utter naturalness. The thought was afterward to occur to me that it was decidedly unimaginative on my part to expect them to be anything else. Still, the notion that they would be imposingly formal and reserved was in the back of my mind, and to find that Royalty lights a cigarette in much the same way as other people do and employs much the same gestures and mannerisms and in addition could be highly agreeable was for me an astonishing revelation.

Thelma must have put the Princes on notice that I was an American and that Ernest had been educated in the United States because in a most casual way they talked to us about life there, and the Prince of Wales in particular expressed his admiration for Americans and the American outlook. It was done with such easy grace that I momentarily forgot about my cold and my dread vanished.

Prince George's friends, with whom he was to spend the week-end, presently called for him. He left after shaking hands with the rest of us, an attention requiring from me another curtsy that I might well have forgotten had he not first said good-by to Thelma. By then it was eight o'clock, and I felt no better. We went upstairs to dress for dinner. When we were alone in our room, Ernest remarked on the charm of the two brothers, their beautiful manners, and the deftness with which they put others at their ease. "I have come to the conclusion," he added, "that you Americans lost something that is very good and quite irreplaceable when you decided to dispense with the British Monarchy." There was no question but that Ernest's admiration of the Royal Family had been profoundly enhanced by even this brief encounter; and after I had had a long soak in the tub and taken two aspirins, my own sense of pleasure began to rise in anticipation of the evening.

The first guests began to arrive shortly after we went downstairs. It turned out to be a large party—at least thirty people, and dinner was late, even by European standards. As I had feared, Ernest and I knew not a soul while everyone else plainly knew one another extremely well. It is a trying experience for a couple to be plunged into a roomful of people who have known one another for years; and the feeling of isolation was accentuated for the reason that the talk was mostly about hunting, and Ernest and I had only the most superficial knowledge of that sport or, for that matter, of horses.

Among the guests were several Americans—the Robert Strawbridges, of Philadelphia, and the F. Ambrose Clarks, of New York and Long Island—who had houses at Melton and who hunted with the well-known local packs of hounds. At dinner Thelma sat on the Prince's right. Ernest and I, as comparative unknowns, were lost in the lower ranges of the spectrum of precedence. After coffee there were cards—poker and bridge. Ernest did not play poker and considered me, perhaps inaccurately, a better bridge player than he was. "You uphold the family honor," he whispered. "I'll be quite happy to sit and talk."

The poker players went off with the Prince and Thelma to a connecting drawing room. I found myself at a bridge table playing for stakes that, by Bryanston Court standards, were frighteningly high. I could see the week's marketing money and more lost by the evening's end. Fortunately, there was time for only a rubber or two and I counted myself lucky to escape with a loss of eight pounds. From the cries of delight alternating with groans of disappointment that came from the next room I judged that the Prince enjoyed poker and played spiritedly. About midnight he came through the room to say good night, explaining that since he had had a hard week of work he wanted a good night's sleep. The rest of the guests left shortly afterward.

Next morning I slept late. My breakfast was brought to my room. When I went downstairs shortly before lunch, the Prince and his equerry, Brigadier-General Gerald F. Trotter, whom everybody called "G," were just returning from a look at the hunters in the stables. "G" Trotter had lost his right arm in the Boer War. He was of medium height, of military bearing, and had thinning gray hair cut very short. He was the soul of geniality and was obviously devoted to the Prince of Wales, to whom he always referred as "my master." At luncheon I was seated beside the Prince. He was afterward to recall that we discussed, among other things, the differing British and American attitudes toward central heating. If so, I can't imagine how the subject ever came up, unless he experimentally introduced it in the hope of finding a common ground of conversation. The truth is that I was petrified, and in the foreground of my mind, censoring all lighter impulses, were Maud Kerr-Smiley's enjoinders, conveyed to me over the telephone the day before, that Royalty must be allowed to lead in any conversation and that I must eschew mention of politics and controversial matters—a restraint which by habit and temperament I was ill equipped to exercise.

There was another but much smaller party that evening. Again there were cards afterward. I played cautiously and successfully, recouping not only the eight pounds lost the evening before but also winning a modest sum besides. Benny, Ernest, and I were up early the next morning to take the train to London. The Prince, who was himself leaving later in the morning on official business elsewhere in England, said good-by to us.

During the train ride back to London, my thoughts kept returning to the events of the weekend. From my fox-hunting Warfield and Montague forebears and connections I had marshaled memories of the idiom of the hunting field; and I therefore was able to join in the conversation, even though timidly. I had discovered, among other things, that in addition to the Quorn and Cottesmore Hunts, the rolling countryside around Melton also afforded sport to a third— the Belvoir, which, needless to say, was pronounced "Beaver." Otherwise the weekend had been instructive principally for the glimpse it had afforded me of Royalty in a state of relaxation. I decided that the Prince was truly one of the most attractive personalities I had ever met. He had a rare capacity for evoking an atmosphere of warmth and mutual interest, and yet it was hardly bonhomie. The unvarying deference accorded even by those who shared with him the hazards of the hunt, the "Sir" that imparted a conscious rigidity to every response, the curtsies, the quick turns and shifts of conversation at his lead—all the formalities of etiquette high-lighted the aura that surrounds and isolates a Royal person. Having watched the smooth skill with which the two brothers undertook to bring Ernest and me into their conversation, the thought occurred to me that their perfectly schooled manners were Royalty's way of acknowledging that others could never be altogether at ease with them. The princely brothers plainly enjoyed their friends and loved to exchange quips, but there was no mistaking the fact that between them and even the friends with whom they galloped across country in the closest of companionships was a barrier that could never be breached.

There was another aspect of the experience that lingered in my mind. I had been fascinated by the odd and indefinable melancholy that seemed to haunt the Prince of Wales's countenance; his quick smile momentarily illuminated but never quite dispelled this look of sadness.

"Do you suppose that he is really a happy man?" I asked Benny.
"I suppose he enjoys himself on occasions like this weekend,"
Benny answered. "He loves to ride, and he's a fine horseman. But
when you stop to think of the kind of life he has to lead—the business of always being on show, the daily drudgery of civic affairs,
Empire-selling junkets, and all the rest—it's hard to imagine that he
can have much to be happy about."

"Do you suppose he'll ever marry? It seems too bad he doesn't
have someone with whom to share these duties."

"Perhaps he might marry sometime," Benny replied. "He has
been in love with several women. There are various stories. But
nothing ever comes of these situations. I rather doubt that he'll
ever marry now, having waited so long."

Thus I judged the Prince an altogether charming and remote
figure, not quite of the workaday world—a figure whose opportunities and behavior were regulated by laws different from those to
which the rest of us responded. I had already dismissed from mind
the possibility of our ever meeting him again. A woman with the
sniffles and a croaking voice would scarcely be judged a desirable
addition to the bright company that revolved around the Prince of
Wales.

As a matter of fact, I did not see the Prince again until the spring
of 1931, nearly six months later. He had meanwhile left London the
previous January on a long tour that took him through much of South
America. The object of the trip, which was lavishly reported in the
press, was to repair British prestige and reinforce British commerce
in an important market where cut-rate German and Japanese competition particularly had been making increasingly serious inroads.
It was only natural that after the weekend at Melton I should follow
the newspaper accounts of his journey with more than a casual interest; and, as I studied the photographs taken of him in the course
of his duties and pleasures in far-off cities, the thought grew in me
that his inner nature was a good deal more complicated than the
popular legend of the golden-haired bachelor Prince allowed for.
As at Melton, I found myself wondering about the strange, sad
expression that fleetingly manifested itself in the otherwise unmarred
gallery of smiling or laughing vignettes. For all the surface spon-
taneity, he must really be, I decided, a withdrawn and solitary spirit,
importuned and harassed by too many to have confidence in more
than a very few. About that time, too, from Ernest's friends in the

shipping business who had connections in South America, I began to hear other things about the Prince. He was inclined to be headstrong, impetuous, and independent in a rather unroyal way—unroyal, that is, in contrast to the mechanical passivity that otherwise regulated the public life of the other members of his family. When the schedules of his tours were submitted to him, he thought nothing of eliminating engagements and affairs he considered a waste of time. Some of my British friends did not approve of the informality that was coming to be recognized as one of his fundamental characteristics; and there was, I believe, some headshaking in the British press at this time over his tendency to fit matters to his own propensities rather than vice-versa. I, for one, rather admired him for that. It suggested to me that he was a man of spirit and independence. But these were idle speculations on my part. He was still for me a figure of mystery and for a long time would remain so.

Then on the Prince's return from South America, Thelma Furness gave a large afternoon reception at her house on Grosvenor Square at which he was present. Ernest and I were invited. We greeted Thelma and then moved on to one of the smaller drawing rooms where we found some of our friends. After a while Thelma came in with the Prince. All of us rose at his entrance. As they moved through the room he greeted people he knew. As he passed close by his glance happened to fall on me. He then nudged Thelma, who was standing beside him, and seemed to be asking her in a whisper, "Haven't I met that lady before?" In any event, he presently came over to where Ernest and I were standing to say, "How nice to see you again. I remember our meeting at Melton." I thought he looked finely drawn, as if the long trip had exhausted him. He made a remark or two about his trip before moving away. It was a mark of attention that was flattering to us both.

In June of that year I was presented at Court. Maud Kerr-Smiley first suggested the idea, but she couldn't present me herself as she had just presented her debutante daughter and Court etiquette did not permit her to make another presentation for three years. Shortly thereafter a friend of mine, Mildred Andersen, an American married to an Englishman, brought up the idea again and offered to present me herself, which she could do as she herself had been presented. Since I had become British by marriage, I would have to be presented by an Englishwoman, and not through the American Embassy, as would be the case with citizens of the United States.

[162]

I was reluctant to be presented because I would have to buy special clothes for the occasion, and I didn't feel justified in such an extravagance. But all my friends told me I would be foolish not to accept this generous invitation of Mildred's and convinced me I would regret it later. In any event, I accepted; but I was determined to get through the ceremony in the most economical manner. Connie kindly lent me the dress she had worn at her own presentation, and Thelma provided the train, feathers, and fan, which had also been used by Connie.

The presentation was a magnificent set piece of pageantry too often described, down to the smallest detail, to bear repeating here. What impressed me most, to the point of awe, was the grandeur that invested the King and Queen, sitting side by side on identical gilt thrones, the King in full-dress uniform, the Queen in a beaded evening dress and bedecked with the magnificent Crown jewels, each wearing the star and blue ribbon of the Order of the Garter. Ranged behind the two thrones were the Prince of Wales, one of his brothers, and their venerable great uncle, the Duke of Connaught, also in full-dress uniform. As our names were called Mildred and I each swept to the floor in a deep curtsy, first to the Sovereign and then to the Queen, and then we withdrew sedately from the Presence. Once out of sight, everyone moved into the adjoining State apartments in order to obtain a point of vantage from which to watch the Royal Family as they left in procession at the end of the Court. I was standing with Ernest in the front row as the King and Queen walked slowly by, followed by the members of their family. As the Prince of Wales walked past, I overheard him mutter to his uncle, the Duke of Connaught, "Uncle Arthur, something ought to be done about the lights. They make all the women look ghastly."

Thelma had invited Ernest and me to drop in at her house afterward, and we did. Perhaps a dozen people were there, including Thelma's husband, Lord Furness, whom I met for the first time. A prominent figure of the City, he was the son of the founder of the large shipping line that bears his name. He was a good deal older than Thelma. He was short with a pointed nose and sandy hair. It was well known among their friends that he and Thelma had gone their own separate ways. The other guests were friends of Thelma's—there was no one there connected with the Court. Presently the Prince arrived, accompanied by "G" Trotter. Over a glass of champagne, which he barely touched, he spoke admiringly of my gown.

"But, Sir," I responded with a straight face, "I understood that you thought we all looked ghastly."

He was startled. Then he smiled. "I had no idea my voice carried so far."

The custom, of course, when Royalty is present is for all others to remain until Royalty has left. After a brief stay, the Prince departed with General Trotter, saying that he was on his way to the country and was already late. After what we judged to be a reasonable interval, Ernest and I took our leave. To our surprise, the Prince and "G" were standing by their car, engaged in conversation. Catching sight of us, the Prince hastened forward to ask whether he could not give us a lift. I said, "Thank you, Sir, very much."

Ernest and I entered the Prince's car—the same one in which I had fleetingly seen him on St. James's Street. Chatting easily, and obviously in high spirits, the Prince mentioned that he and "G" were on their way to his country place, Fort Belvedere, near Windsor Great Park. As every newspaper reader in the country knew, it had been loaned to him by his father the year before; and he had become absorbed in the pleasure of fixing it over—a preoccupation that had induced widespread speculation that he might be preparing to end his imperial wanderings and settle down, perhaps with a bride of his still-secret choosing. The place, the Prince explained, had fallen into ruins; and, as he talked about his plans for restoring it, a sensitive side of his nature came into view, revealing a perceptive and imaginative spirit not ordinarily associated with the hard-riding, night-clubbing Prince of Mayfair gossip. "All the time I was in South America," he said laughingly, "I kept thinking how much work remains to be done at the Fort. And tomorrow morning I want to put in two or three hours in the garden before going back to my work in London." I was utterly absorbed, and all too soon the car arrived at Bryanston Court.

As the Prince helped me out of the car, I asked whether he and General Trotter might not like to come up for a moment and have a drink before continuing on to Sunningdale. The Prince, I had observed at Melton, had occasionally taken a nightcap. However, the Prince declined. "I'd like very much to see your flat one day," he said. "I'm told it's charming, and seeing it might give me some ideas for brightening up the Fort. But I have to be up so early. Still, if you would be so kind as to invite me again, I'd like to do so." Then he drove off.

That was how it all began, to lead in five short years to a terrible conclusion of which I had not and could not have had the slightest intimation. The polite suggestion that he might return I put down to Royal civility. I expected him to forget about it before the car was out of sight. No doubt he did. The summer passed, autumn came and went, and another winter was well advanced before I saw him again.

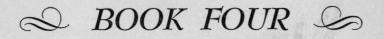

BOOK FOUR

THE CRESTING WAVE

CHAPTER XVI

The Enchanted Fort

THE YEAR 1931 WAS OTHERWISE QUITE UNEVENTFUL FOR ME. To be sure, Ernest and I managed a summer holiday in the south of France, where we visited Herman and Katherine Rogers; and later we had ten days in Scotland. But on the whole the year was a somber one. The great economic depression was casting an ever-deepening shadow over England, our own affairs included. Nor was my outlook helped by an unwonted sense of malaise that came over me. I felt strangely depleted. My doctor finally decided that my condition stemmed from infected tonsils. In early November I went to Lady Carnarvon's nursing home to have my tonsils removed. But it was Christmastime before I felt my old self. Anne and Charles Sackville had us at Knole for New Year's Eve—a fancy-dress affair, with the guests in Tudor costumes and the gold service up from the strong room in celebration of the occasion.

Then out of the blue, about the middle of January, 1932, came an unexpected invitation—a note from the Prince of Wales asking us to spend the weekend of January 30 with him at Fort Belvedere. Ernest was no less delighted than I, and the pleasure of my maid, Mary Burke, when I informed her that she was to go with me, could hardly have been greater if the summons had come directly to her from His Royal Highness. Thelma, I was sure, suggested that we be included, for I learned almost immediately from Connie Thaw that she and Benny would be there, too.

That was more than twenty-four years ago, and it is with a lump in my throat that I begin to write about this place that will always be the most romantic house I have ever known—that half-enchanted castle that David has always called the Fort, never Fort Belvedere, or Belvedere, just the Fort. It was there that the events that supply the heart and meaning of these recollections were in due course to have their first delicate and wholly improbable beginnings; it was from there just five years later, lacking two months, on a gloomy, wintry evening not unlike the one through which I first discerned the Fort, that I despairingly took leave of England—and, I was not sure then, of my present, my future, even my past. I would hesitate to call the Fort mine in the way that women sometimes feel that they have an emotional claim to a setting where they came to share profound love in all of its' strange and overpowering beauty. The Fort was singularly David's; it meant more to him, I suspect, than anything else in the world save honor, the honor with which he was so rashly, yet so gallantly to invest the love he came to have for me. Still, I will say this: a part of me remains in the vicinity of the Fort, and history is herewith given fair warning that one day a pale and anonymous phantom may be observed in the shadows along the Cedar Walk that is such a distinctive feature of the property, perhaps even after Herne the Hunter has tired of his haunting.

From my reading of the British press I had come to know quite a good deal about the Fort before I ever saw it. Numerous photographs had been published of the exterior in the press. The Fort was one of the so-called "Grace and Favour" houses on Crown property bordering Windsor Great Park. Though these are not the private property of the King (as are Sandringham in East Anglia and Balmoral in Scotland), they belong to the Crown and are at the disposal of the Sovereign for the accommodation of relations or senior courtiers. The Fort's origins go back to the early eighteenth century and William, Duke of Cumberland, third son of George II. For some time it was known as "Cumberland's Folly," presumably because the Duke, having made a pretentious and costly start with an imposing structure, seemed to have forgotten exactly what he had in mind—whether a residence or an architectural whimsicality. Later, George IV commissioned the famous Sir Jeffry Wyatville, who restored Windsor Castle during the early part of the nineteenth century, to finish and enlarge the building. The stone structure started by the Duke of Cumberland had been designed around three stone towers; it was Wyatville's inspiration to add another. During Queen Victoria's time the Fort was uninhabited and fell into partial ruin until George V undertook extensive repairs and modifications early in his reign. An old friend of the Family had then lived there for some years, without much comfort and with waning enthusiasm.

The photographs suggested a towered pile of beige-colored stone aspiring to be Gothic. My British friends could not understand why the Prince of Wales, who otherwise exhibited so modern a turn of mind, should have chosen such a strange example of architecture for his country place, with so many fine houses in England to choose from. But remembering how eagerly he had once described the Fort to Ernest and me, I was curious to see what he had done with it.

Sunningdale is about twenty-five miles west of London; Ernest and I drove out in the late afternoon, timing our pace to arrive at six. It was dark when we approached the Fort. Our headlights picked out a gravel driveway winding in graceful turns through a wood; suddenly there materialized a fascinating, shadowy mass, irregular in outline and of different levels, the whole surmounted by a soaring tower bathed in soft light thrown up by concealed flood lamps. Even before the car ground to a stop, the door opened and a servant appeared. An instant later the Prince himself was at the door to welcome his guests and supervise the unloading of our luggage, an attention which I was to discover was a habit with him. The Prince led us through a narrow hallway into an octagonal hall with white plaster walls in each of the eight corners of which stood a chair upholstered in bright yellow leather. The floor was of black and white marble. We then moved into the drawing room. Thelma, the Thaws, and "G" Trotter had preceded us. I was instantly struck by the warmth of the room, which, like the hallway, was octagonal. Curtains of yellow velvet were drawn across the tall windows; the walls, which were paneled in natural pine, were hung with handsome paintings, which I later identified as Canalettos; the furniture my by now quite experienced eye recognized as mostly Chippendale, except for a baby grand piano and a gramophone; and opposite the fireplace on one wall were shelves of books in beautiful bindings.

The Prince himself insisted on taking us to our room on the second floor, and I could not help noticing that before he left he swiftly appraised the condition of the room with the practiced glance of a careful host, a side of his character that was totally unexpected. Having assured himself that all was as it should be, he left us, saying he would expect us down shortly for cocktails.

Another small surprise came as we returned to the drawing room. The Prince was sitting on a sofa, his head bent over a large flat screen, his right hand rapidly plying a needle from which trailed a long colored thread. I could scarcely believe my eyes—the Prince of Wales doing needle point. He must have caught my first glance of unabashed incredulity because he was laughing as he rose. "This is my secret vice," he explained, "the only one, in any case, I am at pains to conceal." Partly with amusement, partly in pride, he showed us the bright pattern that was just beginning to take form. "This is to be a covering for a backgammon table," he said.

"Sir," I replied, "I am fascinated and impressed. But where, if I may ask, and how did you ever acquire this accomplishment?"

"From my mother, when I was growing up" was the amiable answer. "At Sandringham my brothers and sister and I used to sit around her at teatime. While she talked to us, she was either crocheting or doing some kind of embroidery; and because we were all interested she taught us gros point." He paused, then added almost apologetically, "I'm the only one of the four brothers who has kept it up. I find it relaxing and more useful than detective stories. But it would never do to have my hobby become widely known. It might shock the country."

I decided then and there that he must have a really sweet and even tender side to his nature. And this judgment was steadily reinforced in many ways. Two cairn terriers, Cora and Jaggs, tussled at the Prince's feet. Cora, in fact, snarled at Ernest and made a furious but futile rush at his ankle. Snatching her up, the Prince administered a mild spank on her rear. "Cora is always this way when anybody new appears," the Prince explained. "Now Jaggs has a much more hospitable temperament." I was not so sure. When I made a tentative gesture in Jaggs's direction, he stalked off stiffly and assumed an attitude of cold hostility on the far side of the room. The Fort, I decided, was strictly a bachelor's stronghold; even the Prince's dogs were determined to hold strange women at bay.

My first view of the Prince's private life can in truth be described as a continuous surprise—a surprise because the reality was so much at variance with what surmise had led me to expect. Compared to the stately routine of Knole the Princely existence at the Fort was amazingly informal, even though everyone dressed for dinner—Thelma, Connie, and I in our simplest evening dresses. The Prince was wearing a kilt—a gray and red tartan checked with black, which Ernest decided must be the Balmoral tartan designed by the Prince Consort—with a skean dhu, a form of small dirk, stuck into the hose on his right leg, and a silver-mounted sporran from which I was amused to see him presently produce a small cigarette case. There were cocktails, and then we went in to dinner. The dining room was by no means as large as the drawing room. It likewise had walls of natural pine and contained a walnut table and two Georgian mahogany sideboards. The dining-room chairs were of mahogany and ten in number—all the walnut table would seat. On the walls were paintings of horses by George Stubbs, the famous British equestrian painter. The food was simple but delicious—oysters that the Prince explained came directly from his own oyster beds in the Duchy of Cornwall, an excellent roast of beef, salad, a sweet, and a savory.

Thelma and "G" Trotter kept up a running conversation in which the rest of us joined. I knew from the newspapers that the Prince during the preceding months had traveled extensively through the depressed areas of England, but never once did he mention anything about himself or his work. He seemed tired, in fact, and the impression formed in my mind that there must be a tacit understanding in this place and in this company that he would deliberately put aside his official concerns. However, something that Ernest said brought a flash of interest. It had to do with an incident in history. The Prince, like Ernest, fancies himself a lay student of history; in a moment dates and circumstances were flying back and forth across the table like ping-pong balls.

After dinner there was coffee in the drawing room. There were cards for those who wanted to play. Otherwise, the Prince suggested, those who preferred a more rigorous test of mental skill might try to put together an extremely complicated jigsaw puzzle of which the pieces were scattered on a long table in front of the main window. The Prince invited the rest of us to play "Red Dog" with him, a game I had not played in years.

The Prince kindly offered to coach me. I happened to be lucky; good cards fell to me. After several hands the Prince smilingly said, "I don't think you need any more instruction from me. I'd better look after myself."

It was the first notice that he had taken of me that could be described as other than a formality.

Thelma was standing beside the gramophone, going through some records. "I feel like dancing," she said.

A look of pleasure came over the Prince's face. "Perhaps we all do," he suggested. The gramophone started; and, as Thelma turned, the Prince was moving toward her, with outstretched arms, to dance her into the octagonal hallway off the drawing room. I have a poignant memory of the melody. It just happened to be "Tea for Two," and as I danced with "G" Trotter my mind traveled back to Shanghai and the hotel with the sunken garden on Bubbling Well Road, and my

English beau, and the chain of circumstances that had brought me to England, on the other side of the world.

The Prince danced briefly with Connie and me in turn. I found him a good dancer, deft, light on his feet, and with a true sense of rhythm. Then, all of a sudden, he appeared weary. "This being your first visit to the Fort," he said, "perhaps I should tell you about the rules. There are none. Stay up as late as you want. Get up when you want. For me this is a place of rest and change. I go to bed early and get up early so that I can work in the garden."

Well before midnight he said good night. The rest of us lingered only a moment or two, then departed for our rooms. That was my introduction to the private life of the Prince of Wales—a model of sedateness.

"I can't get over it," I remarked to Ernest when we were upstairs. "Over what?" asked Ernest, abstractedly.

"Where is the Prince of Wales I've heard about—the bachelor Prince who never goes to bed before dawn?"

"I daresay he has his Bohemian side," Ernest decided. "What we're seeing is the lover of the countryside. I can understand his wanting to come here for weekends to get away from the routine of public life."

After the lights were out, I lay reflecting on the evening, and my mind kept returning to an engrossing puzzle. What kind of man was this Prince of Wales who seemed endowed with so many contradictory sides, at once charming and yet aloof, so quickly responsive to lightness and gaiety, yet with so much of his nature hidden in shadow? I could not decide.

The next day was of a piece with the evening before. The maid who brought breakfast told us that His Royal Highness had finished his an hour before and had gone into the garden. Shortly after Ernest and I had wandered into the drawing room, I observed advancing up the terrace slope an incongruous figure in baggy plus fours, a thick sweater, hair tousled, and carrying in one hand a billhook, a machetelike tool for cutting brush. It was the Prince, with Cora and Jaggs yapping happily at his heels.

I was prepared for anything, but Ernest, I am sure, was startled, though his expression gave no sign of his inward astonishment.

"Ah," said Thelma, with mock consternation, "I take it your guests are to be ordered out to cut the laurels."

"Yes," said the Prince cheerfully. "I'm always happy for recruits."

"You'll find," muttered "G" Trotter, "that the harder you work, the more popular you'll be."

Because Ernest and I were not in on the little joke, the Prince explained that after coming to the Fort he had occupied his weekends trying to clear away the tangle of undergrowth that had overwhelmed the hillside during the decades the property had lain either disused or neglected. "My particular enemy," he said, brandishing the billhook, "is the laurel, which I have sworn to annihilate, if it costs me my last guest. Come along, if you want to. I can equip you with the necessary weapons."

Ernest glanced at Benny Thaw, who, having previously skirmished with the Prince among the brier-enmeshed slopes below the Fort, made a wry grimace. "It's not exactly a command," interjected "G" Trotter, "but I've never known anybody to refuse."

Exercise, as must by now be plain, was a pursuit that Ernest favored only in the role of a spectator. And his interest in gardening was strictly aesthetic. I was therefore quite taken aback when, with an unwonted display of enthusiasm, he said he'd be delighted to cut laurel.

Ernest went upstairs for a sweater. While he was gone, the Prince took me out on the terrace to show me the grounds. Now I had my first good look at the surroundings. From where we stood, the land sloped gently toward a lovely lake in the distance, known as Virginia Water. Just below us the green lawn ended in a semicircular stone battlement in which were emplaced thirty or more eighteenth-century Belgian cannon, their muzzles pointed in the general direction of London. Directly below the battlement on one side was a large swimming pool, where once had been a lily pond, and on the other side a dirt tennis court. We went out into the grounds. A flagstone path led from the side door to the tennis court. This walk had a wide herbaceous border on the right. Interesting semicircular steps led down from the battlement, in the crannies of which rock plants nestled. Farther down was a long walk lined with magnificent cedars, among which were planted rhododendrons and azaleas.

He walked me around the grounds, pointing out the improvements he had made, showing where he had felled yew trees so as to let in light and open the view, and where he had unearthed three fine granite George III plaques, which he had set into a wall at one end of the swimming pool. He tried to sound casually matter-of-fact as he described what he had done; but his inner pleasure over what he had found and restored to life and beauty burst through the guise

[175]

of nonchalance, despite all his efforts. "It's certainly not a beautiful place, as houses in Britain go," he said, shooting a quizzical glance at the strange conglomeration of turrets on the hill. "My father always speaks of it as 'that queer old place,' as if it were still some deserted ruin. But for me it has unusual charm, and I've found more pleasure in fixing it up than—" he checked himself. "There is no reason why I should bore you with this."

The others just then overtook us, and the Prince went off with the men to equip them with billhooks and heavy gloves. When they returned, each armed with a murderous-looking weapon, they looked more like a band of revolutionaries about to assault the barricades than the Prince of Wales and his weekend guests preparing to deal with offending flora. With the Prince showing the way, we started down a path through a woodland of birch and magnificent cedar. All this had until recently been an impassable mass of laurel; now it was given over to rare and lovely rhododendrons, many of which he had planted with his own hands. Narrow footpaths wandered off in search of some interesting glen or vista; these had also been the Prince's conceit. Then the path we were following ended abruptly in a dense wall of laurel.

"Here we are," said the Prince briskly. "You can see now what I have been up against. Well, this is the last bad stretch of laurel. By summer I shall have finished with it." Stooping, he began hacking at the untidy undergrowth with fierce but practiced strokes. At that point Thelma, Connie, and I decided to leave the men to what was clearly man's work.

It was a weary but obviously satisfied group that returned to the Fort two hours later. And they did justice to the delicious buffet lunch that was awaiting them on the two sideboards in the dining room, one laden with hot dishes the other with cold.

Afterward the Prince took Ernest and me on a tour of the house. He was especially proud of the little library, which contained some good pieces of Queen Anne furniture. His own bedroom, off the hall on the ground floor, was a large and charming room, with tall windows hung with red chintz curtains looking out upon the garden. The bed and other furniture, like that in the drawing room and library, were Chippendale. The walls were painted white; and all about were photographs of his family. The upstairs bedrooms, of which there were six, all had names. One was called "Prince George's Room," for his younger brother, who often spent his weekends there. Another was called "The Blue Room," because the predominant shade of the decorations was blue. There was a "Yellow Room," and a "Pink Room," a "Green Room," and even "The Queen's Room," so named for some reason lost in the mists of time. In view of the relative shortage of bathrooms in British houses, the Prince was rightly proud that he had managed to provide, despite the handicap of the ancient walls, a bathroom for practically every room. But what fascinated me was the architectural wizardry that had been exercised in imparting to the interior of this sprawling fort such an atmosphere of warmth and informality. I was to decide that, for a bachelor's country house, the whole effect was astonishingly warm and attractive.

The end of the day produced its final small revelation of the habits of the Prince. He had gone off alone for a tour of the property with the gardener. It was dark when he returned, and from the drawing room I heard him slam the front door and enter his own room. A little later I heard the door open again and saw him disappear down the stairway to the basement.

Thelma smiled. "It always happens exactly at this time. He's gone to take his steam bath."

"Steam bath?" I asked, astonished. "Does he really have a steam bath in this house?"

"Yes, indeed," said Thelma. "He's almost as proud of it as he is of the central heating."

A little while later the Prince appeared, wearing a bright yellow turtle-neck sweater that rose to his chin and sporting a scarlet face, radiating utter contentment. It was the disclosure of that personal convenience that astonished Ernest more than any other aspect of the weekend, and I confess it was something of an eye opener to me.

That is all there was to my first weekend at the Fort. As we drove back to London, I realized with a slight measure of disappointment that I would have to revise my romantic notions of Royalty, or at least that aspect represented by the Prince of Wales. Without having seen him at the Fort I would never have suspected that so brilliant a personage would find satisfaction in working outdoors with his hands and puttering around a garden. For a long time I would carry in my mind the odd and incongruous picture of a slight figure in plus fours loping up the slope of the terrace, swinging the billhook and whistling.

The year 1932 was a dismal one. Great Britain and the rest of the world lay in the trough of the great depression. Although our own circumstances fortunately were not too much affected—Ernest's father appears to have been foresighted—the shipping company, nevertheless, suffered with other businesses, and Ernest worked long hours at the office. In March we went to Tunis in connection with the firm's affairs. We were back in London for the spring. I suppose we went to the Derby and Ascot, but I have no memory of going, and my engagement book is blank. Then in July Ernest and I left for the Continent on a trip that was partly business, partly pleasure—France and Austria. I was not well; an ulcer was causing me considerable suffering. We returned to London in mid-August, somewhat sooner than we had intended, and I was under a doctor's care at our flat for several weeks. I suppose the ulcer came from nerves, as I always kept the day-to-day tensions of living bottled up inside me.

Later, during the fall, we were twice at the Fort—once for tea and again for a weekend. Those were the only occasions when I saw the Prince that year. In December I was in bed for several days, the ulcer having flared up again, in spite of careful attention to my diet. Then, again, we were asked to the Fort for several weekends—once in January, 1933, twice in February, and again in March, just before Ernest and I were to sail for the United States. If the Prince was in any way drawn to me I was unaware of his interest. Thelma was always there, and often Prince George, whom I found on closer acquaintance to be altogether as attractive as his brother. He played the piano very well, knew all the latest jazz, and loved to bang away at the keys while the rest of us danced after dinner in the octagonal hall. Saturday evenings at the Fort were usually a little livelier when Prince George was on the scene; he was a natural mimic and loved to do caricatures of people he knew well, and often the Prince of Wales joined in. I had a distinct feeling, as I watched them together, that the older brother was at times a little worried, even anxious, about the younger, perhaps because he was too lighthearted.

CHAPTER XVII

The Indefinable Boundary

ERNEST AND I SAILED FOR NEW YORK ABOARD THE *Mauretania* LATE in March. The Isle of Wight had scarcely dropped below the horizon before a messenger came dashing up with a radiogram, which I judged from his agitated manner to be of the utmost importance. It was a *bon voyage* message, signed Edward P., wishing Ernest and me a safe crossing and a speedy return to England. From the respectful treatment that we were thereafter accorded by the ship's company we gathered that the grapevine had carried the word that the Prince of Wales had sent us a personal message. Let me be candid: the attention was flattering. I enjoyed every minute of it.

Ernest's business with the New York branch of the firm kept us in the United States nearly two months. This gave me time to renew old friendships and see my relations in Washington and Baltimore. We were back in London in mid-May, and life resumed its pleasant round, including several weekend invitations to the Fort soon after our return.

June 19 is my birthday. To my surprise the Prince gave a dinner party for me at Quaglino's, a famous restaurant just off Jermyn Street. The Prince gave me a lovely orchid plant. He assured me that it would bloom again within a year if I faithfully followed certain instructions as to its care. I set the plant in the sunniest window at Bryanston Court. For a year I watched it; nothing happened. Meanwhile, the Prince had become a frequent visitor. And one afternoon the plant came beautifully into flower exactly as he had predicted. I was afterward to feel that there was something symbolic about this.

One thing had begun increasingly to trouble Ernest and me: how could we possibly repay the Prince's hospitality? It was obvious that we could not decently delay much longer. The Fourth of July was now approaching; this anniversary has always been the occasion for celebration among Americans in London. So we decided to give a dinner party; and it was with trepidation that I wrote out the Prince's invitation. He accepted almost immediately.

This news threw my staff into an acute state of panic. My cook, Mrs. Ralph, and Cain, the parlormaid, were beside themselves with excitement.

During our growing acquaintanceship I had observed what the Prince seemed to like to eat. His preference was for simple and uncomplicated dishes—smoked salmon, game, grilled sole, and meats of all kinds. In view of the occasion I decided to give him a typical American dinner: black bean soup, grilled lobster, fried chicken Maryland, and for the sweet a cold raspberry soufflé, and as a concession to my English guests, a savory of marrow bones. In my excitement I was bursting to tell my fishmonger and greengrocer, who had seen me through earlier and simpler crises, that now was truly the time for every Englishman to do his duty. Alas, I had acquired too much British restraint; to the later disappointment of the neighborhood gossips I kept my secret to the end.

Ten of us sat down for dinner—the Prince at the head of the table and Ernest at the foot. I was sure that if the lights didn't fail, Cain certainly would trip with a soup plate and scald either Thelma or Connie. But everything, I am happy to say, went very well. The Prince particularly seemed to enjoy his American dinner and paid me the compliment of asking for my recipe for the raspberry soufflé.

Not long afterward Ernest and I departed for Ireland on a trip with Mr. Simpson. Later that summer we went to Norway, where the firm had important connections. On this excursion we were able to combine pleasure with business. Benny Thaw had been transferred to Oslo, where he was Counselor of the Legation; while there, we saw a good deal of him and Connie. We were not back in London until late in September.

The afternoon of the day we returned to Bryanston Court I received a call from the Prince's equerry inviting us to the Fort for the weekend. The Prince had himself been away most of the summer, enjoying a holiday at Biarritz. During our travels he and his activities had more or less slipped into the back of my mind. I was never quite certain about the durability of his interest in either Ernest or me. He had permitted us to share with him the simple pleasures of the Fort; he seemed to find Ernest's comments on America, American and

British politics, history, and commerce stimulating, and his wit entertaining. As for myself, I gathered he was amused and diverted by my wholly American outlook on the subjects under discussion and was somewhat surprised by my independence of view. I had no reason to believe that he ever looked upon me as other than a member of the special group of friends he had drawn around him at the Fort, or to fill out a casual supper party at the Embassy Club or Sartori's.

Thus we found ourselves becoming permanent fixtures at the Fort weekends. The association imperceptibly but swiftly passed from an acquaintanceship to a friendship. As much as anyone I was mesmerized by the aura of splendor that surrounded the British Royal Family and even more by the undoubted glamour emanated by the Prince of Wales as a figure of popular legend and as the quintessence of youthful charm. I was glad to be even a minor satellite in the company revolving around him.

The Prince was still a mystery to me. A reserve surrounded him that was like an intangible protecting film. Even in his most relaxed moments at the Fort he seemed to be two different kinds of man: on the surface, he appeared to be the attentive and appreciative and lighthearted host, but underneath that polished outer guise one sensed a curiously serious and elusive and altogether different kind of man. Once he remarked to me, "I have my own special name for this place. I call it my Get-Away-from-People house." I had already observed that while he undoubtedly had many friends going back to his childhood—friends who must have truly wanted to share their lives with him —few were ever encountered at the Fort. Only occasionally did members of his official Household turn up there. Of these "G" Trotter was the most constant visitor; another who was sometimes invited was David's equerry, Major (now Sir) John Aird. "Jack," as we called him, was a Grenadier Guardsman; being then a bachelor, he lived at York House; he was tall and lean and had an amusing but biting wit. Another former associate who sometimes was a guest at the Fort was Major Edward Metcalfe of the Indian Cavalry, known as "Fruity," which is an English nickname for someone who is the life of the party. "Fruity" had been one of the Prince's A.D.C.'s in India. Returning from there in 1922, he had become an equerry at York House, until his marriage to Lady Alexandra Curzon, daughter of the famous Viceroy and statesman, in 1925. Like most Irishmen, "Fruity" was a fine horseman; he had also been one of the Prince's companions of his fox-hunting days at Melton Mowbray.

Of his four brothers only Prince George was a steady visitor. The

Prince of Wales, I came to realize, was a spirit apart, and the Fort symbolized the isolation and privacy for which he longed as a respite from his official duties. The Fort was his refuge, the place where he could relax in the company of friends and without having to watch his every "and," "the," and "but."

I had, of course, been seeing a good deal of Thelma. We often lunched at the Ritz or at Claridge's, sometimes alone, more often with other women. Our relationship was friendly and easy but scarcely intimate; neither of us, I suppose, was given to exchanging confidences. Around the turn of the year she announced that she was planning a trip to the United States. The day before she sailed she asked me for cocktails. We rattled along in our fashion; as we said good-by she said, laughingly, "I'm afraid the Prince is going to be lonely. Wallis, won't you look after him?" I promised that I would, but privately doubted that he would be in need of solace.

I was happy that in spite of Thelma's absence our association with the Prince continued much as before. The weekend after she left we were back at the Fort, and in the middle of the week the Prince came to Bryanston Court for dinner. A few days later Cain came hurrying into my room. "Madam, the Prince of Wales wishes to speak to you on the telephone." It was the first time he had ever called in person. He wished to ask us to a dinner party that he was giving at the Dorchester for two old American friends, Fred and "Gebe" Bate. Fred was the Western European representative of the National Broadcasting Company, and I had met them at the Fort.

That dinner was memorable for a special reason. Before, the Prince had never dwelt upon his duties and the particular function that he fulfilled in the imperial scheme of things. In fact, I had formed an impression the times I had seen him that he deliberately kept the conversation from these topics, as if the subject of his working hours was something to be thrust aside in hours of relaxation. But on this particular evening some chance remark of mine broke through his barrier, and suddenly, while the others, as I recall, were away from the table dancing, he began to talk about his work, the things he hoped to do, and the creative role he thought the Monarchy could play in this new age, and also dropped a hint of the frustrations he was experiencing.

I was fascinated. It was as if a door had opened upon the inner fastnesses of his character. What I now saw in his keenness for his job, in his ambition to make a success of it, was not dissimilar to the attitude of many American businessmen whom I had known. I cannot claim that I instantly understood him but I sensed in him something that few around him could have been aware of—a deep loneliness, an overtone of spiritual isolation.

"But I am boring you," he said, as if ashamed of revealing so much about himself.

"On the contrary," I answered, "I couldn't be more interested. Please, please go on."

While he was still looking at me questioningly, as if gauging my sincerity, the music stopped and the others began to converge on the table. Then he said a surprising thing. "Wallis, you're the only woman who's ever been interested in my job." A little later on, as we were dancing, he asked if I would mind his dropping in at Bryanston Court for a cocktail now and then when his other engagements permitted.

He seemed to find stimulation in the changing company in front of my little cocktail table. In the beginning he stayed but briefly. Then one evening he stayed on and on. The other guests, one by one, had to excuse themselves. Finally, only the three of us were left—Ernest, the Prince, and I. By now it was long after dinnertime, and finally in desperation I suggested, "Sir, would you care to take potluck with us?"

The Prince jumped up. "Good Lord," he exclaimed, "I had no idea it was so late. I'm terribly sorry."

"I know that beef stew," I said, "is not very inspiring, but I can assure you that we have more than enough."

The upshot was that in a few minutes the Prince was seated at the table between Ernest and me. This was the beginning of many such potluck dinners. We never knew when he was coming or how long he would stay. Sometimes he came once in a fortnight to stay only for a few moments; other times he was back twice in a week and would remain all evening. It always seemed to happen that he picked the evening when Ernest had brought home some work from the office or the evening we had set aside for going over the household accounts. After a succession of these disruptions of Ernest's routine, he developed the art of tactfully excusing himself and retiring to his room with his papers. The Prince seemed to have a new enthusiasm every visit, whether it was a new housing project that he was sponsoring or a design for a new planting at the Fort or a scheme for promoting a British trade drive in some part of the world, or even the latest American jazz record. During weekends he increasingly singled me out as his partner during the dancing.

Thelma's absence stretched into weeks. Finally, he asked me whether Ernest and I would like to bring some of our friends to the

Fort. I was delighted to have the chance to bring Corinne and George Murray, the Hunters, Mike and Gladys Scanlon, and such others of our friends—mostly Americans—as we thought would interest him.

Thelma returned in the early spring. Something had happened between her and the Prince. She was back at the Fort once, but the former warmth and easiness of their relationship were plainly gone. One afternoon she came to Bryanston Court. It was an unhappy call. She told me that the Prince was obviously avoiding her—she couldn't understand why. He would not speak to her himself on the telephone. No more invitations to the Fort were forthcoming. Finally, she asked me point-blank if the Prince was interested in me—"keen" was the word she used.

This was a question I had expected, and I was glad to be able to give her a straight answer. "Thelma," I said, "I think he likes me. He may be fond of me. But, if you mean by keen that he is in love with me, the answer is definitely no."

The spring advanced; Ernest's life and mine were by now almost completely caught up and submerged in the Prince's private world. He had us at the Fort with a few friends for Ascot week. The Royal procession from Windsor Castle onto the racecourse was always a brilliant piece of pageantry—the King, the Queen, their family in the open landaus, with the bewigged postillions astride the gray horses. But that year, as I watched from the Royal Enclosure, I felt an odd surge of pride and admiration when I saw that fleeting, boyish smile directed at us from under his gray topper.

By now I had begun to take a real interest in the Fort. And the Prince, who admired the way I did things at Bryanston Court, encouraged me to make suggestions about all manner of household things that seem to elude and defy a man's mind. I was soon helping to suggest additions to the menu, new arrangements for the furniture, and various other small innovations. Osborne, the butler, distrusted these feminine interventions. His intrinsic opposition to any further interference with his long-established regime was manifest on the occasion when I presented the Prince with a small and inexpensive tray on a folding stand that I thought would simplify the serving of tea. The Prince told me afterward that when at his insistence Osborne finally brought in the afternoon tea the butler snapped the tray into position with a vicious jerk, announcing contemptuously, "Your Royal Highness, this thing won't last twenty-four hours."

Part of my affection for the Fort extended to the Prince's cairns, Cora and Jaggs. When the men were off golfing, I often took them with me for a walk through the grounds, and we became good friends. Unknown to me the Prince had observed the growth of our friendship. One afternoon he turned up at Bryanston Court with a cairn puppy under his arm. "This," he said, "is Slipper. He is yours."

Not long afterward he mentioned casually that he was planning to return to Biarritz in August and take a house for his summer holiday. "Won't you and Ernest come and stay with me?" he asked. Delighted as I was, I had to decline, explaining that Ernest had to go to the United States on business and Aunt Bessie had already arranged to stay with me during his absence. Though regretting Ernest couldn't join the party, he nevertheless brushed aside my other reservation, namely, that a lady in her seventies would be a damper on the Prince and the young friends he had around him. "Nonsense," he said. "I'd love to have your Aunt Bessie. From what you've told me about her I'm sure she'll be the life of the party." And so it was arranged. In early July Aunt Bessie arrived, and a week later Ernest sailed.

The first of August found us on our way with the Prince and the rest of his guests. It was a small party, initially composed of his Assistant Private Secretary, Hugh Lloyd Thomas; "G" Trotter and John Aird, his equerries; Lieutenant Commander and Mrs. Colin Buist; in addition to the Prince, Aunt Bessie, and me. The Prince had rented a commodious villa called Meretmont, overlooking the ocean. As at the Fort, life was simple—swimming and sun bathing, golf, sometimes a little bridge. Soon the Prince and I fell into the habit of leaving the others once a week and dining alone at one or another of the little bistros whose *spécialités* he had come to know and appreciate on previous visits.

Later in the month we were joined by Mrs. Kenelm Guinness, whose husband was an inventor. "Posy," as we called her, was an old friend, and she was young, blonde, vivacious, and pretty. She was a cousin by marriage of Lord Moyne, a son of Lord Iveagh, of the famous Guinness brewing family. Lord Moyne was then a leader of the Conservative Party and was later assassinated while British Resident Minister in the Middle East during the war. At this time he was cruising nearby in his yacht, *Rosaura*. Posy suggested that it might be fun to take a cruise with him, and she was sure that he would be delighted to have us. Having by now had enough of Biarritz, the Prince jumped at the idea, and very soon a formal invitation was extended by Lord Moyne. Aunt Bessie had planned to take a motor trip into Italy and —wisely, as it soon turned out—refused to be diverted.

The yacht was a converted channel steamer. Her owner was a

distinguished, almost ascetic-looking Irishman with an intelligent face surmounted by thinning gray hair. He immediately made a point of impressing us with her seaworthy qualities. Without quite boasting he, nonetheless, let us know that the *Rosaura* could ride out any Atlantic gale. As a matter of fact, it was blowing a full gale when we went on board. We assumed that no one would dream of putting out to sea under such conditions. But Lord Moyne immediately ordered the vessel to get under way, remarking unconcernedly: "I have yet to see the storm that could keep me in port."

As we cleared the harbor, the full fury of the gale struck us; the wind shrieked through the rigging; the seas boiled up. As the yacht buried her bows deeper and deeper with each pitch, our party, one by one, melted away to their cabins, until only Jack Aird was left behind with our host to enjoy the true pleasures of the open sea.

I am normally a good sailor, and I did not get seasick even now. But it was far too rough to move safely. I flung myself on the bed after staggering into my cabin; my trunk was charging back and forth across the room. As the storm mounted in violence, I was sure that Lord Moyne had finally met his match and would prudently head for the shelter of the nearest port. But I had misjudged our host's Viking spirit. Sometime during the night, when a steward looked in to see how I was faring, I inquired hopefully how soon we should be in port. He all but finished me off with a contemptuous response. "I've never seen his Lordship in finer fettle. He has just ordered caviar and grouse and a bottle of champagne for Mr. Aird and himself."

So far as I was concerned, the final straw was supplied by the untimely incursion of Lord Moyne's pet, a terrifying monkey that had the run of the vessel. Just when I had decided that I had endured all I could bear, there was scrabbling and chattering in the skylight over my head. A moment later, a furry, twisting object hurtled down, landing on the foot of my bed. Then I let out a scream that must have carried to Lord Moyne on the bridge; for a steward came rushing in. After one look he beat a hasty retreat. Finally a sailor who had the monkey's confidence appeared and coaxed him away.

I don't know what would have become of us if the Prince, who was in dire straits, had not summoned his last reserve of strength to go up to the bridge himself, where he exercised his best diplomacy to have the yacht headed into Corunna, which was fortunately nearby.

No doubt that surrender cost us face with our host, but Posy and I were convinced that the Prince had saved our lives.

After a day in port the storm blew itself out, and we were sufficiently restored to resume the voyage down the Spanish and Portuguese coasts. What followed was altogether pleasant. Each day found us in a new and fascinating bay or inlet. The speedboat would be lowered, a picnic lunch would be put aboard, and we would be off for a day of sun bathing, swimming, and exploring rarely visited shores. The informality carried into dinner. Posy and I wore simple frocks; the men dispensed with coats. No one played cards; no one felt like dancing to the gramophone. By the end of the day most of us were so drugged with sun and exercise that before the coffee was cleared away heads were nodding.

Often the Prince and I found ourselves sitting alone on deck, enjoying the soft evening air, and that unspoken but shared feeling of closeness generated by the immensity of the sea and the sky. Perhaps it was during these evenings off the Spanish coast that we crossed the line that marks the indefinable boundary between friendship and love. Perhaps it was one evening strolling on the beach at Formentor in Majorca. How can a woman ever really know? How can she ever really tell?

Only eleven days after leaving Biarritz we reached Cannes. Now in a rush the world came crowding back upon us. There were friends to see; countless little chores to attend to; and problems to be faced. One evening, after we had been with Herman and Katherine Rogers for dinner, the Prince took from his pocket a tiny velvet case and put it into my hand. It contained a little diamond and emerald charm for my bracelet.

CHAPTER XVIII

The Two Roads

BY THIS TIME I WAS BEGINNING TO REALIZE THAT UNDERNEATH THE royal reticence there was an elusive quality, something unexpected, about the Prince of Wales. When the mood was on him, he could be almost forbiddingly formal. On Royal business he was unfailingly the quintessence of protocol. Whether in a gray topper for Ascot, or Guardsman's bearskin cap and scarlet tunic for Trooping the Colour, or white tie and tails for a civic banquet, he was always faultlessly turned out. This, however, was what might be called the public side of his character, the aspect demanded of him by his position. He was plainly less than happy with it.

Once he had remarked to me, "I like my work. Best of all, I enjoy getting around the country and meeting new people. But I get very bored with all this dressing up." On the *Rosaura,* for example, his relief at no longer being on show expressed itself in an unexpected form. From being the world's fashion plate he reverted joyously to the simplest of clothes with a beachcomber's indifference to outward appearances. His favorite costume was a pair of shorts, a shirt, and sandals. After we reached Cannes the greatest combined powers of persuasion of the rest of us were required to induce him to change into linen slacks and a coat. "But I'm on holiday," the Prince protested. "Why can't I dress like any other human being in a hot climate?" The only possible answer to that was, holiday or no, the tourists who at this season swarmed over the French Riviera would be looking at the Prince of Wales, and his appearance in an advanced state of deshabille was hardly calculated to create a desirable impression. In the end we won him over, but the victory gained at Cannes was lost at the Borromean Islands when the Prince's

[188]

determination to relax and be like everybody else presently gave rise to a somewhat embarrassing incident.

The original plan was for our party to disband at Cannes, and I was going to rejoin my Aunt Bessie at Lake Como, in the north of Italy, and go back to Paris with her. At the last moment, however, the Prince suddenly decided that as we were all having such a good time it would be a pity to end it so abruptly. He therefore invited Herman and Katherine Rogers to join us and go on to Lake Como. As Lord Moyne had offered to let us continue in the *Rosaura* as far as Genoa, we sailed there the next day; then we motored up to the lake. On an earlier visit to Italy, I had stayed at a lovely villa on a tiny island in nearby Lake Maggiore, and there had lingered in my memory an impression of a gem in a setting of unequaled beauty. On a mildly romantic impulse I had told the Prince about it, and he insisted on taking the party to the lake so that they, too, could see a place of such matchless charm.

Unfortunately, the villa had been sold during the intervening years to the great conductor, Arturo Toscanini. He was away; the house was shut up, and we had to content ourselves with a walk around the island. Finally, with the indulgence of the suspicious caretaker, secured only with the assistance of a substantial *pourboire,* we were allowed to picnic on the terrace. Since it was still early, we decided to employ the remaining hours of the day by taking in the famous Borromeo Palace on the nearby Isola Bella. The day was hot and we were dressed accordingly—Katherine, Posy Guinness, and I bare-legged, and in simple cotton dresses and flat-heeled shoes; the Prince, Jack Aird, and Herman in shorts and sandals. The Prince was sure that he would not be recognized; and, on paying a small fee at the gate, we lightheartedly joined a straggling company of tourists whom a guide was marshaling for a trip through the castle.

Although the tourists were ignorant of the Prince of Wales's presence, some sharp-eyed member of the Borromeo staff must have recognized him. While we were wandering idly about the magnificent gardens, a side door opened and there emerged a gentleman of striking appearance, dressed in a morning coat, striped trousers, and stiff white collar. Walking briskly up to the Prince of Wales, he made a low bow and introduced himself.

"Your Royal Highness," he said, "I am Prince Borromeo. Would you and your friends do me the honor of joining me for tea in my apartments?"

For once the Prince of Wales appeared nonplused. "Well, that's very nice of you," he finally said, "but I happen to be here—well, incognito, or even more so. Look how we're dressed."

Prince Borromeo brushed aside the Prince's embarrassment. "Sir," he pressed, "the House of Borromeo would be deeply shamed if you would not accept our humble hospitality."

It was a long time before I could recall the memory of that tea without laughing—Prince Borromeo and his family assembled in a stately drawing room, all dressed as for a formal reception, and the British Heir Apparent and his party looking for all the world like a collection of castaways who had just stumbled back into civilization.

The Prince of Wales's aplomb, I must say, was more than equal to the occasion. Comfortably installed in a massive Renaissance chair, his slim, tanned legs outlined with startling incongruity against the brilliant brocade, he talked lightly and easily on the pleasures of our voyage, the complexities of the international situation, and whatever other subject popped into his head, precisely as if he were back at York House conversing with an ambassador. I was already beginning to understand that there was an intangible something about a Royal upbringing that the rest of us could never attempt to achieve. That afternoon confirmed it.

September was nearly over, and the Prince had a long-standing engagement to join his father and his mother, who was going to perform the ceremony of launching the *Queen Mary* on the Clyde. We stayed at Lake Como for a week; and then we went to Arona to board the Orient Express for Paris. There the Prince and Jack Aird left us to fly back to London, leaving the rest of us to do a little shopping in Paris.

On the night of September 26, 1934, Aunt Bessie and I boarded the *Manhattan* at Le Havre, she to return to the United States, while I would get off at Southampton. Although the Prince had vanished, with a gay wave of the hand, the spell of the cruise lingered on. Whatever had happened, if indeed anything really had, seemed altogether unreal. Was I allowing myself to drift into a dangerous situation? Or had it all been only a Mediterranean summer night's dream?

My always perceptive aunt must have sensed my underlying preoccupation. As we were having dinner, and while I was telling her about the cruise, she asked in what she hoped would appear to be an offhand way, "Wallis, isn't the Prince rather taken with you?"

I knew my aunt all too well. She was certainly not what is sometimes called the interfering type of relation. With the single exception of registering her strong objection to my divorce, she had never attempted to direct my life or even to proffer gratuitous advice. This question, I knew, could only have come from a deep concern for me.

"Whatever makes you think that?" I asked.

"These old eyes aren't so old that they can't see what's in his every glance."

Aunt Bessie's forthrightness shook me. I did not know what to say, nor did I know what I really thought. Was the Prince really attracted to me—or was he only attracted by the enchanted weeks that we had shared together amid romantic surroundings away from his world, and away from mine?

"Aunt Bessie," I finally answered, "I would like to think that he is truly fond of me."

My aunt looked hard at me. "Isn't all this very dangerous for you? If you let yourself enjoy this kind of life, it will make you very restless and dissatisfied with everything you've ever known before."

"You don't know what you're talking about," I said. With true Montague arrogance I added, "I'm having a marvelous time. It's all great fun. You don't have to worry about me—I know what I'm doing."

My aunt sighed. "Very well, have it your own way. But I tell you that wiser people than you have been carried away, and I can see no happy outcome to such a situation."

On this foreboding note we finished our dinner, leaving me with much unsaid and far more still unresolved in my own mind. My common sense could not believe that the illusion created by the past weeks was anything more than that—but my not-so-common sense could argue equally that the emotion I had sensed in him, however ephemeral, could not really be an illusion. As I well knew, and as, within the limits of masculine discretion, the Prince had already told me, there had been several attachments and even infatuations before our meeting.

Searching my mind I could find no good reason why this most glamorous of men should be seriously attracted to me. I certainly was no beauty, and he had the pick of the beautiful women of the world. I was certainly no longer very young. In fact, in my own country I would have been considered securely on the shelf.

The only reason to which I could ascribe his interest in me, such as it was, was perhaps my American independence of spirit, my directness, what I would like to think is a sense of humor and of fun, and, well, my breezy curiosity about him and everything concerning him. Perhaps it was this naturalness of attitude that had first astonished, then amazed, and finally amused him. Then, too, he was lonely, and perhaps I had been one of the first to penetrate the heart of his inner loneliness, his sense of separateness. Beyond this point my speculations could not carry me; there was nothing else that was real or tangible to nourish them.

I had no difficulty in explaining to myself the nature of the Prince's appeal to me. Over and beyond the charm of his personality and the warmth of his manner, he was the open sesame to a new and glittering world that excited me as nothing in my life had ever done before. For all his natural simplicity, his genuine abhorrence of ostentation, there was nevertheless about him—even in his most Robinson Crusoe clothes—an unmistakable aura of power and authority. His slightest wish seemed always to be translated instantly into the most impressive kind of reality. Trains were held; yachts materialized; the best suites in the finest hotels were flung open; airplanes stood waiting. What impressed me most of all was how all this could be brought to pass without apparent effort: the calm assumption that this was the natural order of things, that nothing could ever possibly go awry. That evening, as I turned over these matters in my mind, it seemed unbelievable that I, Wallis Warfield of Baltimore, Maryland, could be part of this enchanted world. It seemed so incredible that it produced in me a dreamy state of happy and unheeding acceptance.

Ernest was at Southampton to meet me. In reply to his questions about my trip I said, "I can't describe it. All I can say is that it was like being Wallis in Wonderland."

Ernest looked at me quizzically. "It sounds to me," he said thoughtfully, "indeed like a trip behind the 'Looking Glass.' Or, better yet, an excursion into the realm of Peter Pan's Never-Never Land."

From then on the Prince was always "Peter Pan" to Ernest. He meant no disrespect; in fact, Ernest genuinely liked the Prince, and truly revered him as the man who would one day be his King. I laughed, but even so, I felt a slight annoyance.

Our life resumed its now familiar pattern. The Prince had gone on to Balmoral to spend a few days with his parents after attending the launching of the great Cunard liner named after his mother. Soon after his return he came to Bryanston Court for dinner and invited Ernest and me to the Fort for the weekend. With his most impish smile he mentioned to me as he was leaving, "I have a little surprise waiting for you out there." I couldn't imagine what it could be, and when he finally disclosed his secret, it was the last thing I ever expected.

The Prince and indeed his entire family loved the wild music of the pipes. He himself had mastered this difficult instrument and often at the end of dinner at the Fort joined the King's piper, Pipe-Major Henry Forsyth, in marching around the table. On this particular occasion, the Prince arose at the end of dinner, and, without a word, left the room in an obvious state of suppressed anticipation. He was gone for some time; and the rest of us had begun to look at one another wonderingly when, from somewhere deep within the recesses of the house, there came a familiar pipe march, one that I had often heard before. A moment later, the Prince in a kilt, followed by the imposing figure of Forsyth, marched into the dining room, with a deafening skirl. They came to a halt, there was a moment of silence. Then from both instruments issued the most curious melody I had ever heard from the bagpipes in all the times we had been at the Fort—a haunting refrain, almost lyric. It was quite brief and charming; and, when the Prince finished, he looked shyly across the table. "G" Trotter spoke up. "Sir, I thought I knew my pipe tunes, but I can't place this one. I don't know where you found it, but I must say it's delightful."

The Prince's face lighted up. "As a matter of fact, I wrote it myself. It's called 'Majorca.'" As he said this, for a fleeting second his glance rested on me. He told us that the melody had begun running through his head on his way up to Scotland; and as soon as he reached Balmoral he had asked his old instructor, Forsyth, to help him work out the arrangement. "We really slaved over it, didn't we, Forsyth?"

Without cracking a smile, the piper replied, "Indeed we did, Sir. You had me marching up and down the terrace with you all one rainy afternoon. I'll never forget what His Majesty—" Forsyth suddenly checked himself.

The Prince roared with laughter. "I think I know what he started to say. Just as we were getting the thing down pat, my father suddenly threw open his window, thrust out his head, and roared, 'David, stop that infernal noise. If you can't play proper Highland music, I think you'd better give up playing the pipes.' I apologized and with a grunt my father withdrew. A moment later his head popped out of the window again. 'David,' he bellowed, 'what *was* that damn tune you were torturing? In my sixty years of listening to the pipes I've never heard anything quite like that!' Standing there in the rain, I told him rather cautiously that it was a little composition of my own. With this my father, in his best quarterdeck tone, roared, 'I should have suspected it. Don't do it again. My advice to you is to leave this art to the Highlanders. They know what they're doing.' "

This same fall I gained further insight into the character of the Prince. His favorite brother, George, who for many years had been his most intimate friend and companion, sharing his roof at York House and very often at the Fort, was married on November 29 at Westminster Abbey to the Princess Marina of Greece. Because it was the first Royal marriage since that of the Duke of York eleven years before, all England was excited. But, as I watched the Prince during the weeks preceding it, it seemed to me that a sadness began to envelop him. He and his younger brother were very close, and the bonds of blood were strengthened by an unusual kinship of spirit. Prince George, however, was more tempestuous. In the years before I knew him he had sowed his share of wild oats; but the Prince of Wales had taken him in hand, drawing him back once again into the accepted pattern.

Before his wedding Prince George was at the Fort almost every weekend. So, for that matter, were Ernest and I. I rather suspected that, with Princess Marina still in Paris with her parents, selecting her trousseau, the Prince, who was to be best man at the wedding, thought it was just as well to keep a close eye upon the bridegroom-to-be until he had been safely led to the altar. We all had great fun together. Prince George was genuinely in love with Princess Marina, a most beautiful woman, whom I had met earlier at the Fort; and he was also delighted at the prospect of at last having his own home.

He and the Princess were deluged with costly presents from all over the world, and it amused me to observe how meticulously Prince George checked the influx of wedding presents and the joking way in which he estimated the probable worth of the day's deliveries. Royalty can be just as interested in the cost of things as the rest of us.

I particularly remember one amusing passage with Prince George just before the wedding. It was at dinner. After the dessert, he asked me, "Wallis, what is the most expensive kind of fur?"

"What an odd question," his brother cut in with from the head of the table.

George replied, "Not at all. I'm trying to solve a problem for a very rich friend who wants to give Marina a fur coat for a wedding present. Now, Wallis," he continued, addressing me directly, "which is the most expensive fur?"

"Chinchilla," I answered.

"Fine," said George, "I wouldn't want my friend to make a mistake."

"Damn it, George," said the Prince of Wales, "you're beginning to sound like an auctioneer."

"Prince George," I interposed, "will suffer no such anxiety from the Simpson offering. I have already chosen two lamps, at ten guineas apiece, from Fortnum's. They were reduced in a sale and are not exchangeable."

Many brilliant dinners and soirees were held for the young and popular couple, culminating in a state reception given by the King and Queen at Buckingham Palace a day or two before the wedding. Ernest and I were invited. We took our places in the line of guests that by custom forms on either side of the reception rooms on the approach of the Sovereign and his Consort. As they proceed with great dignity down the room, members of the Royal party follow in their wake, stopping now and then to speak with friends. The Prince of Wales brought Prince Paul, Regent of Yugoslavia, and also brother-in-law of the bride, over to talk to us. "Mrs. Simpson," said Prince Paul, "there is no question about it—you are wearing the most striking gown in the room." It was a simple dress, designed by Eva Lutyens, daughter-in-law of Sir Edwin Lutyens, the famous architect, but the violet lamé material with a vivid green sash made it outstanding.

This reception was rendered truly memorable to me for the reason that it was the only time I ever met David's father and mother. After Prince Paul had left us, David led me over to where they were standing and introduced me. It was the briefest of encounters—a few words of perfunctory greeting, an exchange of meaningless pleasantries, and we moved away. But I was impressed with Their Majesties' great gift for making everyone they met, however casually, feel at ease in their presence.

The wedding took place at 11:00 A.M. on November 29, and the Abbey was crowded with foreign royalty, members of the British and Dominion Governments, the diplomatic corps, and many other dignitaries. The ceremony was solemn and moving. The Prince had provided Ernest and me with very good places on a side aisle, from which we had an uninterrupted view of the altar. The British Royal

Family were, as always, impressive, and I was particularly struck by the classic good looks of the Greek Royal Family.

Now that Prince George, newly created Duke of Kent by his father, was out of the Prince's life, I became aware of a deepening of the sadness—perhaps pensiveness is really what I mean to say—in the Prince's mood. To be sure, there was no outward change in his spirit, but as I watched him, I sensed that he was attempting to bridge a void that was no less difficult for him to accept emotionally now that it was a fact. I would try to divert him with some irrelevancy, or plunge into a serious discussion on a current topic that I knew interested him. It was curious to see a man of such dynamic qualities, a man so active and so often filled with the true joy of life, suddenly disappear before my very eyes into uncertainty. Whether he was aware of this, or would even have admitted it to himself, I do not know, but I do know that he was reaching out for something that was as yet unknown to him, something to which he could anchor his personal life. It was easy for the rest of us to change or rearrange our lives, but for him it was not only difficult, it was also well nigh impossible. And this poignant seeking for an absolute in his life was very moving to me, more moving than I perhaps realized.

There was a certain dualism about it—a nostalgic reaching backward for those old familiar values he had drifted away from and, at the same time, a hopeful reaching out for new certainties that he had not yet quite attained.

This was also the time of certain changes at the Fort, a subtle re-emergence of those who before my time had been part of the Prince's circle. Aside from the faithful and orderly alternation of members of his Household, only one member of the Prince's family was now a fairly constant figure there—his cousin, Lord Louis Mountbatten, now Earl Mountbatten of Burma, First Sea Lord. "Dickie," as he was known everywhere, was no stranger to me. I had met him with his beautiful wife, Edwina, during my Washington days; and I had always thought him one of the handsomest of men, his good looks being coupled with an arresting physical presence and an extraordinary drive. Indeed, when they came to Washington on their honeymoon in 1922, I was instantly impressed by the unusual circumstance that so attractive a man would be married to so attractive a woman.

Dickie, like the Prince, was a great-grandson of Queen Victoria, and was the son of the distinguished Prince Louis of Battenberg, who had been the First Sea Lord at the outbreak of the First World War.

The tragic story of his forced retirement, because of his German birth, has been too often told to need repeating. Dickie, like the Prince, had been bred to the tradition of service in the Royal Navy, and I had been told by the Prince that the ambition of Dickie's life was to vindicate the honor of his father as well as that of the house of Mountbatten, the name to which Battenberg had been changed during the First World War.

Although I had known a good many naval officers, Dickie belonged to a breed unfamiliar to me. Practically all of the officers I had known were wrapped up in the specialized techniques of their craft and the intense politics of their special world, but Dickie was different. It was evident that he was more than proficient in his profession, but no one could be with him any length of time without sensing that the Navy occupied only a part of his total interest. Dickie bubbled with ideas on every conceivable subject—housing, relieving unemployment, new strategies of attack in polo, or how to cure the chronic maladies of the British Exchequer. The more baffling these problems were to the experts, the more convinced Dickie was that he had a fundamental contribution to make and was determined to make it. He bombarded the Prince with pamphlets, books, and clippings all carefully annotated or underlined and all urgently commended to the Prince's attention.

Dickie was never content with the usual or conventional. He had persuaded Edwina to rebuild the imposing mansion in Park Lane that she had inherited from her financier grandfather, Sir Ernest Cassels, and to convert it into apartments. They retained for their own use the two top floors, which were sumptuously furnished with priceless paintings and furniture and magnificent jade. The surprising exception was Dickie's bedroom. This was an exact replica of an officer's cabin in one of His Majesty's warships, with a bunk for a bed, a ship's clock on the wall, and windows suggesting portholes. He was entranced by mechanical effects. He told me how he had trained his footman, on hearing the ringing of the doorbell, on the street floor, to synchronize his walk from the pantry to the apartment door with the time it took the lift to ascend. The purpose of these elaborate calculations and drill was to assure that the footman would be there to effect the simultaneous and apparently magical opening of the door at the instant of the lift's stopping at the door of the apartment.

In spite of all Dickie's exuberance and ingenuity, the gap in the Prince's life caused by his brother's marriage was not easily filled.

Nor did the usual round of visits that the Royal Family were accustomed to make, staying at the various country seats of the great families, do much more than politely interest him. This round of Royal visits was considered by the Prince's brothers, and even more so by their father, to be quite the best way of life. Knowing how much the Prince loved to hunt and shoot, it took me a long time fully to understand why he found something lacking in this finest of all possible worlds into which he was born. I discovered that much as he respected what this splendid tradition represented, he felt intuitively that it was already beginning to fade into the past. Perhaps the experience of independence that he had derived as a soldier during the War of 1914 and on his world travels, or perhaps the restlessness that seemed to have infected a whole generation of his countrymen had made him discontented with the old ways. He was seeking something more, something more in tune with the new world, of which he was perhaps the first of his family to achieve an instinctive awareness.

Often I felt I somehow had became part of this search. Each day drew me more intimately into his life. Our dinners alone together were more frequent. Hardly a day passed without his telephoning, perhaps only to tell me of some idea that had occurred to him during his duties, perhaps to retell an anecdote, or only to ask my advice about some housekeeping problem at his beloved Fort.

Until now I had taken for granted that Ernest's interest in the Prince was keeping pace with mine, but about this time I began to sense a change in his attitude. His work seemed to make more and more demands on his time in the evening. Often he would not return in time for dinner, or when the Prince suggested afterward dropping in at Sartori's or the Dorchester for an hour or so of amusement, Ernest would ask to be excused on the plea that he had an early appointment or that papers from the office needed his attention. He also seemed less and less interested in what I had to say about the Prince's latest news and interests.

I first realized how far Ernest and I had grown apart when the Prince invited us to Kitzbuehel in February for the winter sports. The Prince was fascinated with skiing, which was only then beginning to attract the more venturesome of the English. I naturally accepted for both of us.

When Ernest returned home that evening, I told him excitedly about the trip to Austria. He was unresponsive and abruptly cut me off with an announcement that he had no interest in skiing and moreover had urgent business that would require his presence in New York at that time.

Later that evening, after a rather silent dinner, he asked me whether my mind was definitely made up to go. I remember answering, "Of course. Why not? I wouldn't dream of missing it."

He got up from his chair and said, "I rather thought that we might have gone to New York together. I see now that I was wrong." I asked if he couldn't come out for at least some of the time. He answered that it was quite out of the question.

With that he went to his room, and for the first time I heard his door bang.

CHAPTER XIX

The Prince Becomes King

THERE CAN BE NOTHING LESS IMPORTANT THAN THE DETAILS OF a skiing trip, and I shall not therefore dwell on mine. I had taken for granted from what I had seen in the news reels that skiing was largely the monopoly of the Scandinavians, the Swiss, and the Austrians. Never having been on skis, I felt as if I were being carried off into a highly adventurous undertaking. I was secretly of the opinion that once in Austria I could never be induced to entrust my life to two boards of unmanageable hickory.

We left early in February. The Prince's party consisted in addition to me, of Bruce Ogilvy and his pretty wife, Primrose; her younger sister, Olive; and Commander James Dugdale, an old friend of David's.

As always, the Prince's arrangements for our comfort were perfect. We stayed at the Grand Hotel, situated at the edge of the ancient town of Kitzbuehel with an excellent view of the Kitzbuehler Horn and of the Grosse Aache Valley below. I must say, however, that in spite of the glowing descriptions the men brought back each afternoon of the glories and challenge of the upper slopes, I was never tempted to try them. It was solely to avoid being put to shame by young Olive that Primrose and I ventured out upon the gentlest of the nursery slopes, and only then in the charge of a young but most experienced *Skilehrer* named Count Kari Lamberg, who pledged his honor that no harm would come to us. I would not think of claiming that I ever learned to execute more than a passable *Christiania* turn, but I came to understand the appeal of the sport and to look forward to my days on the snow. Even so, the pleasure of a successful downhill run never quite equaled for me the pleasure of the afternoon rendezvous of our party in a village inn, sipping hot chocolate before a blazing wood fire and watching the sun fall behind the mauve peaks. And our days always had a simple and leisurely ending with dinner at a local *Weinstube,* usually to the accompaniment of mountain folk tunes picked out on a zither and an accordion, and when we knew the songs—the Prince knew more than any of us—we would join in the singing.

Our prearranged fortnight at Kitzbuehel passed all too quickly. Then with an impulsiveness that no longer surprised me the Prince announced that we were off not to London but to Vienna—"I feel like waltzing, and Vienna's the place for that."

And so in the effortless manner at which I never failed to marvel we went by train through the Alps and to the Bristol Hotel in Vienna. The Prince's days were largely spent with the British Minister, Sir Walford Selby, making formal calls. But the evenings, happily, he reserved for Strauss. There was a brief but delightful interlude of this; and then one evening the Prince spiritedly asserted that "while these Viennese waltzes are wonderfully tender, there is nothing to match the fire of the gypsy violins." It now seemed only natural that next morning we were on our way to Budapest.

The fascinations of Budapest have been extolled in song and story. But nothing that I had ever heard or read had quite prepared me for the strange, almost hypnotic quality of the gypsy violins. Across the river, in Pest, was a little unpretentious, in fact almost dingy, tavern to which we were all taken one evening by a young man in the Hungarian Foreign Office. He promised us that here was played the best gypsy music in all Hungary. I remember a dim room lit by flickering candles, rough wooden tables on which stood bottles of sweet Hungarian wine, intent faces wavering in and out of the changing shadows, and the Prince and I sitting together as the music of half a dozen violins sobbed and sighed and exulted with a soulful outpouring. One song still lingers with me—something with the incredible name of "Chi, Chi, Chi." Yet it summed up all the world's melancholy. Our Hungarian friend informed us that the song told of the sound and meaning of the rain falling softly on the roof tops. I had the feeling of being torn apart, of being caught up in the inescapable sadness and sorrow of human suffering; and the look in David's eyes told me that he was in the grip of the same deep flow of feeling.

Waltzes (even of Viennese perfection) and gypsy music (even of Hungarian wildness) can hardly be considered the sturdiest handmaidens of reality; rather they are the stuff dreams are made on and from which illusions spring. And at this stage I was scarcely in a condition to differentiate these two worlds between which I giddily swung, hoping to have the best of both, but not quite sure whether I could maintain my footing in either.

Nor were my uncertainties diminished on my return to Bryanston Court. Ernest had undergone a change; the shadow that had fallen across our parting had taken on substance; it was almost palpable. This time he was not at all curious, even indifferent, about the details of the trip; and, if anything, he was more uncommunicative about his sojourn in New York. There can be nothing more baffling in a human relationship than silence, the dark loom of doubts and questions unexpressed. This was the situation in which Ernest and I now found ourselves—a situation from which we were never to emerge as long as we were together.

I was troubled, but my concern was no more than a tiny cloud in the growing radiance that the Prince's favor cast over my life. I became aware of a rising curiosity concerning me, of new doors opening, and a heightened interest even in my casual remarks. I was stimulated; I was excited; I felt as if I were borne upon a rising wave that seemed to be carrying me ever more rapidly and ever higher. Now I began to savor the true brilliance and sophistication of the life of London.

However, I was to discover that contrary to the happy assertion of a popular song of the hour that "the best things in life are free," my introduction to the best things in London under the Prince's auspices was far from free. It is, I judge, an old royal custom never to carry pocket money on the person; the business of tipping and paying restaurant checks is left to an equerry. On the occasions, therefore, when David and I dined by ourselves or perhaps dropped in at the Embassy Club or the Hungaria, David was invariably startled to find that his pockets were empty, and I was constantly dipping into my handbag for a pound note for the headwaiter, and a half crown for the doorman. In the course of several evenings of going from place to place, the drain on my pin money could become quite severe, and one evening I laughingly remarked to David that I was afraid I would have to stop going out with him: "I just can't afford to uphold the standards of largesse expected of the Royal Family."

Among the people I came to know at this time were two of the best-known hostesses of the day—Lady Colefax and Lady Cunard. Sybil Colefax's house in King's Road was called Argyll House; Emerald Cunard's mansion stood at the corner of Grosvenor Square; and both were focal points of the wit, the wisdom, and politics of Great Britain, and, indeed, of the world.

Wit and wisdom gleam fitfully even in Mayfair, but the political fires are never banked, and in the spring and summer of 1935 they were roaring. That year the first Labour Prime Minister in British history, the forsaken Ramsay MacDonald, finally succumbed to Stanley Baldwin, the self-appointed embodiment of John Bull, who, as such, would presently draw a curtain between me and the world I had just begun to enter. Hitler was on the move; Mussolini's legions were poised menacingly on the frontiers of Ethiopia; and the keener minds in British political circles were dismayed, disturbed, and divided. It was at Sybil Colefax's house that I first met Winston Churchill, then at one of the lowest ebbs of his political fortunes. The star attraction of that party was an American journalist, the late H. R. Knickerbocker. He had visited the Soviet Union and most of the capitals of Europe. The conversation turned to Russia and the European political scene. Sitting beside me, slumped back in his chair, the old statesman finally took exception to some of the visitor's opinions. When he could stand no more, like a battleship going into action, he turned on Knickerbocker to crumple him under extemporaneous salvos of logic and irony that would have done Winston proud on the floor of the House. A little later, as if regretting the expenditure of such powerful ammunition, he growled to me, "You know, Mrs. Simpson, I don't get a chance to do this sort of thing very often since my break with the Tory leadership. As a matter of fact, this is the first time Clemmy and I have been invited out this year."

Watching the tilting of the British knights of Fleet Street, Whitehall, and Westminster, I sometimes felt, although by no means a Yankee, a little like one at a modern King Arthur's Court. In the light of the terrible disasters that were already beginning to descend upon the world, I was afterward to conclude that these quick and learned minds were often more interested in scoring off each other than in resolving the momentous issues that they batted back and forth so zestfully across the dinner tables. In fact, Sybil Colefax, a rather tall, trim woman who was always gowned simply and in good taste, was a master of the art of touching off these verbal fireworks; she knew precisely when—whether between the soup and the fish, or the dessert and the savory—to toss out the apple of discord. Her forte was the intellectual luncheon, for which she collected a mixed bag of M.P.'s, journalists, authors, and whatever lion of the moment was within reach.

Emerald Cunard, on the other hand, went in rather more for artistic and musical figures, although one encountered much the same group at both houses. She was an American, but by the time I met her she had already been so long a part of London life as to be almost indistinguishable from those around her. After the Prince's interest in me became known, she took a great fancy to me. Emerald was tiny, birdlike, full of animation and more than a touch of mischief. She had been christened Maud but later decided that this name did not suit her personality; and, under the guidance of a numerologist, she appropriated the name of Emerald as more expressive of her nature. She numbered among her intimate friends and admirers George Moore, the distinguished novelist, and the eminent and temperamental conductor, Sir Thomas Beecham. Her parties were famous for their variety; and on some evenings there was an interlude of chamber music, often with Sir Thomas playing. In spite of her deep love and appreciation of music and opera, Emerald's mischievousness refused to stay curbed. I remember one evening, after Sir Thomas had been playing Handel in his finest vein for a considerable time, her going up to him with an expression of perfect innocence and saying, "So lovely, Thomas. Now, if you aren't too tired, won't you give us a little Handel?"

Sir Thomas blanched and almost despairingly blurted out, "But my good woman, I've been playing Handel all evening."

"Have you?" was the airy response, accompanied by a look of contrived contrition. "And to think I didn't recognize it. We must have that piano tuned tomorrow."

Almost before I realized it I was receiving invitations from the most distinguished hostesses of London. Among those I recall were Lady Portarlington and Helen Fitz-Gerald, whose sister had been married before her death to Lord Beaverbrook. These and other women for a time were my friends, and one whom I remember today with particular affection, not unmixed with awe, was the late Margot Asquith, Lady Oxford and Asquith, the widow of the renowned liberal statesman and Prime Minister, Herbert Henry Asquith. There was the look of the eagle about her; her eyrie was a great bare house in Bedford Square; she had been a noted horsewoman and rider to hounds in her time; and after four decades at the heart of affairs she still rode down her political quarries with the same gusto she had displayed in the hunting field. I was truly overwhelmed by her knowledge of politics and world affairs; I felt almost like a schoolgirl at her table. Yet in spite of her brusqueness, in spite of what must have been her impatience with my political naïveté, she was extraordinarily kind to me. Perhaps more than anybody else whom I met at this time, she taught me the little I ever did know about the workings of the British political mind. In fact, it was she who once suggested that I should be careful not to blurt out my own views. "There are those, my dear," she said, "who will not understand your American woman's habit of independent thinking. They will assume you are reflecting the Prince's views."

While I was under many illusions, I was not deluded about the reason why I was now being taken up by so many influential people. The word had clearly gone abroad that the Prince was interested in me. No doubt there was a good deal of curiosity as to what sort of woman had captured the attention of the Prince of Wales and what she was like. Even at this time I knew that these skilled maneuverers considered me important only as a possible bait to bring their elusive Prince more frequently into their own gatherings. Implicit in these invitations was the unexpressed hint and hope that I would say, "May Ernest and I bring the Prince?" or "Would you mind if the Prince dropped in after dinner, on his way home from the Fishmongers' banquet?"

It may seem incongruous that the Prince's compatriots should have looked to me, an American, to bring him closer to them. There is a simple explanation. Without in the slightest way ever losing touch with his countrymen, he had got out of the habit of attending many of what might be called the purely social functions. For one thing, his arduous and prolonged overseas journeys, with their social and civic demands, had surfeited him. For his very self-preservation he felt a deep need, while in Britain, to have some private life of his own, away from the protocol and formality. Once when I asked why he didn't entertain more, he replied, "I have to attend enough formal occasions as it is."

Perhaps an even more persuasive influence in this withdrawal had been the instinctively self-protective desire of the former recipients of his affection to surround him with their own friends. Perhaps their purpose had been served all too well by David's gentleness, his desire to please those who are close to him. His emotional roots had been transplanted too many times to have a firm grip. It was for this reason, I surmised at the time, that the Fort had come to mean so much to him: it was here that he hoped to find firm and continuing lodgment for his life.

Having gradually come to realize that David looked for fulfillment in the company of those whom he loved and their friends, I now quite unintentionally found myself filling the void that had been left in his life. In addition, I discovered that he rather took for granted that Ernest and I would be on hand to help him with the small, semi-official dinners he gave from time to time at York House. These were often given for personalities in politics or the professions or from abroad with whom he had dealings or whose ideas interested him.

I must in all fairness to Ernest say this: whatever he may have been thinking or feeling, he loyally played his part. At Eastertime, David proposed taking the Hunters and us to Cornwall to see the famous camellia and rhododendron gardens at the height of their bloom. Ernest could not have been more charming. It was almost like the trips into the English countryside when he was first teaching me about his country. Nor did he ever show a sign of strain or stress in his demeanor during our weekends at the Fort, which were now constant.

There was a good deal of activity at the Fort that spring. With the laurel finally beaten back, David was able to concentrate on the plantings, particularly the perennials, of which he is a connoisseur. I remember an amusing happening. David had spent a weekend at Trent Park, a country house belonging to Sir Philip Sassoon, of the famous banking family. Trent Park was renowned for its gardens; David had happened particularly to admire the delphiniums.

I was at the Fort on the morning after David's return. We were just having coffee when the butler announced that Sir Philip Sassoon was outside with a car and a gardener. "What can have brought him here at this hour?" David exclaimed as he rushed out the door. "Come along."

Sir Philip, a tall man with a slim figure and a handsome, intelligent face, was pacing importantly up and down the driveway. The motor and gardener were not in sight. "Ah," Sir Philip exclaimed as he caught sight of David, "I'm so glad to have found you at home, Sir. I've brought you some of those delphiniums that you admired at Trent."

"That's very nice of you, Philip," said the Prince as he glanced around in puzzlement. "But where are they?"

"As a matter of fact," Sir Philip responded with the satisfaction of a man who has performed a good deed, "my gardener must have just about finished putting them in."

"Putting them in?" repeated David in consternation. "But where?"

"A little distance down the driveway" was the bland response. "My gardener and I saw the right spot as we drove in."

"Good God!" shouted David. "What are you thinking of? I'm the only one who could possibly know where I want them planted." As if shot from a catapult David took off down the drive, with Sir Philip puffing and expostulating at his flying heels.

I arrived just in time to see a chastened Sir Philip directing a surly gardener who was in the process of relocating the prize delphiniums at a place a yard or so away that had been designated by an indignant Prince. While Sir Philip was thus occupied, David whispered, "As a matter of fact, he picked out about the best place, but I couldn't resist being a little difficult all the same."

The delphinium incident, as we afterward referred to it, had an even more astonishing finale. As David said good-by to the visitor, we had a glimpse of the interior of the car. It was loaded with packages. Sir Philip must have seen the question in the Prince's eyes, because he announced almost apologetically, "Sir, as I was going to be in the neighborhood anyway, I thought it would be just as easy to include a few presents for the King and Queen at Windsor Castle, and for your brother at Royal Lodge." He seemed almost in a hurry to be off. Watching the receding vehicle, David murmured thoughtfully, "Philip certainly isn't missing any tricks this morning. He's just about filled a royal flush."

This was the year of the Silver Jubilee, the national celebration of the twenty-fifth anniversary of King George V's accession to the British Throne. Never have I witnessed such an outpouring of public respect, admiration, and love. Dominion Prime Ministers, Indian princes, African potentates, sheiks, tribal chieftains, and other lords and masters of the Empire assembled from the far corners of the earth to pay homage to a greatly beloved sovereign. By day there were drives in an open landau through the streets, the King and Queen each time taking a different route and not ignoring the shabbier districts; and in the evenings there were state dinners, balls, and celebrations of every sort.

Because of David, Ernest and I were invited to the State Ball at Buckingham Palace on May 14. After the King and Queen had made their entrance and taken their seats on the dais at the end of the room, the dancing began. As David and I danced past, I thought I felt the King's eyes rest searchingly on me. Something in his look made me feel that all this graciousness and pageantry were but the glittering tip of an iceberg that extended down into unseen depths I could never plumb, depths filled with an icy menace for such as me. Also through the panoply of pomp I discerned that here was a frail old man. The King was then only a few days away from his seventieth birthday, and David had told me more than once of his concern over his father's failing strength. A premonitory shiver ran through me at the thought of what his passing might bring, the startling and immeasurable changes that of necessity would come to all of us. In spite of David's gaiety and the lively strains of a foxtrot, the sense of foreboding refused to lift; in that moment I knew that between David's world and mine lay an abyss that I could never cross, one he could never bridge for me.

Yet the wave that was bearing me surged faster and ever higher, driven by the gala spirit of the Jubilee Year. There was scarcely an evening we were not together at the theater or at one of the great houses or at an embassy reception. On July 10, the Prince, Ernest, and I attended a large dinner at the German Embassy given by the Ambassador, Dr. Leopold von Hoesch. I remember remarking to Beatrice Eden during the course of the evening, "I never see you anywhere except at these things."

Beatrice laughed and said, "These days I never seem to have time to go anywhere else."

It has been widely publicized that this was the time I met Joachim von Ribbentrop, who had come to London as Hitler's special envoy; but such is not the case. I saw him only twice and both times at Emerald Cunard's. The first time was at a large luncheon; the second at a supper party later the same week. All through the luncheon, in his best champagne-salesman manner, he held forth on the great things Hitler was doing for the unmarried mothers of Germany. Winston Churchill was also present. This time, however, he kept his heavy guns silent, although those of us nearby could hear him rumbling ominously. As he and Emerald were talking together, after von Ribbentrop's departure, I heard him say, "Emerald, I hope we never have to hear that broken gramophone record again."

Trooping the Colour, the Derby, Ascot—these marked the rapid passing of the spring of 1935. David decided to go to Cannes for his summer holiday. He took the villa of Lord Cholmondeley, who was married to Sir Philip Sassoon's sister. We were a small party— Lord and Lady Brownlow, Helen Fitz-Gerald, Lord Sefton, the Buists, and Jack Aird. The pattern of the preceding summer at Biarritz was largely repeated. We took a cruise on the Duke of Westminster's yacht, *Cutty Sark,* to Corsica; later, Daisy Fellowes lent us her yacht, *Sister Anne,* for a cruise along the coast as far as the island of Porquerolles. Not unexpectedly, David decided one day that we ought to revisit the delights of Vienna and Budapest, taken this time in reverse order. As Jack Aird struggled to organize a mass movement that taxed severely the *Wagons-Lits* facilities, he finally complained, "Sir, you'd better send to London for the Master of the Horse. This is too big for me; I'm only an equerry."

It was early October before I was back in London. Ernest had, of course, been invited to be a member of the Cannes party, but had again declined. During my absence he had made a trip to the United States. I had the feeling that more than business was now drawing him back to America. We were both going our separate ways; the core of our marriage had dissolved; only the shell remained—a façade to show the outer world.

The rest of that fall and winter I was very busy. When not at the Fort for the weekend, I was at one or another of the country houses of my ever-widening circle of new-found friends.

Only one of these visits stands out in my mind. It was to the country house of Sir Robert (now Lord) Vansittart, then the Permanent Under Secretary of State for Foreign Affairs. His house, Denham Place, in Buckinghamshire, was near Trent Park. I had met the Vansittarts occasionally at various affairs in London; and late in December, 1935, having learned that I was to spend the weekend at Sir Philip Sassoon's, they asked if I would stop over an extra night at their house. I was more than a little surprised by this invitation, as they were the most casual of acquaintances. They were very pleasant, but something in the atmosphere made me nervous. Sir Robert was a diplomat and civil servant of the highest attainments. It did not take me long to realize why I was under his roof. He was looking me over, dissecting me, no doubt, in the light of what he had been reading about me in his Foreign Office digest of the overseas press.

David, as was his unfailing custom, spent Christmas with his family at Sandringham. We were all at the same house party at Melton for New Year's. The year 1936 began pleasantly enough, with no visible indication of the catastrophes that would engulf us before its close.

The first ominous turn of events came in a fortnight. I could not describe it better than David has done in his book, *A King's Story:*

On Thursday afternoon, January 16, I was out shooting with friends in Windsor Great Park. An urgent note from my mother was brought to me in the field. "I think you ought to know that Papa is not very well," the note began, and in the calm way that I knew so well my mother went on to say that, while she herself did not consider the danger immediate, Lord Dawson (the King's physician) was "not too pleased with Papa's state at the present moment." She therefore suggested that I "propose" myself for the coming weekend at Sandringham, but do so in such a casual manner that my father should not suspect that she had warned me of his condition.

I happened to be at the Fort that afternoon and was in the drawing room when he came in with the note in his hand. Without a word he gave it to me to read. He disappeared, and I heard him telephoning his pilot to tell him to have his airplane ready the next morning to fly him to Sandringham.

I returned to Bryanston Court. That evening David telephoned from Sandringham. His word was discouraging. He told me the King was dying; that he could not live more than two or three days; and that he himself was motoring to London in the morning so to advise the Prime Minister.

On Monday evening I attended a movie given for charity with the Lawson-Johnstons. During the showing, Lord Dawson's famous bulletin was read out: "The King's life is moving peacefully to its close." At the end of the performance, when "God Save the King" was played, the old familiar words had a deeply personal significance to everyone who heard them.

The Lawson-Johnstons persuaded me to return to their place for a bite of supper. Shortly after midnight, as I was getting ready to leave, I was called to the telephone. It was David speaking from Sandringham.

"It's all over," he said.

I could think of nothing better to say than, "I am so very sorry."

Then he said, "I can't tell you what my own plans are, everything here is so upset. But I shall fly to London in the morning and will telephone you when I can."

It was only as I hung up that I realized that David was now King.

CHAPTER XX

"Somewhere, Sometime, Somehow"

NEXT AFTERNOON, JANUARY 21, DAVID WAS BACK IN LONDON FOR his Accession Privy Council, the first ceremony at the beginning of a new reign. The Privy Council met at St. James's Palace. After it was over, David telephoned, and I thought he sounded very tired and overwrought. I wished profoundly that there was something I could do, but obviously there was no place for me at such a time and under such circumstances. Reading the newspapers that morning and listening to the radio, I had begun to sense that the impenetrable barriers that custom and veneration hedge about a king were already rising around David. And my sense of this was heightened when David, as by an afterthought, asked if I would like to see him proclaimed king by the Heralds. I told him that of course I would very much like to. He then said one of his aides would make the arrangements.

Godfrey Thomas, David's private secretary, who had been with him for years, called up the following morning to say that one of the four Proclamations of the Accession in London would take place at St. James's Palace, and he added that "His Majesty"—and it gave me a start to hear so familiar a voice using this awesome title—was also inviting some of our friends, Helen Fitz-Gerald and the Hunters among them.

From an unused apartment that looked out on Friary Court, I watched the Garter King of Arms, attended by Heralds, Pursuivants, and Trumpeters, dressed in their medieval costumes, flashing with silver and gold, come out on the palace balcony. To my amazement, David suddenly appeared beside me. If I was startled, Godfrey Thomas and David's assistant private secretary, who were both with us in this room, were astonished. Helen Fitz-Gerald, the first to recover from her surprise, made a flustered curtsy. As soon as I could pull myself together I made mine. Turning to Godfrey Thomas, who was finishing his bow, he remarked lightly, "Godfrey, this may strike you as somewhat unusual, but the thought came to me that I'd like to see myself proclaimed King."

This surprising episode ended with the Guards' band in the courtyard playing "God Save the King." The majestic strains reverberated from the courtyard walls, their power intensified by their compression in that small area. It was almost impossible to believe that by the divine right of kings all this was now for David. Tears came to my eyes, and David, standing beside me, was also deeply moved.

As we made our way down, I could not help saying, knowing how much was on his mind, "How thoughtful of you to bother thinking of me and to ask me here. This has made me realize how different your life is going to be."

He gently pressed my arm. "Wallis," he said, "there will be a difference, of course. But nothing can ever change my feelings toward you." Then with a sudden smile, he was gone.

During the next few days he was absorbed in the sad pageantry of a King's funeral, and I heard from him only occasionally, perhaps a brief word on the telephone or a hastily scrawled note delivered by his chauffeur. With Helen Fitz-Gerald, the Hunters, Hugh Sefton, and a few other friends, I watched the funeral from St. James's Palace, from a window in the room that had been until recently occupied by Sir Frederick Ponsonby, who had served as Private Secretary to three generations of British sovereigns, beginning with Queen Victoria. What affected me profoundly, as the great procession rounded the corner of Marlborough House, was the sight of the heavily veiled women of David's family: his mother, Queen Mary; his sister, the Princess Royal; and the wives of his brothers, riding in State coaches.

The pressure of the King's business was all but crushing during the first few weeks. His mother remained at Buckingham Palace, and he had no desire to hasten her move to Marlborough House, which was to be her future home. Nor did he wish her to tax herself with the depressing business of gathering up the innumerable treasures that she had acquired over a lifetime. In fact, never having liked "Buck House"—as he and many of the Guards' officers called it—he was more than content to remain on at York House. However, he did transfer his office to a small room on the ground floor of the Palace so as to be in direct touch with the King's Secretariat, presided over by his father's old Private Secretary, Lord Wigram.

The Court was in full mourning; and, since David was not appearing in public except on official business, there were no more little dinners for us at restaurants. To be sure, the weekends at the Fort continued, but with a difference. There was a perceptible stiffening in protocol, a heightening of formality. It was no longer possible for David to shut out the affairs of state, or to exclude entirely those who by custom had the right of attendance upon the Sovereign. The red dispatch boxes containing State documents requiring the King's scrutiny or signature followed him to the Fort; there was less time for the garden, and the forays against the last remaining stands of laurel all but came to an end. David's every move became a matter of public interest, requiring more elaborate preparations; whom he saw and where he went were recorded daily in the Court Circular; and the Royal Standard flying over whatever residence he might be occupying at the moment informed the world of his whereabouts.

It was not easy to adjust myself to this changed atmosphere. I felt isolated. I hid my feelings; there was nothing else to do with them. As I watched David becoming absorbed in his duties, it seemed to me there was little left of Peter Pan; he had become the prisoner of his heritage.

Then there was something else. David's bachelorhood had long been a matter of some anxiety to his parents. He had once told me that his mother had raised the subject several times, usually after a family dinner, and while he was alone with her in her boudoir. It was always done, he said, with the tactfulness at which his mother was unexcelled—never anything obvious, but rather a mild suggestion that perhaps it was time he married and settled down with a "suitable" princess of his choice. By this time I knew David well enough to be able to visualize, without his telling me, how he must have put his mother off. He, too, was an expert in the art of the tactful evasion. I could imagine his saying, "Oh, Mama, let's not bother with that now. You know that I'll get around to it at the proper time."

If this pressure upon him had been uncomfortable before, it was now bound to become relentless; for one of the prime duties of kingship is to provide an heir to the throne. In the back of my mind I had always known that the dream one day would have to end—somewhere, sometime, somehow. But I had characteristically refused to be dismayed by this prospect. Perhaps the only brave—or, more accurately, reckless—thing about me is a heedlessness of consequences. I was prepared to take whatever hurt was in store for me, when the day of reckoning came.

In the meantime Ernest had gone off to New York again. It was now made unmistakably clear to me that he had found a new emotional center for his life. There was another woman. The details are unimportant; the situation became known to me through one of those coincidences that are stranger than fiction—a letter meant for Ernest that was inadvertently misaddressed to me.

This disclosure forced me to face up to what both Ernest and I had long known. Even the outer shell of our marriage had disintegrated. Ernest should be free to pursue his new happiness, relieved of the weight of a dead marriage. I had divorced Win because he was destroying his own life and I was afraid he might carry me down with him. Now I might be imperiling my own life, and I did not wish to gamble with Ernest's. All in all, I felt it would be better for me to be free to follow my uncertain destiny in my own way without further involving him. So I reasoned, and not under any illusion that I was a misunderstood woman.

Once my mind was made up—and there were several days of painful reappraisal of my life—I determined to seek legal advice. Having no solicitor of my own, I told David of my decision the next time he came to Bryanston Court and asked if he would recommend suitable counsel. He said gravely that, of course, it would be wrong for him to attempt to influence me either way, that only I could make the decision. "You can only do," he finally said, "what you think is right for you."

He arranged for me to see his solicitor, now Sir George Allen. A day or so later I went to his office in Finch Lane in the City. He heard me out with the cool detachment of his profession. Then he asked, "Are you quite sure, Mrs. Simpson, that you want a divorce?" I assured him that my mind was made up. "As you know," he said, "I'm not a divorce solicitor." He went on to say that he would try to find a solicitor for me who specialized in such matters but that it might take some time. Several weeks later he called me to say that Mr. Theodore Goddard would take my case. And from then on I acted on Mr. Goddard's advice.

While events were thus moving toward the breakup of my old life, I was becoming more and more immersed in David's new existence. Practically every evening, on his way home from the Palace, he stopped at Bryanston Court for a cocktail and a brief chat. I was fascinated by the eagerness with which he entered upon his kingly duties. There are those who have said that he did not want to be King, that he had no appetite for the rigid, highly organized pattern of life followed by his father and grandfather before him. This is simply not so. In all my countless hours with David I never once heard him say that he did not wish to be King. All his talk was the other way—what he would do when he was King. Now he was excited and challenged by what he took to be his mission to modernize the monarchy within its traditional glory and strength. This was extremely important to him, and he talked about little else. And it puzzled and angered him that the modest innovations that he began to introduce were met by the Court functionaries with unyielding and unimaginative opposition. Even I, remote as I was from the Court, could feel their cold, serried resentment.

The veneration David felt for the historic grandeur of the monarchy always welled up whenever he took me, as he several times did, to Windsor Castle. He loved to walk through the galleries and halls and state rooms, discussing the Rubens and Van Dykes and Zoffanys. He knew from his mother the stories connected with the priceless porcelain and the gold and silver services in the Plate Rooms; and one of his favorite exhibits was the now world-famous doll's house started by his mother, and furnished throughout with miniature pieces of the most exquisite workmanship. On Saturday evening he sometimes took the Fort house party over to the Castle for a showing of movies in the Green Drawing Room. His affection for Windsor was all the deeper for the reason that much of his childhood had revolved around the Castle and Frogmore house nearby.

That spring David bought a new American station wagon, a type of car then almost unknown in Great Britain. He was extremely proud of it and lost no chance to show it off to his friends. One afternoon, David said, "Let's drive over to Royal Lodge. I want to show Bertie the car." There were three other guests staying at the Fort that weekend, and they went along with us.

Turning into the entrance of Royal Lodge, he made a complete swing around the circular driveway and drew up to the front door with a flourish. The Duke and Duchess of York met David at the door. David insisted that they inspect the station wagon. It was amusing to observe the contrast between the two brothers—David all enthusiasm and volubility as he explained the fine points of the machine, the Duke of York quiet, shy, obviously dubious of this newfangled American contrivance. It was not until David pointed out its advantages as a shooting brake that his younger brother showed any real interest. "Come on, Bertie," David urged, "let's drive around a little—I'll show you how easy it is to handle." It was quite a sight to see them drive off, the King at the wheel, his still skeptical brother sitting beside him.

After a few minutes they returned, and we all walked through the garden. I had seen the Duchess of York before on several occasions at the Fort and at York House. Her justly famous charm was highly evident. I was also aware of the beauty of her complexion and the almost startling blueness of her eyes. Our conversation, I remember, was largely a discussion of the merits of the garden at the Fort and that at Royal Lodge. We returned to the house for tea, which was served in the drawing room. In a few moments the two little Princesses joined us. Princess Elizabeth, now Queen, was then ten and Princess Margaret Rose was nearly six. They were both so blond, so beautifully mannered, so brightly scrubbed, that they might have stepped straight from the pages of a picture book. Along with the tea things on a large table was a big jug of orange juice for the little girls. David and his sister-in-law carried on the conversation with his brother throwing in only an occasional word. It was a pleasant hour; but I left with a distinct impression that while the Duke of York was sold on the American station wagon, the Duchess was not sold on David's other American interest.

Spring advanced, with all its slow unfolding of a gladness restored. One day in May at the Fort while we were walking in the garden David mentioned that he was inviting the Prime Minister to dinner at York House and he wanted me to be present. Then he paused, and after a moment, with his most Prince Charming smile, added, "It's got to be done. Sooner or later my Prime Minister must meet my future wife."

I had long known, of course, that the idea of our marrying someday was in his mind, but he had never before put it directly into words. And one reason, perhaps, was that he himself had not been quite sure. As a Prince his loneliness could be assuaged by passing companionships. But as King he was discovering that his loneliness was now absolute; there was no longer an easy passing through the barriers of his position. "To every thing there is a season," we are told, in Ecclesiastes, "and a time to every purpose under the heaven: ... a time to weep, and a time to laugh ... a time to rend, and a time to sew ... a time to love, and a time to hate. ..." And

[216]

for David the time had come to marry. The man who had dismissed marriage as something for the ever-receding future now felt the need of a wife to share his burdens. It was my fate to be the object of his affection at the crucial moment of his decision. But what had hitherto seemed a pleasant daydream, while tantalizingly remote and evanescent, now filled me with apprehension.

"David," I exclaimed, "you mustn't talk this way. The idea is impossible. They'd never let you."

My concern, let alone the obvious practical difficulties, failed to change his mood. "I'm well aware of all that," he said almost gaily, "but rest assured, I will manage it somehow."

As we walked along, I tried to dissuade him from harboring this thought. But he turned aside my every sensible objection with light-hearted insouciance.

Finally, I said, "There's your family. There's your mother."

The smile vanished. A look of pain crossed his face. "Yes," he said, "that may be difficult."

And being convinced that even his strongest hopes would be unavailing against her unwavering principles, I could not take his aspirations seriously.

David went ahead with his plans for the Baldwin dinner. As usual, I helped him plan the menu and the table decorations. The guests included Dickie and Edwina Mountbatten; Lord and Lady Wigram; Duff and Diana Cooper; "Joey" Legh, David's equerry, and his wife Sarah; Emerald Cunard; Admiral of the Fleet Sir Ernle Chatfield and Lady Chatfield; and Colonel and Mrs. Charles Lindbergh. David often sat in the middle of the table at large parties, so it happened that Ernest was at one end and Emerald at the other, and Mrs. Baldwin sat on the King's right. The Lindberghs were just back from Germany, and the Colonel's Cassandra-like forebodings of the growing superiority of German air power could hardly have added to the pleasure of the Prime Minister's evening.

The Prime Minister's biographer, G. M. Young, in his book, *Stanley Baldwin,* has written that Mr. Baldwin was "intrigued" by the encounter. The biographer goes on, "Mrs. Baldwin's comments, then and after, were less bland. For her, and for women like her throughout the Empire, Mrs. Simpson had stolen the Fairy Prince." My recollection of that evening is that the Baldwins were pleasant but distant. As so often before in the company of those of power and influence, I was conscious of the assaying glance, the unspoken, probing question beneath the polite surface of the conversation.

As best I can recall, this was the last time that Ernest and I were publicly together in David's company. Not long afterward I told Ernest that I was starting divorce proceedings. He moved to the Guards' Club.

Having made my difficult and painful decision, I refused to look backward. I had little time for regret; my every hour was taken up by expanding social activities in London and the weekends at the Fort. Nearly always the same group—"G" Trotter, the Hunters, the Buists, Helen Fitz-Gerald, Hugh Sefton, and an old friend of mine whom I had known in Paris, "Foxy" Gwynne (so called because of her reddish hair), later to become Lady Sefton—were alternately there, augmented often by some new and interesting personality whom the King thought would add variety to the company. Ascot, however, was not quite the same this year, because the King, being in mourning, could not go to the races. I still carry in my mind the picture of the departure of our party from the Fort for the races and of the King, in old trousers and a sweat shirt, scything the long grass that had grown up along the driveway; as we drove by, he lifted the scythe and swung it in mock salute.

There was one other happening of this period that perhaps should be mentioned, if only because of the furore it created among certain circles—a furore of which neither David nor I was aware at the time. David decided to give another dinner at York House on July 9. On this occasion his principal guests were Sir Samuel Hoare, later Viscount Templewood, the newly appointed First Lord of the Admiralty, and the Right Honorable David Margesson (now Lord Margesson), the Government Chief Whip in the House of Commons. Sir Samuel Hoare was one of Mr. Baldwin's chief lieutenants and a senior statesman of the Conservative Party. Only a few weeks before he had emerged from the wilderness into which he had been relegated by the popular outcry over the Hoare-Laval proposal for the partition of Ethiopia, which he had co-sponsored as Foreign Secretary. Mr. Margesson was another power in Tory councils, and because of his strategic parliamentary position, his influence could be most important in any legislative situation. The Duke and Duchess of York were present; and among the guests were the Marquess of Willingdon, the most recent Viceroy of India, and the Marchioness; Lady Diana Cooper; Lady Oxford and Asquith; Major Alexander Hardinge, whom the King had just appointed as his Private Secretary, and Mrs. Hardinge; Mr. and Mrs. Winston Churchill; Sir Edward and Lady Peacock; Lady Colefax; and several others. The

Court Circular duly recorded all the guests, and it did not pass unnoticed that Ernest was not present.

As I had before at the dinner for Mr. Baldwin, I felt the same
well-bred but not so well-concealed curiosity. The Hoares, like the
Baldwins, gave no indication of their inner judgment. I was interested,
therefore, to find only recently this comment in Viscount Templewood's book, *Nine Troubled Years:* "In the notes that I made at the
time I described her as very attractive and intelligent, very American
and with little or no knowledge of English life." The compliment
aside, it was an acute observation.

By this time the question of David's summer holiday was in his
mind. His father had always spent August at Balmoral; the "Glorious
Twelfth" unfailingly found him on the moors for the opening of the
grouse season. But grouse shooting had little appeal for David compared to the sun of the Mediterranean coasts; and his tastes for the
European watering places being more akin to those of his grandfather, he planned to rent Maxine Elliott's villa on the French Riviera,
near Cannes. Unfortunately for this plan, France had meanwhile been
caught in a wave of civil turmoil brought on by Blum's Popular
Front; in fact, David was informed by his worried Ambassador that
the Red Flag had been flown in plain sight of his intended abode.
Since it would be impolitic for him to appear under such circumstances, he gave up the idea of the French Riviera and chartered a
yacht, the *Nahlin,* belonging to Lady Yule. He decided now to explore new waters—the Dalmatian Coast, Greece and the Aegean
Isles, and the Bosporus. His hope was to recapture the carefree spirit
of our last two summers, and perhaps build up a little diplomatic
good-will in a region of growing concern to his Government.

It was David's original inspiration to dispatch the *Nahlin* ahead
to Venice and to have his party board the yacht in that most pleas-
urable of places. However, the politics of the international situation
did not accord with the fancies of a monarch starting his vacation.
Mussolini's conquest of Ethiopia and his intervention in the Spanish
Civil War had aroused British opinion; the Foreign Office tactfully suggested to the King that under the circumstances his presence
on Italian soil, however briefly and unofficially, might be misin-
terpreted. David acceded to the Government's wishes, but not without a flash of irritation. That was not to be the only occasion connected with the voyage of the *Nahlin* that the Royal temperament
would be in evidence.

David having arranged for the yacht to proceed to Sibenik, on the coast of Yugoslavia, the main party assembled in France with the exception of the Duff Coopers and Herman and Katherine Rogers, who joined us after the cruise was under way. On the evening of August 8 we departed in a private car on the Orient Express. Our number fluctuated between eight and twelve. For at least part of the cruise the party consisted of Helen Fitz-Gerald, Hugh Sefton, Humphrey and "Poots" Butler, Godfrey Thomas, Alan Lascelles, Assistant Private Secretary, later Private Secretary to King George VI, and the invaluable Jack Aird.

On the following night we were due to arrive at Zagreb, Yugoslavia, where our car was to be shunted over to the local train to the coast. En route, however, David was bombarded with telegraphic invitations from Prince Paul, the Regent. The Prince was insistent that our party break the trip and visit him. David finally consented to hold our car in the little town of Kreinberg, near Prince Paul's country seat, long enough to have tea with him and Princess Olga before continuing on our way. The meeting between the Balkan Prince and the British monarch was hardly calculated to hearten either Foreign Office. In a Slavic style worthy of his mountain-chieftain forebears, Paul led us in a wild motorcade through the countryside, scattering peasants and chickens in a flurry of blouses and feathers, curses and cackles. David had a number of comments on the excursion; the one that really amused me was "This is just about what I expected. The only thing that bothers me is that I can't figure which he cares less about, the peasants or the chickens or us."

Prince Paul brought us back in time for dinner to our railroad car, which was attached to the Yugoslav royal train on which he accompanied us as far as Ljubljana. About breakfast time next morning we arrived in Sibenik.

Until we arrived up on the quay, none of us, including David, had seen the *Nahlin*. She was trim and gleaming white as she rode alongside the dock; and to come upon her so, in a picture-book setting of mountains and sunlit sea, made me appreciate as never before the pleasure and power that attended those in the company of a king.

We were there a few hours before getting off. The Premier and many local dignitaries greeted David. Twenty thousand persons from all parts of Dalmatia dressed in their colorful native costumes swarmed around, all laughing and shouting kindly words of greeting to the British King. To my surprise, I found myself almost as much the object of their attention as was he. Eyes turned from him to me and back again to him, and there seemed to be in the air an unspoken understanding and approval that imparted a festive note to the welcome. That should have been a warning to David and me. It meant that our feelings had ceased to be our private secret; they were becoming the property of the whole world, even of the remote peasants of a faraway kingdom. But David and I were oblivious to the dangerous undercurrents of this charming and seemingly irrelevant incident. Since nothing as yet was really settled between David and me—since in the nature of things nothing could be, until fact and fantasy had been resolved by the impersonal workings of the constitutional process—it delighted both of us that strangers of uncomplicated hearts should spontaneously wish us well.

In any event, as the *Nahlin* made her way down the Yugoslavian coast to Albania, putting into little Adriatic ports at our leisurely whim, that whole incredible coast seemed to be ringing to the tidings of our progress. Our privacy vanished in a gala outcry of welcome and shouts of "Long Live the King!" One clear, warm starlit evening, while our yacht lay at anchor off a tiny fishing village below Cetinje, surrounded by mountains that rose straight up from the sea, David and I, spellbound and enchanted, watched the vast, sleeping shadow of the mountainsides come to life at an unheard command and begin to stir with the serpentine movement of lights as thousands of peasants carrying flaming torches filed up and down the steep trails. Across the silent water and echoing from the cliffs came refrains of folk songs, sometimes sad and sometimes gay.

"I suppose," David said, "you think this is for me."

"Of course," I answered, unwarily. "Who else would it be for?"

"You're wrong," he said, half mockingly. "It's all for you—because these simple people believe a King is in love with you."

"This is madness," I expostulated. "If you're not more discreet, you'll have everybody else knowing that."

"Discretion," he said, almost proudly, "is a quality which, though useful, I have never particularly admired."

Earlier there had been a most amusing but, at the same time quite ominous moment of revelation at Dubrovnik. Helen Fitz-Gerald and I had gone ashore with David to look around and shop a bit. As we turned a corner I heard down the street a sudden burst of sound made up of shouts and cheers; advancing in our direction was a large, loosely disposed crowd of men and women. They came surging around us and swept us along at a half trot. Although laughing and in good humor, David was plainly surprised at so much attention in

[221]

so small a town. The rollicking mob followed us everywhere we went; through the cheerful uproar I distinctly heard the cry, *"Zivila Ljubav"*—Long live love. It was then that I realized that matters were on the verge of getting out of hand. A little while after we had returned to the yacht, I found David reading on the afterdeck. I looked at him sternly and said, "David, you have spoken a good deal about the desirability of this very democratic approach to monarchy. It seems to me that what I saw this afternoon calls for some re-examination of your theory."

David chuckled. "Perhaps you have something there. My father often used to say that while monarchy had to move on, things may move too fast and too far."

Two small incidents made me realize for the first time how very headstrong David could be. The first episode occurred when we were passing through the Corinth Canal on our way to Athens. The canal reminded me of a sword thrusting through the middle of Greece, with the walls of the cut rising sheer on either side of the current running swiftly through. David was engrossed in the captain's seamanship as he maneuvered the ship under these tricky conditions. The day was very hot; David was on the bridge in shorts, with no shirt, and a pair of binoculars suspended by a strap around his neck. Again the word of our coming had mysteriously preceded us; the banks of the canal were swarming with Greeks, all cheering, some snapping cameras, and others waving gaily colored kerchiefs. So narrow was the passage in places that it seemed as if the spectators had only to reach out to touch the King. The bucolic charm of this scene entertained me, but I soon found out that Diana Cooper and Jack Aird were not amused. In fact, they were appalled at the spectacle of their King on public exhibition without a shirt.

An argument ensued as to which of them would undertake the unpleasant duty of remonstrating with His Majesty. Neither being willing to broach so delicate a subject, Diana turned to me and said, "Wallis, look at all these people. Do you think you could possibly get the King to at least put his shirt on until we get out of sight of the Greeks?"

"After you, my dear Diana," I said. "If this were my President, I might. But you have had more experience in dealing with kings."

Needless to say, nobody stirred, and the King and the Greeks, each in their own way, thoroughly enjoyed the *Nahlin*'s passage through the Corinth Canal.

Maybe the concern over this episode laid the groundwork for a really embarrassing situation between Jack Aird and me after we reached Athens. Lord Dudley, an old friend of David whom I had often met while with him, was in Piraeus, the port of Athens, in his yacht *Anna Marie*. As we entered the harbor, he sent a signal, inviting us to join him ashore for dinner. Eric Dudley's choice was a tiny and picturesque garden café. Because the Greek political situation was at that time most unstable, King George II having only recently returned to the throne after a long exile, Jack Aird immediately implored me to use my utmost influence to dissuade the King from accepting the invitation.

"But, Jack," I protested, "I can't see any harm in the King's dining in a café. On the contrary, it strikes me as a nice democratic gesture."

Jack turned with ill-concealed anger. "It's undignified. Can't you understand that? You must use your influence."

"You know as well as I do, Jack," was my answer, "that he'll make his own decision. But if it will make you happier, I'll bring up your objections."

But when at what I thought was an opportune moment I attempted to raise Jack's point, David dismissed it in his airiest manner. That evening we dined with Eric Dudley at the café. Jack dined alone aboard the *Nahlin*.

From Greece we continued by leisurely stages to Istanbul, taking advantage of such secluded coves as we could find along the way for a morning dip and the hour's rowing in the ship's dinghy that David insisted upon for exercise. In Istanbul we were entertained by Kemal Atatürk, who impressed me as one of the most forceful men I have ever met. The call had diplomatic overtones; the Foreign Office was anxious to strengthen relations with Turkey. As soon as David had concluded his business, we started the return journey, leaving the *Nahlin* and taking Atatürk's private train, which he had lent David to take us as far as Vienna. In Bulgaria King Boris met us, and the next stage of the trip was made memorable for me by the fact that we had two kings in the cab of the engine, with King Boris, whose delight was driving locomotives, officiating at the throttle. When we finally retrieved David at Sofia, I asked him how things had been up front. "Fine," he answered with a chortle. "Boris is a virtuoso at the throttle, and he let me blow the whistle at the crossings."

There was a stop at Belgrade. Having already seen Prince Paul at the beginning of the trip, David felt that diplomatic courtesy had been satisfied. However, since we had to make at least a brief halt there in any event, he accepted the Regent's invitation to visit his town residence and to see the late King Alexander's palace nearby. The most striking feature of this building is an up-to-date motion-picture theater complete in every detail that King Alexander had had installed not long before his assassination. The memory of this tragedy cast a shadow over the trip, and it was with a sense of relief that we reboarded the train and continued on our way to Austria.

Whatever dispiriting effects the Belgrade interruption may have had upon David's spirits were quickly dispelled by the now familiar atmosphere of Vienna. Here in this ancient and urbane capital on the Danube, with its long tradition of royalty and sympathy for romance, our happy summer reached its high noon. But I was sure then that my wave was still far from reaching its crest.

Early in September we parted in Zurich, David returning by air to London while I went to the Hotel Meurice in Paris for a few days. It had been decided that the Rogerses and I would join him at Balmoral later in the month.

BOOK FIVE

IN THE EYE OF THE STORM

CHAPTER XXI

A Letter and a Choice

A DAY OR TWO AFTER ARRIVING IN PARIS I CAME DOWN WITH A SEVERE cold, and all else had to be put aside. While recuperating, I caught up with my mail. Included in the letters from my family and friends were a number of clippings from the American newspapers and periodicals. Reading them, I was amazed and then shocked. The world beyond the narrow seas was seething with conjecture about somebody called Mrs. Simpson. Who was she and what was her role in the King's life? What heretofore had been purely personal between David and me was now a topic of dinner-table conversation for every newspaper reader in the United States, Europe, and the Dominions.

There were also several letters from Aunt Bessie in Washington— warm letters, each, however, drawing attention to a particular article or clipping. None of the enclosures was accurate or reassuring.

I was troubled, and when David telephoned, as he did nearly every day, I told him of my deepening misgivings and of some of the wilder things concerning us that were being bandied about. But David refused to attach any importance to what he called American newspaper gossip. "I've been all through this before. It was the same thing when I visited Long Island years ago. It doesn't mean a thing." To reassure me further, he reminded me that the British press was ignoring this nonsense, and insisted that the furore would soon die down. My disquiet was lulled by his confidence, and I tried to put the matter out of my mind.

After a week, Herman and Katherine Rogers joined me, and I felt well enough to start for Balmoral. David was already there. On the way I stopped off in London long enough to see my solicitor, Mr. Goddard. At the end of July he had commenced divorce proceedings against Ernest. He had decided that the case should be tried out of

London, and his choice was the Ipswich Assizes in the county of Suffolk. Mr. Goddard's reasoning was that the case would attract less attention in a quiet provincial town and could be disposed of more expeditiously and smoothly than in the crowded Divorce Court in London. This arrangement, however, would necessitate my taking residence within the jurisdiction of the court, and my solicitor had already picked a suitable cottage, called Beech House, near Felixstowe, for the purpose. I agreed to these arrangements, and just that simply matters were finally settled.

Having disposed of this piece of business, and having meanwhile given up Bryanston Court, I spent the night with the Rogerses at the Fort. Next day we all took the train to Aberdeen, and David met us at the station, a thoughtful act toward me that was to drive another spike in the growing structure of public misunderstanding. Some months previously the Aberdeen authorities had asked him to dedicate some hospital buildings, but he had declined, being still in deep mourning for his father, and had delegated the duty to his brother, the Duke of York. By another of those unfortunate coincidences, my arrival at Aberdeen was on the day of the ceremony, and many Scots, on learning of the King's presence in Aberdeen, chose to misconstrue his absence from the ceremony as being due to his desire to meet me. Later on, I was to reflect that this mischance was to be typical of the way everything went from this point on.

My week at Balmoral was important to me chiefly because it gave me an insight into a side of David's life of which until then I had had only glimpses. Here in the gray-granite, pseudo-Gothic castle— which the Prince Consort had conceived as a Highland fastness for his beloved Victoria—David continued the ways of his forebears, ways of life that had remained unchanged for nearly a century. By custom the Monarch at Balmoral surrounded himself with the age-old associates of the Sovereign: the Primate, the Prime Minister, Cabinet Ministers, and friends of the Royal Family. David, in his first and only experience of being host there, departed from this tradition and invited instead a number of his friends who had extended to him their hospitality over the years. Among his guests when I was there were the Duke and Duchess of Marlborough, the Duke and Duchess of Buccleuch and Queensberry, the Duke and Duchess of Sutherland, and the Earl and Countess of Rosebery, who—like their ancestors before them—had been perennial guests there. Other members of the Royal Family gathered at the Castle, or, as in the case of the Dukes of York and Gloucester, at their lodges, Birkhall and Abergeldie Mains, nearby. However, David's talent for innovation persuaded him that this grouping would be improved by a leaven of less exalted but nonetheless stimulating people such as he had entertained on the *Nahlin*. When the arrivals and departures of the guests were duly published in the Court Circular, there were raised eyebrows from Inverness to Penzance.

For myself, I can only say that I enjoyed every minute of my stay. The day's events, revolving as they did around the deer stalking, moved in a time-honored routine going back to the days of Queen Victoria. At a fairly early hour the King's guests gathered around the sideboards in the big dining room to help themselves to a hearty breakfast from an array of steaming dishes. At ten o'clock, the men who were going out stalking, each with a stalker and two gillies, would drive off separately to some beat on the "forest." I contented myself with long walks about the glorious Scottish countryside, with its clear, fast-running burns and wooded glens now turning their autumnal gold. Deer stalking is an all-day affair, and the men would not return until nearly dusk.

The evenings were more formal. Everyone dressed for dinner—the men in dinner jackets or the tartans of their clan, the women in simple evening dresses. There were always twenty or more guests, including friends from the neighborhood; and the dinner, again according to ancient custom, always ended with a colorful touch—five pipers, led by the King's Pipe Major, marched around the table. Afterward, for those who did not wish to play cards, there were movies in the ballroom hung with curtains of Royal Stewart and Balmoral tartan.

My contribution to the traditional grandeur of Balmoral was the introduction of the three-decker toasted sandwich as a late supper item, after the movies. This proved so popular that it created a minor crisis in the kitchen through the heavy demand for repeat orders. I am sure that this innovation, so patently mine, hardly endeared the new reign to the household staff.

On the first of October I was back in London, with many urgent matters pressing upon me. Foremost among these was preparing my imminent move to Felixstowe for the divorce case. I was also in the midst of completing arrangements for moving into a new home. Before leaving on the *Nahlin* cruise, I had taken a charming furnished house of four stories at 16, Cumberland Terrace, Regent's Park. Because my lease did not start for a week or so after my return from Scotland, I stayed at Claridge's. David, too, was in the process of re-establishing himself. His mother had finally completed her move into Marlborough House, the Duke and Duchess of Gloucester had taken over York House, and David, none too happily, was installed at Buckingham Palace.

It was necessary for me to go to Felixstowe some weeks in advance of the hearing of the divorce petition. George and Kitty Hunter had kindly offered to stay with me during the period of waiting, and early in October we drove down in my Buick. My first glimpse of the little house at Felixstowe was dismaying. It was tiny; there was barely room for the three of us, plus a cook and maid, to squeeze into it. There is nothing drearier than a seaside resort town after the season. The only sounds were the melancholy boom of the sea breaking on the deserted beach and the rustling of the wind around the shuttered cottages. The date for the hearing had now been set for October 27; and while the imminence of the case was already producing profound repercussions in the inner circles of the Government and causing con-cern among the Palace secretariat, no hint of this distant concern penetrated Felixstowe. When the Hunters and I walked down to the town for the mail and the newspapers, not a head turned at our passage. On fair days, we used to walk alone along the beach, and for all the attention anyone ever paid to us we could have been in Tasmania. While this atmosphere did not make the tedium of the waiting easier to endure, it had a lulling, almost soporific effect upon my inner anxiety as to the outcome of the proceedings.

Whatever the circumstances, whatever the reasons, a divorce is an unpleasant experience. The night before I was to appear at the Ipswich Assizes I could not sleep; I paced the small floor for hours, wondering whether I was doing the right thing, whether my recklessness of consequences had betrayed me, whether I was right in my confidence that what I was about to do would bring no harm to the King. Finally, a measure of calmness came; it was too late for me to turn back.

My case was to be presented by the distinguished barrister, Mr. Norman Birkett, K.C. (now the Right Honorable Lord Justice Birkett), with whom I had conferred before leaving London. On the morning the case was to come up, Mr. Goddard with his partner, Mr. Stenson, called for me in his car to drive me to Ipswich. As I decided to return to London directly from the Assizes, I had packed my suitcases the night before; the Hunters were to bring them up in my car.

When we arrived at the Assize Court, there were some reporters standing about—perhaps twenty or so. I was relieved that they made no attempt to question me. It was not until I had taken my seat in Court, beside Mr. Goddard at the Solicitors' table, that I began to realize that there was something unusual about the procedure. I had expected the clutter of lawyers and clients and curiosity-seekers of the American courtrooms I had visited; instead the room was strangely silent and only partially filled; even more surprising was the absence of women. There were only two, sitting together in an otherwise empty gallery above the Judge's dais; and Mr. Goddard, on seeing my gaze turn in their direction, whispered, "It's the judge's wife and a friend."

I was much too tense to pay attention to my surroundings, or even to follow the details of the proceedings, which lasted only a few minutes. About all that I remember of that ordeal was the hostility of the judge as he scrutinized me while I was testifying, and his obvious attempts to discomfit Mr. Birkett. For a terrible moment I felt sure that he was determined to deny me my divorce. Then I heard him say to my counsel, almost reluctantly, "Very well, decree *nisi*." A moment later, Mr. Goddard had me by the arm and was guiding me out of the courtroom and into the car. We started at once for London. The decree *nisi* that I had been granted required under the British law of that time a six months' wait before the divorce would become absolute and my marriage dissolved.

On the long drive back to London, Mr. Goddard exuded an air of quiet triumph. But for me there was no triumph—only a sense of relief. And that was to be short-lived.

I now faced six long months of waiting before I was really free. Fortunately, I had provided somewhat against that prospect. With one of my rare flashes of foresight, I had earlier persuaded Aunt Bessie to postpone her planned summer trip to Europe until the fall. She was to leave New York in early November, and I would soon have her company and counsel.

Mr. Goddard dropped me off at my new house at Cumberland Terrace, where I had spent only a few days before going to Felixstowe. During my absence my cook and Mary Cain, who had been with me since my earliest days at Bryanston Court, had made good use of the time. The house really looked settled; my things were all properly in place; I felt life in my new status was off to a good start.

Shortly after I arrived, David telephoned from the Palace. He had already heard the news from Ipswich. As he was not going to the Fort until later, we were able to dine together at Cumberland Terrace. The evening started off as a happy reunion. But it was not long before I realized that something was troubling David. Beneath his gladness over my having successfully cleared the hurdles at Ipswich, I detected a certain reservation, a suppressed anxiety. Bit by bit, as he described his own activities over the previous days, the reasons for his worried air came out. Several disturbing and important things had happened.

A week before, the Prime Minister, at his request, had been to see David at the Fort. David had been taken aback by Mr. Baldwin's desire that the request for an audience be kept private. David told me, with obvious distaste, that the Prime Minister's purpose in seeking the interview was to express his concern over the divorce and to suggest pointedly that the King use his influence to persuade me to drop the proceedings.

My first reaction was one of utter bewilderment; then as I began to grasp the enormity of what was on Mr. Baldwin's mind, I was appalled. For there could be only one explanation for his unasked-for and unprecedented intervention: he had clearly made up his mind that David wanted to marry me and he wished to foreclose such a possibility, once and for all. In an attempt to avoid a head-on collision with the Government at this delicate juncture, with the divorce petition not yet even heard, David had replied that my divorce was a matter that involved only me and that he would not and could not properly attempt to influence me.

That had been one development, and it was connected with another. The Prime Minister had warned David that, in view of the seething speculation in the press overseas, the divorce petition, if carried through, might well force a disastrous rupture in the reticence with which the British press traditionally surrounded the private affairs of the Monarchy. David had, in fact, foreseen that possibility. Several days before the Prime Minister's visit to the Fort, and shortly after my move to Felixstowe, he himself had moved unobtrusively to prevent a bracketing by the press of my divorce with the sensational rumors that were abroad concerning him and me. Through the help of two powerful newspaper publishers, Lord Beaverbrook, owner of the *Daily Express* and the *Evening Standard,* and Esmond Harmsworth, now Lord Rothermere, publisher of the rival *Daily Mail* and *Evening News,* both his personal friends, he had arranged a "gentleman's agreement" with the body of the British press that the divorce at Ipswich would be reported in a routine way.

For the first time I was frightened. David tried to reassure me and minimized the importance of the Prime Minister's call. He said, "Don't be alarmed; I'm sure I can fix things." David's reassurance notwithstanding, I was still convinced that we had not heard the last of Stanley Baldwin.

Aunt Bessie arrived early in November. Casual as she tried to be, her conversation brought home to me as nothing else had done before, the lengths to which the American press had gone in its reporting of the King's interest in me. However, Aunt Bessie's account of some of these newspaper stories was not without its humor. My Warfield relations, she said, were not half so concerned over me as they were over the wild canards being circulated that my family had come from the wrong side of the tracks in Baltimore, that my mother had run a boardinghouse. "You'd think," said Aunt Bessie with some heat, "that we'd all come right out of *Tobacco Road*."

Well, there wasn't much I could do about that. Moreover, I was beginning to be seriously disturbed by the reaction of people much closer to home. I could no longer go out—even to my hairdresser's— without having people stop to look at me. Obviously, despite the silence of the British press, the London circles in which I moved were now well aware of what the world outside Great Britain was saying. David laughed off these public embarrassments, insisting that they would soon blow over.

Now out of the darkening sky came a thunderclap, all the more shattering because of the unexpected quarter from which it came.

During the second week in November, David left London for a brief visit to the Home Fleet. He invited Aunt Bessie and me to spend the weekend of his return at the Fort—the one beginning Friday the thirteenth. That Friday was truly to be a day of ill omen. My aunt and I drove to the Fort in the late afternoon. David arrived shortly thereafter. He was in high good spirits, pleased by the enthusiastic reception accorded him by the Navy and stimulated by the renewal of old friendships. However, after greeting us and giving the briefest account of his trip, he excused himself, explaining that an urgent dispatch from the Palace was waiting for his attention.

It was some time before he rejoined us. The moment he entered the library I knew that something was seriously wrong. He was preoccupied and his manner abstracted. All the upwelling of joy that he had brought back from the Fleet was gone; the dispatch had plainly induced some kind of shock. But he gave no hint or sign of what was troubling him. He has always had an extraordinary capacity for

[233]

keeping his inner tensions locked up inside his mind and heart. During the evening he seemed to shake off his depression. After dinner we played three-handed rummy, and his normal buoyancy appeared fully restored.

David had friends at the Fort for lunch and dinner on Saturday. We were invited to the Duke and Duchess of Kent's Sunday afternoon for tea at their home, Coppins, in the village of Iver in Buckinghamshire, not far from Windsor. Shortly after lunch David mentioned that he had something to do at the Castle, something, as I recall it, concerning the rehanging of some portraits. It was arranged that I should call for him at Windsor an hour later and that we should continue on to the Kents'.

On the way back from tea, just to make conversation, I asked him about the pictures he had hung.

"Pictures?" he asked vaguely. "What pictures?"

"Why, David, isn't that what you went there for?"

Then he said, gravely, "Darling, I must confess that my going to the Castle had nothing to do with pictures. I wish it had. I really went there for a private talk about a serious matter with my old friend Walter Monckton."

I had met Walter Monckton, now Sir Walter Monckton, Minister of Defence, once or twice in David's company and knew him to be a distinguished barrister who had been to Oxford with David and who for some years had been Attorney-General to the Prince of Wales and also to the Duchy of Cornwall, the Royal properties that appertain to the eldest son of the Sovereign.

"My reason for seeing Walter," David went on, "was to discuss with him an important letter that I received Friday evening—a letter I'll show you when we get back to the Fort. It is very serious. I didn't want to tell you about it until I had discussed it with Walter, and so I met him secretly at Windsor."

On returning to the Fort, he took me directly to his study and closed the door. On his desk stood one of the red dispatch boxes, which he opened with a key. From it he withdrew a letter. Handing it to me, he said, "Wallis, I want you to read this alone. After you've read it, I think you'll agree that there is only one thing for me to do—send for Mr. Baldwin."

With that he left the room. The letter was on Palace stationery, and it was from the King's Private Secretary. It said:

Buckingham Palace,
13th November, 1936.

Sir,

With my humble duty.

As Your Majesty's Private Secretary, I feel it is my duty to bring to your notice the following facts which have come to my knowledge, and which I *know* to be accurate:

(1) The silence of the British Press on the subject of Your Majesty's friendship with Mrs. Simpson is *not* going to be maintained. It is probably only a matter of days before the outburst begins. Judging by the letters from British subjects living in foreign countries where the Press has been outspoken, the effect will be calamitous.

(2) The Prime Minister and senior members of the Government are meeting to-day to discuss what action should be taken to deal with the serious situation which is developing. As Your Majesty no doubt knows, the resignation of the Government—an eventuality which can by no means be excluded—would result in Your Majesty having to find someone else capable of forming a government which would receive the support of the present House of Commons. I have reason to know that, in view of the feeling prevalent among members of the House of Commons of all parties, this is hardly within the bounds of possibility. The only alternative remaining is a dissolution and a General Election, in which Your Majesty's personal affairs would be the chief issue—and I cannot help feeling that even those who would sympathize with Your Majesty as an individual would deeply resent the damage which would inevitably be done to the Crown, the corner-stone on which the whole Empire rests.

If Your Majesty will permit me to say so, there is only one step which holds out any prospect of avoiding this dangerous situation, and that is for Mrs. Simpson to go abroad *without further delay,* and I would *beg* Your Majesty to give this proposal your earnest consideration before the position has become irretrievable. Owing to the changing attitude of the Press, the matter has become one of great urgency.

I have the honour, etc., etc.,

ALEXANDER HARDINGE

P.S.—I am by way of going after dinner to-night to High Wycombe to shoot there to-morrow, but the Post Office will have my telephone number, and I am of course entirely at Your Majesty's disposal if there is anything at all that you want.

I was stunned. This was the end I had always known in the back of my mind was bound to come. Such a letter, emanating as it did from a man whose duty it was to maintain the closest contact with the King's Ministers, could mean only that the Government was preparing for a crisis with the King. Clearly, there was only one thing for me to do: it was to leave the country immediately, as Hardinge had implored, and I so told David when he returned a few moments later.

Almost peremptorily he said, "You'll do no such thing. I won't have it. This letter is an impertinence."

"That may well be. But just the same I think he's being sincere. He's trying to warn you that the Government will insist that you give me up."

"They can't stop me. On the Throne or off, I'm going to marry you."

Now it was my turn to beg him to let me go. Summoning all the powers of persuasion in my possession, I tried to convince him of the hopelessness of our position. For him to go on hoping, to go on fighting the inevitable, could only mean tragedy for him and catastrophe for me. He would not listen. Taking my hand, he said, with the calm of a man whose mind is made up, "I'm going to send for Mr. Baldwin to see me at the Palace tomorrow. I'm going to tell him that if the country won't approve our marrying, I'm ready to go."

It was the first mention between us that he had ever entertained any thought of stepping down from the Throne.

I burst into tears. "David, it is madness to think, let alone talk, of such a thing."

"In any event," he said, "I've got to have it out with the Prime Minister. Walter and I were agreed on that point this afternoon. Because of Hardinge's attitude, I can no longer use him as my official channel of communication with the Cabinet. Walter's going to act for me. I am far from giving up. There are things I still can do."

Among the things he had it in mind to do was further to test the temper of the Cabinet by consulting several of his friends among the Ministers. He particularly had two in mind. One was Sir Samuel Hoare, First Lord of the Admiralty, whom he had known since the First World War, and who had recently been shooting at Sandringham, and who only a few days before had been his Minister in Attendance during the visit to the Fleet. The other was the Right Honorable Alfred Duff Cooper, Secretary of State for War, a friend of almost equally long standing, who with his wife had been with us on the *Nahlin*. Because of the delicate situation that now prevailed, constitutional etiquette required that he obtain the Prime Minister's consent to seek such advice.

I was afterward to reproach myself for being deflected from my decision to leave England immediately. I should have realized that this was the fateful moment—the last when any action of mine could have prevented the crisis. What kept me from going? The answer to that hinges on a misconception on my part and, I suppose, the fundamental inability of a woman to go against the urgent wishes of the man she loves.

The misconception sprang from my failure to understand the King's true position in the constitutional system. The apparent deference to his every wish, the adulation of the populace, the universal desire even of the most exalted of his subjects to be accorded marks of his esteem—all this had persuaded me to take literally the ancient maxim that "the King can do no wrong." Nothing that I had seen had made me appreciate how vulnerable the King really was, how little power he could actually command, how little his wishes really counted for against those of his Ministers and Parliament. David did nothing to disabuse me of these misconceptions. And, too, right to the end it seemed utterly inconceivable to me that the British people and the Dominions would ever allow anybody who had served and loved them so well to leave them.

As for my second point, I can only say that David was determined that I stay; he insisted that he needed me, and as a woman in love I was prepared to go through rivers of woe, seas of despair, and oceans of agony for him.

CHAPTER XXII

The Crisis

ON MONDAY MORNING, NOVEMBER 16, I MOTORED BACK TO CUMBER-
land Terrace with my aunt. It was a tense day. As I went through
my small activities, my mind was reaching forward toward David's
evening meeting with his Prime Minister. It was almost dinnertime
when he finally called from the Palace. David was always guarded
in his telephone conversations—not only because of his innate reserve, but also because he could never be sure that someone was
not listening in. This evening he was even more noncommittal than
usual. I could only gather that nothing important had been lost,
but that no progress had been made. However, there had been one
faintly encouraging development: Mr. Baldwin had agreed to David's
consulting his friends in the Cabinet.

The succeeding days were extraordinary. I knew that momentous
happenings were going on all around me; that the issue was fully
joined between David and the Cabinet; that decisive actions were
impending. But to me, waiting alone at Cumberland Terrace, these
were only dimly outlined shadows. I knew that David was meanwhile
seeing his mother and his three brothers, one after the other, but
he never revealed what he was telling them. All that he ever said
about all these various moves and countermoves, his discussions with
his family and the Government and his own advisers, was "I must
work things out my own way." In the midst of it all, with his whole
future trembling in the balance, he had to go off on an official tour
of the depressed areas in South Wales.

While David was away, Esmond Harmsworth, whom I had known
for some time, invited me to lunch with him at Claridge's. I knew,
of course, that he and his father, Lord Rothermere, were sympa-

thetic to David and to me. Esmond was chairman of the Newspaper Proprietors' Association and, as such, in co-operation with Lord Beaverbrook, had been instrumental in restraining the British press's handling of the divorce suit. During the early part of the meal we chatted aimlessly. Then, suddenly, the purpose of the lunch became clear. In a matter-of-fact way, Esmond said he knew that the King wanted to marry me and of the difficulties involved. Then he asked whether any thought had been given to the idea of a morganatic marriage.

His directness quite took my breath away, and I wasn't sure that I understood what he meant. The term morganatic was one that I remembered from my history books—something romantic having to do mostly with the Hapsburgs. Still uncertain as to what Esmond was driving at, I asked him to tell me what was on his mind. He then explained that this form of marriage was not infrequent among foreign royalty: it was one whereby a king or a prince could contract a legal marriage with a woman outside the royal circle, with his wife, however, not sharing her husband's position and titles.

Esmond had obviously done a good deal of research about this curious institution. He cited chapter and verse at considerable length. He finally concluded that he was advancing the idea in the thought that a morganatic marriage might be the only acceptable compromise solution for David and me, since there could be no question of my ever being Queen. "I realize, Wallis," he said, "that all this is not very flattering to you. But I am sure that you are one with us in desiring to keep the King on the Throne."

The whole idea was so astonishing and so filled with incalculable implications that I could not possibly express any opinion as to its feasibility or desirability. And I frankly told him so.

Esmond then urged that at least I pass on the idea to the King. Almost as an afterthought he suggested that a suitable title for me might be that of the Duchess of Lancaster—an ancient and subsidiary title adhering to the Sovereign.

I was now completely at sea. Parting from Esmond, I was sure of only one thing: that I knew less than ever of the marvelous workings of the British political mind.

Thursday night, November 19, David returned to London from his tour of the coal fields. As I had not expected him back until the next day, I had gone to dinner with some friends. The front door had no more than closed behind me when, as I learned later, the phone rang. It was David back at the palace. When he was told that

I was out, he asked to speak to Aunt Bessie. He both charmed and startled her by inviting himself to dinner *à deux,* but she took this development in her stride. It so happened that she had a fondness for snipe, and I had arranged with Mrs. Ralph to serve them as a special treat. They also happened to be a favorite of David's. It was toward the end of the snipe course that Aunt Bessie's aplomb almost deserted her. She became aware of the King eying hopefully the untouched heads on her plate.

"Aunt Bessie," he asked briskly, "you don't intend to leave those heads, do you?"

My aunt gasped, "Why, Sir, I wouldn't dream of eating them!"

"Why," he exclaimed, "the brain is the best part of the snipe. Do you mind if I take them?" Whereupon he reached across the table, skillfully severed the necks, impaled the heads on his fork, and transferred them to his own plate.

Aunt Bessie's description of her evening with David was the last amusing episode she and I were to share for a long time.

We joined David the next evening at the Fort. He looked exhausted and, more than that, harassed; the tension of inner struggle was obviously eating into his soul, and I felt that the appalling strain he was under could not be allowed to go on. Therefore, but with many misgivings, I brought up the subject of Esmond Harmsworth's proposal. David's face showed his distaste. The custom of morganatic marriage, he said, had long since ceased to be acceptable in Britain, and the last example in his family nearly a century before had been lamentable. "Whatever may be the outcome of our situation," he declared, "I can't see a morganatic marriage as right for you."

Needless to say, I shared his distaste and could foresee the humiliation that would inescapably adhere to such an ambiguous role. I understood his attitude. Nevertheless, having turned the matter over in my own mind, I now told him that if there was the slightest possibility that Esmond Harmsworth's proposal might ease the crisis and keep him on the Throne, it was our duty to consider it, regardless of our own feelings. Perhaps my putting the matter to him in this way, and at this time, was a mistake. He sighed wearily and said, "I'll try anything in the spot I'm in now."

No doubt it was all a romantic fantasy. But in any case David moved. The following Monday, or thereabouts, on his return to London, he sent for Esmond. For reasons I never quite understood then, and even today still find inexplicable, David and Esmond decided to try it out on the Cabinet.

The first step was an informal call by Esmond upon Mr. Baldwin to lay the idea before him. Esmond reported to David that the Prime Minister was interested but wary about committing himself. At this point I became alarmed. David was obviously allowing his better judgment to be swept aside by his impatience to break the deadlock. I began to suspect that the whole idea, however well meant, would turn out to be in reality a trap. He would be putting his head on Mr. Baldwin's chopping block. For the formal presentation of the morganatic proposal would give Mr. Baldwin the constitutional right to proffer the King advice and the King would have to take it.

Once David was in the grip of an idea, wild horses could not hold him. He brushed aside my alarm, saying, "I've got to do something. At the very least I'll get my head in a more comfortable position on the block."

So on Wednesday, the twenty-fifth, David saw Mr. Baldwin again, to ask him whether he had considered the Harmsworth proposal. Both David and the Prime Minister have described at length their conversation on this critical occasion. Here it will suffice to say that David requested that Mr. Baldwin submit the question of the morganatic marriage formally to the Cabinet and the Dominions. Two days later the Cabinet met; and, although no formal word was transmitted to David about the outcome of its deliberations, he had learned before the end of the day that the morganatic-marriage proposal had been overwhelmingly rejected.

As I have said, these complex and, for David, desperate maneuverings, were scarcely known to me. What little I knew at the time— and, remember, not a word about the breach between the King and his Ministers had yet appeared in the British press—came to me in bits and snatches from David, by now seemingly withdrawn even from me. But as that terrible week wore on, even I, remote as I was from the center of the storm, could feel the mounting menace in the very atmosphere. It was by now almost impossible for me to get about the streets without strangers turning to stare, and this was an eerie, unnerving experience. It was as if some mysterious and silent means of communication was carrying the story of the hidden crisis into ever-widening circles of the British public. My house was rapidly becoming a focus of attention; my aunt, looking out through the curtains, discovered that there was scarcely a moment during the day when strangers were not loitering on the sidewalk, peering up at the house and noting our comings and goings.

Worse still, I began to receive strange letters—some signed but more anonymous—mostly critical and some even threatening. This was my first experience with notoriety, and nothing can be more dreadful. I began to feel like a hunted animal. Knowing the ordeal that David was undergoing, I did not wish to add to his burdens by confiding to him my growing difficulties and apprehensions. Now, however, David was informed of a rumored plot to blow up my house. On the Friday morning of the Cabinet meeting he sent me a note by hand saying that he thought it would be wiser if Aunt Bessie and I got out of London for a bit and stayed at the Fort, where we should not be bothered. He added that he would pick us up in his car in the late afternoon and in a P.S. advised that I instruct the servants not to disclose our whereabouts.

About six o'clock that evening Cain entered the drawing room to announce that the King's car was waiting. Aunt Bessie and I hurried out. As we had packed for only a few days, it was but the work of a moment for the chauffeur to stow our bags away in the luggage compartment. David emerged from the darkened interior to help Aunt Bessie into the car and to squeeze my hand reassuringly. Then we were off on the familiar road to Sunningdale and the Fort. As the lights of London receded into the distance behind us, little did I know that this was the last time I was to see them for nearly three years.

The instant I entered the Fort I sensed the vast change that had come over its atmosphere in the short space of a week. The faces of the servants were drawn. No sooner had we entered the house than David was called to the telephone. There came to me the realization that this was no longer the enchanted Fort; it was the Fort beleaguered.

All through the weekend the tempo of activity mounted around David. There were constant comings and goings, between the Fort and London, of advisers, aides, and couriers. The telephone was never quiet. With so much clearly visible, it was not possible for David any longer to conceal from me the true magnitude of the crisis. On Sunday afternoon, after a lengthy conference with Walter Monckton and George Allen, David took me into the library and told me how things really stood. It was a somber recital. He had seen Sir Samuel Hoare and Duff Cooper; neither had held out any hope that the Government would allow him to marry me. Though sympathetic to David personally, Hoare had told him that he had only two real choices—renunciation of me or abdication. Duff Cooper confirmed Sir Samuel's analysis of the Government's position; there was no possibility of changing it. The course of action that he advised was an immediate withdrawal of the marriage proposal from the Cabinet's consideration; he urged David to proceed with the Coronation and at some more favorable period in the long future to reopen the question of marriage again.

David had also consulted Lord Beaverbrook, who had generously returned from abroad to lend his powerful assistance and who I believe was in touch with Winston Churchill. Both had basically concurred with Duff Cooper, "So, you see, darling," David said in conclusion, "I'm trying to do everything within my power. Nothing is yet final. I still think something can be worked out. In any case, I haven't stopped trying."

I was crushed. I felt unutterably sorry for him in the dilemma into which his love for me had brought him so early in what had promised to be a glorious reign. David had mentioned that if there was only some way by which he could make his position known to the people of Britain and the Dominions, their decent and loyal sentiments would be felt in Downing Street, and the present picture would be quickly reversed. The thought struck me that possibly the only way, and certainly the most effective way, considering how far matters had already progressed, was for him to make a radio broadcast to the nation and to the Empire, telling his story and letting them hear his voice. In suggesting this idea, I was not unmindful of the extraordinary impact on public opinion of President Roosevelt's "fireside chats" and, indeed, of the famous Christmas broadcasts of David's father.

David was immediately interested. His face lighted up with a flash of his normal enthusiasm. "Darling, it may be grasping at a straw— but I'm going to try it. It's a damn good idea. But I'll have to get the Cabinet's permission, and that will take some doing."

During the next few days the idea matured in David's mind, in long discussions with his principal advisers, Walter Monckton, George Allen, and Major (now the Rt. Hon. Sir) Ulick Alexander, Keeper of the Privy Purse. They added to the basic idea of his telling his story a strategic touch. It was that he withdraw from England while his people considered the issue, meanwhile delegating the Royal power to a Council of State.

With something concrete to do, David threw himself feverishly into the writing of the broadcast. He decided not to request formal permission of the Cabinet until he had heard from Mr. Baldwin the final replies of the Dominions to the morganatic-marriage proposal that had been submitted to them.

All this time my aunt and I were still at the Fort. On Wednesday, December 2, David motored to London and received Mr. Baldwin at the Palace. David was back in time for a late dinner. One look at his face told me that the worst had happened. Not wishing to alarm Aunt Bessie, for whom he had formed a deep affection, he made no mention during dinner of the events of the afternoon. Afterward, he suggested we step outside for a little air. It was a foggy night. As we walked up and down the flagstone terrace, he told me what had gone on between him and the Prime Minister. The answers from the Dominions were not yet all in, but Mr. Baldwin was certain that their verdict would be an emphatic rejection of the morganatic marriage. Nor was his Government prepared to introduce the necessary legislation for such a marriage in the British Parliament. This door was now forever closed. "So it now comes to this," said David. "Either I must give you up or abdicate. And I don't intend to give you up."

As I had said to him so many times before, I now repeated that abdication was unthinkable. His place was at the head of his people. He was scarcely listening. His mind was far away. Now, with everything on the final brink of disaster, with the Throne tottering and David beyond my reaching, I realized that the time had come for me to take matters into my own hands to the extent that I could.

"David," I said, standing there in the darkness, "I'm going to leave. I've already stayed too long. I should have gone when you showed me Hardinge's letter. But now nothing you can say will hold me here any longer."

To my great relief, he did not argue with me. On the contrary, it seemed as if I had unknowingly lifted a weight from his mind.

"It will be hard for me to have you go," he finally said. "But it would be harder still to have you stay." Then he told me that among the other dire developments of that day in London was the collapse of the "gentleman's agreement" that had kept the press silent on the question of our affairs. The next day's press, he warned, would be ablaze with every conceivable rumor and speculation about the two of us. "Wholly apart from anything else," David concluded, "your situation here would now become harrowing beyond belief. You are right to go. I must handle this in my own way, alone."

After we went back inside, I told Aunt Bessie of my decision and the reasons for it. In her wise and intuitive way she had come to much the same conclusion.

I was braced for a blow; but nothing had equipped me to deal with what faced me on my breakfast tray in the morning. There in big black type in paper after paper were the words "Grave Constitutional Issue," "Grave Crisis," and "Constitutional Crisis." The dam was broken; I felt unnerved; self-reproach flooded through me. Everything that David and I had created between us—everything that David in his tenderness had seen in me—was about to be rendered public and common. Through my mind ran the question: *Why? Why? Why? Why didn't you follow your first instinct? Why didn't you go when you first knew that was the only thing to do?*

I dressed quickly. David was in the drawing room, at his writing table. As he heard me enter, he pushed aside the heap of newspapers at his elbow. "Don't bother, David," I said, "I've seen them."

He rose and took me into his arms. "I'm sorry, darling. I had hoped you wouldn't see them."

All that I could say—and it was inadequate enough—was "Dearest David, I am sorry I've done this to you."

His answer was "What's done is done. We've got things to do right now."

"You're right," I answered. "I must be out of England before this day is over."

David said he had already given thought to how my departure should be handled. His idea was that a trusted friend should accompany me; my privacy was gone; the hounds of the press would now be baying in pursuit, wherever I might go. But where? That was the question.

We discussed several possibilities. Then it occurred to me that there was only one sanctuary within immediate reach—Villa Lou Viei, the house of Katherine and Herman Rogers at Cannes. David agreed that this was the answer.

With no further discussion, David had a call put through to them. When Herman came on the line, I told him, as deviously as I could, that I was leaving England rather soon and would it be an imposition if I stopped with him and Katherine. Herman grasped my meaning. "Of course" was his answer. "You must come to us."

After I had hung up, David said that his choice of a companion for me was his Lord in Waiting, a former officer in the Grenadier Guards, Lord Brownlow. "Perry" Brownlow and his charming wife, Kitty, had been frequent visitors at the Fort. Furthermore, I had spent a weekend at their country seat, Belton, near Grantham in Lincolnshire, not many months before. David's choice was a happy one—perhaps the happiest during all the unspeakable trouble.

Knowing that every road from the Fort would be watched by the press, David arranged to put into operation a set of evasive tactics. His trusted chauffeur, George Ladbrook, with whom David and I had so often driven to and from the Fort, would take my car to Newhaven, where it would be put aboard the night ferry to Dieppe, on the French side of the Channel. He would send along his most suave and least identifiable detective, Inspector Evans, of Scotland Yard, to deal with any awkward contingencies, if such should arise. As part of this plan, as it developed during the morning, Perry would come to the Fort under cover of darkness and conduct me to the steamer in his car, which no one would connect with my flight.

The rest of the day was consumed in a whirl of preparations. There was no chance for me to try to make any arrangements about my house at Cumberland Terrace, or the servants there, let alone to tidy up my affairs. All that I dared to do was to send Mary Burke back to London to pick up a few clothes.

The only other thing I did was to draw up a new will. This was an afterthought and therefore had to be done hurriedly. George Allen and I repaired to my bedroom, where in a matter of minutes he wrote the document on Fort stationery. I made a bequest of money to Mary Burke and Cain. All my personal clothes, silver and china, and a bequest of money, I left to Aunt Bessie. I appointed David and George Allen my executors.

By then the day was gone. Perry Brownlow arrived from London just as tea was being brought into the drawing room. All that afternoon, despite the distractions attendant upon my departure, David had been polishing the final draft of the broadcast. He had already summoned the Prime Minister to the Palace for an evening audience to seek his assent for presenting his case to the people, and it was his plan to leave for London as soon as I was off.

Hurried as were my last moments at the Fort, they were nonetheless poignant. I think we all had a sense of tragedy, of irretrievable finality. As for me, this was the last hour of what had been for me the enchanted years. I was sure I would never see David again.

Almost as hard as leaving David was saying good-by to my dear Aunt Bessie, who had so loyally supported me all these years, and whom I was now leaving behind in the forlorn wreckage of my life.

We had to leave by seven o'clock to catch the boat. At the last moment I decided, because of the uncertainties ahead, that I could not take with me the little cairn, Slipper, whom David had given me at the beginning of our friendship and whom I had come to love dearly. We came out the door as the last bag was being put in the luggage compartment; Perry tactfully moved to the far side of the car.

David embraced me. His parting words were "I don't know how it's all going to end. It will be some time before we can be together again. You must wait for me no matter how long it takes. I shall never give you up."

CHAPTER XXIII

Lord Brownlow's Proposal

THOSE WERE THE CIRCUMSTANCES OF MY LEAVE-TAKING. THE night mist swiftly engulfed the outlines of the Fort, an intimation that the same darkness was closing around my hopes, my love, my life. France was my destination, but for me France at that hour meant the beginning of oblivion. I was sure that I would not come back, that I would never see England again.

The night ferry left at ten o'clock. We had none too much time, and Perry's chauffeur, Field, drove fast. It was drizzling, the car windows were fogged over, and every now and then a yellowish blur would tell me that we were passing through a town. For a long time Perry and I sat together in silence. The parting had been deeply affecting, and both of us had withdrawn into our private thoughts.

For, as it was later to turn out, Perry, too, had a good deal on his mind. A fantastic circumstance had injected him into the situation not alone as the King's friend but also in the clandestine role of a kind of double agent. The evening before, Perry had received an invitation from Lord Beaverbrook to come to Stornoway House. It was a men's evening—many people passed in and out. After dinner Lord Beaverbrook drew Walter Monckton, Esmond Harmsworth, and George Allen—all devoted partisans of the King's cause—into his library. Lord Beaverbrook had called them together, at this eleventh hour, in the hope of averting the constitutional crisis that was about to burst upon the country. Their one idea was to keep the King on the Throne and to extricate me with dignity from my appalling situation. As the trusted friend of David and me, Perry was charged by the others with approaching me to explain the situation and to persuade me to give up the King since he would not give me up, and also to leave the country while there was still a chance to save us both. This mission Perry was uniquely qualified to perform since, as Lord in Waiting to the King, he had entree to the Fort. The friendly conspirators, if I may use so melodramatic a term for men of such honorable intentions, knew that the King would be in London the next day, December 3, to conduct his business and to see Mr. Baldwin. The scheme, as it was developed at Stornoway House, was for Perry to pass the King on the Great West Road and seek me out at the Fort. Actually, the following morning, while I was packing, Perry, Walter Monckton, and George Allen were meeting at the Windham Club to give the final touches to the strategy. Just as Perry was about to start for the Fort, his wife, Kitty, reached him on the telephone with word that the King was trying to get in touch with him. Shaken, even alarmed by this startling coincidence, Perry called the Fort, to be told by the King, as I have already described, of the plans for my leaving.

At this stage I was, of course, wholly ignorant of Perry's other and secret undertaking, and he did not immediately take me into his confidence. When, therefore, breaking the silence, he asked what had induced me to leave so suddenly, I told him the reasons—my fears for the King and my resolve to remove myself from a position that had become insupportable. As Perry and I talked, a note of relief became apparent in his voice.

"Wallis," he finally said, "this is the way I always was sure you felt about the King." Then he put a surprising question. "Do you still think it wise for you to leave England?"

"I have only one desire now," I answered. "It is to go just as far away as I can just as fast as I can—to finish it."

"You are the only person who can influence the King," Perry said thoughtfully. "Has it not occurred to you that by leaving him to make up his mind alone you will almost certainly bring to pass the conclusion that you and all of us are so anxious to avert?"

My brain was spinning. Almost in desperation, I said, "You have me utterly bewildered. What are you getting at?"

"Things are much more critical than you realize or than I did until I talked to the King just prior to our leaving. Before we go any farther, we'd better make sure that we're doing the right thing in light of what I now know." He signaled the chauffeur to pull over to the side of the road and stop. For some minutes we talked in whispers, in order not to be overheard by Field and Inspector Evans sitting in the front, their eyes straight ahead.

Perry weighed his every word. "What I'm getting at is simply this. With you gone the King will not stay in England."

The idea seemed preposterous. "He will stay," I insisted. "He has to stay. They will never let him go."

"That's where you're wrong," Perry said somberly. "The King told me that his mind is made up. He intends to leave the country unless and until the Government gives way. In fact, he mentioned going to Switzerland with Joey Legh until the crisis is resolved." Perry said hesitantly, "I can see only one outcome—abdication."

The possibility of abdication had hovered implicitly over David's negotiations with the Prime Minister, but I had assumed he was testing Mr. Baldwin's resolution, that it was only a move in a dangerous game, not one invested with finality. Even in our last hours together David had given me to believe that a way would somehow be found out of the impasse.

"What can we do, Perry?" I asked in my despair.

Perry now proposed a possible course. It was for us to give up the idea of continuing on to Cannes and to go instead to Belton, which was only about a hundred miles from London. "Your nearness," Perry said, "will give the King comfort. You will not be completely cut off from him. From Belton you can bring your influence to bear and restrain him from any hasty and irretrievable action. Meanwhile, Kitty and I can look after you."

"Wait a minute," I said, trying to adjust my mind to this startling idea. "You know what David is like when he's crossed. Any change in his plan, in the state he's in, will drive him wild."

"I've thought of that," Perry said soberly. "I know it will almost certainly cost me the King's confidence and lose me his friendship; but that's a risk I'm prepared to take to keep him on the Throne."

This was the core of Perry Brownlow's proposal. In the distress of the moment I could not see how my going to Lincolnshire, rather than Cannes, could possibly affect the situation. My separation from David would be nearly absolute, whether the actual distance between us was one hundred miles or seven hundred. Knowing David as I did, I was more than doubtful that anyone, including me, could change his mind. If I stayed and my pleas failed, I should always be accused of secretly urging him to give up the Throne. I told Perry, therefore, that I did not see how his plan could work. If I were to go to Belton, I told him, and if I were to remain there during the King's negotiations with the Prime Minister, and if, in the end the King should decide to abdicate, the blame attaching to me would be even more bitter than was already the case. It would be said that I was afraid of losing the King; that, having left him at the Fort, I had lost heart and run back in order to hold him.

"You must remember," I said, "that until this morning I was an utter stranger to all but a handful of people in Great Britain. There is no one to speak up for me. I am sure there is only one solution: that is for me to remove myself from the King's life. That is what I am doing now."

Whether or not my reasoning convinced Perry I had no way of knowing. At any rate he told Field to drive on. The British are an insular and an ancient race. As Sir Winston Churchill is fond of reminding us, their insularity has armed them with a closed system of moral judgment that is as impervious to outer appeal as their coasts are invulnerable to the beating of the seas. And, being an ancient people, they have long memories. Just about anything that could possibly happen has a remembered precedent in their past; and having experienced just about everything they are inevitably cynical about what can be done with the generality of human beings, including themselves. In the back of every Englishman's mind is a kind of Domesday body of moral principles that continuously sits in judgment upon the affairs of others; and yet, the English, more than any other race, have an ingrained reluctance to interfere. Perhaps this is really what is meant by British reserve. And so, in my particular situation, profound as were his misgivings, Perry ceased to press his point. He never again raised the question of my returning with him to Belton. On the contrary, he conceded that he himself was of divided mind about the wisdom of such an action.

I am far from certain that I did the right thing in leaving Great Britain; indeed, today, in the long view of hindsight, I am ready to concede that, in all likelihood, Perry was right and I was wrong. The instant I started across the Channel, I had ceased to exist, so far as my being able to influence the King's mind was concerned.

All the rest of the way to Newhaven we discussed the ways open to us for persuading the King to give up the idea of marriage and thus end the crisis. Perry and I went down the list of his friends to whom he would possibly listen. We agreed upon Lord Derby, whom David greatly respected and who had been a friend of his father. For my part, I promised to telephone Lord Derby from the quay. But we were late and there was no time even to call David. Perry hurried me into the cabins that had been reserved for us in the name of "Mr. and Mrs. Harris," and the opportunity was lost.

CHAPTER XXIV

"Voilà la Dame"

To our relief, Ladbrook was already aboard the ferry with my Buick. That was the end of our good fortune. Thereafter everything seemed to go wrong. At Dieppe, on the French side of the Channel, as Perry accompanied Ladbrook to deal with the French customs, he discovered, to his horror, that the papers for the car were still in my name. The customs officers were polite but knowledgeable; I was conscious of heads turning as I entered the car. "You've been found out, Mrs. Harris," Perry said in a stage whisper. "It may be difficult to shake off the posse."

From Dieppe to Cannes down the length of France, the distance is about 650 miles—too far to be feasibly undertaken in a straight run. Perry suggested stopping at Rouen, about two hours beyond Dieppe. A few hours' rest, an early start, and with luck we should be in Cannes by midnight of the second day.

It was about two o'clock in the morning when we arrived at the Hôtel de la Poste. The lobby was deserted. The sleepy clerk at the reception desk did not even so much as glance at me as Perry asked for two rooms and registered in the name of "Mr. and Mrs. Harris." Perry took me to my room to make sure that I was all right. "Good night," I said. "You have been a true friend."

I was too tired to undress and threw myself on the bed, intending to rest a moment. The next thing I knew Perry was knocking on the door. "Wake up, Wallis. Wake up. I'm most frightfully sorry; I've overslept," he called. I longed for a bath and to change my clothes, but dared not delay. He had intended to be off by the first light, before the hotel had bestirred itself, but now it was daylight. Perry had tea and rolls sent to my room. I had a sip of one and a bite of the other.

Then behind Perry's protecting back, I crept downstairs; and, as I entered the lobby, the few people there seemed to recognize me. I moved toward the door with Evans walking ahead of me. Perhaps our attempts to be unobtrusive gave us away. Perhaps it was the Buick at the door. In any event, there was a crowd around the car. An unfortunate contretemps arose. A young girl—she was blonde and laughing—stood in front of the car door. Evans asked her to move aside. The girl said something, half mockingly, in French and pointed a camera at me. Evans's arm flashed out, and the camera flew from the girl's hands. She screamed. Evans and Perry pushed me into the car and jumped in as Ladbrook pulled away from the curb.

"Evans," I cried, "why did you do that?"

"I am under the King's orders," he replied. "How could I be sure that the girl did not have a pistol in her camera?"

It was, I am sure, the only mistake that this competent detective ever made in his long career, but there was no time to go back for an apology.

The one thing on my mind now was to find a place where I might stop and telephone David. I wanted above all to implore him not to be carried away by his emotions, to do nothing impulsively, to seek advice. But that incident in front of the Hôtel de la Poste and the realization that all the journalists in France must be mobilizing along our route had thrown our plans askew. We dared not take the direct way to Cannes. Once beyond the outskirts of Rouen, Ladbrook left the main road and started off on a roundabout course to the south, hoping thereby to shake off pursuit.

Perry had a map spread out on his lap from which he called out directions to Ladbrook. The new route took us, about lunchtime, to Evreux, in Normandy, a charming town where I had stopped for the night some years before. I remembered there the Hôtellerie du Grand-Cerf, in former times a coaching inn, with a large courtyard where the car would not be visible from the main room. It would be a good place from which to make my call to David. Perry and I entered the inn together, leaving Ladbrook and Evans to watch the entrance. The dining room was already quite full. Nobody looked up. The telephone was in a booth near the bar. Before I left the Fort, David and I had worked out a simple code in which he was identified as "Mr. James." While Perry was putting the call through to "Mr. James" at the Fort, I sat at a table and jotted down on a piece of paper what I wished to say. The first sentence was, *"On no account is Mr. James to step down."* There were other points: *You must get advice. You must* *bring in your old friends. See Duff Cooper. Talk to Lord Derby. Talk to the Aga Khan.* Do nothing rash.*

Perry was beckoning from the booth. "The King's coming on," he whispered. "The connection is abominable. You'll have to shout."

David's voice came to me as from another planet, asking why we were in Evreux. I answered that we were trying to shake off the press; he couldn't hear me and seemed to be trying to give me some sort of warning. (What he tried to tell me, I learned afterward, was that the press, having discovered my presence in France, had correctly guessed my destination as being Cannes and was already dashing toward the Rogerses' villa.) I begged David to listen to me carefully. I went over and over my scribbled list of points, hoping by sheer repetition to make myself heard and understood. At the end I was screaming, and so, too, were Perry and Evans outside the booth in an anxious effort to drown out what I was saying and to keep it from being understood by the few Frenchmen in the bar. I could only hear David asking repeatedly what Perry and I were doing in Evreux.

There comes in moments of despair an agonized feeling that one's voice is fated never to be heard, that a malign power is bent upon defeating the most desperate efforts to make oneself understood. I had that feeling at Evreux. It was with a sense of utter hopelessness that I hung up.

Perry had ordered something to eat: hors d'oeuvres, cheese, coffee. A Frenchman sat across from us, sorrowfully contemplating a glass of red wine. Once I thought I caught his glance lingering speculatively upon us. When we rose to leave, he was still lost in his private reflections.

We took to the road again, intending to make another attempt to telephone at the next town. We had gone perhaps five miles when I suddenly remembered the notes I had scribbled in the inn at Evreux.

I reached into my coat pocket. They were not there. I searched through my handbag. "Lost something?" Perry asked languidly. He watched with amusement as I emptied the contents of the bag on the lap robe. "The notes," I said. "The notes for my talk with the King. I must have left them in the booth."

For once Perry's *savoir-faire* deserted him. "It would be unkind of me to say how like a woman," he said, "but, Wallis, I'm going to say it anyway. Now we are in a hole. If we go back you're almost

---

* I included the name of this sagacious and experienced religious leader at Perry Brownlow's suggestion. The Aga had been a close and admired friend of George V, who often consulted him privately on political matters.

certain to be recognized this time. Yet if we leave those notes—if they should be found and given to the press—well, I don't have to tell you how Fleet Street will deal with them."

In the end we decided not to go back after the notes. The chances were that if they were noticed the paper would probably be tossed aside as meaningless jottings, and even if they were to be picked up by a reporter, he would be unable to make sense of it, or be sure that it was my handwriting. The episode of the lost notes, as David has recorded in his book, had an interesting aftermath. They were not lost. The *hôtelier* found them after I left, and being a chivalrous man, kept them to himself. Some years later, the British author, Sir Harold Nicolson, happened to stop at the same hotel. Knowing him to be a distinguished man of letters, the *hôtelier* showed him the scrap of paper, which had been carefully put away in an envelope, and insisted that he take it. Sir Harold, whom I had met at Sybil Colefax's, generously returned the paper to me.

Not far from Evreux Ladbrook somehow took the wrong road. Perry suddenly discovered, from the road signs, that we were headed toward Deauville, back to the coast. By the time the car was turned around we had lost twelve miles. Now we headed for Orléans, on the main road south. It was nearly dusk when we reached there, and I was disturbed over what moves David might meanwhile be making. Fearful of attracting attention, we hurried off into a side street, stopping at one *brasserie* after another in search of a telephone booth. None was to be found, and with considerable apprehension I decided to risk entering a small hotel, the name of which I have forgotten, and telephoning from there. It had a tiny lobby, barely wide enough to turn around in. Perry asked the concierge where the telephone was. He pointed to an ancient instrument on the counter. Perry shook his head.

"Let's go to the Police Station," he said wearily. "Maybe I have enough influence to persuade the local authorities to let you use their telephone in privacy." But I did not want to do that. Before I had left the Fort, David had said that he could not with propriety ask the French Government to assist me, and I was therefore determined not to ask for official favors, however small.

For an hour I tried to get through to Buckingham Palace, but the circuits were impossible. I might just as well have been shouting into a bottomless well. All the while the concierge sat at my elbow, fussing over his keys and his accounts. I finally gave up and, depressed in spirit and physically exhausted, returned with Perry to the car, to resume the journey south.

The others, too, were tired, particularly Ladbrook. Perry suggested we stop for dinner at Blois, in the valley of the Loire, a little further on. It was past seven o'clock and very dark and snowy when we finally reached there and went to the Hôtel de France et de Guise. We decided that, in view of the bad weather, the only thing to do was to stop there for the night. While I waited in the car, Perry arranged for accommodations. As we relaxed in the sitting room, Perry remarked, with unexpected cheerfulness, that as a special mark of the *patron's* esteem, we had been given the room in which the Duc de Guise, a leader of the Catholic nobility in the sixteenth-century political and religious intrigues that had rent France, had slept the night before he was murdered—"And we're sitting in it now."

Just before I went to bed, Perry returned from reconnoitering the lobby with dismaying news: more than twenty reporters, photographers, and newsreel cameramen were encamped in the lobby, stretched out on sofas, tables, and chairs. To throw them off the track, he had told Evans, loudly enough to be surely overheard, that our party would be off at nine o'clock in the morning. "Now, Wallis," he said, wearily, "that means we've got to be out of here well before dawn." He had bribed the porter with 10,000 francs to bring us coffee at 3:00 A.M. and to guide us out through the kitchen, without alerting the reporters. Next morning at that hour we tiptoed down the backstairs, and, without the reporters' being aroused, successfully made our way to the Buick. In front of it a reporter had shrewdly parked and locked his car. Ladbrook was equal to the emergency; using full power and with great skill he inched the other car out of the way with so little noise that even then the overconfident reporters did not wake up.

It was still snowing and sleeting, and the roads were treacherous. Four hours later we reached Moulins, where we breakfasted. Before we started out again, Perry sent two telegrams. One was to the Rogerses, saying that we expected to arrive that night. The other, as I later learned, was in code to Walter Monckton in London for Lord Beaverbrook. In this message Perry expressed his confidence that the crisis would be solved if the King could be persuaded to drop all thought of marriage until at least a year after the Coronation.

As I try to retrace in my mind's eye the details of that December ride with Perry Brownlow, the feeling of desperation that was my invisible and relentless companion during the entire trip is not difficult to recapture. On the whole, it was for both of us an agonizing experience; yet it was not lacking in its moments of unconscious humor.

A former Grenadier Guardsman who had sensibly observed that a reasonable provision for personal comfort was not necessarily inconsistent with the discharge of duty, Perry had equipped himself for the long ride with a warm fur-lined coat with an astrakhan collar. While he and I were debating whether to make one more attempt to reach the King, I became aware of a powerful odor of what was unmistakably Scotch whisky. "Perry," I exclaimed, "what is this smell of whisky in the car?"

Perry's face fell, and he clutched at his pocket. "You're quite right, Wallis," he replied. "Excellent whisky—St. James's from the King's cellar. And now," he moaned, "only the aroma remains. I've suffered a major disaster."

With the idea of fending off the chill of the road, he had slipped a flask David had given him into his pocket before starting out that morning. A bump in the road had jolted him against the side of the car, breaking the bottle without his realizing it. Perry began to pick the fragments of broken glass out of his pocket. Before he had finished, the liquor had seeped through the coat, into his suit, and down into the upholstery. The odor was overpowering. In what was reputed to be a hilarious account of this episode, which Perry subsequently devised for the entertainment of our mutual friends in London, I am supposed to have been so overcome by the fumes as to have ordered Perry to rid himself of the offending coat and to stow it in the luggage compartment, forcing him to finish the journey bundled up in the lap robe. All I really did was to suggest mildly to Perry that he open the window on his side of the car until the fumes had cleared. Thereafter, more than once, I observed Perry morosely sniffing his coat.

We drove at a fast clip down Route Nationale No. 7 into the valley of the Rhone. On the outskirts of Lyon, Ladbrook became momentarily lost, and, at Perry's direction, pulled up at a corner to inquire of some pedestrians the way back to the main road. A man politely volunteered the necessary information. Standing beside him was another man who peered idly into the car. His eyes fell upon me. Suddenly his face was convulsed with emotion—it was like watching a scene in a movie. He uttered a shrill cry, *"Voilà la dame!"* and I realized in consternation that he was pointing directly at me. From the others near him came a sound that might have been a gasp of surprise. Ladbrook drove on.

"Voilà la dame!"—for a long time afterward that curious cry was

to reverberate in my memory. This, I reflected bitterly, was what I had finally been brought to—no longer Wallis Simpson, no longer just another woman, but *the* woman. I was marked.

I thought we should never get through Lyon. Perhaps it was a trick of the imagination, but I would almost swear that the man's piercing cry, echoing through the streets, was picked up and relayed ahead of us, stopping people along the way, causing them to turn and stare at the Buick, which was hedged in by traffic. Worse still, there was a hubbub of horns behind and around us. Several cars whirled up alongside, dangerously close, and faces peered intently into ours. Perry nodded glumly. It was the press, which had again caught up with us.

There was no shaking off the pursuit now, and for an hour we drove in the company of our unwanted escorts, a long line of cars moving almost bumper to bumper at breakneck speed. Every now and then one of the pursuers would roar past for a closer look at the quarry.

Directly on our route, and only a short distance ahead, was the town of Vienne, famous, among other things, for the Restaurant de la Pyramide, which has one of the finest cuisines in the world. From my previous travels in this region I had come to know its proprietors, M. and Mme Point, upon whose discretion and solicitude I was sure I could count. We arrived there, finally, about three o'clock in the afternoon, our pursuers breathing down our necks. They followed Perry and me inside but kept their distance. Nobody tried to force me into giving an interview. But there was no mistaking the look of triumph on the faces of the reporters as they trooped into the building. They had run me down and did not propose to let me get away again.

Mme Point took me up to her own room. I was desperately tired. She asked if I had had lunch. I told her that I had not eaten all day and would be grateful for something simple, an omelette. While waiting, I finally succeeded in reaching David on the telephone. The connection this time was almost intelligible. I repeated the gist of the message I had tried to get through to him from Evreux. David was reassuring but noncommittal. So that our party would not be bothered, Mme Point insisted on serving our lunch in her private banqueting hall, a room large enough to seat at least forty. In this setting of lonely grandeur Perry and I lunched together at the far end of the room, while Evans ate alone at the other end, with his eyes trained on the door.

It was Mme Point who came forward with a brilliant scheme for rescuing us from our pursuers. The press was also hungry. They had ordered en masse a meal that must have made formidable inroads upon their employers' bank accounts. Although otherwise the essence of modesty, the proprietress had sufficient confidence in the excellence of her husband's cuisine to be certain that the meal in preparation would engross their exclusive attention for several hours. "Meanwhile, Madame," she said, "there is a back stairway leading down to the kitchen, and on one side of it, easily reached from the top of a table, is a not-too-small window from which one might drop, without real difficulty, into a narrow alley not likely to be known to these strangers. If Madame will give the necessary instructions to her chauffeur, Monsieur Point will undertake to guide the motor unobtrusively into the alley; and if Madame herself is not opposed to a course which, while perhaps lacking in dignity, nevertheless will—"

"Madame Point," I interrupted, "I'm ready to try anything. And I am sure I can also speak for Lord Brownlow."

And it was in this manner that I made my escape from La Pyramide, squeezing myself through a tiny window above the sink, while Mme Point and Perry Brownlow braced a kitchen table beneath my feet, and M. Point and Evans, disposed like acrobats outside in the alley, maneuvered to catch me as I slid down. It was a feat that would, I am sure, have brought a nod of approval from Miss Charlotte Noland, my girlhood gym instructor of Arundell days. And Perry Brownlow, after he had wriggled his way through the window in his turn, remarked dryly, "Too bad Stanley Baldwin missed that little scene."

In any case, the ruse worked. As we entered the car, there came to us faintly from the restaurant the sounds of the press bloodhounds enjoying their fine luncheon.

Through the rest of the afternoon, in sleet and rain, over twisting roads, Perry took turns driving with Ladbrook. The day had wearied us all; talk ceased; even the vigilant Evans dozed in his seat as the car sped down the all but deserted highways, past the shuttered towns. I felt most frightfully alone. It seemed that I had been gone from the Fort not for two days but a lifetime. All that had happened to me there now took on an unreal and remote aspect.

Because of the storm, the roundabout route, and the time lost in Vienne, we were still three hours from Cannes, and I was afraid that the Rogerses, thinking we must have stopped on the road for the night, might be about to go to bed. It was then about eleven o'clock; we were approaching a town called Brignoles, and Perry decided we should telephone Herman. But Brignoles was shuttered for the night as tightly as only a French provincial town can be. The post office, where public calls are ordinarily made, was pitch dark. Perry banged with his fists on the big front door. Suddenly, shutters flew open, at least four heads popped out of windows, and there was directed at Perry a fusillade of Gallic indignation that could have started the cobblestones from the street. Perry finally broke through the barrage and made known his desire to use the telephone. An elderly gentleman with fierce mustachios bellowed back that the telephone was in plain sight in a box on the wall a short distance down the street. He recommended that Perry use it, if, on further thought, he could find any rational justification for telephoning respectable people at such an outlandish hour.

Perry made his way to the box while Ladbrook and I followed slowly in the car. Anyone who has ever tried to make a long-distance call from a street telephone in a small French town in the middle of the night will sympathize with the almost impossible task that Perry had so lightly undertaken. His French was rough and ready, and his difficulty in making himself understood, combined with the agitation spread throughout the system by the unseasonable call, led to what even at the time struck me as one of the funniest scenes I have ever witnessed. Perry went slowly but magnificently mad. Standing in the headlights, brandishing the receiver, he cursed the French communications system in general, and its Brignoles representatives in particular, all the while pounding his fist against the side of the blue box in which the instrument was housed. As an example of a man running amuck while rooted in one place, it was a masterpiece. Eventually, through dogged British perseverance, Perry muddled through to Herman. He had been expecting us and would wait up. He warned that the reporters were already encamped around the villa, but he had sent for the French police to clear a way for us through the gates, which would be left open.

It was about two-thirty in the morning of December 6, as we mounted the steep, winding road behind Cannes to Lou Viei. The story has been published that as the car shot through the gates I was crouched on the floor, with a rug over my head. This is correct. Perry had spotted a crowd at the entrance and had warned me to get out of sight. I slid off the seat, pulling the lap robe over me. Herman and Katherine were at the door. They must have been taken aback to see me emerge disheveled from under my camouflage. Katherine put her arms about me and led me inside where a fire was blazing in the living room. I was back among friends.

CHAPTER XXV

I Attempt to Give Up the King

FOR DAYS SEVERAL HUNDRED REPORTERS AND PHOTOGRAPHERS WERE deployed around the house like a besieging army. The Rogerses were followed wherever they went; inquisitive telephone operators, in the pay of the reporters, listened in on their telephone conversations; and attempts were made to bribe their servants. The eavesdropping on the telephone became so bad that Perry had to protest to the Préfet of the Department of the Alpes Maritimes, and in consequence the French Foreign Office in Paris sent down two of its own operators to the Cannes exchange to handle telephone traffic with the villa. Katherine and Herman bore the burden they incurred from my presence as their guest with unfailing kindness. I have reason to be grateful to them as perhaps to no one else on earth, with the exception of Aunt Bessie.

Katherine gave up her bedroom to Inspector Evans, and Herman took the bedroom next to mine. I was thus well guarded against possible interlopers. A place was made for Ladbrook in the servants' quarters. It was quite a load suddenly to put upon a small household, the more so as Lou Viei now became, so far as the press was concerned, the principal focus of its attention.

The villa was a twelfth-century monastery upon which Katherine and Herman had lavished loving care and imagination. It is situated on a stony ledge slightly below the crest of a hill. Photographers equipped with long-range lenses had stationed themselves on the higher ground, and some were even perched in the trees. If I wished to preserve my privacy, Katherine warned, when she joined me in my room for Sunday breakfast, I had better be careful to stay away even from an open window. "The French police want to be helpful, and

Herman will do his best," she added, "but for a while, at least, you had better regard yourself as a prisoner." In seeking to escape from one trap I had run blindly into another. Worse still, I was coming to realize that the crisis enfolding David was at the explosion point.

That day there were a number of telephone calls from David at the Fort. Necessarily our talks were guarded and we resorted—I suspect sometimes to the compounding of our mutual misunderstanding—to our code. At first David seemed more optimistic, more sure of regaining control of the situation. Mr. Baldwin had consented to his consulting Winston Churchill, and the two had dined together at the Fort Friday evening. Mr. Churchill and Lord Beaverbrook were working in close harmony.

David meant to be reassuring. He tried to make me understand that the issue was now in the hands of the Cabinet, and in that sense the outcome was no longer entirely under his control. Much would depend upon how Mr. Churchill and Lord Beaverbrook were able to present the constitutional argument—the former in the House of Commons and the latter in the press. All this, David suggested, provided some grounds for hope. But, as I tried to grasp the real meaning of David's words through the double-talk of the code, a different conclusion formed in my own mind. If Lord Beaverbrook and Mr. Churchill were still fighting, then it meant only one thing: they must think that they could prevail upon the King to withdraw the marriage proposal, at least temporarily, and to be crowned as scheduled in May, and then, with Mr. Baldwin outmaneuvered and the King secure on his Throne, the question of the marriage could be raised later if he still persisted in the idea. There was an anguish in his voice that ambiguities of language could not conceal.

"David," I pleaded, abandoning the code, "please listen to your friends."

"I will," he promised somewhat unconvincingly.

At that moment I had the sensation of talking to a stranger. "You must listen," I went on. "Nothing will be lost, nothing will be changed, by your waiting."

His voice was barely audible as he said, "You can trust me. However, I must deal with this situation in my own way."

He had turned remote and unreachable. His inner defenses had gone up in a manner that I had observed in other, less fateful circumstances.

A sense of helplessness of unimaginable scope came over me. The French telephone system thwarted me; everything that I wanted to say, that I had to say, and everything that David was trying to tell me was lost or distorted into a howl of subhuman squeaks and squawks. I now realized how sound had been Perry's advice in urging me to go to Belton; there David and I could at least have made ourselves understood to each other. I had the sensation of sinking in quicksand, and the futility of my situation was made all the more excruciating by the reports that Perry was receiving from London and the correspondents hovering around Lou Viei. Despite David's reassurances, it was becoming tragically clear that the balance was tipping toward abdication. Perry was in despair. As gently as he could, he conveyed to me his realization of how deep was the breach that was opening up between the King and his subjects, both in the United Kingdom and in the Dominions. "As I see it now," he said, "there is only one possible way of stopping this dreadful drift. It is for you to renounce the King."

Ever since that awful last day at the Fort much the same idea had been taking shape in my mind: I must wrench myself entirely out of David's life. Since he would not give me up, I would have to give him up and in a way that would leave him no choice but to accept this decision. However I put the matter, he would be hurt. It would be difficult, if not impossible, to make him understand. But I had no alternative. Apart from the moral considerations affecting his Kingly position, my own self-respect was at stake.

Perry was convinced that only a strong and unequivocal public statement of this intention would stave off the abdication. My withdrawal would confront the King with a blank wall. But I was not altogether persuaded by Perry's reasoning. More than a public disavowal on my part would be needed to restrain David. He would at once suspect that my course was dictated by exhaustion and outside pressures. He would refuse to believe that I would voluntarily desert him. I would have to count on David's solicitude for me. No good would be served by my trying to appeal to his sense of duty. He would tell me, as on countless occasions before, that he knew where his duty lay; but that duty was a complex and subtle compulsion, presenting many different paths; and that a man, in his choice of paths, must differentiate between the mere form of duty and its inner substance. There would be no deflecting him on that score. My only hope was to make him realize that the price of marriage would not be just the forfeiture of the Throne. The final cost would include as well the destruction of my reputation. If I left undone anything within my power to prevent his abdicating, I knew I could never again look into the mirror of my conscience.

Perry and Herman helped me prepare a statement to be issued to the press. It was purposely short:

> Mrs. Simpson throughout the last few weeks has invariably wished to avoid any action or proposal which would hurt or damage His Majesty or the Throne.
>
> Today her attitude is unchanged, and she is willing, if such action would solve the problem, to withdraw forthwith from a situation that has been rendered both unhappy and untenable.

Perry viewed the statement with mixed feelings. He doubted that the language was sufficiently strong. He wanted a forthright declaration that I had no thought of marrying the King. From my knowledge of David's nature, I shrank from dealing him so cruel a blow—he had already been through about as much as a human being could be expected to endure.

So Monday afternoon, December 7, I telephoned David at the Fort to tell him of my decision and to read him the statement. At first he was unbelieving, then hurt and angry. The connection, as always, was noisy and uncertain. He asked if I had the statement ready. I said yes. He inquired whether Perry and Herman had seen it. I replied that they had helped me with it. He then asked me to read it to him. This I did. After I finished there was a long silence. I thought that David in his anger had hung up. Then he said slowly, "Go ahead, if you wish; it won't make any difference."

That evening, at seven o'clock, Perry gave the statement to the press. On his return to Lou Viei, he was heartened; the reaction of many of the correspondents was that my statement would end the crisis. A terrible weight lifted from my mind. That night, for the first time since leaving the Fort five days before, I slept soundly.

I awakened the next morning, refreshed and hopeful, only to be confronted before long by a new complication. In the afternoon there was an agitated telephone call from David. The solicitor who had handled my divorce, Mr. Goddard, was already en route to the south of France in Mr. Baldwin's official airplane and was due to arrive that evening. "I don't know what his purpose is," David warned. "All I know is that Baldwin is behind it. Don't be influenced by anything Goddard says. Better still, do not see him at all."

Now I was completely at sea. What could my own solicitor and the Prime Minister possibly be up to? The only explanation I could think of for the injection of my lawyer into the situation at this hour was that he must be carrying a message of some kind to me from Mr. Baldwin. But what message could Mr. Baldwin want to send me? I couldn't even guess. This was the most fantastic development of a fantastic week.

I waited in confusion and anxiety. The day wore on with no sign of Mr. Goddard. That evening, after dinner, I sat with Perry and Herman, discussing the latest ominous news that Perry had received from London and what more I might still do. In the midst of our talk, David telephoned again to assure me that no irrevocable step had been taken. But I was to learn all too soon that in his gallant way he was determined to spare me any pain, any responsibility, for the grave decision that he had all but made. Perry, however, was not convinced. From his own sources he had gained a strong feeling that not only had the King set in motion the machinery of abdication but also that the Government was prepared to let him go.

Our discussions really got nowhere. About two-thirty Wednesday morning, just as we were about to go to bed, Inspector Evans brought to Perry a note signed by four British correspondents. It was a bombshell:

> Mr. Goddard, the well-known lawyer who acts for Mrs. Simpson, has arrived at Marseilles by special plane. He brought with him Dr. Kirkwood, the well-known gynecologist, and his anaesthetist.

Standing impassively in the drawing room, Evans added that the reporters at the gate were anxious "for any comment we might care to make."

I was shocked to the core of my being. Gynecologist? Anesthetist? Had the Prime Minister and my solicitor taken leave of their senses? Somebody had obviously gone mad.

Perry went livid with rage, exclaiming, "Herman and I have done everything in our power to protect your dignity, your good name and peace of mind, and the prestige of the King. This is the last straw." Whirling on his heel, and saying, "Wallis, I'll deal with this," he rushed out of the villa. Confronting the reporters, he hotly denied the report and all its imputations, improvising on the spur of the moment a story that Mr. Goddard was coming to take up matters connected with the disposition of the lease on my house in London.

Mr. Goddard turned up shortly after breakfast time Wednesday, having motored during the night from Marseilles to Cannes. When he unsuspectingly telephoned the villa to ask for an appointment to see me, Perry let him have it. When Mr. Goddard finally recovered from the blast and realized its cause, the explanation he gave added the final touch of absurdity to this entire episode. Mr. Goddard had a weak heart. The alleged gynecologist was his personal physician, who had insisted on being with him on so long a flight, and the alleged anesthetist was actually one of his law clerks. Still wary, Perry finally consented to let him come to the villa, but only under rigorous conditions: first, he was to come alone; second, he was not to carry any brief case or anything resembling a physician's bag; and third, he was to have his taxi stop a full hundred yards from the Rogerses' gate and walk openly through the ranks of the waiting press. "That," said Perry, as he finished, "should dispose of all this nonsense."

It was a chastened Mr. Goddard who was ushered into the drawing room not long afterward. After apologizing for the embarrassment he had in all innocence caused me, he got down to the reason for his visit. It was to urge me to withdraw the divorce action, which would not become absolute for another five months. If I could persuade myself to do this, he explained, all possibility of the King's marriage would fall to the ground and the crisis would thus be resolved. At the same time he pointed out that such an action—"rescission," I believe, was the term he used—would not be simple and would take several weeks to effect. Furthermore, any reinstatement of my petition in the future would be complicated and "possibly somewhat untidy."

"Mr. Goddard," I said, "any question of inconvenience is now irrelevant. I will do anything within my power to keep the King on the Throne."

"That is what I was sure you would say, and I so informed Mr. Baldwin." The Englishman in Mr. Goddard had triumphed over the solicitor; his expression was that of a man conscious of playing a crucial and successful role in a historical situation.

"Do you mind," I asked him, "if I call in Lord Brownlow, the King's friend, who is with me, and ask his advice?"

"Not at all," answered the solicitor. "This is a most serious step, and you should reflect on it."

Perry listened gravely while I explained what Mr. Goddard had advised me to do. Perry was dubious whether such a complicated action could be initiated in time to affect the King's decision, and convinced that, in the event it failed of its purpose, it would present both the King and me with a vista of endless frustration. "If the King does abdicate," he concluded, "his object, as we all know, will be marriage; and for you to scrap your divorce will produce a hopeless anticlimax and an all-round tragedy."

I knew Perry spoke from the heart, but in spite of the logic of his argument, I felt that I had to try even this uncertain expedient. I left the room and put a call through to the Fort. David was not immediately available. A little later, around noon, he called back. I told him that Mr. Goddard was with me and that he and I had agreed to institute proceedings to withdraw my divorce petition. There was a long silence. Then with emotion David answered that matters had already gone much further than I realized and that he would ask George Allen to speak to me.

I now repeated to Mr. Allen what I had told David. In his crisp, lucid way Mr. Allen advised me not to withdraw my petition. The King, he went on, had made up his mind to abdicate immediately and in fact was already in the process of doing so.

I still could not believe it. When I returned to the room and told Mr. Goddard of the conversation, he seemed to sag. "If this is indeed so," he said, "there is nothing more I can do. However, to be certain I shall call Allen before leaving Cannes."

Hardly had the visitor taken his departure than there was an urgent call from Esmond Harmsworth, who was at his mother's villa near Monte Carlo. He said he had received important news from London and it was vital that we confer. Because his mother was ill, he could not come to Cannes and asked if we would go to him instead.

Perry and I started out in the car. It was the first time I had been outside the villa since my arrival. Esmond had strange news. He was convinced that a solution was in the making—one involving, among other things, the creation of a Council of State and the King's withdrawal abroad until the crisis simmered down. Knowing what we did, Perry and I found this almost impossible to believe.

On the drive back to Cannes, Perry talked to me gently but with a directness he had never before employed. "The hour is very late," he said solemnly, "and the mills of the gods are grinding fast. You must now begin to think of the position in which you will find yourself if the King does abdicate." I who had sought no place in history would now be assured of one—an appalling one, carved out by blind prejudice.

I knew he was not exaggerating the picture. This would indeed be my fate. I cried, "What would you do in my place?"

Perry thought a moment. "If I were you," he answered, "I'd leave Europe at once. There's just a chance that would still save the situation. And if you should decide to leave, I'm ready to go with you."

At the end of my tether, my mind exhausted, my every fiber crying for an end to the intolerable strain, I told Perry that I was ready to leave that very afternoon, if he could make the arrangements.

"Good," said Perry. "I'll start working on it as soon as we reach Lou Viei." It was already in his mind that our best chance of catching an imminent sailing was from Genoa.

My earlier attempt at renunciation having failed of its purpose, something more summary, more drastic was required to check David from taking the final step. I would have to withdraw from his furthermost reach. The gulf between us would then be real, and I could count upon David's pride to restrain him from a humiliating pursuit, with the world watching. I dreaded the prospect of trying to lose myself among strangers and was momentarily tempted to return to the United States. But having had some experience with the resourcefulness of the American press, I put aside the idea. China was the only other distant country that I knew, and it seemed the best choice. Some of my friends of Peking days were still there. They would take me in, and at that distance "the Mrs. Simpson" would soon be forgotten.

As soon as we were back at Lou Viei, Perry sent Evans into the town to engage a private railway car to take us to Genoa. With matters thus in motion, Perry and I sat down with Herman to prepare a final statement for the press, telling of my complete and total withdrawal and of my departure for distant parts. (Only recently Perry told me that he still has the draft of the statement.)

Then came the dreadful ordeal of breaking the news to David, of burying my love forever. When he came on the line, having carefully rehearsed exactly what I would say, I outlined my plan and the reasons why. For once he cut me short. "I can't seem to make you understand the position," he said. "It's all over. The Instrument of Abdication is already prepared. If I can't make you understand, maybe George Allen can. Wait." A minute or two passed. Then David's voice was back on the line. "Listen to what George has just written down for me to read to you."

This is what he read: "The only conditions on which I can stay here are if I renounce you for all time." Waiting a moment for the import of the statement to sink in, he added, "And this, of course,

[268]

I will not do. The Cabinet has met twice today, and I have given them my final word. I will be gone from England within forty-eight hours. Now, I want you to listen to George."

In measured tones George Allen repeated the words he had written for the King.

I was crying when the conversation ended. I was conscious only of having failed tragically. Katherine tried to comfort me. "You have done everything," she said, "that could be expected of a woman in this situation. No one will blame you." I could not seem to grasp the meaning of what David had done. I found myself whispering as to another self that nothing so incredible, so monstrous, could possibly have happened.

Now silence descended upon the Villa Lou Viei. We were no longer part of the drama. Far away in England events ground to their remorseless conclusion. Thursday afternoon, the tenth, about dusk, Perry read to me a telephoned summary of Mr. Baldwin's statement in the Commons announcing the King's Abdication. Fortunately only Perry was in the house at that moment to witness my flood of tears.

I was shocked to learn from David the next afternoon that he was planning to take up temporary residence in a hotel in Switzerland. It filled me with fury that the British Government could be so indifferent to his new vulnerability, so ungrateful for his splendid services, as to fail to provide him with the privacy and protection he would desperately need in the first months of readjustment. Here, at least, I was able to help him. Friends of ours, Baron and Baroness Eugène de Rothschild, had a castle, Schloss Enzesfeld, near Vienna. I telephoned to ask if they would invite David to visit them. They consented instantly and graciously.

I asked Herman to telephone David. His personal operator, William Bateman, at the Palace reported that he was dining with his family at Royal Lodge. Herman finally got the message to Walter Monckton, who promised to relay it.

That night I drained the dregs of the cup of my failure and defeat. It was the day of the Abdication. As the moment approached for David to make his farewell broadcast, everyone in Lou Viei, including the domestic staff, gathered around the radio in the sitting room. David's voice came out of the loud-speaker calmly, movingly. I was lying on the sofa with my hands over my eyes, trying to hide my tears. After he finished, the others quietly went away and left me alone. I lay there a long time before I could control myself enough to walk through the house and go upstairs to my room.

❧ CHAPTER XXVI ❧

The Aftermath

A DAY OR SO LATER PERRY BROWNLOW LEFT FOR ENZESFELD, TO join David. This was a characteristically thoughtful act of Perry's. Realizing that David would be distraught and lonely, he felt that the appearance of an old friend might cheer him up. I was loath to see Perry go. He had been a wise and sympathetic friend. As he was leaving, he said to me, "I shall tell them in London how you tried to stop this tragedy. They may not believe me—they may not want to believe me—but I was witness. I wish, for your sake, let alone my country's, that you had succeeded. You, no less than the King, have paid heavily for happiness. With all my heart I hope it comes to you."

Now, with David in Austria and his brother on the Throne, the excitement quieted down. The army of reporters and photographers around Lou Viei drifted away, except for a handful of rear guards. The siege was lifted. Aunt Bessie came from London, bringing my clothes and my maid, Mary Burke. Aunt Bessie stayed at the Carlton Hotel in Cannes. Appreciating the strain that I was imposing upon the Rogerses' household, I wanted to join her there, but Katherine and Herman would not hear of my leaving them. "You would have no privacy in a hotel," Herman advised. "Here, at least, we can protect you."

Herman never told me until many years later that he feared a lunatic might attempt to kill me. Directly upon my arrival at Cannes there followed a fantastic volume of mail, a great deal of it from strangers, much of it anonymous and threatening in tone. I had asked Herman and Perry to go through it for me and pick out those letters that deserved an answer. One series of letters that came in after Perry had left worried Herman. An anonymous writer, who identified himself only as an Australian, swore that he was on his way to France to kill me. He sent half a dozen such letters, spaced a day or so apart, all postmarked London, but from different districts. What troubled Herman was that the writer was patently no ordinary crank; the handwriting and choice of language identified him as being of some education. Herman turned the letters over to Inspector Evans, who dispatched them to Scotland Yard for investigation. If the writer was ever tracked down, I was not told. But fear that this madman or someone else of the same warped mentality might actually turn up in Cannes induced Herman to keep a loaded pistol close at hand at night.

Even if I was spared the knowledge of this particular series of letters, I did not lack examples of the fury and hatred that the human race is capable of mustering in a flash. Of all the strange and dismaying things connected with the coupling of my name with the King's, nothing shook me so much or hurt me more than the discovery of the scorn, even hatred, that many felt for me. I do not wish to suggest that no friendly voices were raised in my behalf. Many were. From strangers all over the world, and even from Britain, came warming letters of sympathy. But these were in the minority. The most abusive, oddly enough, came from Canadians, from English people residing in the United States, and from Americans of British birth or connections.

During my first weeks at Cannes I must have read several thousand letters. With my breakfast would come two or three trays heaped high with the day's delivery. It is no exaggeration to say that my world went to pieces every morning on a tray. Everything that I stood for was condemned. The presumption was that I had in some way gained an ascendancy over a beloved King. The vocabulary of vilification and abuse is a good deal more extensive than I had until then supposed; there can be few expletives applicable to my sex that were missing from my morning tray.

Let me make myself clear: I knew that in view of the enormous uproar of which I was the center, with the whole world seething with controversy and speculation about me, I was bound to be the target for every imaginable attack; and therefore I had tried to steel myself for what was certain to come. Still, the enormity of the hatred I had aroused and the distorted image of me that seemed to be forming in minds everywhere went far beyond anything I had anticipated even in my most depressed moments. Whatever else may have been absent from my make-up, spite and envy certainly were; and I had assumed

[271]

the same of others. But the daily bombardment to which I was subjected at Cannes taught me that my judgment of human nature had been woefully innocent. The human race, or at least that segment given to firing letters at public figures, includes an astonishingly high proportion of jealous, vindictive people, some of whom appear to be actually crazed.

Perhaps naïvely, having little knowledge of governments and journalism, I became obsessed with the notion that, in a manner impossible for me to comprehend, a calculated and organized effort to discredit and destroy me had been set afoot. Otherwise, there was no accounting for the relentless pounding. Herman Rogers, I was afterward to realize, was much more sensible in his judgment of the situation.

"Whether you like it or not," he said to me one day, "the world is discovering you."

"Discovering me?" I exclaimed. "You mean destroying me!"

"Wallis," he said quietly, "you'd better learn to live with these things, because from here on you must expect more rather than less. It's not just that you've become a celebrity; you've become a historical figure, and a controversial one. You are in for a miserable and unhappy life unless you learn to ignore the lies and inventions, and to say to yourself over and over again, I won't let it get me down."

"But it *is* getting me down. It hurts."

Herman went on. "You can't run away. And there's no place left where you can hide. You've got to learn to rise above all this. Put it out of your mind. Much of what is being said concerns a woman who does not exist and never did exist. Perhaps it would be just as well if you stopped reading about her."

Herman was a good philosopher. But despite his schooling in self-discipline, I was a long time attaining an attitude of detachment from criticism. To be accused of things that one has never done; to be judged and condemned on many sides by people ignorant of the controlling circumstances; to have one's supposed character day after day laid bare, dissected and flayed by mischievous and merciless hands —this, I submit, is the most corrosive of human experiences. The natural impulse is to lash back at one's tormentors. But how could one hope to prevail against so many? How could the small, dull facts of a previously respectable anonymity be expected to contend with the monstrous inventions of those who, unwilling to acknowledge the simple human emotion that had persuaded the King to do what he did, now found it necessary to attribute diabolical intentions to the woman he had chosen? In enduring this ordeal, I, who had always been impatient, learned something of the virtue of patience. Yet I am moved to say that I have not observed that the meek have come much closer to inheriting the earth. Nor has my own experience convinced me that presenting the other cheek is the most effective answer to one's detractors. However, I suppose that the real meaning of those ancient admonitions is to take counsel, first of all, of one's inner resources. I survived at Cannes by mastering my own emotions. What is called for is a kind of private arrangement within oneself—an understanding of the heart and mind—that one's life and purposes are essentially good, and that nothing from the outside must be allowed to impair that understanding. Such an internal adjustment came to me in the course of my bitter experience at Lou Viei; I learned that one can live alone.

Perhaps, on second thought, I should modify that judgment. One can never live alone and be said really to live at all. This realization was brought home to me in a most unexpected way. About ten days after David abdicated, while going through the letters on the morning tray, I recognized with incredulity one addressed in a familiar hand. It was from Ernest Simpson, and it said in part, with the gentleness I knew so well:

I did not have the heart to write before. I have felt somewhat stunned and slightly sick over recent events. I am not, however, going into that, but I want to believe—I do believe—that you did everything in your power to prevent the final catastrophe.

My thoughts have been with you throughout your ordeal, and you may rest assured that no one has felt more deeply for you than I have.

For a few pence each day I can keep *au courant* with your doings. . . .

Later there was another:

. . . . And would your life have ever been the same if you had broken it off? I mean could you possibly have settled down in the old life and forgotten the fairyland through which you had passed? My child, I do not think so.

BOOK SIX

IN SEARCH OF A LIFE

CHAPTER XXVII

"I Have Taken You into a Void"

WITH THE PRESS GONE, I WAS NOW ABLE TO WALK IN THE GARDEN without having my every step spied upon. On warm afternoons, Katherine and Herman would take me on a drive into the hills, and we would walk the dogs. Aunt Bessie, unsparing of herself as always, came to see me every day, using her inexhaustible fund of family reminiscences to turn my mind from the bleakness of the present to the fun of the past. Somerset Maugham had me for Christmas at his beautiful villa at Cap Ferrat. A few of my old London friends, including Sybil Colefax, were there. Daisy Fellowes invited me to her villa at Cap Martin, near the Italian frontier.

It was good to be able to move about the world again and to discover that so few doors had been slammed shut. But for a long time my sense of liberty remained precarious. One afternoon I made the mistake of going to Cannes to shop. While making a purchase, I became aware of a commotion outside. A crowd was pressing against the shop window, and other people were hurrying across the street to see the show. Taking pity on me, the manager led me into a back room and eventually managed to have my car brought around unnoticed to a side entrance from which I made my escape.

Thereafter I stayed away from Cannes. In an attempt to divert me during the long winter evenings, Katherine and Herman often had friends for dinner. But I must have been a depressing companion. If one recollection of Lou Viei can be properly said to overshadow all others, it was the experience of a prolonged blankness of the mind and spirit. Just as the sounds and violence of a hurricane can numb one into insensibility, so the storm that had howled around the person of "Mrs. Simpson" had left me spent. For hours, I remained in my room, staring, I suspect, into space. At night sleep would not come.

My personal folk tale had gone disastrously awry. Given the circumstances under which it began, I had never been certain what the ending would be, but I had at least been encouraged to believe that it would be reasonably happy. In my darkest moments at the Fort, I had never visualized anything like this—David by his own choice a virtual outcast from the nation over which he had ruled, and each of us condemned to wait in idleness and frustration on our separate islands of exile until my divorce became absolute in early May.

David had thought that after spending a little time in Austria he might move to France. The Duke of Westminster, an old friend of his, had indeed offered him his hunting lodge in Normandy. But when David broached the idea of his going to France, even with a substantial amount of geography between him and me, his legal advisers were alarmed. Any suspicion of a meeting between us during the period of waiting for my decree to become final could jeopardize it under the existing laws. Even though people in England under the same circumstances could live in the same city without risk, our lawyers insisted that we keep a national frontier between us. Mr. Baldwin had, in fact, reminded David at one of their meetings that under English law anyone could bring to the attention of an official called the King's Proctor any matter that might affect the validity of a divorce. Any such allegation had to be considered and investigated by the King's Proctor, before the decree could be made absolute. Indeed, a formal intervention was actually made, only a day before the Abdication, by an aged solicitor's clerk in London, named Stephenson. Neither David nor I was told of this action at the time, but David's legal advisers and mine had, of course, been put on notice and were worried. They were worried not at all by the possibility of there being any authentic legal basis for challenging the divorce—there could be none—but rather by the possibility that this strange action was symptomatic of a vengeful desire to prevent David's marriage to me as a final reprisal. Unhappily but unprotestingly, we bowed before the sentence of separation. After all that had happened, there could be no doubt of our feelings about each other. Yet, to save the one thing left to us, the thing for which David had given up everything, we would faithfully play our roles in the bitter legal farce until the six months' interval of waiting should run its course.

During these long months there was never an evening that David and I did not talk to each other on the telephone. The fear of possible eavesdroppers imposed a restraint upon our discussions and exchanges of confidences; still, we managed to support each other and to assuage our loneliness, though not without great effort on our part and no little inconvenience to Herman and Katherine.

The Rogerses' telephone was in the hall near the dining room. David's call from Schloss Enzesfeld in Austria usually came through about seven o'clock. The butler would by that hour have laid the table for dinner and withdrawn to leave me in privacy. At the appointed time, I used to go into the dining room to wait, moving the telephone, which had a long cord, to the dining-room table, so that I could prop myself on my elbows and bellow into it. The circuit between Cannes and Austria was, in those days, hardly more than an acknowledgment of the possibilities of long-distance communication. David and I had to shout at each other to make ourselves heard at all. In my excitement I would unconsciously pound the table with my elbows, and this gesture produced a succession of small but lamentable catastrophes. The Rogerses had brought with them from China some very pretty soup spoons with fine coral handles. Unerringly my elbow would come down upon one of these spoons, and there would be a horrible crack as the coral handle snapped. I don't know how many times I had to tell Katherine, "I'm so sorry, I've broken another of your lovely spoons." Katherine finally decided that at the current rate of destruction she would be out of coral spoons long before I should be off their hands, and the butler was sternly instructed not to place the soup spoons on the table until after the call from Austria had been completed.

Those evening telephone calls must have been among the major inconveniences that my presence imposed. The smooth routine of their household was interrupted; the calls came through at a time when the butler should have been in the dining room doing something about dinner. Often, because of trouble on the circuit, the calls were delayed as much as three-quarters of an hour. Worse still, the connections were uncertain, and we would be repeatedly cut off. My command of French, even now more vigorous than elegant, was in those days embarrassingly weak. Unable to cope with the French operators, who had a tendency to fly into a fine frenzy whenever the mechanics of the situation proved intractable, I would have to call to Katherine downstairs in the living room with Herman to come and help me. Katherine would rush up the narrow, winding flight of stairs to the dining room, where, taking command of the situation, she would scream back at the operator in fluent French until David had been brought back on the line.

Even Katherine's patience finally gave out. After one such episode she said to me sternly, "Wallis, this is ridiculous. All you need to know is one French phrase, *Je n'entends pas*—I can't hear. Just keep repeating that and everything will be fine. Here, I'll write it out for you." She printed the phrase in large block letters on a piece of paper and fastened it to the telephone. Thereafter, when David called, I had that marvelous phrase in front of me. If anything went wrong, I would repeat into the mouthpiece, *"Je n'entends pas. Ecoutez, mademoiselle, je n'entends pas."* Invariably it precipitated a torrent of explanation of which I understood scarcely a word. Nevertheless I kept chanting the phrase, as Katherine had instructed, and in due course the connection would be miraculously restored.

Katherine and Herman, who both spoke excellent French, tried to persuade me to take lessons. They thought that studying the language would help to divert me. But, though I tried in desultory fashion, I had no better luck than with Chinese in Peking; my mind was too preoccupied with other things.

Of the two of us, it was David who had by far the worse time, although in his reticence he rigidly held in his grief. His relations with his brothers, once so intimately revolving around the bright sun of his personality, turned increasingly formal. His mother continued to write to him, and he to her; the affection between them remained to the end; but their relationship had subtly changed. There is something steely and inhuman in the monarchical principle. No form of discipline can be more repressive of the simpler instincts of the heart than that of a monarchy in defense of its institutional self. It is and always has been: "The King is dead. Long live the King!" By watching what happened to David during the first months after he left England I came to appreciate the almost absolute transfer of emotion implied by that phrase—not just in a national sense, but also within the Royal Family itself. A light goes out; another flares in the darkness. Even Queen Mary, for all her love of her eldest son, could not make room in her heart for something that had altered the natural order of monarchy. David had put aside what he had been born to fulfill until he died; now in his mother's eyes he had become something different and apart. Her love remained; but his place at the hearth had gone, along with his place on the Throne. As for me, I simply did not exist. And on the very eve of my marriage the King, his brother, would, by an unexpected exercise of his historical prerogative as the Fountain of Honour, exclude me as a member of the family.

In various pointed ways, David, alone in Austria, was made to realize that a velvet and ermine curtain was going down between him and his past. To be sure, he could not reasonably have expected to save much of what had been; in his farewell broadcast to the British people he had announced his intention of withdrawing from public life, and he had readily assured his brother that there would never be conflict between them. David stood ready to serve the new monarch as devotedly as any other British subject. Above everything else David was, and remains, a Britisher; his hope was to return one day with me to Britain and to make a new home, and to help his brother in any way he could. Little by little it was made evident that he could never resume his place in the family circle.

No doubt there was a good reason for all this. What is finished is done; and the internal laws of the British monarchy are of iron. But it was a terrible thing to watch. David had taken leave of his family in sorrow but in a hopeful spirit, leaving many matters to be composed in what he assumed would be an equally cordial and compassionate atmosphere. Now he said to me, "The drawbridges are going up behind me. I have taken you into a void."

Spring comes early to the Côte d'Azur. The long night of waiting slowly lifted; my aunt returned to the United States to attend to her own neglected affairs. Soon the mimosa spread its lovely yellow haze over the hills behind Cannes; and by early March I was increasingly occupied with the preparations for my wedding.

David and I decided to be married in France—partly because both of us knew and liked the country, and partly because the French, being a highly civilized people with a fastidious regard for privacy, could be relied upon to accord us a greater measure of that luxury than we were likely to find elsewhere. The thing we feared most was that the press, descending once again in a locust swarm, would turn the occasion into a roadside carnival. So we needed a place that could not be overrun by intruders. And David insisted on being married in a place of charm and beauty.

With David determined that the ceremony should be performed as soon as legally possible, the job of finding the right place fell to me. Various friends, surmising our difficulties, offered their houses. My choice was a handsome white villa, called La Cröe, at Cap d'Antibes, only five miles or so from Cannes. It was owned by a retired British newspaper executive, Sir Pomeroy Burton, who was willing to rent it to us. Herman Rogers received another offer. He was slightly acquainted with a French industrialist named Charles Bedaux, who had a country place, the Château de Candé, near Tours. He and Katherine had seen it and judged it to be an ideal setting—not too large, remote enough to discourage sight-seers, well protected by a wooded park, and in a storybook setting. At that time I had never met the ill-starred Charles Bedaux or, for that matter, ever heard of him; but he had written to Herman that he had followed the Abdication with intense interest, was deeply sympathetic with David's position and mine, and would like to offer us his château for our marriage. Herman wrote to his brother Edmund, a prominent New York banker, to ask whether, if the Château de Candé should be considered for the marriage, there was anything in its owner's background that might render it inappropriate. His brother replied that to the best of his knowledge Charles Bedaux enjoyed a good reputation in the business world and, so far as he was able to determine, his private life was blameless.

I passed on the various suggestions to David, who decided that the choice lay between La Cröe on the Côte d'Azur and the Château de Candé. David then asked his brother for his reactions. The King was not enthusiastic about our being married on the Riviera, because of its reputation as a playground, and he favored the old château in the center of France as the more dignified setting. That was how Candé came to be chosen. After the King had expressed his views, Herman Rogers wrote Charles Bedaux that his offer was being accepted, pointing out at the same time that the selection was bound to give rise to widespread publicity and that, therefore, if Mr. Bedaux had any skeletons concealed in his cupboard, he would be well advised to measure the consequences—in his own interest as well as in the interest of the Duke of Windsor and Mrs. Simpson. The answer must have been reassuring, for Herman informed me that Candé was at our disposal.

Early in March Katherine, Herman, and I left for Candé, at six o'clock one morning. In another car following behind us were two French detectives of the Sûreté, whom the French Government had thoughtfully assigned to protect me (Inspector Evans had long before returned to Britain), as well as Katherine's personal maid and mine. It was pouring rain as we left, and we traveled in a downpour all the way north. We stopped overnight in Roanne, finally arriving at the château, in the gray dusk of the next afternoon. To avoid reporters who, we had been warned, were already posted at the main gate, we entered the grounds by a back entrance, and my first glimpse of Candé was pleasing—gray walls and slim turrets in the slanting rain.

Mrs. Bedaux was at the door to greet us. She struck me as an unusually handsome woman, graceful and poised. "I was afraid," she said, "that this rain would delay you. You must be tired and chilled. Tea is ready, if you want it." My first favorable impression of Fern Bedaux was to be deepened and strengthened by our subsequent association. Her physical beauty and charm were the outer manifestations of a generous spirit. Whatever her subtle husband may have expected to gain from the loan of his château, I am convinced that she was innocent of any ulterior purpose. Seldom in my life have I known a person to show more kindness to a stranger. Within a few years she was to experience a personal tragedy—her husband, suspected of being disloyal to his country, came to an untimely end.

Fern Bedaux led us through a small entrance hall into what she called the library—a large paneled room, with a handsome fireplace in which several large logs were blazing. We were famished; the tea refreshed us. Among her other admirable qualities Fern exhibited tact of a high order. She asked nothing about my wedding plans, simply remarking that she would be leaving the next day and she hoped I would stay at Candé as long as I desired. "Now, let me show you around," she said. "The château is not quite so large as you may think. There will be time for you to rest before dinner."

The drawing room, spacious and high-ceilinged, with oak paneling, was more formal and, I thought, less attractive than the library. At one end was an organ. Off this room was a smaller salon, very French, with pale paneled walls and Louis Seize furniture. I instantly decided that this was the room in which I would be married. The dining room was downstairs—a kind of taproom, with immense hand-hewn beams, very old, and with an equally ancient oak table flanked on either side by long, low benches. Adjoining the main part of the house, and reached by a narrow passage and a flight of stone steps, was a small guest apartment. Fern Bedaux suggested that the Duke might like to have this apartment when he came from Austria.

Then she showed me her own bedroom, a rather spacious room, with a cream-colored *boiserie* and having an excellent view of the grounds. Since she would not be there, she asked me to use it as my own. Adjoining the bedroom was a small sitting room with a day bed that Mr. Bedaux used. Herman decided to take this for himself.

He had slept in a room adjoining mine with a gun under his pillow ever since I had arrived from England, more than three months before. Upstairs were several other bedrooms, of which Katherine took one.

Having shown us around, Fern Bedaux left us to change for dinner. The long ride in the rain had tired me, and I lay down on the big bed, hoping to snatch a nap before my bath. But my mind persisted in running haphazardly over the innumerable questions in my life and David's that still were unsolved. Where would we start our life together? What to do about our things in Great Britain? Would there ever be a reconciliation between David and his family? How to deal with the renewed onslaught of the press that the marriage was certain to bring?

There was another question that troubled me still more. Who would marry us? Under French law there had to be a separate civil ceremony, apart from a religious ceremony, if the latter was performed. We should in any case be married by the *maire* of the nearby town of Monts. But David was anxious to be married in a church as well. He has a deeply religious side; he wanted to be married by a minister of the Church of England, and with its blessing. The knowledge that David was being cut off not only from his family but also from the blessing of that Church of which as King he had been Defender of the Faith added to my worries.

I had much to think about, and there were no tolerable solutions. More than ever our affairs seemed to be becoming increasingly involved rather than less so. The thought took form that marriage, far from ending these complexities in which we now found ourselves, would inevitably confront us with new ones that neither of us had ever foreseen. Sitting in that unfamiliar room, I felt a shiver pass over me at the realization that my marriage to a man who had been sovereign of the world's greatest empire would take place, not in a setting long connected by birth or family association with either his life or mine, but rather in a land foreign to us both, in a turreted castle belonging to strangers. This was to be the conclusion of the events put in train by the Abdication. The drawbridges across which we had passed so many agonizing months ago had indeed, in David's bitter words, been drawn up against us. In the midst of these melancholy reflections the telephone rang. It was the butler to say that *"Son Altesse Royale"* was calling from Austria. "Darling," came a clear voice across the width of Europe, "I am so glad to find you safely at

[284]

Candé. Was it a difficult trip?" The gray mists lifted from my spirit
I ceased to be afraid.

The next two months were trying. There were innumerable details that needed to be attended to, and many required David's opinion or approval. Despairing of ever settling these matters over the
telephone, he asked his advisers if he might visit me in France, if only
for an afternoon, to deal with them. Their advice, as before, was that
such a meeting, even at so late an hour, could jeopardize the divorce.
I was left to complete all the arrangements as best I could. Without
the stabilizing presence and the help of Katherine and Herman, I
should have been hard pressed.

Meanwhile the press had once more thrown its encircling lines
around me. The day after we moved into Candé the concierge discovered half a dozen reporters and photographers camped outside the
gate. They stayed there until the wedding. No one could come or go
without passing under the surveillance of these patient observers. I
never could understand why newspapers went to the expense of keeping presumably competent and useful men at such an empty task.
Herman, who made it his business to see them from time to time and
to answer their questions, gathered that the press suspected that I
might suddenly go off to meet David at some rendezvous for a secret
marriage or that he might suddenly turn up in France. But, as they
should have realized, such romantic excursions were wholly out of the
question for us, whatever our inclinations might have been.

Spring, which we had left behind at Cannes, now caught up with
us again in the valley of the Loire; but spring in central France can
be capricious. It rained a good deal; the stones of the château held a
residual winter chill that the logs blazing in the fireplaces failed to
dispel and that penetrated to my bones. Yet Candé had its brighter
moments. At Lou Viei I had been in a state of semiparalysis. At
Candé I gradually came alive again. The château sits on a hill; on
the slopes below were winding wooded paths; I walked a great deal.
There was also a golf course on the property, and on fine afternoons
I played with Herman and Katherine. In the evenings we talked or
read. Occasionally friends came down from Paris for the weekend.
The country thereabouts, with its magnificent châteaux, is as beautiful
as any to be found on this earth. I had been through it before, as a
tourist, but now I was glad to see it again; and during my stay at
Candé I made several trips in the company of the Rogerses to visit
places of interest, stopping for lunch at little inns picked out from the
Guide Michelin.

All in all, it was scarcely an exciting life. For me indeed, it was no life at all, just a dull marking of time. Katherine used to relieve the tedium by short trips to Paris. But Herman never left me. He accompanied me on my afternoon walks. He continued to manage the correspondence. He listened to my problems. If he was ever bored, if he ever reflected—as he must have done, being of a thoughtful disposition—upon what had become of his own previously well-ordered existence, no word or action ever betrayed his inner impatience. His calmness consoled and steadied me.

David must have guessed something of my inner state. One evening, he telephoned to say that he was sending back to me my dog Slipper, to be a companion on my walks. A rarity among animals, Slipper seemed to find equal joy with either of us. Two days later, Chief Inspector Storrier, of Scotland Yard, who had been assigned to David in Austria, arrived with certain important papers and the cairn. The dog's joyous recognition was like a signal to me that, along with Slipper, David had sent part of himself.

Next afternoon a terrible thing happened. Bernard Rickatson-Hatt, an old friend from London, was stopping at Candé. He and the Rogerses decided to play golf, while I chose merely to walk around the course with them. Slipper tagged along behind. Katherine and Herman had a pair of Scotties, and shortly after we started down the second fairway, Slipper and the Scotties suddenly tore off into the woods, in pursuit of a rabbit. The Scotties reappeared, but Slipper was missing. That struck me as a little odd; Slipper was always at my heels. We went on to the next tee. Still no Slipper. I became worried. "It's not like Slipper to run off," I remember remarking to Herman, who whistled and whistled in the notion that Slipper was probably rooting in the underbrush close by. Then, with Bernard, I started back through the woods to look for him. As we emerged near the first green, I saw what seemed to be a gray rag on the grass. It was Slipper. I called; he did not move. But on coming closer I saw that his eyes were open and staring. When I tried to come near he raised himself as in a spasm. I had a dreadful time picking him up. He twisted and tried to bite me. There was no mistaking what had happened to Slipper. In his foray into the undergrowth he had run afoul of a viper. And I realized as I half-ran to the car that it was already too late to save him.

Slipper died early that evening at the veterinary's in Tours. He was a tiny creature; the poison must have gone rapidly to his heart. I cried. His loss on the eve of my reunion with David seemed to me a frightful omen. He had been our companion in joy and trouble; now he was gone. Was everything that I loved to be destroyed?

April slowly ran its course. By then David and I, despite the vagaries of the international telephone, had worked out the plans for the ceremony. Our one desire was to be married in peace and as quietly as possible. To invite all our friends was out of the question. David had asked his old equerry, Fruity Metcalfe, to be his best man. And there were other old friends whose hearts and loyalty had remained steadfast in his time of trouble—Hugh Lloyd Thomas, Walter Monckton, George Allen, Lady Selby, Randolph Churchill, and, of course, Lady Alexandra Metcalfe, and Eugène and Kitty de Rothschild.

But more than all these, David longed to have his sister and his brothers, and most of all his mother, near him at his marriage. As is his habit, he kept his feelings to himself in that regard; a Royal upbringing, whatever else it may do to the heart and mind, confers a kind of unbreakable pride. But I knew without his ever saying so how deep was his disappointment. The unspoken order had gone out: Buckingham Palace will ignore our wedding. There would be no reconciliation, no gesture of recognition. That also meant that many of the friends with whom David had made his life would find it "awkward" to come to Candé. It was as if a glacial current had begun to flow between us and our accustomed associations. But overriding all this only one feeling was paramount: our impatience over our seemingly endless separation.

CHAPTER XXVIII

David and I Are Married

FINALLY, ON THE MORNING OF MAY 3, THERE WAS A TELEPHONE call from George Allen in London. My divorce decree had now become absolute. I telephoned David in Austria. "Wallis," he said, "the Orient Express passes through Salzburg in the afternoon. I shall be at Candé in the morning." That afternoon I went walking with Katherine Rogers in the woods below the château. There was a warmth in the air. The fruit trees were in blossom; the meadows were lush and sprinkled with flowers. Katherine was thoughtful. Stopping in the path and prodding the earth with the point of her walking stick, she said, softly, "Remember that he has been through a good deal. He has been hurt —he may be changed." I was not afraid on my own account. I was afraid only that the upheaval in his life might have crushed a valiant spirit.

David arrived at lunchtime with his equerry, Dudley Forward. David was thin and drawn. I could hardly have expected him to look otherwise. Yet his gaiety bubbled as freely as before. He came up the steps at Candé two at a time. His first words were "Darling, it's been so long. I can hardly believe that this is you, and I'm here."

Later, we took a walk. It was wonderful to be together again. Before, we had been alone in the face of overwhelming trouble. Now we would meet it side by side.

But as David's brother was to be crowned on May 12, we both felt that we should prefer to wait until June to be married.

On the morning of the Coronation, David mentioned casually that he was going to listen to the broadcast of the ceremonies from London. It was a silent group that gathered around the radio in the Château de Candé. David's eyes were directed unblinkingly at the

[288]

fireplace. He had heard the service twice before—first when his grand-father was crowned, then his father. Was he thinking of those other occasions? Was he thinking of himself in the Abbey? He never said. The words of the service rolled over me like an engulfing wave; I fought to suppress every thought, but all the while the mental image of what might have been and should have been kept forming, dis-integrating, and re-forming in my mind.

When we were briefly alone afterward, he remarked in substance only this: "You must have no regrets—I have none. This much I know: what I know of happiness is forever associated with you."

In these first days together at Candé we began to plan for the future. While at Enzesfeld, David had taken for the summer the Castle Wasserleonburg, near the Wörther See, in Carinthia. It belonged to Count Paul Münster, who was married to a cousin of Eric Dudley. We also decided later in the autumn to look for a house in or nearby Paris. There was, of course, nothing to prevent our settling down in England; David and I were free to come and go as we wished. But strong as was our desire to keep our lives rooted in Great Britain, he did not think it would be fair to his brother to return immediately.

Now came a cheering development. Herman received a letter from the vicar of St. Paul's, Darlington, the Reverend R. Anderson Jardine, offering to come to France and perform the marriage ceremony. David was delighted and telephoned George Allen in London to get in touch with the clergyman and, if George thought well of him, to make the necessary arrangements for the Reverend Mr. Jardine to come to Candé. He arrived at the château the day before the wedding, ap-parently a typical country parson in appearance and manner. I thought it rather brave of him to defy his Bishop in order to marry us, and David and I gratefully welcomed him as a man of God.

Somehow the preparations got done. Mainbocher made my trous-seau. From his sketches I chose for my wedding gown a simple dress of blue crepe satin. Reboux made a hat to match. I asked Constance Spry, the prominent London florist, to come to Candé and do the flowers for the wedding. She was a person whom I knew and admired. She brought her assistant with her, and in a matter of hours they had transformed the atmosphere of the house. I love flowers, and there can be few to equal Constance Spry in the art of arranging them so that the effect seems to be entirely natural. I was enchanted. This was her wedding present to me.

Other preparations, beyond our control, were also going forward. The press was congregating in the nearby city of Tours. Herman

Rogers returned to the house from his meeting with the reporters one afternoon with the news that a huge trailer was parked on one of the approaches to Candé and that it was inhabited by Cornelius Vanderbilt, in his role of correspondent. David was incredulous. "A Vanderbilt reporting from a trailer! My father never would have believed this."

David hoped that, once the Coronation was over, his family might soften its attitude, and that at least some of them would attend the wedding.

But yet another blow was in preparation, one especially humiliating to him. Sir Ulick Alexander, David's former Keeper of the Privy Purse, and a steadfast friend, telephoned David to say that Walter Monckton was coming to the wedding and would bring with him a letter from the King that would contain, as I recall the phrasing, "not very good news." In his letter the King said that he had been advised by the British and Dominion Prime Ministers that when David had renounced the Throne he had also given up the Royal titles. As he was no longer in the line of succession, according to the King, he had furthermore lost his right to the title of Royal Highness. But the King wished him to enjoy this title, and therefore he was re-creating him H.R.H. However, he could not, he went on to say, under the terms of Letters Patent of Queen Victoria, extend this title to his wife. The King concluded by saying that he hoped this painful action he had been forced to take would not be considered an "insult." David would henceforth be known as His Royal Highness, the Duke of Windsor, and I would be simply the Duchess of Windsor. The effect of this decision was to debar me in defiance of all custom from taking my place alongside my Royal husband and to bar any offspring of our marriage from inheriting his title.

The letter enraged David. He exclaimed, "I know Bertie—I know he couldn't have written this letter on his own. Why in God's name would they do this to me at this time!"

The distinction did not seem particularly important to me. David had given up the most exalted of titles. It hardly seemed worth while to me to quibble over a distinction in a lesser one. But nothing in the aftermath of the Abdication hurt David more than that gratuitous thrust. In his eyes it was an ultimate slur upon his wife, and, therefore, upon himself. He could not bring himself wholly to blame his brother, who, he knew, had bowed to strong pressure. But this action made for a coolness between them thereafter. There is considerable question that the King's action in this regard was legally sound. David was so advised, a few months later, by Sir William (later Earl) Jowitt, who became Lord Chancellor in Mr. Attlee's Government. Nevertheless, the barrier stands, and, so long as it stands, David will never be reconciled.

Our wedding day, the third of June, was beautifully warm and sunny. Herman Rogers gave me away, and it must have been with a profound sense of relief that he saw me become the responsibility of another.

Here I shall say only that it was a supremely happy moment. All I had been through, the hurt I had suffered, were forgotten; by evening, David and I were on our way to Austria. En route we would stop briefly at Venice between trains.

The first thing I learned about David as a husband was that he was much more thoughtful and attentive than I had expected. Having picked Wasserleonburg on his own, he was jittery over whether I would like it. And as the Buick labored up a steep hill, following a rough and narrow road, I began to have misgivings myself. Then abruptly, the climb was over, and before us was a most fascinating house—not a castle in the British sense, but rather a magnificent manor house in the Austrian style, with a wide courtyard paved with cobblestones, a tennis court, and a swimming pool. All around were magnificent peaks of the Austrian Alps.

David had indeed done well. On hand in addition to Dudley Forward was a staff he had selected himself—a chef and a butler from Vienna, various Austrian servants from Count Münster's establishment, as well as a British secretary, Mrs. Bedford. Dudley Forward, a handsome young man with a black mustache and black hair, had been with David ever since Enzesfeld. He dealt most effectively, even though he couldn't type, with the official correspondence and the running of the household.

There was chamois stalking in the mountains; we walked every day, swam, played tennis, and visited friends. David sometimes used to satisfy his passion for exercise by climbing a rocky peak back of the castle, called the Dobratsch, and signal to me with a small mirror from the summit while I lunched on the terrace.

It was an idyllic interlude; for the moment one could almost forget the winter's pain and separation. Many of our old friends kept turning up to visit us, and we made friends with our Austrian neighbors who lived nearby. Only one thing marred our happiness: after the first burst of joy in rediscovering each other and being together we found our minds turning back in interminable post-mortems concerning the events leading up to the Abdication. I suppose this is a common reaction of all couples who have endured a rending personal crisis. *If I had only done this; if you had only done that; if you had only listened to me; if I had only known.* This endless rehashing of the lost past became almost an obsession with us until one evening David said despairingly, "Darling, if we keep this up we are never going to agree, so let's drop it for good." Then and there we vowed we never would discuss the Abdication again, and to this day we never have.

I was relieved to observe how smoothly David adjusted himself to his new way of life. Indeed, he seemed almost unaware of the many problems with which his changed status was certain to confront him. This attitude rather amused a good friend of David's, former King Alfonso of Spain, who was spending a few days in the neighborhood. King Alfonso had married one of David's cousins, Princess Victoria Eugenie, one of Queen Victoria's granddaughters; and David when Prince of Wales had visited the Spanish Court during Alfonso's reign. This last monarch of the Spanish Bourbon line, who had lost his throne some six years earlier, was indeed a striking figure of a man —tall, lean, saturnine of countenance. David admired him particularly for two reasons—for his well-known personal courage and his prowess as a sportsman. Another distinction that set Alfonso apart even among the small company of monarchs was the fact that he had been born a king. One evening he came to dinner with us at Wasserleonburg, and knowing that he had had to face much the same problem of readjustment when he left his own country, I gained the impression that he now was quietly amused by David's almost naïve attitude toward his future.

Smiling quizzically, Alfonso said, "David, you're not going to find the attitude of the Courts of Europe toward the members of our little club of former monarchs quite as pleasant as you may think. Let me tell you a story. For many years, as you know, while I was still on my throne, I used to go to England every year. You will also recall my great interest in polo, and I made it a point to watch the match for the Champion Cup at the Hurlingham Club, of which I was a member. The Committee always gave me seats in the box reserved for the British Royal Family. Well, a year or two after the revolution in Spain I went to England for the polo matches as usual. The Club very thoughtfully sent me tickets for my old place in the front of the Royal stand. Before the game had even started one of the Club officials appeared at my elbow to ask apologetically whether I'd mind yielding my seat to one of my British cousins-in-law and moving back another row. I didn't mind this at all, but when the same fellow reappeared a few minutes later and repeated the request—perhaps even more apologetically, and with a few extra 'Your Majesties'—I began to get a little miffed. This went on all afternoon. David, I never realized you had so many relations until I found myself at the beginning of the last chukker in the last seat in the last row."

David roared with laughter. "I suppose, Alfonso, this is what they mean when they say somebody's being kicked upstairs."

CHAPTER XXIX

We Visit Hitler's Germany

AFTER SPENDING THREE MONTHS AT WASSERLEONBURG AND TAKING several short trips about Austria and into Hungary and Czechoslovakia, we decided to go to Paris. There we took a small apartment in the Hotel Meurice—two bedrooms and a sitting room, overlooking the gardens of the Tuileries—to use as a base while we searched for a house. This promised to be a difficult undertaking because David preferred the country while I liked the city, and there was no logical way of combining the two.

While we were in the midst of finding our way back into the world and establishing a home for ourselves in France, there came an interruption—one that was to have unforeseen repercussions: We decided to make a trip to Germany as David was anxious to see the developments in low-cost housing there.

The idea for the trip originated with Charles Bedaux, and he first broached it to David at the Château de Candé, just before the wedding. Mr. Bedaux knew of David's interest in housing projects in Britain and of his visits to Austria, France, Denmark, and Sweden to study pioneering experiments in this field. When, therefore, Charles Bedaux suggested that David might find it stimulating to see the remarkable things that were being done by the Germans in this field, David's curiosity was instantly whetted. In the course of his imperial tours, he had come to know the world in a way that few of his contemporaries could match, and now that he was a private citizen he looked forward to exploring it afresh, even to the nooks and crannies from which he had previously been fenced off by reason of his position. Moreover, an idea had been evolving in David's mind that he might carve out a useful and dignified career in fostering large-scale

[294]

housing developments, either in Europe or in the United States. So he agreed to give some thought to such a trip, possibly after our return from our honeymoon; and Mr. Bedaux on his side undertook to sound out his highly placed business connections in Germany about possible arrangements for the visit.

David forgot about the invitation, and nothing more was heard about the proposed trip until, in September, we stopped with Charles and Fern Bedaux at their shooting lodge in Hungary. Mr. Bedaux now informed David that he had heard from his German industrialist friends that they would be glad to show David the more important German housing innovations.

He insisted that all this could be done without David's having to worry about becoming involved in any Nazi propaganda schemes. David was well aware of some of the sinister aspects of the Nazi regime and of the growing concern with which the world regarded Hitler's jingoistic gestures. However, David no longer had any official position, and in his view he was perfectly free to visit any foreign country he chose to without prejudicing his country's diplomatic relations. In fact, we had only recently spent a week in Venice, which had caused no adverse comments in the press despite the fact that Mussolini was anything but *persona grata* with the British Foreign Office. Therefore, it never occurred to David that this purely private trip could become a cause of public concern. On this basis, after receiving renewed assurances from Mr. Bedaux that we should travel under the auspices of private German citizens, David agreed to make the trip, and said that the details could be worked out after we reached Paris.

We started out by train early in October, and went straight to Berlin. That the British Government was dissociating itself from our visit was evident the instant we got off the train at the Friedrichstrasse Station. While a number of German officials headed by Dr. Robert Ley, the leader of the Nazi National Labor Front, were on the platform to welcome us, only a third secretary from the British Embassy, Mr. (later Sir) Geoffrey Harrison met us. He brought with him a note from Sir George Ogilvie-Forbes, the chargé d'affaires. Ogilvie-Forbes said in the note that the Ambassador, Sir Neville Henderson, had rather unexpectedly left Berlin and that he himself had been directed by the Foreign Office to take no official cognizance of our presence and therefore he regretted his inability to meet us at the station, but he would call on us as soon as we were settled at our hotel.

This was a disturbing development, and David's disquietude was heightened by the conversation he had with Ogilvie-Forbes. He is a

Scot of independent mind, whom David had known when he was Prince of Wales. With obvious embarrassment, he described the instructions he and the Embassy staff had received and expressed his great regret that he could not therefore receive us at the Embassy. For himself, however, he could not leave the matter there. "I have come, Sir," he told David, "to pay my respects to my former King and to help behind the scenes in any way I can."

It now turned out that our German guide was not to be an industrialist, as Bedaux had assured us, but Dr. Ley, who was also the Nazi official responsible for housing projects. Ogilvie-Forbes had drawn a depressing picture of this strange man. If not actually an alcoholic, Dr. Ley was a noisy, chronic drinker. In this respect, at least, our guide lived up to his advance billing. We saw a great deal of him—too much, in fact. David soon discovered that Dr. Ley fortified himself periodically during the day with infusions of schnapps. By evening he was usually in what might be described as the schnapps equivalent of the fifth Martini stage—unsteady, emotional, and bombastic. His ugliest side would then come into view, and he would boast about what he had done for the German working class, unmarried mothers (this seemed to be a matter of particular Nazi pride), and the younger generation whom he was organizing in the "Strength-through-Joy" movement. We had been told that Dr. Ley, as a young man in the chaos of Germany after the First World War, had been a fanatic Communist who had switched around to become a Nazi, an anti-Communist fighter, and a wrecker of the Weimar Republic. To me he appeared to be the archetype of the revolutionary—a man driven by sheer evil to undermine the existing order, whatever it might be, and who would lend his ugly talents to any enterprise dedicated to such an end. He had bright blue eyes, a florid complexion, and a squat bear-like build. To my American eyes, he was a fourflusher.

Dr. Ley was a menace in another respect. His official car was an enormous black Mercedes-Benz, half as long as a city block. In this shiny juggernaut he loved to whiz through Berlin, scattering lesser traffic with an ear-piercing blast of the siren. On our second day there Ley called for us at the hotel to take us to a housing development on the outskirts of the city. The glittering Mercedes-Benz was at the entrance—the top down, two SS guards in black uniforms on the front seat. With Dr. Ley sitting between us, obviously relishing the public display, we roared through the city. On the open road the speed increased until I was afraid of being blown out of the back seat. It was a hair-raising ride that brought to mind the one we had

had with Prince Paul of Yugoslavia. All the while, above the roar of the wind, a radio blared out German tunes to which Dr. Ley kept time by rolling his head from side to side.

Our meeting with Field Marshal Goering, which followed a few days later, presented us with a less strenuous view of Nazi life. An invitation to join him and Frau Goering for tea at Karinhalle, his country place forty miles from Berlin, was extended to us out of the blue. A Luftwaffe officer came to fetch us. A steady rain was falling; we drove perhaps an hour, entering a magnificent forest. Through this the car pursued a winding road, then suddenly came into a clearing in which stood an imposing stone house, with a thatched roof reminiscent of an ancient baronial hall. Goering, in an immaculate white uniform, with rows of medal ribbons across his tunic, and Frau Goering met us at the door. They had just come from a funeral for one of her relatives and apologized, on that account, for not having their friends in to meet us. They led us to a large hall with contemporary furniture, and we had tea at a massive round table wide enough to dance on. Being fluent in German, and having had an opportunity to brush up his command of the language during his long stay in Austria, David was able to hold up his end of the small talk with grace and spirit. Fortunately for me, Frau Goering spoke English, and I conversed with Goering in French, a language he spoke quite well. However, the one bit of intelligence I abstracted from that discussion was Frau Goering's whispered confidence, after I had complimented her about something or other, that she was expecting her first child.

I was eager to see the rest of the house, and Goering, pleased by my show of interest, volunteered to show us around. His bedroom was a small, dark chamber, in which stood a sturdy four-poster bed. Over it was hung a painting that I understood him to say was a Rembrandt. By contrast Frau Goering's bedroom was spacious and sunny and decorated with bright chintzes.

By any standards Karinhalle was quite a house. It contained, among other features, a private gymnasium in the basement, equipped with weight-lifting apparatus, an electric exercising horse, horizontal bars, and a massage apparatus bearing the Elizabeth Arden trademark— a gadget one would scarcely have expected a Field Marshal to use. Goering was especially proud of the fine quarters he had provided for his large staff of housemaids. Their rooms all had good furniture, gay cretonne curtains, and the occupant's name, embellished with painted flowers, on the door; and the housemaids' dresses were of peasant design, with pleated skirts and smocked blouses.

The entire attic was given over to a playroom for the children of the Goerings' relations and friends. It was stocked with enough children's toys to equip a shop. Spread around the room was the most elaborate toy railway I have ever seen—yards and yards of intricately connected tracks, dozens of switches, coal tipples, charming little stations, and any number of locomotives and cars of different types. The Field Marshal, kneeling down in his white uniform, showed us how it worked. The deftness with which he directed the trains up and down the tracks, opening and closing switches, blowing whistles, and averting collisions, suggested that he must have spent a good part of his time in the attic.

Only once did international politics intrude during the course of the visit. In the library, above the mantel, was a map of Germany, with its national frontiers marked off, and Germany colored green. While Goering was showing me a trophy from his days as an ace in the First World War, David strolled across the room to study the map. Just then a servant entered the library to hand a message to the Field Marshal. While he was reading it, I caught a signal from David. As I joined him beside the map, he whispered, "Look quickly at Austria. Frontier's gone."

The green of Germany had indeed overflowed the entire expanse of Austria, clear beyond Vienna.

"Why don't you ask him about it?" I whispered.

David nodded his head. "I certainly will," he said.

Goering came across the room. David said, *"Exzellenz,* this is a very interesting map."

Obviously pleased, Goering replied, "I've just had it made—a fine example of the new German cartography."

"So I see," said David quietly. "In fact, your German cartographers seem to have novel, and I might add, expansive ideas."

The rolls of flesh on Goering's face puckered into mirth. "Ho, ho," he cried, "you refer, Sir, to the incorporation of Austria into Germany. Well, I needed a new map, and since Austria will soon join Germany—voluntarily, of course—it seemed more economical to anticipate the event. Saves the trouble of having to have the map done over again."

When the *Anschluss* took place five months later, David remarked, "Those German cartographers certainly had it right. But Goering has a strange idea of what 'voluntary' means."

Still under the aegis of the flamboyant Dr. Ley, David and I went on to Dresden, Nuremberg, Stuttgart, and Munich, looking into workers' houses, hospitals, and youth camps. On the way, we met many leading Nazis, among them Heinrich Himmler, boss of the Gestapo, whose bespectacled meekness would have seemed more befitting a minor civil servant, a clerk caught up in politics. Rudolph Hess, who was then being pointed out as Hitler's Heir Apparent, was a different sort—charming of manner and good-looking. Goebbels, the club-footed mastermind of the Nazi propaganda mills, impressed me as the cleverest of the lot—a tiny, wispy gnome with an enormous skull. His wife was the prettiest woman I saw in Germany, a blonde, with enormous blue eyes and a flair for clothes. Seen together, they reminded me of Beauty and the Beast.

I had never before been thrown in with such a strange, ill-assorted company of men. They both repelled and fascinated. Having read about them in the press, and knowing something of their individual reputations, I had the curious sensation of wandering about the vast backstage of an opera house, watching a cast assemble for a Wagnerian opera. Yet for all their swashbuckling airs, they seemed to be ridden by secret doubts. One thing was sure: they were a humorless lot. Once, while riding down a Berlin street, I remarked to a Nazi official how charming was the German custom of setting flower boxes in the windows. "That depends upon the point of view" was the solemn response. "We had those things dropped on our heads by the Communists when we entered Berlin, and I still carry a scar from that time."

On the day before we were to leave Germany, while we were in Munich, we were suddenly notified that the Fuehrer would like to have us for tea at Berchtesgaden that afternoon and that his special train would be at our disposal.

Fortunately, we had by this time passed from under the auspices of Dr. Ley, and the trip to Berchtesgaden was made in the company of Rudolph Hess, who was to give us a dinner at his home in Munich that same evening. At Berchtesgaden we were met by Hitler's famous interpreter, Dr. Paul Schmidt, and Hitler's car. In this we were whirled up a steep mountain road to his Bavarian lodge. The famous Eagle's Nest had not yet been built.

We entered a large drawing room, one entire side of which was given over to an enormous window looking out over the Bavarian Alps into the sunny valleys of Austria. Dr. Schmidt pointed out to us the more interesting landmarks. The room was decorated with the dark, rather heavy modern furniture that had recently made its appearance in Germany. While we were standing in front of the great window, admiring the view, an aide appeared to say that the Fuehrer would receive the Duke of Windsor, and David went off with Schmidt.

The interview was supposed to last half an hour. I stayed behind with Hess, who tried to entertain me with talk about music, which he loved. The half hour passed and then became an hour, with no sign of David. Hess became agitated, thinking of the dinner guests who would presently be assembling at his house in Munich. Excusing himself hurriedly, he went off to telephone his wife that we should be late. While he was gone, David returned with Hitler, who was talking energetically.

We had tea in front of the fire. Since Hitler spoke neither English nor French, the conversation, which David insisted on continuing in German, despite the presence of Dr. Schmidt, was entirely over my head. I could not take my eyes off Hitler. He was dressed in his brown Party uniform. His face had a pasty pallor, and under his mustache his lips were fixed in a kind of mirthless grimace. Yet at close quarters he gave one the feeling of great inner force. His hands were long and slim, a musician's hands, and his eyes were truly extraordinary— intense, unblinking, magnetic, burning with the same peculiar fire I had earlier seen in the eyes of Kemal Atatürk. Once or twice I felt those eyes turned in my direction. But when I tried to meet their gaze, the lids drooped, and I found myself confronted by a mask. I decided that Hitler did not care for women.

On the way back to Munich, when we were momentarily alone, I asked David whether he had had an interesting talk with Hitler.

"Yes, very," he answered, riffling through the pages of a magazine.

"Did you get into international politics?" I asked, curiously.

"Now, darling," he protested. "You know my rule about politics. I'd certainly never allow myself to get into a political discussion with him!"

"You were with him one hour. What did you talk about?"

"He did most of the talking."

"Well, what did he talk about?"

"Oh, the usual stuff. What he's trying to do for Germany and to combat Bolshevism."

"What did he say about Bolshevism?"

"He's against it."

And that was about all that I ever did get out of David about his meeting with Adolf Hitler. In one respect, at least, men are pretty much alike. Statecraft is an art into which they will not readily initiate women, no doubt on the theory that it is over their heads.

Back in Paris in late October and still, in effect, living out of trunks and suitcases, we resumed the search for a house, interrupting it for a short stay on the Riviera for Christmas. Katherine and Herman Rogers, who were away, kindly put Lou Viei at our disposal, and we had a pleasant week there. David had always had a special fondness for the Côte d'Azur, and now decided that in addition to a house in Paris we should have one there, on the Mediterranean. After looking around a bit, we learned that the same château, La Cröe, at Cap d'Antibes, which had been offered to us for the wedding, would be available the next summer for renting, and we were tempted to take it. However, we decided, on second thought, to withhold a final decision until we had become more settled.

At this stage we were still not sure that France would suit us as a permanent home. Neither of us spoke the language easily; nor did we know many French people. Then, too, David had in mind the possibility of our living in the United States, where we had many friends. Therefore we concluded that it would be wiser to rent, rather than to buy, for the time being.

That winter of 1937–38 was gray and dreary. Every day I was out in the environs of Paris, tramping through houses of all kinds and styles of architecture. Needless to say, this time-consuming process bored David, as it does so many men. He always managed to evade any personal inspection until I had lined up three or four possibilities; then he would rush through each in turn, always ending up with the same comment: "Darling, this won't do at all," and leaving me more in the dark than ever as to what would really please. Either the houses were too big or too small, or the ceilings were too high or too low, or, most of all, the gardens were too formal or not formal enough. David insisted that he had a very clear picture in his own mind of the kind of house we needed, but he never succeeded in communicating the picture to me.

Finally, when I was on the verge of despair, I happened to show him a house in Versailles. To my utter astonishment, he exclaimed, "This, though not ideal, will do until we get this country versus city living straightened out between us." I suppose his real reason for settling on this particular house—Versailles is only twenty minutes from Paris—represented a compromise between his desires and mine. The house was nicely furnished; it had a pleasant garden and grounds.

It was such a relief to be in a house of my own again. With the aid of Dudley Forward things were soon running smoothly. As a matter of fact, David was doubtful of the necessity of having an equerry in his new circumstances and was not too sure he could any longer afford such a luxury now that he no longer had official engagements. Much more useful in his opinion would have been another secretary who could handle his personal correspondence as well as business letters. But it took David some time to make this change. In the meantime he put a typewriter in the little room he used as an office. It struck me as somewhat incongruous, even though David really preferred typing his own letters, to see the equerry gracefully taking his ease in the drawing room while the former King was pecking away at the typewriter upstairs.

Late in the spring of 1938, having vacated the Versailles house, we returned to the Riviera to make up our minds about La Cröe. The softness of the Mediterranean spring made the decision for us; we took a ten-year lease on the château. While waiting for it to be redecorated and for our furniture to arrive from England, we stayed nearby at the Hôtel du Cap, Eden Roc, run by the famous André Sella. La Cröe is a beautiful white villa standing on a small eminence overlooking the sea; it had a tennis court, a swimming pool cut into the rocks on the shore, and a garden. The feature about the house that promptly caught the attention of the press as soon as our signing of the lease was announced was a huge bathtub in the shape of a swan and reputedly made of gold. There is no disputing the swan shape, but the gold was nonexistent, and in any case the presence of the bathtub long antedated my occupancy of the house. My principal contribution to the *décor* was a blue and white color scheme, to harmonize with the blue of the sea and the white clouds that drift lazily across the perpetually azure sky.

On second thought, however, I feel I can properly claim a somewhat larger measure of credit. La Cröe was partly furnished; and between David's possessions at the Fort and York House and what I had at Cumberland Terrace there seemed to me quite enough to make an adequate beginning. Our effects had meanwhile been collected by David's long-time chief clerk, Mr. Thomas Carter, and stored at Frogmore, in Windsor Great Park, while awaiting our final choice of a house. Mr. Carter had from time to time traveled to Paris in connection with David's private business. On his every visit he produced from his brief case a number of inventory sheets for our inspection. Out of long habit David would run his eye over the sheets, occasionally exclaiming in pleasure over the rediscovery of a cherished item. One of the hidden skills upon which David prided himself and which until now I had never suspected was his mastery of organizing paper work. First, he would deftly stack Mr. Carter's sheets in order; then, seizing the punch that was always upon his desk, he would stamp out a hole through the upper left-hand corner; and finally he would thread them into a folder by means of a corded red string at either end of which was a tiny brass rod. Being accustomed to the American practice of performing such an operation with staples or paper clips, I once asked David why he bothered with such a complicated threading operation. A look that was almost patronizing came over his face.

"Darling," he said, "this is the way I've always filed my papers. These are India tags." And from the way he said it I gathered he was sure that they are what had held the British Empire together, at least since the time of Disraeli. (To my knowledge, he has never wavered in this faith. I have yet to see him capitulate to the stapler or the paper clip.)

Perhaps I was so bemused by the skill with which he handled the papers, or so lulled by his confidently reiterated assurances that "Mr. Carter will take care of everything," that I failed to appreciate the magnitude of the logistics that I was becoming involved in, as the wife of a former King. My awakening came late one afternoon when Mr. Carter rolled up to La Cröe at the head of a convoy of vans. Before I fully grasped what was going on, the lawn had practically disappeared under an avalanche of crates, linen baskets, furniture, trunks of clothing, bales of draperies, chests of silver. David charged up and down the lawn, happily identifying favorite pieces. "Don't worry, Wallis," he called from the far edge of the lawn, "Mr. Carter is very good at sorting." This was a confidence that Mr. Carter clearly did not share. He was a small, precise gentleman who had grown gray in David's secretariat. After the last van had rolled away, he came to me, looking wan but determined to preserve to the end the Royal tradition of imperturbability in the face of obvious disaster. "Ma'am, everything here was on my inventory sheets. I am sure you know just where you want it all put. Perhaps we should begin with the silver."

At that point I felt faint. I replied, "Yes, Mr. Carter, an excellent suggestion. We shall begin with the silver." Several days later, as the last crate went through the front door, David announced triumphantly, "Now, darling, I hope you understand why Mr. Carter and I swear by India tags."

Although there were moments when I felt almost like a curator of a museum, it still gave a lift to my spirit to see David rejoicing in the re-creation of his familiar surroundings at the Fort and at York House —the treasured mementos of his youthful service with the Brigade of Guards, the hard-won trophies of race riding, and, most of all, his truly magnificent collection of old silver, much of which consisted of pieces inherited from his ancestors or of the plate presented to him by the corporations and guilds of London and other cities in recognition of his services.

Eventually a measure of order was established where all had been chaos. While I could not hope to reproduce on the Riviera the splendor of the life into which David had been born, at least he seemed happy in his new role of husband and man of the house. However, I must in frankness say that he continued to see the role in somewhat Royal terms. Eager as he was to do everything for himself and for me, it was some time before he understood how ordinary things really get done. The rule of his father's life had always been a man and a half for every job. That applied to butlers, valets, gardeners, maids, and chauffeurs. The trouble was that the extra half man was not present in his new and reduced scheme of things. Nor had his experience ever prepared him for negotiating with plumbers, electricians, and tradesmen in general; and the Royal economics had never gone beyond the principle that things were cheaper by the dozen, whether it be screw drivers, thermos bottles, or thermometers. While I was loath to curb David's zest for exploring these to him new and exciting frontiers of experience, I nevertheless was obliged, from time to time, to intervene, if only to keep us both from being inundated. However, there was one area in which David was invincible. He was unshakable in his conviction that he was a master of the mechanical arts, especially anything having to do with heat, power, or water. He was never happier than when superintending the operations of half a dozen artisans in making household repairs. I was never sure whether our salvation lay in David's actual understanding of the intricacies of the machinery that he was having overhauled or whether it lay in the inability of the French artisans to understand him and their going about the work in their accustomed way. In fact, there was for David a rather crushing episode. While he was explaining to a small task force of French plumbers, in what he considered his most eloquent and precise French, the maladies of the hot-water system, the foreman of the group interrupted to say, *"Pardon, M'sieu le Duc, je regrette, mais je ne comprends pas l'anglais."* Still, in the end everything seemed to work.

By the end of the summer La Cröe was in order. In the autumn, having given up the house in Versailles, we went back to the Hotel Meurice for the winter. During the next several months I resumed the search for a really suitable house in or near Paris.

During that fall there occurred an episode to which I attached little significance at the time, but which I later came to realize was prophetic of the ambiguous status that was to be David's lot as the former monarch of Great Britain. It was always in David's mind to retain his British ties; the idea of becoming an expatriate had never occurred to him. All the same he had the sensitivity to understand the desirability of letting his brother's position on the Throne become thoroughly consolidated before he reappeared, however briefly, on the British scene. David would have liked to help his brother and from time to time take some of the burden off his shoulders. This idea, as I say, had been maturing in the back of his mind, but he did nothing about it until that fall. It happened that the British Prime Minister, Mr. Neville Chamberlain, who had succeeded Mr. Stanley Baldwin, was to come to Paris to consult with the French Government. David decided to take advantage of Mr. Chamberlain's presence in Paris to have a talk with him.

This seemed to David a simple and direct way for him to ascertain the feelings of the Palace and the Government on the question of his returning to Britain. But it was unclear to me whether it was a matter for the King or the Government to decide; and when I asked David where the competence lay, I was astonished to have him say that he couldn't give the answer. "In fact," he said, "I doubt whether anyone can. Because there's no precedent, this is a twilight zone, and that's where we are right now. My instinct is that it's best to take up this question with the P.M."

In due course Mr. Chamberlain arrived in Paris and came to see David at the Meurice. I was not present at the interview. Afterward David told me that Mr. Chamberlain had been cordial, interested, but noncommittal. At the conclusion of their talk, the Prime Minister had said, "I shall be very glad to discuss the matter with my colleagues and, if desirable, with His Majesty. As soon as we have examined the matter I shall advise you."

David waited hopefully. Weeks passed. No word came from 10, Downing Street or from the Palace. David finally made inquiries. All that he could ever find out was that the Government considered that the question of David's returning to Britain was a private matter between him and the King, and the Palace considered it a matter in which the Government should tender advice; and there things lay. In one of his rare resorts to cynicism David remarked one day, "I'm afraid we'll be too old to cross the Channel before my brother and the P.M. stop batting the ball back and forth."

We spent the Christmas of 1938 at La Cröe. As many of our friends were spending the holidays nearby, we decided to have our first big party in our new home. It was to be a dinner followed by dancing. We engaged a band to provide the music. David offered, in his still novel capacity as head of the house, to handle all the necessary financial arrangements; but remembering from our London experience his innocent disinterest in the importance of cash payments, I was somewhat dubious about the wisdom of entrusting him with such responsibility. It was therefore with some uneasiness that I clipped together 5,000 francs (then equivalent to about $150) with which he was to pay the band. I last saw it disappear into his trousers pocket just before we went down to greet our guests.

The evening was a great success; the band outdid itself. I was congratulating myself on how everything had gone when David, who had been escorting the band leader to the door, suddenly came rushing back to exclaim, "Darling, where's that 5,000 francs? I don't seem to have it on me."

"But, David," I replied in horror, "I gave it to you. I saw you put it in your pocket."

"Are you sure?" he asked in genuine bewilderment. "I certainly haven't got it now." One by one he turned his pockets inside out. There was no sign of the money, or even the gold clip.

Only for a moment was David nonplused. "Ah," he decided, "of course, the money must have dropped out of my pocket while I was sitting down, and fallen back of the cushions." Then his executive instincts surged back and took command. Mobilizing the few remaining guests, he started a methodical dismemberment of the sofas and chairs. The missing money was not found; and unable to stand the mounting devastation, I dashed upstairs to my room where I was fortunate to find enough money to pay off the band. From that point on I attended to these matters myself.

Aside from his blithe assumption that the logistics of life would take care of themselves, I discovered that David had endearing qualities that were rare in my experience. There was not a mean bone in his body or a snide thought in his mind. Gossip rolled off him like rain off a slate roof; he never allowed gossip to warp his healthy faith in human nature. He had an extraordinary resiliency of the spirit. He had somehow achieved the capacity—I suppose it was almost a necessity for one brought up in the glare of his twentieth-century princely role—to expunge instantly from his brain the cares of the day; however harassing might be the problems on his mind, he could always go to sleep the minute his head touched the pillow. This was a form of self-discipline I envied.

David had another attribute that I also envied. For some time after our marriage I was puzzled by the fact that while he was the acknowledged leader of men's fashion, he rarely bought a new suit. To be sure, he had a dozen or so, most of which I vaguely remembered having seen before, although each time I saw what I thought was the same one, it was oddly different. I happened to mention this phenomenon to Mr. Carter one day. He replied, "There's no mystery to this at all. Take, for instance, that tartan dinner suit His Royal Highness wore last night at dinner. According to the tailor's marks on the inside pocket, it was made for his father in 1897. Now, I am happy to see the suit still looking so well, after being refitted to His Royal Highness, even though I never did hold with His late Majesty's insistence on having his trousers creased on the sides."

But along with the thriftiness and conservatism that were so innately a part of David's inheritance went an extraordinary outgivingness and trust in those about him. I came to realize that this was an expression of his sunny disposition, his difficulty in bringing himself to believe ill of anyone. Perhaps, at a critical time for him, this quality was his salvation; believing, as he does, that all human experience should be a challenge, it was impossible for him ever to think that any change in circumstances could be a defeat.

The one fundamental lack in his new life as it first began to take shape may have been the absence of the ordered round of duties, the calendar blocked out as much as a year ahead, and the daily inflow of red boxes from Whitehall bringing to him the never-ending business of State. It now devolved upon me to attempt to fill for him this perhaps unfillable gap. I sometimes used to say to myself that today I have to be Canada, tomorrow I shall have to be New Zealand, and perhaps the next day the Fiji Islands.

Finally, early in 1939, we found in Paris a house that seemed to suit our needs—or at least by my definitions. It was on the Boulevard Suchet at the end of Avenue Henri Martin, not far from the Bois de Boulogne. The location was certainly not country; the camions bringing the produce of the country to the markets of the city rattled and backfired under the windows all night. But it was airy and sunny, in the Louis Seize style, with windows all around and a charming courtyard, and when I showed it to David he smiled and said, "I see that it's going to be the city for us, after all."

With relief that David was reconciled to the impossibility of combining in one abode in Paris the country charm of the Fort and the metropolitan convenience of York House, I completed negotiations with the owner for a long-term lease. The rest of the winter and through the spring David and I were absorbed in plans for redecorating and furnishing the house, and making a real home of it. After the plans had been completed, and after the work was safely under way, we returned to La Cröe for the summer.

It was an uneasy summer. While most of our American and British friends insisted that war was unthinkable, still our French friends, with that sixth sense of impending disaster that has been bred into them by centuries of war and invasion, somehow seemed to feel otherwise. Outwardly their lives continued unchanged; but, as the summer wore on, the assurance drained away, to be replaced by a weary, almost cynical fatalism. David was increasingly on the telephone to London; he spent more and more time listening to the news broadcasts from London, Paris, Berlin, and even Washington. And then in late August came the stunning announcement of the Russo-German nonaggression pact, to be followed in a matter of days by the German invasion of Poland. Until that moment David had held to the hope that diplomacy and sound judgment would intervene to prevent the catastrophe of a general war. In the spring he had even made a broadcast from the battlefield of Verdun, appealing to the good sense of the statesmen of Europe to further this objective. But as he listened to the radio bulletins telling of the German smash across the Polish frontier, he suddenly said, "This is beginning to smell like 1914 all over again."

BOOK SEVEN

THE WAR WITHIN A WAR

CHAPTER XXX

War and a Summons from the Palace

SEPTEMBER 3, 1939, WAS A HOT AND HUMID DAY, EVEN FOR THE Côte d'Azur at that season. The morning news broadcasts over the French radio left no doubt of the imminent disintegration of the Polish forces. That same morning one of the French footmen and the assistant gardener received in the mail the fateful little cards ordering them to report for military duty. They asked if they might see *Monsieur le Duc* before they left. David went to the door to say, good-by. He gravely shook their hands and wished them well. Now convinced that Britain and France would be at war with Germany in a matter of hours, David tried to reach his friends in London; but the French telephone circuits were hopelessly clogged. Giving up the struggle, he shrugged his shoulders, saying "There's nothing we can do from here right now. I'm sure that I shall hear from my brother the moment any decision is taken. Let's go for a swim."

Fruity Metcalfe was staying with us. Just before noon, as we all started down the lane toward the sea, a servant hurried after David to tell him that the British Ambassador was calling from Paris. Fruity and I went on. About ten minutes later, David joined us. Walking straight to the edge of the pool, he said in a quiet voice, "Great Britain has just declared war on Germany, and I am afraid in the end this may open the way for world Communism." Then there came a splash; he had dived into the pool.

From this moment on, the question uppermost in David's mind was how he might serve. In his farewell broadcast, David had said he would return to the service of his country if there should ever again be need of him. He would not consider staying in idleness on the French Riviera while his countrymen were hurrying to the colors. He finally got through to Walter Monckton in London, saying, "I want to offer my services in any capacity my brother deems appropriate, and I must return to Britain."

By reason of his earlier role as David's liaison with the Government during the Abdication, Walter had continued to act for David in London. Next day Walter telephoned to say guardedly, being mindful of possible eavesdropping by German agents, that he had had promising discussions and would be seeing us presently. He appeared at La Cröe three days later, having flown from London in a Government airplane. He brought from the King word that David and I were to return to London at our earliest convenience and that the King would be glad to send out his own airplane for the trip. Walter further informed David that he could have the choice of two jobs—either as a member of the British Military Mission attached to the French General Headquarters at Vincennes, or as Regional Commissioner of Wales, a civil-defense job that would obviously require our taking up residence in Britain. David was to inform the King of his preference on his arrival in London.

David was impatient to be off immediately. He would have preferred, I realized, to accept his brother's offer of the airplane. But I could not face the prospect of so long a flight. The distrust of planes that I had formed at Pensacola twenty years before had become a fixation with me. I told David that even if the German panzers were at the gates of La Cröe, I still would not entrust myself to an airplane. "I'm ready," I said, "to cross the Channel in a submarine, a destroyer, or, if necessary, a rowboat. But in an airplane—never."

"Well," said David patiently, turning to Walter Monckton, "that ends that."

Yet even so simple a matter as David's return in time of war to the service of his country was made difficult by the family cleavage that was to us the most unfortunate consequence of the Abdication. Fruity Metcalfe, who was still with us, invited us to stay with Baba and him at their home, Hartfield House, in Sussex. The house was close enough to London for David to be able to motor back and forth during the day and conduct his business with his brother and government officials.

Later that day, David received a rather mysterious telephone call from the Ambassador, Sir Ronald Campbell, in Paris. Sir Ronald advised that the Government wished us to start north by motor for the Channel Coast and to stop and telephone the Embassy again. At that time we should be given directions for the final stage of the journey.

[312]

David interpreted these directions to mean that a naval vessel was being sent from Britain to pick us up, and he decided upon Vichy, almost in the exact center of France, and equidistant from the ports of Calais, Cherbourg, and Le Havre, as the place to head for.

There followed an afternoon and night of feverish preparations. Because of the danger of France's being overrun, I was determined to take advantage of the expedition to transport certain valuable possessions, mostly David's, to England for safe storage. To save weight and space I had them wrapped in brown butcher's paper and put into cardboard boxes.

We started north on the afternoon of September 8, David, Fruity Metcalfe, and I, in our car, with our three Cairns, Pookie, Preezi, and Detto, and our baggage in a station wagon. I included the dogs with some misgivings. British law requires that dogs brought into Britain from foreign parts be quarantined for six months, and, being well aware of the regulation, I was sure that our beloved pets would fall victim to it. But neither David nor I could bear to leave them behind.

We reached Vichy the second evening, having stopped the first night at Avignon. David telephoned the Embassy, only to be told that the arrangements for the last stage of the journey had not been completed, and we were to remain where we were for further instructions. We waited another day and another night, and all the while David's impatience mounted. Deciding that a personal appearance at the Embassy would galvanize matters, he had the rest of us up early on the third morning and on our way to Paris. Entering the city during the early afternoon, we drove directly to the British Embassy, where David saw the Ambassador. The cloak-and-dagger atmosphere was preserved to the end. Sir Ronald said that we were to continue to Cherbourg, where at the office of the Admiral Commandant of the Port a British officer would take us in charge. David thanked the Ambassador, hurried back to the car, and by nightfall we were at Evreux and the Grand-Cerf—the little inn where in December, 1936, I had left the notes of my conversation with David. The same proprietor was still in charge, and I was able to thank him personally for his kindness in turning over the lost piece of paper to Sir Harold Nicolson. Next morning we continued on to Cherbourg.

The Admiral was on the lookout for us, but he was obviously demoralized by our unsightly array of baggage. Unwilling to have his neat drawing room encumbered with my cardboard cartons, he suggested politely that they might better be stored in the garden until

[313]

the British officer responsible for us put in an appearance. David was supervising the unloading of the two cars when into the garden strode Dickie Mountbatten, in the uniform of a captain in the Royal Navy. Dickie is a striking figure, and thus encountered on the Admiral's lawn, he personified at once the majesty and tradition of the British Navy. In his wake clattered and clanked another martial figure, Randolph Churchill, in the uniform of the lieutenant of the 4th Hussars.

Both were old friends—David and I were glad to have them with us under these circumstances. Randolph had been delegated by his famous father, by this time re-established in the Cabinet as First Lord of the Admiralty, to represent him and to escort David back across the Channel. The choice of Dickie Mountbatten, the King's Naval Aide, to command the destroyer that was to take David back to England, was an affecting example of Winston Churchill's sense of historical appropriateness. David's trained eyes, however, did not fail to notice that Randolph's spurs had been strapped on upside down.

The reunion in the garden at Cherbourg was heart-warming. The presence of Dickie and Randolph meant to us that Winston wanted David's return to his native land to go off well and smoothly; and David was grateful, on his account and mine, for this sign of regard.

Dickie had crossed the Channel under cover of darkness the night before in H.M.S. *Kelly*—the destroyer in which he was presently to achieve fame in the fierce fighting off Crete. His orders were to make the return run at night, so as to avoid risk of possible interception by German aircraft or submarines. Our destination was Portsmouth, and Dickie estimated that we should arrive there about midnight.

David assured Dickie we should be ready to leave just as soon as our "things" had been stowed aboard the *Kelly*.

"Good," said Dickie. "Where are your things?"

David waved an apologetic hand at the pile on the Admiral's lawn —suitcases on one side, the cardboard boxes on the other. For a long instant Dickie's aplomb deserted him, as his eyes ranged over this unsightly array.

"Do you mean to tell me," he demanded, pointing at the cardboard boxes, "that those things are yours?"

"They certainly are, Dickie," I answered.

I knew enough about naval customs to appreciate how irritating it was to a commanding officer's sense of fitness to have his tidy vessel cluttered up with what must have looked to him like the odds and ends of a rummage sale. Moreover, Dickie protested that David was to be piped aboard the *Kelly,* and for David to arrive at the gangway with that collection would ruin the effect.

"Well, Dickie," I finally said, "just because we're the first refugees you have seen is no reason for the Royal Navy to turn up its nose at us. These are my clothes and David's things. You can arrange this any way you want—take David out first and then, when nobody's looking, send the launch back for me. But these things go with us." Dickie capitulated.

Dusk was darkening the western sky as the *Kelly* moved out of the harbor. Soon we were rushing through the night at high speed, zigzagging to evade any U-boat that might be lying along our course. Dickie left his post on the bridge only long enough to join David, Randolph, and me for a hasty supper in his cabin. As he started back to the bridge, he asked David if he would like to join him there. David followed him. He was gone some time. It was an eerie sensation to sit in that tiny cabin, making small talk, while the ship rushed furiously through the darkness, the sea making a swishing sound against the vessel's steel hull, and the atmosphere inside taut with the hum and howl of mysterious machinery.

When David returned, he was thoughtful and abstracted. It was not hard for me to guess what must have been passing through his mind. It was not quite three years since he had left England in another destroyer, in the night. He was wondering what he would find on his return, and how his family would treat him and me, and whether it would be possible for him to find a really useful job in his country's service. The coldness that had settled down between him and his family had hurt him more than he could bring himself to admit. He had paid in full the price exacted for his choice, and now he longed to share, as he had done before, his country's perils, and to end the separation. As he sat in silence, thinking his thoughts, the speed of the ship slackened; there was a banging of metal doors, a clatter of boots on the deck.

"We must be entering the harbor," David said. He came to the divan on which I was sitting. "I don't know how this will work out," he said quietly. "War should bring families together, even a Royal Family. But I don't know." He pressed my hand, turned quickly, and walked out of the cabin.

Although Portsmouth was completely blacked out, David was accorded full honors as he stepped down the gangway. A red carpet was spread for him; a naval guard of honor, at the foot of the gangway, snapped to attention. Even in the pitch darkness the little ceremonial was beautifully carried off, as only the British can manage such things. David was stirred. He remarked later, "Of course, I have seen hundreds of guards of honor, but I don't think I was ever prouder of inspecting one."

Admiral Sir William James, Commander in Chief at Portsmouth, and his wife, put us up for the night at Admiralty House. They gave us some refreshments, and we chatted with them a little while before going to bed. They were very nice to me, almost desperately polite. However, under the politeness, I became aware that it was I, rather than the former King, who was the object of their covert curiosity. When I was chatting with one, I could feel the sidelong glance of the other, charged with speculation, roving searchingly over me. In the oblique scrutiny there hovered the unasked question: *Can this really be the Mrs. Simpson who caused it all? Can this be the woman who took from us our King?* Under other circumstances the curiosity masked by politeness might have been flattering, even mildly challenging. So much depended upon the outcome of our trip—David's future, and mine with his. If only the rift between him and his family could be healed! I privately sought the answer to our dilemma in the Admiral's bright blue eyes set in boyishly pink cheeks. But there was no way of telling what he or his wife really thought of me. And deep in my heart I knew that I would never know what they or any other Briton thought.

Next day we motored to the Metcalfes' house. While I stayed behind with Baba, David drove to London the following afternoon for a talk with his brother at Buckingham Palace. David had meanwhile decided that he would prefer the Regional Commissioner's job in England to the one with the military liaison group in France. The art and technique of war, he realized, had radically changed since he had last served with the British Army; and it seemed to him, therefore, that his particular gifts could be most advantageously employed working with community organizations on civil defense and civilian morale. When David returned from the Palace he was sanguine. His brother appeared to agree with him that the Regional Commissioner's job was the right choice. In any case, the King had observed that there was no hurry about making a decision. "Let's see how things go," he told David at the end. "Meanwhile, I'll discuss your ideas with the Government."

So far as David's family or the Court were concerned, I simply did not exist. The fact that our love had withstood the tests and trials of three difficult years made no difference. Neither did his desire to share, however humbly, the wartime burdens of the Royal Family and the hazards that war would present to us all. Nothing was ever said. It was simply a case of our being confronted with a barrier of turned backs, rigid and immovable. For the first time I saw David's face set itself into a mask barely concealing his deep-smoldering anger. But because he was determined to do something useful for his country, he put aside his personal feelings and went about his appointments in London with good grace.

Among others, he saw Winston Churchill at the Admiralty. Now directing the affairs of the Royal Navy and already marked as the embodiment of the martial spirit, Winston said to David, "I know, Sir, that you and I have not always seen eye to eye on foreign policy— but we're all in this war together, aren't we?"

"Yes, indeed," said David. "That's why I'm here."

"I know that," said Winston. "And we all want you back."

Sometimes I drove up to London with David for the day. One afternoon we went out to Sunningdale for a sentimental visit to the Fort. The lawn was overgrown; the garden in which we had spent so many happy hours together had become a mass of weeds; and the house itself, shuttered, damp, and dark, was slowly decaying. It was a sad visit.

On our trips in and out of London, David was often recognized by passers-by on the sidewalks. They lifted their hats to him. There were occasional cheers and heartening echoes of the familiar nickname going back to his Edward, Prince of Wales, days: "Good old Ted; good to see you back."

Perhaps reports of these small but heartfelt demonstrations of affection reached the Palace. In any event, David one day was suddenly summoned to the War Office, to be informed by Field-Marshal Sir Edmund Ironside, then Chief of the Imperial General Staff, that he was to be assigned to the British Military Mission at Vincennes and was to report for duty as soon as possible. David heard nothing more from his brother. The civil defense job was never mentioned again. David and I suspected—perhaps unfairly—that some of the older members of the Court had recommended that, rather than encourage any possible revival of the former King's popularity, he be posted safely and obscurely outside the country.

Naturally, David was disappointed, but he chose not to make an issue of the matter. He still retained the rank of Admiral of the Fleet and of Field-Marshal in the Army, and Marshal of the Royal Air

[317]

Force. Rather than confront the War Office with an awkward problem, he cheerfully agreed to waive temporarily his rank and accept that of Major-General.

We remained in England only long enough for David to be briefed on his new duties. One forenoon late in September, we left Portsmouth in the destroyer *Express,* under command of a young officer who was anxious to finish without delay his mission and be off for his war station in the North Sea. The voyage was terribly rough— the roughest, in fact, I have ever experienced, although that impression may be colored by the fact that it was my first trip in a destroyer in a heavy sea. During most of the crossing, I sat on the floor of the captain's cabin, while our suitcases careened from one bulkhead to the other. We were put ashore at Cherbourg in the late afternoon. Several officers attached to the Military Mission were at the dock to meet us. Fruity Metcalfe had returned with us, in major's uniform, to be David's A.D.C. Our Austrian chauffeur had had to return to his own country when war became imminent, or risk internment by the French. Fortunately, Ladbrook, who had left us at Wasserleonburg two years before, was too old for military service; now he was glad to resume his old duties and accompanied us back to France.

CHAPTER XXXI

The Debacle

DIRECTLY ON OUR RETURN TO FRANCE, DAVID REPORTED TO HIS
Military Mission at French General Headquarters outside Paris. The
head of this mission was a professional soldier, Major-General Sir
Richard Howard-Vyse. Because David would have to live at Headquarters and travel a great deal, and as there was no telling when
the lull following upon the collapse of Poland would explode into
furious action, our first decision was not to open the house on the
Boulevard Suchet. We decided to stay at the Trianon Palace Hotel
in Versailles, and, being anxious to do my bit, I joined a French relief
organization, the *Colis de Trianon,* that had been started by the indefatigable Elsie Mendl. Its purpose was to distribute comfort kits
among the French troops, containing among other things a knitted
sweater, socks, soap, gloves, cigarettes, and toilet articles. The various items were collected and packed by volunteer workers like me,
and we put in long days at Versailles on the kits.

Now followed that odd interlude known as the Phony War—a
period when the *Wehrmacht* stood silent and menacing behind the
Rhine and along the northern frontier of France. A considerable
part of the French Army had meanwhile disappeared into the concrete casements of the Maginot Line, braced for the blow that was
mystifyingly held in abeyance. Paris, or rather the part of Paris that
I knew, waited as on tiptoe for the next paroxysm. The town houses,
for the most part, remained shuttered and empty as they had been
left at the beginning of the war; the men had gone off with their
regiments, the women and the children to the relative security of the
country.

Wearying of hotel life, I soon decided to take a chance and

move back to the house on the Boulevard Suchet. By this time an old friend of David's, Major Gray Phillips, of the Black Watch, had come from England to join our household as Comptroller. He helped me reopen the house. But Boulevard Suchet was never again the same. I left it exactly as the staff had closed it for the summer, with the dust covers shrouding the furniture and the rugs rolled up alongside the walls. The tall windows were hung with heavy black curtains, drawn tightly at night to prevent even a sliver of light from showing.

On my return to Paris I took another job, joining the motor branch, called the *Section Sanitaire,* of the French Red Cross, and contributing my car. This job required my making frequent trips to the hospitals behind the Maginot Line, delivering plasma, bandages, and cigarettes. Between the *Section Sanitaire* and the *Colis de Trianon,* I was busier and perhaps more useful than I had ever been in my life. There were weeks when I did not see David at all, but he telephoned when he could. He, too, was continuously shuttling back and forth between Vincennes and the French lines.

These plasma-delivering expeditions used to take me into the rear areas of the Maginot Line every ten days or so, and the trips themselves lasted, as a rule, three days. A charming French woman, the Countess de Ganay, known to her friends as "Pinky," was assigned to me as driver; we usually had another Red Cross worker along to relieve Pinky at the wheel and to help with the unloading and distribution at the other end. We were up by five-thirty and off before seven o'clock. It was no fun to be on the roads in proximity to the front after dark. Huge camions had a habit of materializing out of the gloom, with nothing to mark their careening progress but a keyhole gleam of light. Pinky was a fast and skillful driver, with a command of language, when the rights of the road were at issue, that would have done credit to any trooper. She conceded nothing to the male prerogative or, if a camion had roused her ire, to superior size.

In Paris it was the unreality of the lull that dominated one's thinking. No bombs fell, and the hope grew that perhaps none would ever be dropped. But on the Maginot Line one gained an entirely different view. There, in the presence of thousands of men concealed under camouflage in the countryside, or at their underground posts in the elaborate chain of fortifications, one sensed that events were under compression, as when a spring is coiled. There was no telling when a button might be pushed, the spring released, and savage violence unleashed.

The winter passed. And still nothing really important happened. David, like me, was all the while on the move. His personal position, I had come to realize, was delicate and even difficult. There was no precedent in British military protocol for regulating the role and position of a former monarch who had taken subordinate rank. There had even been an awkward incident involving his brother, the Duke of Gloucester, also a Major-General but now outranking him as a Royal Duke in the table of precedence. David's liaison duties often took him to the British Army sector near the Belgian frontier. On one of these visits he encountered his brother, who was on the staff of Lord Gort, commanding the British Expeditionary Force. While the two were visiting the billets of a battalion of the Brigade of Guards, a company guard "turned out" to render the honors due to general officers. The Duke of Gloucester had fallen behind to talk to a friend. The guard, consisting of a sergeant and some guardsmen, presented arms as David walked by with the commanding officer. Automatically, David returned the salute. Several days later, after David had returned to headquarters at Vincennes, he was coldly notified that he had violated military etiquette by taking a salute technically intended for his brother. David shrugged the incident off, but the manner in which the rebuke was administered, the fact that so trifling an action had been deemed worthy of notice, was petty to say the least. And it was all the more galling to him for the reason that many of the British officers with whom he was thrown into close contact had served with him during the First World War; they remembered him with affection as a former comrade in arms and would gladly have shown him that, whatever the constitutional issues of the Abdication, they were happy to see him back in uniform and once more among them. In that one respect we had two wars to deal with—the big and still leisurely war, in which everybody was caught up, and the little cold war with the Palace, in which no quarter was given. David has always had a gift for dealing with troops—the gift of the common touch and understanding. His admiration and respect for the fighting man in the ranks are deep, and their roots go back to the trenches of World War I. It seemed to me tragic that this unique gift, humbly proffered, was never really called upon, out of a fear, I judged, that it might once more shine brightly, too brightly.

Spring came early. April was lovely and May even lovelier. The sun shone; the chestnut trees bloomed; flowers suddenly spangled the meadows and paths of the Bois de Boulogne. And with equal suddenness, just when France seemed about to recover its wonted joyfulness, Hitler's forces sprang forward, and before one had really grasped that the Phony War had ceased to be phony, it was all but lost.

All that I could pump from David, when one afternoon he stopped unexpectedly at the house on his way back from the French front, was the closemouthed admission that while the battle was serious the main Allied forces were not yet engaged, and that therefore there was no reason for alarm. Then he said good-by and drove off to Vincennes.

Three days or so later—it was either May 15 or 16—David burst into the house late in the afternoon. I had just returned from the Red Cross. Seizing my arm, he said, "You're leaving Paris this evening. I'll give you two hours to pack, but not a second more."

Having already made one retreat through France, I was not eager to start another on such short notice. Moreover, as I told David, my job was with the French Red Cross, and it would not be seemly for me to take to my heels the minute Paris was in danger. Nevertheless David insisted, and I finally said I would ask the advice of the American Ambassador, my friend, Bill Bullitt.

When I reached Bill on the telephone, he was confidence personified. Nothing, he insisted, could defeat the great French Army. It was invincible. To be sure, it was in some trouble now, but it would presently turn and fight, and everything would be all right. "Remember the stand on the Marne," Bill said, "Remember the taxicabs that turned the tide." However, he finally suggested that it would be just as well if I went away for a while, perhaps into the center of France, until the situation was stabilized.

Before leaving, we got out our battered copy of the *Guide Michelin* to look for a place to head for.

Running my eyes over the map, I noticed the name Blois, in the château country. It was there that I had stopped with Perry Brownlow, on my way to Cannes in 1936. I remembered the charming little hotel and the kindly *patron*. If Bill Bullitt was right, Blois was the logical place to stop while assessing the situation.

David agreed. The roads leading south and west from Paris were crowded as I have never seen roads crowded. There were endless lines of cars, many with a mattress strapped to the roof and, I surmised, jerry cans of gasoline hidden inside. Judging by the license plates, all of Western Europe was on the run—Belgians, Dutch, French. We had a hard, slow trip, with many long waits in the traffic.

Ladbrook drove with his usual skill and patience. It was dusk when we finally reached Blois, and I was discouraged to see the entrance of the hotel blocked with cars, most of them with Belgian license plates. "There'll be no room for us here tonight," I warned David. The innkeeper recognized me as I entered the little lobby, and a smile lit up his face.

"Here I am in trouble again," I said as cheerfully as I could. "But this time I have my husband with me. Could you possibly put us up for the night?"

Weariness had furrowed his kindly face, and he must already have been driven to distraction. "The entire population of Belgium has been trying to crowd into my little inn," he said. "I don't have a bed left. But I'll do something about you."

Eventually, he found two small cots, which he put in a tiny sitting room on the ground floor. There David and I spent the night.

After breakfast the next morning David decided to change the plan and take me to Biarritz on the Basque coast. From there, if the Germans overran France in a rush, it would be only a step to the Spanish frontier. We were off again, and, in the late afternoon, very weary, we drove up to the Hôtel du Palais, which was also packed to the rafters with refugees.

Early the following day David went back to Paris to rejoin the Mission. The German propagandists now played a most unchivalrous trick on me. For no purpose that I could possibly imagine, unless further to demoralize the French by suggesting that Fifth Columnists were everywhere, the German radio blared out the news that the Duchess of Windsor had arrived at Biarritz, and was staying at the Hôtel du Palais. It even gave my room number, and correctly. Instantly I became the most unpopular guest in the long history of the Hôtel du Palais. By my belated appearance I had brought this sanctuary to the notice of the enemy.

David telephoned every day. Through his guarded language I was made to realize that Paris was almost certainly doomed. Then, perhaps a week after my arrival at Biarritz, he called to say that his Mission had been ordered to leave Paris. A new threat had appeared. The entrance into the war of the Italians on the side of the Germans was imminent. David was being given a leave of absence from the Mission to close up La Cröe and also to establish contact with the French forces drawn up along the Italian frontier.

David reappeared the following afternoon with Ladbrook; Gray Phillips had remained in Paris, while Fruity had been ordered back

[323]

to England. Very early next morning we started eastward across France, in a tangle of mixed military and civilian traffic, with Ladbrook doing his best to keep the car moving. The smell of catastrophe was in the air; and everywhere the family car with the mattress lashed on top was in evidence, the symbol of many nations in headlong flight. It occurred to me that we were breasting a tide; all the traffic was headed in the direction we had left, toward the coast. We alone were pointed toward the Italian frontier.

The day we arrived, May 29, was warm and sunny. From my window I had a wide view of the Mediterranean, heaving with gentle glassy swells. Some distance offshore a few fishing boats were working their nets. Otherwise the sea was empty and serene. The war, which in the morning had seemed to be breathing down our necks, now seemed altogether unreal and remote.

During the next few days—days of peaceful calm—I was seldom far from the radio. The Paris bulletins were mere rhetoric.

Then one day at lunch—June 10, to be exact—as we were sitting on the terrace with the French singer, Maurice Chevalier, whom we had invited in the perhaps forlorn hope that he might be inspired to supply a last flash of lightheartedness in that dismal atmosphere, the radio that David had put beside his chair announced that Italy had entered the war and fighting had already started along the French frontier, some forty miles to the east of us. Chevalier hurried off without waiting to finish his lunch. Throughout the afternoon our British neighbors kept calling to tell us that they were packing to leave as fast as they could and urging us to do likewise. But David refused to panic. He knew that strong French forces were drawn up along the Italian frontier, and was confident of their ability to handle Mussolini's reluctant legions.

Nevertheless, the sunny tranquillity of the Côte d'Azur began to disintegrate into melodramatic chaos. Not far from us, at St. Raphael, was a French military airfield. Several times a day a group of aircraft would form over the villa and wheel eastward toward Italy. One night the boom of heavy naval guns came over the water accompanied by brilliant flashes on the horizon—the French fleet, supported by the British, bombarding Genoa. That was a sound David understood and liked. But these distant and ominous concussions did not reassure me; my mind kept returning to the radio bulletins telling of collapse and catastrophe throughout the length of France.

My uneasiness turned into real apprehension several days later when Gray Phillips rejoined us. He looked exhausted; his uniform was rumpled, and he needed a shave. It had taken him four days and three nights to travel from Paris. The railroads were paralyzed; he had hitchhiked rides on French ambulances and military lorries. I noticed that his clothes bulged curiously.

"What have you got in your pockets?" I asked.

"Some of your things from Boulevard Suchet," he said.

Out of his pocket came an extraordinary collection of *bibelots*, including half a dozen George II silver saltcellars that had come down to David from the Duke of Cumberland.

Gray Phillips was famished; while he ate we bombarded him with questions. He was appalled by the suddenness with which France had disintegrated; all capacity for resistance, in his opinion, was gone; the Germans and Italians could range France at will.

I told him that everyone was urging us to leave but we had decided to remain for the time being. Gray agreed with us, remarking that by now he was sick and tired of running from the Germans.

That afternoon Gray went to see some mutual friends of ours. I saw him coming up the driveway on his return, looking very downcast. I called out the window to him and asked where he had been and why he looked so concerned. He replied that he had walked over to see George and Rosa Wood and that he wanted to have a talk with David and me right away.

George Wood had been a captain in the British Army during the First World War; their daughter had married an Austrian, Prince Ernst Hohenberg; and they had been with her and their son-in-law in Vienna when the Prince had been taken by the Nazis. With a fervor born of their firsthand experience with Nazi methods, they had pressed upon Gray the necessity of our leaving immediately.

So persuasive were the arguments they had advanced that they had convinced him that this was the only course to take. After David had listened to Gray, he said to me, "I think he's right; much as we want to stay, I think we had better plan to leave."

Besides, one of the officers of David's Mission had telephoned from Bordeaux several days earlier to say that they were embarking for England immediately.

David then called the British Consul General at Nice, Major Dodds, who informed him that instructions had just come from London to his colleague at Menton, on the Italian side of Monte Carlo, ordering him to burn his papers and evacuate his post. Major Dodds added that he, himself, was preparing to do likewise.

"Where are you going?" David asked.

"To Spain, Sir."

"How do you expect to get into Spain?"

"We have been given a piece of paper by the Spanish Consul here asking that we be passed across the frontier. Can I help you in any way? What are your plans, Sir?"

"I'll let you know as soon as I have decided," said David.

"Sir," the Consul went on, "I urge that you leave with us. Will you call me when you have reached a decision?"

After some little further discussion among the three of us, David went off to telephone Consul Dodds. He informed David that his group, including the Vice-Consul from Menton, would be passing by La Cröe at noon the next day. They proposed to travel in convoy and would be honored to have us join them. In a little while David returned to say tonelessly, "Let's get on with the packing. I've told Dodds we'll be ready to leave with him."

Nearly all of our most cherished possessions—those that were not at Boulevard Suchet—were at La Cröe. There was no choice but to leave them where they were. The American Consul at Nice offered to put the house under the protection of the United States, which was then neutral, and to affix his seal to the door. David disappeared into his penthouse office on the roof to finish going through his papers, putting the important ones in a big tin box that would be taken with us, and filing the others in boxes to be stored in the strong room.

When I went downstairs in the morning, the Buick was waiting in the driveway, and Ladbrook, with his habitual British thoroughness, was calmly directing the storing of the overflow of baggage in a trailer hooked on behind.

Shortly before noon, the Woods drove up the driveway in their Citroën, towing a heavily laden trailer. Not long afterward Consul Dodds and the Vice-Consul from Menton arrived in their cars.

The staff was grouped around the entrance to say good-by. As I was about to enter the car, the gardener stepped forward to press into my arms a huge bunch of tuberoses. "Your birthday present, darling," David whispered. In the confusion I had forgotten the date—June 19. I buried my face in the sweet-smelling mass, grateful for being able to take away with me at least this lovely reminder of La Cröe. Our staff wept as we left; so did I.

The route that Consul Dodds had worked out led across the southern part of France, north of Marseilles, to Perpignan, near the Spanish frontier. But we had no way of telling what conditions would be encountered on the way, or whether we could get through at all.

As we passed through Cannes, I saw in the roadstead two rusty, nondescript cargo ships that had been diverted to pick up the rear guard of the British Riviera colony. Fletcher, the Duke's Scots Guards piper and servant, was sailing aboard one of them, as he was in uniform and would have been subject to internment in neutral Spain.

We made fairly good time until we reached Arles, where we spent the night. Next morning, still in convoy with the Consuls, we were off early, hoping to reach Perpignan by the afternoon. Barricades had been erected across the highway on the approaches to the bigger towns, and Ladbrook was repeatedly obliged to slow down so that our credentials could be inspected. Counting upon being favorably remembered, at least by the older gendarmes, for his service with the French Army during the First World War, David had the inspiration of introducing himself at the barricades with the statement, *"Je suis le Prince de Galles. Laissez-moi passer, s'il vous plaît."* This introduction worked magically with the veterans.

It was late morning when, wearied but exultant over our progress, we arrived at Perpignan, at last in sight of the safe barrier of the Pyrenees. From the concierge of the hotel there we learned that the crossing of the frontier would have to be made at a little town called Port Bou, ten miles away, but no purpose would be served by our continuing on unless we first secured visas for ourselves and the rest of our party. Fortunately, there was a Spanish consulate in Perpignan, and David and George Wood set out hopefully after lunch to arrange matters with the Consul. On their return an hour later, David was the angriest man I have ever seen.

"To put the matter bluntly," David fumed, "the Consul won't let us into Spain. He has the peculiar idea that we might become a charge on the Spanish Government."

It is impossible for David to stay angry long. "Do you know what this fellow had the effrontery to ask?" David went on, with a bleak smile. "He wanted my autograph for his grandchild. I was standing at the counter, holding our passports in my hand. So I shoved them toward him, saying that if he'd put his signature on them, along with his stamp, I'd gladly provide mine for his grandchild. Thought he'd explode, he was so mad. Then I took the autograph book and signed it anyway. Maybe the grandchild will put in a good word for us."

Milling about the lobby and bar of the hotel were scores of other refugees, who, like ourselves, were pulling every possible wire to enter Spain. Understandably, they were in no mood to look on with composure while later arrivals tried to maneuver in front of them. The magic key that finally unlocked the door for us was David's remembering his long-standing friendship with the Spanish Ambassador to France, José Lequerica. Figuring that he had doubtless moved with the French Government to Bordeaux, David returned to the local Consul to try a new gambit. The Ambassador, David said, would unquestionably vouch for us. He therefore proposed that the Consul put in an urgent call to his superior at Bordeaux. Meanwhile, we would go on to Port Bou and wait there, on the French side, until the authorization came through. Softened, perhaps by the earlier gift of the autograph, the Consul agreed, although he at first protested that only David and I could be admitted: the rest of our party would have to remain behind. David stood firm; all would go into Spain or none; the question was one for the Ambassador to decide.

As we left the hotel, two middle-aged couples who had obviously been trying to eavesdrop on David's report to the rest of us got up and followed us to the car. "You going to Spain?" asked one of the women tipsily. David replied evenly that we were going to the frontier but none of us had visas. The woman measured him suspiciously. "I don't believe you," she snapped. "But we're going to follow you. If you get through, we'll be right behind." A little while later Ladbrook informed David that a strange car was tagging after our convoy. We took our place in the double line of cars that was drawn up at the frontier barrier. Nearly an hour later a uniformed functionary ran out to say that the Consul at Perpignan had authorized the passage of our entire party at the request of the Spanish Ambassador.

❧ CHAPTER XXXII ❧

Iberian Interlude

AFTER BEING ON THE MOVE SO LONG, IT WAS A RELIEF JUST TO BE able to sit still for a little while. For two days David and I rested at Barcelona before continuing on to Madrid.

In a material sense, David and I were more or less back where we were in December, 1936—certainly homeless, once more adrift in a strange country, our possessions scattered, David without a post, and our prospects befogged. Precariousness was, of course, no stranger to me, but it was still fairly new to David. On the whole, he adapted himself to this refugee interlude with far more resourcefulness and good humor than I might have expected from a person with no previous experience of this sort of adversity. But he was certainly no Admirable Crichton. It is said that no man is ever a hero to his valet. I decided that it is almost impossible for a Prince to be a hero to his wife without a valet.

David had been unexpectedly philosophical when his valet or rather soldier-servant Fletcher had sailed from Cannes on the morning of the last day at La Cröe. "It may sound like a strange thing for a grown man to admit," David remarked after Fletcher had gone, "but this will be the first time in many years that I've been without a valet. However, I'll manage." David managed, all right: he managed to drive me to the edge of desperation. As his farewell service, Fletcher had packed David's things with the faultless precision of which the British valet is master, the suits beautifully pressed and folded, the ties, handkerchiefs, socks, shirts, underwear, and shoes all in their proper compartments and painstakingly matched. By the second day at Barcelona, David had reduced Fletcher's masterpiece to a shambles.

What wasn't on the floor was scattered about the room—on the backs of chairs, on the top of the bureau.

Having been brought up in a different way, and being familiar from my previous marriages with the male capacity for disorganization, I began one morning, while David was out, to pick up his things and to sort them and to put them in bureau drawers, which it had never occurred to him to use. He was back before I finished.

"Wallis!" he demanded from the door. "What the devil are you doing?"

"Just trying to make room on the floor so that you can walk around," I said sweetly.

"I can't have you doing this," he protested.

"I don't mind," I said. "If you'll just tell me where you put the mate of this shoe—"

Taking the lone shoe from my hand, David said something very nice. "I am ashamed. I curse myself for having become so dependent upon a valet. Now get out of this room," he continued, propelling me firmly toward the door. "I'll deal with it."

In justice to him, I must say that he tried. But the result to me was unnerving—instead of being left on the floor, the clothes were now tossed hopefully into the closet as he discarded them and the door closed to hide the chaos within.

In our general misfortune there appeared at this point a promising gleam of light. David was hopeful that with Winston Churchill, his great friend, at last Prime Minister, an appropriate job would quickly be found for him in his country's service.

Buoyed up by this hope, we continued on to Madrid, accompanied by the Woods and Gray Phillips. By a strange coincidence, the British Ambassador was Sir Samuel Hoare, to whom David had turned early in the Abdication crisis. Our meeting with Sir Samuel in Madrid came off very well, with the past scrupulously ignored by both parties. Sir Samuel arranged for us to be put up at the Ritz and gave us a big dinner at the Embassy, where, for the first time in a month, we had news that we could trust about the course of the war—bad news to be sure.

The Ambassador had important information for us: Winston Churchill wanted David to return to Great Britain immediately by way of Portugal. Toward that end, two flying boats of the Coastal Command were to be sent to Lisbon, on our arrival, to pick us up. He also told us that the Duke of Westminster had offered us the use of his house, Eaton Hall, near Chester. In the light of the urgency

Winston attached to David's return, Sir Samuel suggested to David that we leave Madrid at once.

After all that we had been through, the plan struck me as very sensible, with the flying boats supplying an appropriate Churchillian touch. My fear of flying was forgotten in the prospect of escaping from a Europe that was on the verge of passing entirely under Nazi domination. But David had his back up. Still resentful over the cool reception accorded him on his last visit to London, he made up his mind, without taking me fully into his confidence, that certain conditions would have to be clearly spelled out in advance of his returning. One was the kind of job that the Government had in mind for him—and he was eager to be put to work. The other was the question of whether or not I was to be accorded equality with the wives of his brothers.

However, all that I knew at the time was that cables were flying back and forth between Winston and David, that some kind of row over what David dismissed as "mere details" was brewing between them. In consequence of the conflict over David's conditions, our departure from Madrid was postponed from one day to the next; but meanwhile, thanks to David's family connections and the friends he had made on earlier visits to Madrid, we were never at a loss for things to occupy our time.

One evening we dined on the veranda of the Ritz with Doña Sol, sister of the Duke of Alba, a chic woman but one with a strong personality who completely disconcerted both David and me by rendering the Fascist salute as she crossed the threshold. And one of David's cousins by marriage, the Infante Alfonso, who was married to Beatrice, daughter of the Duke of Edinburgh (Queen Victoria's second son) and a sister of Queen Marie of Rumania, also came to dine with us. A general officer in the Spanish Air Force, he had fought under Generalísimo Franco in the Civil War. The Infante was full of information about German military might. He discoursed endlessly on the number of tanks, airplanes, and so on that the Germans had thrown into the battle.

David listened to his cousin's almost impassioned descriptions with no show of emotion. "Wait a minute," he finally said. "There's still the Channel to cross. Remember that, Ali." There is something about the refusal of the British to take seriously the possibility of their ever being beaten that is surely one of the wonders of the human temperament. Ali's statistics, which had the ring of authenticity, raised my hair. But when I mentioned them to David afterward, he just shook his head. "Hitler doesn't know Winston—and Winston will never give up."

It was desperately hot in Madrid that June. But David could not tolerate an idle moment, and the Spanish siesta custom, so far as he was concerned, was honored chiefly in the breach. When he was not having discussions with officials, he had me off sight-seeing—to the Escorial, to see the tombs of the Spanish kings, and to the outskirts of the city, to inspect the ruins of the Civil War. Meanwhile, nothing having been settled between him and Churchill, David finally agreed, at Sir Samuel's suggestion, to proceed to Lisbon and await there the outcome of the consultations between Winston Churchill and Buckingham Palace.

Still in company with the Woods and Gray Phillips, David and I left Madrid early in July and motored across Spain, taking two days for the trip. We had known the British Ambassador to Portugal, Sir Walford Selby, and his wife in Vienna. He had arranged for us to be put up at the house of a Portuguese banker, Dr. Ricardo de Espirito Santo e Silva, in Estoril, near the town of Cascais, on the coast. We went there directly. Sir Walford was waiting for us, together with our host and hostess. The plan was for us to stay only overnight. In fact, the Ambassador had with him the captains of the two flying boats. Taking David and me aside, he whispered that everything had been arranged for us to leave either the next morning, or, if we wished, to rest after the long drive, the second morning. He was briskly outlining the various details of our departure when David interrupted. "Now, just a minute. I want to talk to you alone."

They walked into the library. After they returned to the sitting room, Sir Walford took his leave. David did not mention their conversation except to say, enigmatically, "I thought it proper to set Walford straight."

There was no doubt that Ambassador Selby had provided for us well. The house was of lovely pink stucco, with a big swimming pool, and the sitting rooms contained beautiful pieces of Lowestoft.

As matters turned out, I had plenty of time, too, for contemplating them. The trouble was that the "mere details" that had irked David in Madrid were now blowing up into a major issue. Although Winston Churchill had not been able to obtain from Buckingham Palace the answers to David's questions about what was to be done about David and me, Winston now pressed David to forget about his conditions and to come home in the flying boats. But David, much as he admired Winston and anxious as he was to be back in England, was not to be persuaded. He informed the Ambassador that he was not stirring from Lisbon until he knew where he stood. Because of the deadlock he requested Sir Walford to have the flying boats sent home immediately.

What followed now seems fantastic and perhaps even a little silly. But David's pride was engaged, and he was deadly serious. When, after some time, he felt it necessary to tell me what was going on, he put the situation in approximately these terms: "I won't have them push us into a bottom drawer. It must be the two of us together—man and wife with the same position. Now, I am only too well aware of the risk of my being misunderstood in pressing for this at such a time. Some people will probably say that, with a war on, these trifles should be forgotten. But they are not trifles to me. Whatever I am to be I must be with you; any position I am called upon to fill I can only fill with you."

It was characteristic of him to hold to such a view. It is one of the reasons why I know that he is a finer person than I can ever hope to be. But his stubbornness worried me as it had worried me on earlier occasions.

I tried as hard as I could to make him see the matter in another light: the importance above everything else of his not allowing his gallantry toward me to interfere with his returning to England in a war job. The question of my position as his wife, I said, could be dealt with later, if it had to be dealt with at all. But, as on more than one earlier occasion in our association, David turned a deaf ear to my argument. And in truth, all that he ever specifically asked for was a fairly simple thing: that I be received, just once, by the King, his brother, and the Queen, in order to erase by that single gesture of hospitality the stigma attaching to my never having been received since our marriage by the Royal Family, his family.

For me to suggest that I did not desire that recognition would be hypocritical. I felt almost as much as did David that I deserved it. But not, however, from a mere desire for social status. Rather, I wanted it for the reason that I dreaded being condemned to go through the rest of our lives together as the woman who had come between David and his family. Yet in Lisbon I felt, deep in my conscience, that it was scarcely seemly for us to make an issue of so private a matter when the rest of Britain was fighting for its life; and, while David agreed that it was undoubtedly a poor time to stand on a point of pride, he nevertheless insisted that it was also a time when old quarrels should be put aside and by a single action be buried forever. Therefore he would not yield.

And so began a day and two nights of what must have been one of the oddest and certainly one of the least satisfactory exchanges in the history of the British monarchy, with Winston firing away from No. 10, Downing Street, in the midst of his other distractions, and David countering from Cascais. Because the messages were all in code, to prevent any hint of the disagreement becoming known to German agents, who were swarming about Lisbon, the negotiations were routed through the harassed Ambassador, whose clerks had to do the coding and decoding. I was up both nights with David, pacing the floor, while he, in his dressing gown, chewing on a pencil, composed his replies. Comparing the exchanges, I was to think more than once that it was a one-sided struggle between master and pupil, and the outcome was not difficult to forecast. It was a hideous time for all of us—for Winston Churchill, with so many other and much more fateful problems facing him; for Gray Phillips, chafing over being kept in idleness while his country girded for the battle; for the Espirito Santos, steaming in the summer heat of Lisbon while their guests conferred interminably at their cool country house by the sea; for Rosa Wood, almost hysterical over the absence of news about her daughter, who was still in a Nazi prison in Austria; and for Sir Walford, who was caught in the cross fire between the Prime Minister and his former King.

The upshot of the exchange was that, no satisfactory answers having come from the Palace, and Winston being unable to achieve a compromise, David finally informed the Prime Minister that he would not and could not return to Great Britain so long as his conditions were ignored but that he was ready to serve anywhere overseas that his brother or Winston designated.

The dispute evaporated with the arrival of a warmly worded cable from Winston, which Gray Phillips telephoned from the Embassy. The message said, in effect, that the King would be pleased to appoint David Governor of the Bahamas.

David came to my room to tell me. "Well, darling," he began, "they've finally found a job for me."

The look on his face made me hold back the obvious question.

"The Bahamas," he added, "Governor of the Colony of the Bahamas—one of the few parts of the Empire I missed in my travels. It's a small governorship and three thousand miles from the war. Well, Winston said he was sorry, but it was the best he could do, and I shall keep my end of the bargain." He telephoned Gray Phillips at the Embassy. "Send Winston a cable telling him that I will accept the post, and we will leave on the first available ship."

While we were still at Cascais, Walter Monckton, who had meanwhile become Director General of the Ministry of Information, arrived by air. From him we gained our first intimation of what had been agitating the Prime Minister throughout the battle of words. British Intelligence had picked up information that German secret agents were plotting to kidnap us.

"But how could we possibly be of any use to them?" David asked, incredulously.

Walter was very serious. "Winston is convinced that Hitler is crazy enough to be tempted, in the event of a successful invasion of Britain, to try to put the Duke back on the throne in the belief that this would divide and confuse the people and weaken their will to resist further."

David was flabbergasted. "Winston couldn't possibly think that," he replied.

"Sir," Walter said, "in war Winston is always ingenious and imaginative. He overlooks no possibilities—however unlikely."

If a plot there was, David and I were afterward to decide that it must have been a pretty simple piece of intrigue. One day we received a call from a distinguished Spaniard. Our visitor said he had come on a confidential mission on behalf of the Spanish Government to offer us a house in Spain.

David thanked him, saying, "I have accepted a post under the British Colonial Office. I intend to serve my country."

What really lay behind this strange offer? We were never sure. It is David's conjecture that the Germans were behind the Spanish Government's offer; that they had in some way learned of, or suspected, the dispute between him and Churchill; that they hoped in some way to exploit his mood of dissatisfaction. David has always considered this plot one of the more amusing examples of the habitual German miscalculation of the British character.

CHAPTER XXXIII

Nassau: Five Fruitful Years

THE BIG DECISION HAVING BEEN TAKEN, WE HAD TO WAIT THREE frustrating weeks while a harassed Whitehall tried to fit our small destinies into the vast jumble of war. Because there was no direct steamship service between Lisbon and the Bahamas, we were confronted immediately by a difficulty. Fortunately, the *Excalibur,* of the American Export Lines, was scheduled to leave shortly for New York, and the line was persuaded by the British Government to divert the ship to Bermuda, where we could count upon connecting with the regular service of the Canadian National Steamship Company to the West Indies. Gray Phillips agreed to continue in David's service as Comptroller, and George Wood offered to accompany David as an aide as long as David needed him.

We sailed from Lisbon on August 1, 1940. The *Excalibur* was crowded with stranded Americans returning home and refugees from the already occupied countries. Among this heterogeneous company were my good friends, Tony and Margaret Biddle. Tony I had met years before in Baltimore during his bachelor days. Recently he had been the U.S. Ambassador to Poland, and I had come to know him and his wife, Margaret, in Paris after their escape the previous autumn with the remnants of the Polish Government. Now that the exile government had been forced to flee to Britain upon the French collapse, Tony was on his way back to Washington to report to President Roosevelt. During the days at sea they told me of their latest diplomatic vicissitudes with governments on the run; their accounts left me more concerned than ever about the Allied fortunes.

It was with regret that I saw the continent of Europe disappear. I felt a sense of being removed from the centers of action, from the main theater of the war and the land in which I had begun to make my new life. Much would be expected of David and even more of me as the wife of the Governor. And I was anxious to do well for David's sake, knowing how much he wanted to make a success of his new post.

At Bermuda we were the guests for nearly a week of the Governor, Lieutenant-General Sir Denis Bernard, while waiting for the Canadian ship, *Lady Somers,* to pick us up. Early on the morning of August 17, we landed at Nassau. David had been on the bridge while the ship entered the harbor, and the Captain had picked out Government House—our future home. When I came on deck, David pointed out to me a large, rambling building on a green knoll. "Darling, there it is. Our home for the duration." At that distance it looked not unlike a substantial Southern plantation house, with spacious verandas, jalousied windows, and surrounded by palm trees. Though the heat from the shore struck me like a blast from a suddenly opened oven, that first prospect was promising.

In an instant we were caught up in the pageantry of an official welcome. The Governor's Executive Council was waiting at the foot of the gangway; behind them were the other colonial officials, all in their tropical white uniforms and helmets, accompanied by their wives; and flanking them was the Bahamas police force, drawn up as a guard of honor. David was still in the khaki uniform of a Major-General; there had not been time for his white uniforms to be sent on from England. David always perspires easily in the heat; but on this occasion, in his heavy khaki, he suffered more than usual. I could see the black patches of wet coming through the back of his tunic before he had progressed halfway down the reception line.

We then walked across Rawson Square to the Legislative Council Chamber, where David was met by the President of the Legislative Council and the Speaker of the House of Assembly. He then took the oaths of allegiance and of office. By this time his clothes were wringing wet. He then had to attest the oaths by signing what was called the Oath Book. I noticed that David was having some trouble; he started his signature, stopped, blotted the paper, started again, only to stop. The bewigged Chief Justice stepped forward to dab the page of the ledger with another blotter; sweat was pouring down his face, too. Between pats of the Chief Justice's blotter and the squiggles of David's pen the signature was finally completed. The Chief Justice then stepped forward to add his as witness, still blotting across the page. When I later looked at the Oath Book, little remained of the signatures but undecipherable blots.

The wives of the leading citizens had done all they could to give Government House a festive look. That morning, in advance of our arrival, they had filled every room with bright tropical flowers. The wives of the officials showed us through the house and tried to make us feel at home. But the flowers could not disguise the need for fresh paint, and the late Victorian mahogany furniture bore the impress of many Governors and their families. As the ladies left, the wife of the Colonial Secretary remarked out of kindness, "I'm afraid you won't find this very comfortable after the houses you are used to in France."

I said, "It is absolutely lovely."

After a week, we decided that we could not live there until the building was renovated. The Legislative Assembly had in fact appropriated some money for essential repairs, and now voted an additional though modest sum toward the repairs and for the addition of a badly needed wing; David and I paid for the decorating ourselves. While Government House was being refurbished, we first stayed in a house generously loaned by Mr. and Mrs. Frederick Sigrist, and later in Westbourne, one of the homes of Sir Harry and Lady Oakes.

This was our quietest period of the war. Except for the short-wave broadcasts from London and the news programs from Miami one might almost have forgotten that Europe's nightmare still continued. That first winter of 1940-41, the United States still being at peace, the American visitors and tourists poured in; business-as-usual was still the rule in the shops of Bay Street. David, from his long experience in official life, was able to fit himself easily into his duties as Governor; and somewhat to my surprise and pleasure I was soon at home with those activities which by custom devolve upon the Governor's wife. By reason of that position I found myself automatically president of the local Red Cross and honorary president of the local branch of the Daughters of the British Empire. Because of Britain's increasing needs, with the Battle of Britain at its height and fighting intensifying in the Middle East, these duties had become far more than perfunctory, and they increasingly occupied my days.

Also, as I came to understand colonial politics—and they could erupt, I discovered, as violently in the local parliament as in the Mother of Parliaments at Westminster—I realized that I could best help David by cementing friendly relations with the wives of the leaders in all factions. In the Colony of the Bahamas, as in most British colonies, there was a traditional struggle between the Governor, as the representative of the British Government, and the elected local Assembly, representing the community. In the nature of the situation this eventually led to a certain coolness between Mr. (later Sir) Kenneth Solomon, the Speaker of the House of Assembly and David. There was, of course, nothing intrinsically personal about all this, although it was occasionally inconvenient for David. One of the advantages of being a woman is that one does not have to become emotionally engaged in the peculiar combativeness that males bring to politics. Mrs. Solomon, a woman who shared my views in this respect, and I soon became fast friends. A happy outcome of this friendship was that, while the Solomons had continued to come to official dinners, they had not attended our informal dinners for some time, and eventually I was able to produce the Speaker and his wife for a quiet, informal dinner. Although David began by being a little leery that a truce could be maintained through the evening, by the time the brandy had been passed and they had lighted their cigars, one would have thought that Crown and Parliament were on their way to being one and indivisible. That episode in a still unfamiliar land more than ever confirmed my long-time belief that a well-chosen dinner is one of the surest eradicators of political bias.

In order to make it easier to visit the out islands, of which there are some seven hundred, we purchased a fifty-seven-foot Elko cabin cruiser. We named her the *Gemini,* after the sign of the Zodiac under which I had been born. In her we went to nearly all the inhabited islands during the next few years.

A few months after Pearl Harbor, Nassau got its first real taste of war. The U-boats suddenly appeared in the Caribbean and off the Florida coast, to prey on the tankers and ore boats coming up from South America. In the space of ten days five shipwrecked crews landed in Nassau. With the other ladies of the Red Cross, I did what I could to make them comfortable while they awaited evacuation. As that terrible spring wore on we began to receive some truly heart-wrenching cases—men who had drifted for days without food or water under the searing tropical sun.

Now everything came with a rush. Under the lend-lease program a large American construction company moved into the island to begin building a large airfield, later named Windsor Field, for the joint use of the U.S. Air Transport Command and the R.A.F. Coastal Command. With the tourist trade cut off, the whole economy of the island became dependent upon these and other war activities. This economic upheaval gravely complicated David's job; the normal trade with the mainland was restricted, and real privation came to the natives, principally on the out islands where there was no war work to replace their accustomed livelihood.

Although it had never occurred to us that we might be in any particular danger, some unknown worrier in the Colonial Office suddenly had the idea that a German submarine might raid our island and seize David and, I presume, me and carry us off as hostages. At any rate, in March, 1942, a company of Cameron Highlanders was rushed in. With commendable zeal they promptly set up barbed-wire entanglements and posted sentries around Government House. More interesting still, the company commander insisted on staging mock raids from different directions. Usually these took place at night, and David and I, watching from the veranda as the stealthy figures slithered past the unsuspecting sentries, came to the conclusion that the Captain's offensive talents far overbalanced his defensive skill; for almost invariably he succeeded in penetrating his own lines, and his delight was to burst into Gray Phillips's room while he was asleep and declare him a prisoner.

David's hardest time came in the middle of that year. By now the construction of the airfield was gathering momentum. The contractors had brought in a considerable group of American technical and supervisory personnel; but for their basic labor force they depended upon recruiting local workmen. In general these were paid an average of four shillings a day—good by Bahamian standards, but low by comparison with the wages being paid to the Americans. Bit by bit the idea took hold in the minds of the local laborers that they were being underpaid, and for some time there had been rumbling of discontent—nothing serious and, in the judgment of David's advisers, no cause for immediate concern.

Late in May, David and I crossed over to Miami in the *Gemini*. David had business to transact with the U.S. naval authorities. Also, to arrange with the Colonial Supply Mission in Washington to provide for our needs, David had to continue to Washington for discussions with the officials. There we stayed at the British Embassy as the guests of Lord and Lady Halifax. On the evening of our arrival they gave a dinner for us, and among the guests were Harry Hopkins and Louise Macy, an old friend of mine from my Paris days with whom Harry was obviously in love and whom he married not long afterward. In the middle of dinner David was called from the table by the Ambassador's secretary. On his return, some minutes later, looking worried, he apologized to our host, saying that he had just received a message from Nassau stating that there had been serious rioting there by the Bahamian workers on the airfield construction project and that he must return immediately.

While David and Lord Halifax were discussing how best this could be done, Mr. Hopkins unobtrusively left the table. Shortly thereafter David was summoned to the telephone, this time with the word that the President wished to speak to him. We had lunched that very day at the White House with President and Mrs. Roosevelt, and I wondered what possibly could be the reason for the call. The explanation was almost immediately forthcoming. Having been advised by Mr. Hopkins of the crisis in Nassau, the President had generously offered to put at David's disposal the Secretary of the Navy's airplane.

David was off next morning from Anacostia Naval Airfield. He insisted that I remain in the United States until the situation had been brought under control. Only later did I learn what David had been through during the next few days. After a difficult flight—the airplane had engine trouble shortly after the take-off, and David had to transfer to another one—he arrived at Nassau to find that the mob had looted the Bay Street shops and liquor stores. Finally the troops had been called out; and the rioters had been driven back into their section of the city, called Grant's Town. There they were still besieging a police station and, in defiance of the orders of the Acting Governor, were terrorizing the community. Directly upon his arrival David made a quick survey of the situation. Deciding that law and order must be restored at all costs, he summoned his Executive Council. Overruling the more cautious members, he announced his decision to use whatever force might be necessary to achieve this end. He then promptly called in the Chief of Police and the Captain commanding the Cameron Highlanders and instructed them to relieve the police station by nine o'clock the following morning. Happily, this show of force succeeded in its objective without bloodshed. The mob scattered; David drove through the streets of Grant's Town; the crisis was over. Later, he was able to bring about a mediation that produced a more equitable wage scale, thus quieting the unrest.

With order restored, David flew back to Washington to complete his business with the Supply Mission. This took only a few days. On the day the trouble in Nassau broke out—as a matter of fact, at the luncheon President Roosevelt had given for us—we had invited Herman and Katherine Rogers to return with us for a visit. Their presence at that luncheon was a thoughtful gesture on the part of the President. He and Herman were lifelong neighbors; their families were among the older residents of the Crum Elbow–Hyde Park area of the Hudson River Valley. To find them at the White House was a delightful surprise for us, and David had impulsively insisted across the table on their returning to Nassau with us. Herman and Katherine exchanged glances, then Katherine said that while they would love to come their passports had expired. From the head of the table, with a Rooseveltian smile, came the quick remark, "Katherine, don't worry, I think I may still have a little influence with our passport lady, Mrs. Shipley." On David's return, therefore, Herman and Katherine were ready to go, their passports in order.

Our return to Nassau was somewhat more dramatic than we had anticipated. We were to make the trip back from Miami in the *Gemini,* and the Commandant of the Seventh Naval District, Rear Admiral James L. Kauffman, whom I had known as "Reggie" in Coronado, had provided us with a sub-chaser as escort across the Florida Straits, and also had asked his air patrol to keep an eye on us. All this was fine; however, no sooner were we out of the harbor than a smashing, blinding, tropical rain squall hit us; so hard did it rain and blow that it was like being in a heavy fog, but one made up of furious, stinging particles. The glass windshield was shattered; green water swashed through the bridge deck. The Captain, David, and Herman struggled to hold the bow up into the sea. Down below, in the cabin, Katherine and I sat on the sofa, clutching the table, which was bolted to the deck, expecting the boat to capsize at any moment. It was a dreadful hour. Then the storm lifted as quickly as it had struck. David looked around for our air and surface escort. There was no sign of either. We finished the voyage under cloudless skies and fortunately without further difficulty.

Two or three days after our return—I connect the occasion with Katherine's birthday—there occurred an even more exciting episode. We had just finished the birthday celebration when, from the veranda, we were startled to see flames leap up into the summer night over the center of Bay Street. As we watched incredulously, the flames flared and spread. "Good God," said David, "the whole town's burning up." On the dead run he headed downtown, with the rest of us following as best we could. By the time we reached the scene an entire block, between Bay and George Streets, was in flames. Near the center of the conflagration was my beloved Red Cross headquarters, already smoldering. A crowd had gathered; among them I recognized some of my co-workers. Deciding that we must try to save the supplies that we had struggled to collect and had made with our own hands, we ran for the building and, more by instinct than by planning, organized ourselves into a kind of bucket brigade to pass the kits and cartons and equipment from hand to hand out the doors and windows and along the line to safety. We were lucky; although the building was soon burned to the ground we managed to save most of the supplies. Meanwhile the fire was gaining momentum along Bay Street and threatening the adjacent blocks. Because the tide was down, the antiquated fire engine lacked sufficient power to pump water far enough to reach the flames. In order to save the Cathedral David authorized the firemen to dynamite the buildings between so as to create a firebreak. That checked the spread of the fire. By dawn it had finally burned itself out, but a good part of the business section was gutted.

While the fire itself seemed serious enough, all of us had a deeper fear that the conflagration marked the onset of another wave of sabotage and rioting. In fact, directly on reaching the scene and conferring with such members of his Council as were on hand, David had caused the Cameron Highlanders to be alerted for possible action. At breakfast time, after we had returned to Government House, David summoned the Executive Council to meet with him as soon as possible to discuss the apparently menacing situation. While he and they were in discussion, the Chief of Police, Lieutenant-Colonel R. A. Erskine-Lindrop, arrived with word that quickly laid the natural fear that the fire was part of an insurrectionary plot. He had found evidence that the fire had been set by a property owner who wanted to collect insurance and who later went to jail for arson. Bay Street was a long time recovering from the damage; but the quickening tempo of the war effort soon made even this episode seem relatively unimportant.

In addition to the worries and difficulties that beset his official life during the year 1942, David also suffered two personal sorrows. In January the Duke of Connaught, his beloved Uncle Arthur, died at the age of ninety-two. Then in August came word that his favorite brother George, Duke of Kent, had been killed in a tragic airplane crash in Scotland. On each occasion a memorial service was held in the Cathedral; and at the second service by David's request his servant and piper, Fletcher, joined by the piper of the Cameron Highlanders, played the moving lament, "The Flowers of the Forest," the same dirge that Pipe-Major Forsyth had played as the body of David's father was borne from Sandringham. I had hoped that under the impact of these two blows so close together there would be a drawing together of the family, a softening of all hearts. But even these shared sorrows proved not enough.

The sorrows of a man run deep; and in the soul of every man lie secret enclaves of affection and sentiment that are beyond the probing of a wife's perceptions. These two deaths brought home to me the essential inner loneliness of every human being. To David the passing of his Uncle Arthur represented the passing of an age—the secure and golden age of the monarchy in which his own splendid youth had been spent. The Duke of Connaught was to David the last of the great Victorians; he had as Queen Victoria's third son served his mother, his brother, and his nephew with an unswerving sense of duty. Heavy as was this blow, the death of the Duke of Kent was a heavier one still. When we first heard the radio report of the airplane crash, David refused to believe it. A little later came two cables confirming the truth—one from Queen Mary and the other from Lord Halifax in Washington. Of all the brothers the Duke of Kent had always been closest to him; that he had been cut off in the prime of young manhood, at the outset of what promised to be a brilliant career, seemed to David almost a senseless caprice of fortune.

Now the oldest and the youngest had both gone; for David it was as if the golden glow of his past had been dimmed at the same time that a bright hope for the future of his family had been darkened.

By the end of summer the airfield was becoming usable; the R.A.F. began to pour in. Before long there were four thousand officers and airmen stationed there in connection with the Coastal Command's training program. In addition, the U.S. Army Air Force sent in a sizable detachment to service the Air Transport Command's operations at Windsor Field.

This huge influx of servicemen on our small island naturally confronted us with the problem of devising wholesome recreation facilities for them. Some sort of canteen seemed the answer, and wondering how best to go about it, I asked David's advice.

"Nothing much to it," he said casually. "First, you set up a Finance Committee, then a Food Committee, and, of course, an Entertainment Committee. Naturally, as my wife, you'll be chairman ex officio of the whole thing, and so I'd suggest you ask one of your more energetic and efficient friends to serve as your executive secretary. Actually, she'll be your wheel horse."

"But, David," I protested, "I've never organized anything, not even a bridge club."

David laughed. "You just start—you'll be surprised how quickly things will solve themselves." David's confidence steadied me, and I plunged ahead. And as David had indeed predicted, my canteen eventually came into being, though it took a lot more doing on my part than David's blithe formula of delegating the work had indicated. Mr. Frederick Sigrist, in whose house we had stayed and who had been a partner in the design and development of the Hurricane plane, owned the Bahamian Club, a former gambling casino. He kindly put it at my disposal for the duration of the war. This solved our major problem.

Now I scarcely had a spare moment. Every morning at the Red Cross, from nine o'clock until noon; each afternoon at the Canteen. Here I did a little of everything; but I found that my real talent was as a short-order cook. I never kept track of the number of orders of bacon and eggs that I served up, but on the basis of forty an afternoon, and three hundred and sixty-five afternoons a year for nearly three years I arrive at a rough total of about forty thousand. And that's a lot of eggs. However, I must admit that this total was affected by an inflationary factor over and beyond young men's natural craving for a snack. One of the military censors confided to me that the principal item of news in the outgoing letters from the troops to their families was their accounts of having just finished a plate of bacon and eggs personally prepared and served by the Duchess of Windsor.

Everyone was considerate of me; everyone helped, whether at the Red Cross, the Canteen, the bazaars and garden parties to raise funds, or the cocktail parties I gave to introduce each new contingent of R.A.F. cadets as they arrived. I was busier than I had ever been; but each day, with its continuing chores, brought the satisfaction of useful work gladly done. I had come to these people as an utter stranger; now I felt almost as if I had always been part of their lives and they of mine.

Moved by this feeling of identification with the island life, David and I decided that the best contribution we could make was to found clinics for the care of expectant mothers and young children. We had observed the woeful lack of such care on the outlying parts of the island of New Providence; therefore we built our first clinic on the western part and another on the eastern. They are, I am happy to say, still being maintained.

By our third year in the Bahamas things had really begun to go smoothly, despite the strains and stress of war and the serious dislocations of the economy of the colony. By this time, too, we had many warm friends. Among the most interesting of these was a famous and wealthy mining magnate, Sir Harry Oakes, a native of the State of Maine, who had made a fabulous gold strike in Ontario some thirty years before. He later became a British subject and a baronet and took up residence in Nassau, where he became active in the development of the island. When David and I came to know him, he was in his middle sixties, a small but impressive man, with gray curly hair. In spite of his great affluence, he affected a scorn for the conventional niceties that normally go with this station; he still preferred the rough garb of a prospector, spurned neckties and coats, and liked nothing better than to take the controls of a bulldozer and level acres of palmetto trees in a series of furious rushes. Lady Oakes, by contrast, was calm, dignified, and gentle; she was a pretty woman, pale of complexion, with unusual green-blue eyes. We saw a good deal of them and often visited them at their home, Westbourne, where we had lived for a while during our first months in Nassau. David, who was always attracted to the pioneering type, was fascinated, watching the progress of Sir Harry's clearing operations. The last time we saw him, only five days before his shocking murder, he was happily engaged in filling a swamp on the edge of his property with a bulldozer.

On the night of his murder, July 8, 1943, it was pouring rain. At seven o'clock the next morning David and I were awakened by a knocking on our door. David opened it and was astonished to find standing there Gray Phillips. Snatches of their conversation came to me—something about a murder. David came back to the room and told me what he had just heard: Harry Oakes had been murdered in his bed. I just couldn't believe it. It seemed incredible to me that anybody could so hate such a good man.

David immediately conferred with the Attorney General and the Chief of Police. There were no clues as to the identity of the murderer; more serious still, the Bahamas police had no up-to-date detection equipment. Their fingerprinting apparatus was inadequate. The need for the latter was crucial because in the high humidity of the island fingerprints and other clues would be quickly obliterated by the dampness. It was obvious to David that the chances of identifying the murderer would be all but lost in a matter of hours, unless an expert with the necessary equipment was brought in immediately. The nearest place where such resources were available was Miami; during the course of his several visits there to confer with Admiral Kauffman, David had been assigned a bodyguard, Captain Edward Melchen of the Miami police, who had impressed him favorably. With the approval of his own officials David telephoned the Miami Police Department and asked to have Captain Melchen with the necessary assistants and equipment flown to Nassau immediately. This was done. Unfortunately, Melchen was unable to develop any fingerprints or run down any other clues of real value. The murder remains unsolved to this day. The sense of shock and horror sent through the colony by this crime and the mystery as to its perpetrator were never quite dispelled during the remaining time we were there.

By early 1944, the war had begun to move away from our island shores. The U-boats had been driven back into the mid-Atlantic; the American Rangers who had been training for the battle of Europe and the British Commandos who had been preparing for the invasion of Burma had moved out. Only the R.A.F. training activities remained at a high pitch. David's duties now became increasingly perfunctory as the colony slipped once again into the backwater of war. Craving more active service and hopeful that his hard work there had been recognized in London and would be considered to merit his assignment to a post closer to the important theaters of war, he wrote to friends in the Government, suggesting a transfer. All that his friend Winston Churchill could do for him was to offer the Governorship of Bermuda. David could see that this would be only exchanging one military backwater for another. Bitterly disappointed, he declined the Bermuda offer and decided to finish out his war service where he was. It was clear now beyond all question that David's family were determined to keep him relegated to the farthermost marches of the Empire.

This attitude on the part of David's family was not unexpected by me; I realized nonetheless how disappointed he must have been at heart. Some considerable time before, I had decided entirely on my own volition and without his knowledge to make one last try to reach his mother and to heal the breach between them. What I thought was a proper opportunity for such an attempt had presented itself on the occasion of the departure for England of the Bishop of Nassau, the Right Reverend John Dauglish. We had formed a warm friendship with him; moreover, as a navy chaplain, he had served aboard the battle cruiser *Indomitable,* in which David's father sailed to Canada in 1908. Because of this old association, Bishop Dauglish, I felt, was certain to be received by Queen Mary. I therefore decided to write a letter for him to present when he went to see her. I still have the rough draft from which I composed the letter. This is what I wrote:

Madam:
    I hope you will forgive my intrusion upon your time as well as my boldness in addressing Your Majesty. My motive for the latter

is a simple one. It has always been a source of sorrow and regret to me that I have been the cause of any separation that exists between Mother and Son and I can't help feel that there must be moments perhaps, however fleeting they may be, when you wonder how David is. The Bishop of Nassau is leaving in a short time for England, having been appointed by the Archbishop of Canterbury, Dr. Lang, as Secretary to the Society for the Propagation of the Gospel, an advancement over his post here. I thought if you wished to hear news of David you might send for him. His name is the Rt. Reverend John Dauglish. He is a delightful man and has been of the greatest help to us here, not only through his understanding but his knowledge of local conditions on this tiny isle. He can tell you if all the things David gave up are replaced to him in another way and the little details of his daily life, his job, etc., the story of his flight from France leaving all his possessions behind. The horrors of war and the endless separations of family have in my mind stressed the importance of family ties. I hope that by the end of summer we will be nearer that victory for which we are all working so hard and for which England has so bravely lighted the way.

I beg to remain

Your Majesty's most humble and obedient servant,

WALLIS WINDSOR

In due course I received from the Bishop a letter telling of his audience with Queen Mary. She had shown keen interest in David's work in the colony and had asked many questions. But when the Bishop had mentioned what I was doing with, I judge, some show of appreciation and approval, there was no response. He met a stone wall of disinterest. Eventually, however, some weeks later there did come a curiously oblique response. David read me a letter from his mother. In it was this sentence: "I send a kind message to your wife."

David was astonished. "Now what do you suppose," he asked in genuine bewilderment, "has come over Mama?" I made no comment; and David never received the answer to his question until I showed him this chapter.

Even though all the familiar roads of duty and service were now hopelessly blocked off to David, we continued to do our jobs to the end of the war in good spirit—David unflaggingly carrying out his official duties, and I carrying on with the Red Cross, the canteens, the clinics, and my social duties. There was one task that I always dreaded, and that was the annual speech I had to make to the Daughters of the British Empire. This always fell in March; I was required to report on the year's work of the local chapter—how many cases of bandages had been sent to England, and that sort of thing. In addition, I had to introduce the practiced speaker that the Canadian Headquarters of the order always sent down to inspire the members to still greater efforts during the coming year. Each winter the prospect of this ordeal began to haunt me in February, and my terror grew with each passing day. Like most women, I never stop talking while sitting down, only to turn speechless the instant I am called upon to stand up before a group. David, with his usual thoughtfulness, tried to help me; and from his years of experience in giving thousands of speeches all over the world and having also been coached by the finest orators in Great Britain, he has developed a superb technique.

"There are only a few really important fundamentals to this business of speaking," he expounded. "Once you've mastered those there's nothing to it. First, put down what you want to say in big type on index-size cards that you can flip over easily. The trick is always to repeat on the bottom of the card the first sentence on the succeeding one so there is no awkward pause while you make the turnover. The other important trick is always to appear casual. Pause frequently; when you have a point to emphasize, make a sweeping gesture with your hand. That always gets them. And then do what Winston Churchill once taught me; when you come to your really big point, hit it hard and then hit it again."

Under David's tutelage I mastered the preliminaries, even to the point of stringing my cards in order on the indispensable India tag that he always insisted upon; but, when the awful day finally arrived and I found myself on my feet, all the good advice, the careful drilling, invariably deserted me. I never dared pause for fear I would not have the courage to start on again; my hand was shaking so that I dared not lift it from my side; and, if my audience was ever aware that I had a main point, it must have been conveyed to them more by mental telepathy than by any rhetorical emphasis I was able to impart to it.

In the spring of 1945, with the war in Europe and David's term as Governor drawing to their close, he concluded, not without regret, that he could no longer fulfill any useful purpose by remaining in Nassau. He tendered his resignation. As we prepared for our departure, which was set for early May, we were touched by the marks of affection shown to us by individuals and organizations throughout the Colony. The leading men of the community gave David a testimonial stag dinner at the Country Club, at which he was presented with an inscribed parchment; and the House of Assembly presented him with an address stating their appreciation of his services. The R.A.F. gave me a touchingly inscribed silver salver and my Red Cross ladies a beautiful silver box. These were but a few of the many expressions of friendship and esteem that came to us from every side; we were astonished and stirred by the genuine regret with which our imminent departure was viewed. There could be no question that David had done a good job. Later, Arthur Creech Jones, Secretary of State for the Colonies in the Labour Government, described David's administration as the best the Bahamas had had in recent times. Be that as it may, our lives in Nassau had been happy and imbued with a sense of purpose that we were sorry to lose.

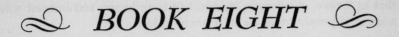

BOOK EIGHT

OF WOMEN AND FATE

⚘ CHAPTER XXXIV ⚘

Of Women and Fate

BECAUSE THE WAR IN THE PACIFIC WAS STILL GOING ON, TRANS-portation back to Europe could not be arranged that summer. It was September, 1945, before we were able to return to Paris. Except here and there on the outskirts, that most beautiful of cities had emerged unscathed from the ravages of war. We were fortunate; our house on Boulevard Suchet was untouched. It had been under the seal first of the U.S. Embassy and later the Swiss Legation; and a French care-taker had remained in undisturbed possession. He reported to us, still with undiminished indignation, that early in the war, a German soldier had entered the house on the pretext of looking it over as a possible billet and had made off with Gray Phillips's riding boots. Now with pride Fernand advised us, "Rest assured, *Madame la Duchesse,* on discovering this outrage, I instantly proceeded to the *Kommandantur* and made the strongest representations. The boots were returned the next day with profuse apologies by a major."

Under our lease we had an option to buy the house if the owner wished to sell; while in Nassau we had been advised that the owner now wanted to do so. Being uncertain of the conditions that might prevail in France after the end of hostilities, we were reluctant to buy it, and in consequence the house had passed into other hands. We waited until April to move out our possessions, and then moved to the Ritz.

Southern France was still under the control of the United States Army; it was not until December that we obtained permission from the military authorities to return to La Cröe. Here we had not been quite so lucky. The Italians, who had occupied the property, had re-spected the house to the extent of quartering their troops in the garage.

Later, the Germans had put a radar on the roof and built several concrete pillboxes on the shore. When we arrived, a gang of German prisoners, under French supervision, were gingerly removing land mines from the property; we counted twenty-four on the front lawn alone. On taking stock, we were relieved to find that only the curtains, several oil paintings, and a few odds and ends had been taken. The silver, which on our departure had been sent to the town of Albi in the interior in the care of a trusted resident, was returned intact.

Though David and I were impatient to reoccupy the house, conditions were still too unsettled for us to be permitted to remain. Food and gasoline were both in desperately short supply; the removal of the German mines, which were thickly strewn along the coast, had just begun; therefore after a few days we were forced to return to Paris, where during the rest of the winter I searched vainly for an apartment or house. Finally in the spring word came from the military authorities that we could reoccupy La Cröe. We spent a busy summer putting the house back in order. But the Côte d'Azur no longer seemed the same. Only a few of our friends came straggling back during the postwar years; the old familiar estates and villas seemed to be passing into unfamiliar hands; a new type of tourist was swarming in. Then, too, David's principal recreation was golf; the grass on the few small courses thereabouts always burned up in the summer for lack of water. Finally in 1949, at David's insistence, I reluctantly parted with La Cröe; but even now, sometimes in summer, I miss that delightful place.

In the spring of that same year I finally found a house in Paris that we could rent, at 85 rue de la Faisanderie, not far from the Etoile. Here we stayed four years until 1953. Then a lovely house in the Bois de Boulogne was offered to us on a long lease. The property of the City of Paris, it had been occupied right after the war by General Charles de Gaulle while he was President. Even though this house had spacious grounds and tall green hedges shielded it from the street, David's craving for the country was not satisfied. Ever since our return from Nassau, I had kept an eye out for a small place in the country within reasonable reach of Paris where we could spend the weekends. By happy chance, a year before we moved to the Bois, I found an old mill with a great deal of charm near the village of Gif-sur-Yvette, on the northern slope of the valley of the Chevreuse, only forty-five minutes' drive from Paris. It was called the Moulin de la Tuilerie; a French painter friend, Etienne Drian, had made it habitable, but had preserved its ancient atmosphere intact. Part of the structure went back to the seventeenth century; the floors of the main hall were paved with gravestones stolen from cemeteries during the French Revolution. Closely grouped around the Moulin itself were a barn, a stable, and several small outbuildings; past them rush the swift waters of the Merantaise, which in earlier times turned the great wooden mill wheel and now fills the air with lovely, untiring sounds.

When I showed the mill to David, he fell in love with it on the spot. While my mind was turning to the formidable problem of what would be involved in remodeling these ancient buildings, with their massive hand-hewn beams and stone walls two feet thick, David was already joyfully marking out with his eye where the herbaceous borders and the plantings of perennials would go; and across the stream, at the foot of a rocky outcropping, he had already begun to visualize a rock garden like the one he had created at the Fort. First we took a lease; then, as the spell of the place grew on us, we finally succeeded in inducing M. Drian to sell the property to us. So at last we have land and a house of our own in a countryside we have come to love.

It is only now, after four years of endless changing and remodeling, that I am beginning to realize that the Mill is nearly finished, and that there can be little more I can reasonably do to it. This knowledge saddens me, for it means that I can no longer enjoy the thrill of creating that so pleasurably filled those years for me. No longer can I justify to myself the endless afternoons given to combing the antique shops and the art galleries of the Left Bank, picking up here a piece of Sèvres or Meissen for a table or a vitrine, there a still life—what the French call *la nature morte*—to hang in the dining room. While I was occupied with the inside of the buildings, David and his gardeners were clearing out the rank growth of weeds and untended vegetables in the old walled garden adjoining what had been the barn. Here, with devoted care and mounting joy, he laid out a true English garden, between two herbaceous borders filled with his old favorites at the Fort —delphiniums, chrysanthemums, phlox, and asters. Almost before these plantings were in hand, he had begun the rock garden on the far side of the little stream. Taking advantage of a spring at the foot of the hill, he created, with the aid of a local stonemason, an artful arrangement of little pools and waterfalls among the rocks; as a final touch he had the inspiration to pipe water from the river to the top of the hill, whence it splashes in a gay cascade down the rocky slope to augment the flow through the pools and waterfalls, overhung with alpine blooms.

Now of an afternoon as I sit on the terrace, watching David as he

[355]

moves from plant to plant with his Alsatian gardener, checking the growth of each, I often think of how well he has succeeded in making a new life for both of us—not quite the kind of life we had envisaged back at Wasserleonburg, but still one that is good. While David always made light of the problem of readjusting himself, I realized better than he knew that it must have been hard at times. For he had been trained as few men have ever been for service to the State; now to find himself cut off in the high noon of life from all chance of using this knowledge and exercising his undoubted gifts must have left him with a haunting sense of waste. In the years immediately following the war David made several trips to London. He led me to believe that these visits were motivated mainly by a desire to see his mother and his brother, to attend to business affairs, and to renew old friendships. But it gradually became apparent that there was more to these trips than this. In a delicate way he was reminding the Government and his brother of his availability and desire for further service. But these hints fell on barren ground. He met the same noncommittal evasions from Buckingham Palace and from the new Labour Government that came to power in 1945 that he had met earlier under the National Government.

Not only did this silent ban apply to service under his own government; it extended to any form of public work in which the British Government might be concerned. Let it not be said that I was unaware of the extraordinary difficulties attaching to service by a former monarch in a lesser post; still, in view of David's generosity of spirit, this need not have been an insoluble problem. Of course, he received many offers to take positions in commerce and industry; appealing as were these exciting fields and long as had been his interest in them, he nevertheless rejected them out of regard for his background.

But for a gallant spirit there can never be defeat. The closing of one road is only a challenge to open another; the death of one hope leads but to the birth of a new one. David had too keen a sense of living, of the infinite variety and texture of life, ever to find it savorless, whatever the changing circumstances in which he found himself. Through the years I have come to feel that this was always the hidden key to his character, the secret of that almost boyish zest with which he welcomes each new situation. Thus in a way rare in my observation of people he is always able to negotiate satisfactory terms with life. Yet, after all these years, there is something about him that still eludes me, an enigma of outlook that sets him apart; an aloofness of spirit that I can only explain as being the inner essence of royalty. Perhaps

✑ MY LIFE TODAY

David and I have two houses in France between which we divide our time. Our Paris house (above) where we spend most of the week is just inside the Bois de Boulogne, near the Porte de Madrid in Neuilly. Weekends we spend at our country house, the Moulin de Tuileries (below) near Gif-sur-Yvette, only a half-hour drive from the Bois. We acquired both of these houses in quick succession only a few years ago. After years of living in rented houses it is wonderful to feel one's roots taking firm hold in places one loves, and I would like to think that we are finally settled.

There is a pattern to a woman's life. After breakfasting in my room and reading the newspapers I deal with the mail. Personal correspondence I answer in longhand; business letters I dictate to my secretary, Miss Hivet. The rest of the morning is generally taken up with household chores: going over accounts, planning meals with the chef, arranging appointments, and directing the work of the domestic staff. When we are alone, David and I lunch off trays out on the terrace (below) whenever the weather is warm. In this picture are the two oldest members of our staff—Anna, who has been with us since 1938, and Sidney, a Bahamian, who entered our service in Nassau in 1940. Afterward I usually go into the city, perhaps to see a new art exhibition or to browse among the antique shops of the Left Bank or to see my friends.

My husband's days are busy and well ordered. In our Paris house, weather permitting, he moves his office out onto the terrace, to which he repairs directly after breakfast. David types many of his personal letters himself. This was a skill that he learned when he was Prince of Wales. After lunch David often plays a round of golf at Saint Cloud, Saint Germain, or La Boulie.

One of life's most dangerous illusions for a hostess is that a meal can be entrusted solely to the judgment of a chef. No one could possibly hold the art of the chef in higher esteem than do I; in fact, I am inclined to place his accomplishments among the fine arts. However, it has been my observation that chefs, like the rest of us, tend to repeat their successes. Leave them to their own devices, and they will evade the unusual and the untried. Moreover, their aesthetic sense, so acutely developed in other respects, does not extend to color as well as to flavor in their creations. Unless the hostess is on her guard she may very well find the entire meal running through the pink-mauve band of the spectrum, from lobster bisque to sherbet, or to all in the brownish black, from bean soup to chocolate sauce.

Here I am with Lucien, my chef (above), who is twenty-nine years old and already a master of his craft. I wanted a chef who is young enough to be daring and who will accept new ideas. Lucien precedes us every weekend to the Mill. Here he is arriving with some of his supplies.

For a hostess, as for the conductor of an orchestra, the test is how effortlessly the finished production comes off. But again, as with the conductor and his orchestra, the outcome depends almost entirely upon the preparation, the untiring attention to detail, the rigorousness of rehearsal, and the *esprit de corps* on the part of all concerned to turn out a flawless performance.

If I find myself faced with the prospect of giving a large dinner—one, for instance, for a French Cabinet Minister, an Ambassador, or a senior officer of SHAPE—I start planning and ordering not less than a week in advance. Not only does such a dinner mean working up the menu with the chef; it also involves deciding the service to be used, and the motif of the table decorations, whether the dominant color is to be iceberg blue or pastel green.

My husband in his man's way is never able to understand why these things take so much of my time. Why, he asks, can't they be delegated? The reason is that in my woman's way I have to see for myself how each effect I have in mind works itself out in practice. I can never really be sure of anything until I see it has come into existence, tangibly, visibly. Thus in preparation for an important dinner I spend a good deal of time in the kitchen with the chef and his assistants and in the pantry with the butler George (left) and in the storeroom selecting table ornaments (right).

The setting of a formal table is to me like a study in still life, with harmony and proportion as its keynotes.

This Meissen service was made for Frederick Augustus II, Elector of Saxony.

No matter what masterpieces the chef may create, no matter how beautifully the table may be set, the success of a dinner party is ultimately dependent upon the company. There is, I am afraid, no reliable rule for finding a perfect combination of personalities who will stimulate without clashing over some unpredictable vagary of politics, economics, or artistic credo. However, from having had my share of dinners blasted by inextinguishable controversies or slowly smothered under the pomposities of stuffed shirts, I have evolved a few simple rules of thumb.

The most important rule is never to have too many brilliant people at one table. They tend to exhaust themselves, not to mention the other guests, in their competition to hold the floor. Faced with such a possibility, the prudent hostess would be well advised to arrange for a judicious ballasting of, well, bores.

Another rule I've followed is never to have more than ten people at one table. Ten, in fact, is for me the ideal number; one that gives scope for variety in personalities, yet still is small enough to allow the conversation to be general. A larger number of guests is best divided among two or more small tables, preferably round (as shown above). Finally, there is one quicksand in which many a hostess has foundered: that of letting the cocktails run on too long before dinner, to the ruin of the meal and the demoralization of the staff. In my house the immutable rule is never more than two cocktails before dinner.

Casualness and informality are the essence of the country, and that's the way we live at the Mill during our weekends there. Here, we are outdoors as much as we can be. Often we have several friends staying over with us, and others drive out from Paris for lunch. When weather permits we lunch and have tea on the flagstone terrace (left), looking out upon the garden. Here (right) is the outside dining room I created in what was one of the storerooms of the seventeenth-century mill. The ceramics on the wall impart a feeling of space to the room.

Here David and I are on our way to pay a visit to our nearest neighbors, Farmer Dubois and his wife. We were amused to find that David's trousers and Madame Dubois's nephew's were both made of matching corduroy.

Every wife should devote one room in her house to the tastes and interests of her husband. I like to think of our main living room (above), in what used to be the old barn, as David's room. Here I've gathered together the mementos of his youth—his trophies won steeplechasing, regimental insignia of the Brigade of Guards, his midshipman's dirk and Field Marshal's baton, and a variety of objects collected on his world travels.

Then, too, I'd like to think that the nicest rooms in my house are the guest rooms. It has always been my habit to look them over carefully before anyone occupies them. I have a check list that I run down (below). This is to help me make sure that there are new books on the bedside table, that the clock is running, that the thermos has been filled with fresh water, that the cigarette boxes and the stationery have been replenished, that the medicine cabinet in the bathroom has been stocked with aspirin and other household remedies, and that the soap in the washstand matches the color scheme.

David's great joy is the garden. When we took possession of the Mill, the garden shown here (above and below) did not exist. It was an abandoned chicken run overgrown with weeds. It took David a full two years of unremitting but devoted labor to achieve the effect he desired. His ideal was the English garden, a type rarely seen in France since the eighteenth century. Whereas the modern French garden stresses the formal and the geometrical, the emphasis of the English garden is all on expanses of green grass broken here and there by apparently random and casual plantings and informal borders. And David still begrudges every hour he cannot spend with his Alsatian gardener, in developing some new vista or sudden surprise.

The rock and water garden, however, is David's tour de force. Across the stream from our terrace is a rocky crag (left) that slopes steeply down to the river that rushes past the Mill. Here David took advantage of a small stream that surfaced on the lower slope, and channeled it through a series of little waterfalls and pools made to look natural by the skillful placing of native rocks. Now they are almost covered by alpine plants and primulas; and the effect of the whole has been enhanced by still another and bigger waterfall down the face of the crag, created by pumping water from the river up the hill through pipes buried in the ground.

While by no means as keen a gardener as David, I eagerly seek the blooms
he produces. Flower arranging is for me one of life's purest aesthetic joys.
I first became fascinated by this art years ago when I was in China. Since
then I have taken advantage of every opportunity to study the techniques
of the experts of Europe and the United States. My house is always full of
flowers, and every morning I go from room to room, arranging and re-
arranging. My personal taste runs to white flowers, tulips, arums, Easter
lilies, stock, etc. The tall arrangements, so effective in big rooms, were my
first fancy. Lately, however, I've become more and more attracted by the
simplicity and charm of detail possible in the newer small arrangements.
I like personally to select the flowers that are to be used from the greenhouse.

David and I are united in our love of dogs. In the beginning we had cairns. Recently our affection shifted to pugs, of which we now have four—Disraeli, who is the eldest, Trooper, Peter, and the puppy, Davy Crockett. We take them with us everywhere. They are true internationalists, equally at home in the French countryside, Paris, the liner *United States,* or high up in the Waldorf Towers. Unlucky is the visitor who unheedingly puts down within their reach a handbag or a sheaf of papers; they'll be off with the loot in a flash. Feeding four such spirited animals is a feat in itself; for each is convinced the other's bowl contains a tastier ration than his own (left). Germaine, our versatile concierge, whose husband is also part of our household staff, keeps a close watch over the driveway gate lest our four rascals decide to explore the Bois.

Throughout my life decorating has been one of my strongest enthusiasms. There are no more wonderful shops than those of Paris, and I love to search through them. Here I am at the Mill with Mr. Travers of Jansen, selecting new curtains for the hall. On occasion I've come upon some unpromising and even unwanted object that I've been able to transform into a decoration of charm. Such a find was a rusting iron figure of a crane. I had the happy thought of painting it gray and white, wiring it, and turning it into a lighting fixture. The effect was so pleasing that I ransacked the shops of the Left Bank until I found its mate. They now occupy places of honor in the dining room at the Mill (above).

In my opinion there is only one important rule about clothes: it is that they should be so simple and unobtrusive as to seem unimportant. Simplicity of line, relieved from plainness by richness of fabric and elegance of detail, is my golden rule. French women seem to be so much wiser than the rest of us; they dress in the style most becoming to their own personalities, regardless of the ever-changing whims of fashion.

This evening dress of shantung is of interest for the reason that while my preference runs, as a rule, to short evening dresses, the simplicity of this one appeals strongly to me. This photograph was taken in the drawing room of our Paris house, and I am standing beside a red-lacquer Louis XV commode, on which can be seen my collection of Meissen pug dogs.

I am wearing (lower right) a pale blue-and-white silk printed dress which has a matching coat. This ensemble I like for summer afternoon parties. In my hair is a summer's excuse for a hat—a cluster of bird's wings repeating the blues of the print.

The suit I have on (below) is over three years old. It is of red and black wool, bound with black grosgrain ribbon. Because of its classic lines the outfit has for me the attraction a well-cut man's suit has—the look of being undated.

Strange as it may seem, the principal activity of my life today has been the writing of this book. When David started his book some years ago, I found it difficult to understand how he could spend so much time staring at a blank sheet of paper. I had often before been a golf widow; this was my first experience of being a literary one. Now the shoe is on the other foot; it is I who have had to cope with the reams of blank paper while David has been off to the links (above). But I must say that, having been through the same ordeal, he has been much more understanding of my difficulties than I was of his. But of an evening when I read him passages of what I have written and he can't resist telling me how he would have described the same scene in his book, I sometimes wonder how the Brownings handled similar, and of course much more important, matters of this kind in the Casa Guidi.

there is one further trait that enables him to translate his adjustment to life into happiness: the Hanoverian romanticism of his forebears fortified by the courage of an island race.

In addition to recapturing the old pleasures of gardening, David has re-established in a somewhat different form his former interest in industrial progress. We spend a part of every year in the United States, where David seeks out the company of men of affairs whom he questions searchingly about the latest developments in their fields. The sense of being in touch with vital affairs that once was brought to him in the red dispatch boxes perhaps now comes to him from these associations and discussions.

Although it was some time before we could bring ourselves to face the fact in its entirety, ours was a most ambiguous and amorphous position. We could never really be private persons, however much we might wish it. While David had stepped down from the Throne, he could never step out of the Royal Family; as the son, grandson, and great-grandson of former Monarchs, and later the brother and now the uncle of a sovereign, he is immutably part of the Royal institution, fixed there forever, like a fly in amber. Perhaps our late friend, Duff Cooper, summed it up best one evening in Paris when he remarked to me, "You and the Duke have none of the advantages of royalty and all of its disadvantages."

These disabilities have presented special problems for me. Not being royal, and in fact being rather pointedly excluded from the position traditionally accorded the wife of a Royal Duke, I have had to live in the knowledge that notwithstanding my anomalous status my every action, indeed even my most casual conversations, is inevitably judged against the fact of my being married to a former king. To fit my life into this context was a long exercise in self-discipline, for by temperament and habit I had been content to live for the hour and the change and surprise the imminent moment might bring. It is admiringly remarked of some people that they have arrived. By this is meant, I suppose, that their affairs have progressed according to some carefully disciplined plan to a desired conclusion. With me, however, it has been a case of just landing, and more often than not in defiance of the maxim of never leaping before taking a prudent look.

Quite apart from other differences, women seem to me to be divided into two groups—those who reason and those who are forever casting about for reasons for their own lack of reason. While I might wish it to the contrary, the record of my life, now that I have for the first time attempted to see it whole, clearly places me with the second group. Women, by and large, I have concluded, were never meant for plans and planning. Men can and do plan their lives, and the good ones manage one way or another to arrive at their chosen destinations, often to the advantage of the rest of us. But it has been my observation that most women have a great deal of Micawber's willingness to believe that "something will turn up." For most of us the best things are those that materialize seemingly out of nowhere, that suddenly and miraculously charge a woman's existence with totally unexpected meaning and light up her landscape as a flash of lightning illuminates the way for the traveler moving through the darkness.

Nowadays as I look around and note the splendid achievements of other women—famous and capable women like Helen Keller, Clare Boothe Luce, Anne Lindbergh, not to mention the young women now making their way in industry and science—I realize how lacking in ambition, how lacking in self-discipline, I really was to cope with the wonderful opportunities that even in my youth were beginning to present themselves to women of the twentieth century. Few women of my generation and background could have had a fairer crack than I at the storehouse of wisdom, worldly and otherwise. I was brought up among cultivated, charming, even witty people, went to good schools, and never lacked good company. I traveled and came to know not only my own country from the Atlantic to the Pacific, but also Europe and Asia. Everywhere I found myself in exciting company. All this was mine; but I was a long time learning that wisdom and experience are things apart; that to taste life is not to be confused with understanding what life is really all about. The shared experiences, the wisdom so freely proffered by others, in words and by example, rarely swayed me for long. Came another day and the import was gone, and only the echo of laughter remained. Experience was a revolving sun in the warmth of which I was content to bask.

But great as have been the achievements of women and wide as have become their horizons in my day, I still instinctively feel that Lord Byron was right when he wrote:

> Man's love is of man's life a thing apart,
> 'Tis woman's whole existence;

Any woman who has been loved as I have been loved, and who, too, has loved, has experienced life in its fullness. To this I must add one qualification, one continuing regret. I have never known the joy of having children of my own. Perhaps no woman can say her life has been completely fulfilled unless she has had a part in the miracle of creation.

Of course, no life that has been zestfully and perhaps even recklessly lived can be said to be all of one piece. A woman's life can really be a succession of lives, each revolving around some emotionally compelling situation or challenge, and each marked off by some intense experience. And of these I have had a woman's full share. All I can say is that, everything taken together, I have finally found a great measure of happiness and contentment.

Index

German Embassy, 208; attends first school, 15; attends state reception at Buckingham Palace, 195; and Aunt Bessie invited to Biarritz by Prince of Wales, 185; Aunt Bessie urges her return to London, 141; back in London, 209; back in Washington with her mother, 92; begins to understand Prince of Wales's loneliness, 182; begs Duke of Windsor to relinquish her, 236; boards *Empress of Canada* at Philippines, 93; books passage on *Chaumont* for Philippines, 92; born at Blue Ridge Summit, Pennsylvania, 3; briefed by Duke of Windsor on speech making, 349; and British etiquette of eating, 130; at "Burrlands," 29-30; christened Bessie Wallis (Bessie-wallis), 4; code for living, 82; compares British and Americans, 135; compares Paris and London, 134; confers with American Ambassador, William Bullitt, 322; considers divorce from Winfield Spencer, 76; considers entering the fashion field, 114-15; consults astrologer, 118, 119; consults Aunt Bessie on divorce, 77-78; consults mother on divorce, 76-77; consults Uncle Sol on divorce, 78-79; cooks first meal, 68-69; Cousin Henry escorts to Cotillion, 39, 40; Cousin Lelia gives tea dance for, in Washington, 44-45; cruises to Corsica, 208; curiosity concerning, 205; dances with Prince of Wales, 174; decides to join Winfield Spencer in the East, 91; decides to try to obtain divorce in U.S. Court in Shanghai, 95; decorates La Cröe, 302; dines at Balmoral, 228-29; disintegration of marriage to Ernest Simpson, 214; divorce decree absolute, 288; draws up will, 246; drinks first cocktail, 69; early memories of, 5, 6; effect of London winter upon, 133; entertains Prince of Wales at dinner at Bryanston Court, 182; and episode of the lost notes, 255; establishes residence in Warrenton, Virginia, 109-10; feeling toward stepfather John F. Rasin, 25, 26; first impression of Prince of Wales, 157; first meets Winston Churchill, 203; first view of Prince of Wales's private life, 172; fondness for Prince of Wales's Cairns, 184; and food, 136; at Fort for Ascot week, 184; and French telephone system, 262-63, 279; friendship with Lady Oxford

and Asquith, 204; furnishes flat in London, 145; and German propaganda, 323; gets advice from Uncle Sol, 37; gives first party at La Cröe, 306; goes to camp in Virginia, 29; goes to girls' school, Arundell, 16; goes to Ireland, 180; goes to London, 1928, 126; goes to Oldfields boarding school, 30; goes to France, 126; goes to Paris with Corinne Mustin, 89-91; goes to Pittsburgh, 117; goes to see mother in Washington, 144; goes to Norway, 180; goes to Shanghai, 95; goes on tour of Fort, 176, 177; goes to Tunis, 178; graduates from Arundell, 30; grandmother's discipline of, 7; granted divorce from Winfield Spencer, 126; hate expressed for, 271-72; helps to fight fire in Nassau, 342-43; Herman Rogers gives away, 291; home at Bryanston Court, 147; honeymoons with Ernest Simpson in France and Spain, 127; honeymoons with Winfield Spencer at White Sulphur Springs, West Virginia, 61; honorary president of Daughters of the British Empire, 338; at house party at Melton, 209; house-hunting in Paris, 305, 354; ill on voyage across Pacific, 109; illness in Paris, 227; imagination as a child, 17; impression of Duchess of York, 216; impression of Prince of Wales, 160; impressions of living in a monarchy, 131-32; impressions of London, 134; influence of sister-in-law on, 132; interest of American press in, 233; interest in household at Fort, 184; invited to Cannes by Prince of Wales, 208; invited to dinner party at the Dorchester, 182; invited by Prince of Wales to Cornwall to see famous gardens, 206; invited to Fort Belvedere, 169, 170; invites Prince of Wales to dinner party, 180; Irish nurse Joe, 10; issues statement to press, 264; joins *Colis de Trianon,* French relief organization, 319, 320; joins friends in Lake Maggiore, 124; joins *Section Sanitaire,* motor branch, French Red Cross, 320; joins Winfield Spencer in Hong Kong, 93; King reads Instrument of Abdication to, 268; learns activities of governor's wife, 345; learns of death of Uncle Sol, 124; leases house in Paris, 308; letter to Aunt Bessie, 22; letter from Bishop of Nassau to, 348; letter to Queen Mary, 347-48; letters of sympathy to, 271; life in London, 128; life in Paris, 319-20; life in Peking, 103-4; life at Pensacola Air Station, 63-72; life with Winfield Spencer, 72-73; lives at Warren Green Hotel, Warrenton, Virginia, 110-12; looks for job in New York City, 116; love of books while in school, 33, 34; love for Peking, 106-7; love for Winfield Spencer, 54; makes home with Aunt Bessie, 6, 14; marries Duke of Windsor, 291; marries Ernest Simpson in London, 1928, 126-27; and mathematics, 19, 20; meeting with "Robbie," 96, 97; meets Fern Bedaux, 283; meets John Barrymore, 73; meets Charlie Chaplin, 73; meets Earl W. Spencer, Jr., 47, 48; meets Prince of Wales, 153, 161; memories of grandmother's home, 7-8, 9; memories of Uncle Sol, 125; misconceptions of the King, 237; morganatic marriage suggested for, 239; moves to Boston, Massachusetts, 66; moves to North Island, San Diego, 68; Mr. Goddard visits, 266; and music lessons, 28; objections to marrying the King, 217; organizes a canteen in Nassau, 344-45; Perry Brownlow's proposal to, 250; personalities remembered by, 10; position as wife of former King, 357; presented at the Bachelors' Cotillion, 38-42; presented at Court, 162-63; president of Red Cross in Nassau, 338; Prince of Wales gives dinner party for, at Quaglino's, 179; Prince of Wales's melancholy makes impression on, 160-61; Prince of Wales visits for cocktails, 183; reading habits while in Warrenton, 112; reads statement to Duke of Windsor, 264; Reboux makes wedding hat for, 289; receives a bracelet charm from the Prince of Wales, 187; receives bulldog "Bully" from her stepfather, 27; receives Cairn puppy Slipper from Prince of Wales, 148; receives help from Mme Point, 259; receives letters from Ernest Simpson, 272-73; receives proposal from Ernest Simpson, 119; receives radiogram from the Prince of Wales, 179; receives telephone calls from the King, 262; reflects on Prince of Wales, 174; remembrance of Eddie, Negro valet-footman, 10-11; remorse of, 245; rents house in Paris, 354; returns to Hong Kong, 95; returns to London, 141, 179, 180;

returns to Warrenton, 119, 126; reunion attempts with Winfield Spencer a failure, 94; sails aboard the *Mauretania* for New York, 179; sails for America on the *Mauretania*, 138; sails for Europe with Aunt Bessie, 1927, 123; sails from Lisbon, 336; schooldays of, 19; seeks sanctuary with the Rogerses, 245; self-analysis, 357-58; shares house in Georgetown, 86; shopping in London, 135; shops for antiques, 145; sight-seeing in England, 141-42; skiing in Austria, 200; social life in Baltimore, 43, 44; social life in Mayfair, 147; social life in Washington in 1920's, 82-83; in Spain, 329; spends Christmas at Cap Ferrat, 277; spends several weekends at the Fort, 178; spends summers as child at Timonium, 23; suggestion of title of Duchess of Lancaster for, 239; suggests the King make radio broadcasts, 243; takes ship from Japan, 108; takes trip to Peking, 97, 98, 99; takes a trip to the Continent, 178; telephones to the King, 253-54; tells Winfield Spencer of divorce decision, 79; tries to prevent the King's abdication, 263; trousseau made by Mainbocher, 289; Uncle Sol gives blessing, 54; Uncle Sol gives her away, 56; upset at Slipper's death, 286; views on marriage, 81-82; visits Denham Place, 209; visits Lady Sackville-West at Knole, 151; visits in Pensacola, Florida, 45; visits Uncle Sol in apartment at Plaza Hotel, New York City, 87-88; visits Winfield Spencer's family, 55; at Warm Springs, Virginia, 18; watches King George's funeral from St. James's Palace, 212; wedding in Christ Church, Baltimore, 56; wedding presents, 55-56; writes to Queen Mary, 347-48

Windsor, Duke of, accepts rank of Major-General, 318; adjustment to new life, 292; asks for recognition of Duchess, 333; attributes of, 306-7; in Austria, 270; builds clinic in Bahamas, 345; buys old mill in France, 355; decides to go to Spain, 326; exchanges messages with Winston Churchill, 334; expressions of esteem given to, 350; and family relations, 280; and German intrigue, 335; goes to Buckingham Palace for talk with his brother, 316; helps in trying to solve murder of Sir Harry Oakes, 346-47; hopes